Wordcraft

Stephen Pollington

Anglo-Saxon Books

Published by
Anglo-Saxon Books
Frithgarth
Thetford Forest Park
Hockwold-cum-Wilton
Norfolk, IP26 4NQ

First published 1993
Reprinted and expanded 1993
Reprinted with additions 1996
Reprinted 1999 & 2002
Revised and Reprinted 2004

British Library Cataloguing-in-Publication Data. A catalogue record
for this book is available from the British Library.

ISBN 1–898281–02–5

To Mines Fæder Gemynde

Contents

Acknowledgements

All entries in the Dictionary and the Thesaurus have been cross-checked from the various texts against Clark-Hall's *Concise Anglo-Saxon Dictionary*.

I should like to record my gratitude here to those who made this book possible: to Janice McKenna, who tested the Dictionary by random searches and suggested areas in need of amplification; to Tony Linsell, who had the foresight to take this project on for Anglo-Saxon Books; and above all to Pearl Linsell, whose tireless efforts at the keyboard, in the face of countless revisions and additions, say more about the strength of her character than any words of mine can.

S.P.
Southchurch,
Essex
July, 1993

Introduction

1. Aim of the Book

The aim of this book is to provide the student of Old English (OE) with a handy guide to the basic vocabulary of the language in a usable format. In order to bring this about, it has been necessary to make choices based, in the end, on nothing more than what I personally thought most appropriate or useful. No doubt sometimes I have got it wrong; I hope that I have got it right most of the time.

The book is particularly for those students who wish to compose original work in OE as a means of familiarising themselves with the inflexional patterns and syntactic structures of the language. Hitherto, the main complaint of students has been that it is nearly impossible to find the right words to express oneself in this dead language; it is hoped that this book will at least provide a useful reference book for them, to be supplemented by their own gleanings from texts.

In cases of uncertainty a more detailed Old English/New English (NE) dictionary should be consulted in order to compare the range of meanings a given OE word may encompass with a modern equivalent. This applies equally to variations in spelling.

2. Content

The core vocabulary of our modern language is very largely OE, with a few Old Norse words. The handful of French terms which have become indispensable are often ones which harmonise well in sound and form with English patterns: face, chair, table; chase, catch; proud, very, vast. This book gives OE equivalents to the bulk of these central concepts, as well as a good many other less immediately necessary words, to form the nucleus of a broad-based basic OE vocabulary.

Items specifically excluded are personal names, nearly all place names (although many of the English counties and some geographical features do appear) and many obviously 'poetic' words, particularly the greater part of that huge slice of OE vocabulary centring on the glorification of warfare. The student soon picks up a great many of these terms, through the Chronicle and Beowulf; while they are interesting in themselves, their inclusion would have meant the exclusion of a wider coverage. Verbs are given in their infinitive forms, so that 'am, art, is, are, was, were' and the like do not appear. Nouns are usually given in the nominative singular, except where only plural forms occur (e.g. names of nations). Adjectives appear in the positive degree, except for a few oddities such as better, best, more, most, etc.

The core of the book is the Word List entries, and it is to these that I have given the greatest attention. Naturally I have included pronouns, etc. in the Dictionary for ease of reference, but at the same time it is assumed that the student is making use of a reliable grammar and does not need separate entries for 'love; loves; loving; loved' which are all deducible from the infinitive form; similarly the relative pronoun is given as 'þe' throughout, ignoring the many ways OE has of expressing this idea – such matters belong to the realms of accidence and syntax respectively.

3. Date And Dialect.

Where possible I have used West Saxon forms in preference to Anglian or Kentish ones, and early forms rather than later ones. This is largely for practical reasons, in as much as, whether we like it or not, the bulk of OE prose appears in a West Saxon guise. Early spellings also tend to be more 'transparent' than later ones – when several vowels fall together in spelling as 'y' (earlier y, i, ie) and others as 'æ' (a, æ). Having said that, where an OE word only occurs in a late spelling or in a non-West-Saxon form, I have not excluded it from this work.

The reader is presented with lists of genuine, recorded OE words of admittedly mixed date and regional colouring. For this I make no apology. Those who care enough to excise everything inappropriate to their chosen dialect and period are welcome to do so – but bear in mind that while OE prose shows clearly regional characteristics, the majority of the poetry shows distinctly Anglian (perhaps Mercian) features, regardless of the provenance of the verse, which rather suggests that OE speakers could cope with variations in 'register' according to the situation, just as we today can recognise and understand the English of, e.g., New York, Cape Town, Melbourne, Glasgow or Dublin in their contemporary forms, and at the same time can read the works of Spillane, Wodehouse, Dickens, Bunyan and Shakespeare without too much trouble.

Furthermore, in some cases, I have ignored very late forms (for example, the names of counties which post-date the Conquest) in an effort to avoid glaring anachronisms. But, conversely, where the names of certain plants are recorded only in late documents – but are clearly OE in character – I have not seen fit to exclude them on those grounds alone.

Finally, it is worth noting here that I have avoided marking palatal *c* and *g* by special characters, partly because these are not separate sounds in OE, but pronunciation variants (allophones) of the non-palatal type. Clearly palatalisation did not proceed with equal speed in all dialects, but in order to mark these sounds it would be necessary to determine a date and place of composition for each text. (N.B. Students who wish to mark these sounds can usually pinpoint them by the i-mutation of the proximate vowel. Modern English pronunciation is also sometimes a guide here.)

4. Layout

In the Dictionary, for the majority of nouns, verbs, adjectives and adverbs, a capital letter code appears beside the OE form; this is the code for the corresponding Word List Section (e.g. WEA(lth) for expressions relating to money, riches and financial matters). Where there is more than one OE word given, the first entry from the appropriate Word List shows the code, and the following entries all have the same code; where there is more than one code, I have endeavoured to segregate the two senses by separate listings, thus :

> **behave** drohtnian *w* WOR
> gebæran *w* MIN, PFM

read as 'drohtnian' in the sense of 'do what is necessary, earn one's living' with the code WOR(k), and as 'gebæran' in the sense of 'conduct oneself personally or have a habitual bearing' under codes MIN(d), PFM(perform).

Equally, where a headword has both verbs and nouns shown after it, the headword has to be read correspondingly in each case, e.g. 'command' has five entries: 'bebēodan *2*, bebod *(n)*, diht *(m)*, hā tan *7*, hæs *(f)*' to be read as verbs ("to issue orders") in the first and fourth instances, and as a noun ("an order") in the others. A word like NE 'still' can belong to any of several parts of speech (verb 'make calm'; adjective 'quiet'; noun 'distillery'; adverb 'yet') although little discretion is required in determining which of these senses is appropriate to the context since they hardly overlap at all in use. Here again, reference to a glossary or OE dictionary will settle any cases of ambiguity.

The Word Lists are grouped to provide a range of vocabulary with a common theme suggested by the title, so that the writer should be able to find a usable word for the context.

5. Abbreviations

The abbreviations used are as follows :–

a	anomalous (irregular) verb
(acc)	accusative case
(dat)	dative case
(f)	feminine noun
(fpl)	feminine noun, plural number
(gen)	genitive case
(inst)	instrumental case
(m)	masculine noun
(mpl)	masculine noun, plural number
(n)	neuter noun
(nom)	nominative case
(npl)	neuter noun, plural number
w	weak verb
1	strong verb class 1
2	strong verb class 2
etc.	

A very small number of nouns belong to more than one gender, and are so marked, e.g. '*(m,n)*' means 'masculine or neuter noun'. Often it is simply impossible to determine the gender of a noun from the few recorded examples of its inflected forms. Adjectives are unmarked, as are conjunctions, adverbs, pronouns and interjections. Where personal pronouns are marked for case I have indicated this in the entry.

6. Grammatical Information

I have made no attempt to indicate for example whether a verb takes the direct object in the accusative or the dative, what case a preposition or adjective governs, and so on. To do so would have involved considerably larger entries than at present, and would have meant either a larger and more expensive book, or the exclusion of many interesting and useful OE words. I did not think this a price worth paying to provide syntactic information which the student will soon acquire through reading or studying the various guidebooks available.

There is a certain amount of blank space provided after each Word List in which the student can record his own discoveries of further relevant vocabulary. I make no claim to exhaustiveness in this book, only to having brought together a basic vocabulary for a wide range of subject matters.

7. Neologisms

A further use of the material herein, and one which will be of especial benefit to those who wish to compose original work in OE, is the opportunity to invent new (i.e. unrecorded) words from OE elements. Sometimes this need be no more than simple extrapolation: from the verb *þingian* (hold talks, settle a dispute, come to terms) one can deduce a noun *þingung* (peace talks, reconciliation) without departing at all from OE practice, since weak verbs of Class II regularly form nouns in this way (*-ian* becomes *-ung*). Equally, on the model *fremman* (carry out, achieve) > *fremful* (effective) one can produce many useful adjectives in *-ful* from verbal stems; and likewise for adjectives in *-sum*, *-lic*, *-ol*, etc. from these and other parts of speech.

OE poetry and prose make great use of compound nouns (e.g. *wēa* 'woe' + *gesīþ* 'companion' = *wēagesīþ* 'a person who shares in one's misfortune') and it is in this area that the intending writer will find this book most useful (assuming that no existing OE word expresses the intended notion exactly). The material presented tends to fall into two categories: the very mundane, such as tools, plants, household items, clothing, etc.; and the emotional and intellectual, including many entries reflecting attitudes of mind, mental qualities and states of emotion, as well as many aspects of speech and thought.

By careful use of vocabulary one should be able to devise compounds to express many notions which we nowadays simply borrow from elsewhere. A knowledge of German would be of assistance here, since it tends to rely on its own (Germanic) resources far more than NE, as did OE. To gloss 'telephone' the German language uses 'Fernsprecher' (far-speaker) – I see no reason not to use OE elements likewise (e.g. *feorrsprecend*).

Old English Pronunciation

The following is a brief guide for the reader who just wants a little help with the often daunting Old English names met with in the early literature and histories. It is important to bear in mind that the speakers of this language were English, and that the language itself was not so very different from that of today. There are very few aspects of Old English grammar, etc., which have not survived into the modern period, though often they appear as very formal, or only in regional dialects.

When pronouncing an Old English (OE) word, the stress usually comes on the first syllable: the name *Alfred* has the same stress pattern now as it had then. This is helpful for an English speaker of English, but variants such as b'**Nard** for Bernard (**Ber**-ned) have to be consciously altered. The main exception to this rule of first syllable stress is the very common and productive prefix '*ge-*' which is never stressed: '*gewitt*' (knowledge, understanding, wit) is 'ye-**wit**'.

The consonants of OE are often pronounced very much as in the modern language. The following can be given normal English pronunciation:–

b   d   l   m   n   p   t   w

The following are also pronounced as in modern English, but are very rare in Old English texts:–

k   x   z

j and *q* did not exist in OE: the sound of *q* was spelt *cw* in words like *cwic* 'quick, alive'.

c had the hard sound of *k*, never the sound of *s*. Before *i* and *e* it was pronounced something like the modern *ch*: *cōl* 'cool', *cinn* 'chin'; there are a handful of exceptions to this rule, where OE has an *e* replacing an earlier *o*, as for example in *cene* 'keen, sharp'. The modern pronunciation is usually a guide if the word has survived.

h at the beginning of a word (initially) was pronounced as now (e.g. *heorte*, 'heart') but it was also used within words (medially) or at the end (finally) to spell a sound like the last sound in Scottish 'loch', and this often survives into the modern spelling with -gh-: *niht* 'night', *flyht* 'flight'.

f was pronounced at the beginning or end of a word like the modern letter, but inside a word it was voiced to a *v* sound: *feoh* 'fee', *līf* 'life', *seofon* 'seven'. But when it is doubled it always has the unvoiced sound: *offrian* 'to offer'.

s (similarly to *f*) was initially and finally *s*, but medially voiced to *z*: *seofon* 'seven', *læs* 'less', *rīsan* 'to rise'. In combination with *c*, the sound was like *sh*: *scip* 'ship', *wæsc* 'wash, moving water'. When doubled it has the soft sound: *præsse* 'army'.

ð and *þ* are letters we no longer use; they would both be represented by *th* in our spelling. Like *f* and *s*, they are initially and finally unvoiced, as in 'thin', 'hath', and medially they are voiced as in 'bother': *ðoht* 'thought', *bæð* 'bath', *lāðan* 'to loathe'. Again, when doubled they are always unvoiced: *smiððe* 'smithy'.

g is a letter with at least three values. At the beginning of a word it has its ordinary modern sound: *gatu* 'gates'. Medially and finally, it has a sound similar to that in 'loch', but voiced: *sagu* 'saying, speech', *fāg* 'hostile'; particularly when it is in final position, the sound is sometimes softened to the *h* equivalent, and the spelling then varies between *g* and *h*: *stāh/stāg* 'he climbed'. But whenever it occurs before *e* or *i*, or after *i*, it has a sound nearer to modern *y*: *gēar* 'year', *gield* 'yield', *blōdig* 'bloody' (this *-ig* suffix is the origin of modern adjectives ending in -y). The digraph *cg* may represent a doubled *g* (*frocge*, 'frog') or it may have been the sound we spell *j* or *dg* (*brycg,* 'bridge').

Unlike modern English, where a number of spelling traditions have been unhappily brought together and produced chaos, OE spelling is generally very straightforward. All the letters have to be pronounced, though sometimes these are digraphs (two letters written to represent one sound, like the modern 'th') e.g. *sc, cg*. There are a few OE consonant clusters occurring at the beginnings of words which appear strange to the modern reader, though when they are pronounced they have a certain grandeur and charm which adds to the effect of the language. Among these are:–

cn	pronounced *k + n*	*cniht* 'boy, knight'
fn	*f + n*	*fnæst* 'blast, wind'
gn	*g + n*	*gnornian* 'to mourn, wail'
hl	(a voiceless *l*, like Welsh *ll)*	*hlæst* 'cargo'
hn	(a soft breathing before the nasal consonant)	*hnutu* 'nut'
hr	(a soft breathing before the trill)	*hring* 'ring'
hw	(a voiceless *w*, as heard in Scots English)	*hwǣr* 'where'
wl	*w + l*	*wlanc* 'proud'
wr	*w + r*	*wrēon* 'to cover'

The vowels of OE are a tricky area, and the following is a rough guide which will serve for practical purposes, but the diphthongs in particular are not easily reconstructed:–

	short	long
a	as in bud (southern English)	as in bard
ae/æ	as in bad	as in has (with full stress)
e	as in bed	as in bayed, bade
i	as in bid	as in bead
o	as in body	as in board, bored
u	as in bull	as in booed
y	as in French su	as in French sur

(The two *y* sounds can be reproduced in English by pronouncing the corresponding *i* sound and rounding the lips at the same time.) *ae* is an early spelling of the sound which later appears as *æ* .

Vowel length is usually marked in printed texts by a macron (¯) over a long vowel, with short vowels unmarked. There were no standard marks for vowel lengths in OE manuscripts. Diphthongs are vowels which glide from one to another without a break: the standard pronunciation of 'I, eye' starts like the vowel in bard and glides to the vowel in bead – try it for yourself! Although diphthongs look ferociously difficult, you have to remember that modern English uses many of the OE ones, and others that the Anglo-Saxons would have found equally mystifying!

ea   something like the sound in bared, Baird, with long and short variants where the first part is either the vowel of bed (short) or bade (long).

eo   similar to the above, but with the glide towards *o* rather than *a*.

ie   similar to the sound of beard with long and short variants.

io   similar to the above but with the glide towards *o* rather than *e*.

Finally, it is worth stressing that, for example, *c* + *h* is not a digraph in OE and has to be pronounced separately: the name *Cwichelm* is *Cwic* + *helm* and pronounced pretty much as in modern quick-helm, not quitch-elm. It is necessary to beware of words like *hātheorte* 'quick-tempered, rash' which is *hāt* (hot) + *heorte* (heart), and where *t* and *h* just happen to stand next to each other.

The above is a brief guide to the standard West Saxon system which is most often met with in histories. There are a good many regional variants, as well as spelling changes in the course of the period, which don't warrant detailed treatment here. Just as an example, the early name *Uualchstod* occurs also in standard West Saxon as *Wealhstod*. The interested reader should consult a reliable grammar for a better understanding, and the following are recommended:–

An Old English Grammar Randolph Quirk and C.L.Wrenn (old but useful, especially regarding the role of prefixes).

Old English Grammar Alistair Campbell (detailed and definitive, especially regarding pronunciation material and inflexions, but not for the beginner).

A Guide to Old English Bruce Mitchell and Fred C Robinson (includes a lot of material on grammar).

Dictionary

Word Hoard

Dictionary - Word Hoard

A

a certain (one) ān
  sum
a great deal micel MEA
  wornfela
a little lyt(hwōn) MEA
  sumes
abandon forlǣtan 7 EVL, GO
abase forbīgan w EVL
abate āswāmian w FAI, GO
  linnan 3
  sweðrian w
abbess abbodisse (f) CHU
abbot abbod (m) CHU
abide ābīdan 1 POS
ability cræft (m) MIN
  mǣð (f)
abject hēan EVL
ablaze fȳren FIR
able, be cunnan a KNO
  magan a PFM
abode hām (m) HSE
  setl (n)
abode of the dead dēaðwīc (n) CHU
abound genihtsumian w GD
about ābūtan
  be
  on būtan
  ymbe (embe)
above bufan POS
  ofer
  (on-, be-)ufan
abroad elðēodige STR
  ūtanbordes
  ūt(e)
absent æfweard POS
  ofhende
absolve scrīfan 1 CHU

absorb bedrincan 3 WAT
abstain forhabban a EAT
abstemious mǣðlic EAT
  sȳferǣte
abundance fyllu (f) GD
  nyhtsumnes (f)
acceptable ðoncwyrðe ASK, THI
accepted folccūð ASK
  freōndlic
accepted (as guilty) geresp ASK
accessible gefēre GO, LAN
accessory gewita (m) LAW
accident belimp (n) EVI
accompany midsīþian w GO
accomplish geæfnian w PFM
accomplishment cræft (m) KNO
  gecneordnes (f) MIN
accord, with one ānmōdlīc MIN
according to æfter
  be
account gerecednes (f) SAY
  racu (f)
accrue ārīsan 1 WEA
  ēacian w
accuse oncunnan w BLM
accuse wrongly forwrēgan w BLM
accuser onspecend (m) BLM
  tēond (m)
  wrēgend (m)
accustom geliðian w MIN
  wenian w
accustomed bewuna MIN
ache acan 6 AIL
  ece (m)
  wærc (m)
achieve æfnan w PFM
  begān a
  gehēgan w
acknowledge (and-)ondettan w SAY
acolyte candelbora (m) CHU

aconite ðung *(m)* PLA
acquaint cȳðan *w* KNO
acquiesce geþwǣrian *w* AGR
    underhnīgan *1*
acquire gestrȳnan *w* WEA
acre æcer *(m)* LAN
across geond
act dǣd *(f)* PFM, WOR
    gewyrht *(n)*
act out plegian *w* PFM
active hwæt PFM
actor trūð *(m)* REC
add ēacian *w* BEC
adder nǣddre *(f)* ANI
addicted to gelenge AIL
addicted to, be
    underðēodan *w* MIN
addition, in on ðǣrtō MEA
addition to, in tōēacan
address tōspēcan *5* SAY
adequate gemēde LAW
    medemlic
adjective nama *(m)* WRI
administer ðegnian *w* WOR
admit andettan *w* SAY
admonish monian *w* BLM
    mynian *w*
    (æt)wītan *1*
adorn   gerēnian *w* ART
    (ge)glengan *w*
    (ge)gyrwan *w*
    hrēodan *2*
    tēon *w*
    weorðian *w*
adorned fāg ART
    gehroden
adulation oferlufu *(f)* LOV, MIN
    twædding *(f)*
adult fullðungen FAM
    fullweaxen
    orped
adultery ǣwbryce *(m)* LAW, LOV
advance stæppan *6* GO
    wadan *6*
advantage fremu *(f)* GD

adverb bīword *(n)* WRI
    wordes gefēra *(m)*
adversary andsaca *(m)* FOE
    wiðersaca *(m)*
    wiðerwinna *(m)*
adversity broc *(n)* EVL
advice mæðel *(n)* AGR
    rǣd *(m)* MIN
advisable rǣdlīc MIN
advise (ge)lǣran *w* AGR, MIN, SAY
    (ge)rǣdan *w* KNO, THI
adviser geðeahta *(m)* WOR
    geðeahtend *(m)*
    geðeahtere *(m)* THI
    rǣdbora *(m)*
advocacy forspǣc *(f)* AGR, SAY
advocate forespeca *(m)* LAW, SAY
adze adesa *(m)* TOO
affable wordwynsum LOV
affinity mægrǣden *(f)* KIN
afflict brocian *w* EVL
    (ge)dreccan *w* AIL
    geswencan *w*
    hȳnan *w*
affliction hefignes *(f)* EVL
afford it, he can
    hē spēdeð tō ðǣm WEA
    him tō ðǣm gehagige
afraid forht MIN
Africans Affricani *(mpl)* STR
after æfter POS, TIM
    on lāst
    siððan
    ðæs ðe
afterbirth hala *(m)* AIL
afterwards æfter þǣm
    eft
    ofer
    siþþan
    þæs
again eft TIM
    ongēan
against on POS
    ongēan
    tōgēanes
    wið

against one's will unðonces MIN
age yldo *(f)* TIM
ago gēo TIM
agree ðingian *w* AGR, SAY, THI
  gecweðan *5*
  geðwærian *w*
agree to geðafian *w* AGR
agree upon āstihtan *w* AGR
agreeable gecwēme LOV
  gemēde
agreement ānnes *(f)* AGR
  geðwærnes *(f)*
agriculture eorðtilð *(f)* LAN
agrimony gārclife *(f)* PLA
ahead forð GO
aid (ge)fultumian *w* GD
  helpan *3*
ail ādlian *w* AIL
  yfelian *w*
air lyft *(f)* SKY
akin (ge)lenge KIN
alas! ēalā
  ēow
  wā
  walāwā
alb halba *(m)* CLO
albumen hwēte *(n)* PLA
alder alor *(m)* PLA
ale ealoð *(n)* EAT
  ealu *(n)*
alehouse ealuhūs *(n)* REC
alien elelendisc STR
  ellende
  fremde
alien spirit ellorgāst *(m)* MON, STR
alight fȳren FIR
  līhtan *w* GO
  onæled
alike gelīc ART
  onlīc
alive cucu LIV
  cwic
all eall MEA
all day long andlangne dæg TIM
allow lætan *7* PFM

allure ōlæcung *(f)* LOV
  spanan *6* ASK
almighty alwealda *(m)* CHU
  ælmihtig LRD
almond amigdal *(m)* EAT
almost fulnēah MEA
  welnēah
alms ælmesse *(f)* ASK, CHU, WEA
along andlang
  be
  wiþ
alongside emnlang POS
  onemn
  tōemnes
alphabet stæfræw *(f)* WRI
Alps Alpīs STR
already īu TIM
already mentioned foresprecen WRI
also ēac
  ealswā
  furðum
altar altare *(m)* CHU
  wēofod *(n)*
  wīgbedd *(n)*
although ðēah (ðe)
alum efne *(f)* MAT
always ā(wā) TIM
  ealne weg
  ealnig
  on symbel
  simble
amazed āmasod MIN
  ofwundrod
amazed, be wāfian *w* MIN
amber eolhsand *(n)* MAT
  glær *(m)*
  smelting *(f)*
ambiguous twifeald SAY, WRI
ambusher færsceaða *(m)* FOE
amid onmiddan POS
  tōmiddes
among betwēonum POS
  mid
  ongemang

amount andefn *(f)* MEA
  worn *(m)*
amphor-full amber *(m,n,f)* MEA
amulet lybesn *(f)* CHU
ancestor ealdfæder *(m)* KIN
  foregenga *(m)*
  foregongel *(m)*
ancestors ieldran *(mpl)* KIN
anchor ancer *(m)* WAT
anchor-chain oncerbend *(m,f)* WAT
ancient duty ealdriht *(n)* LAW
ancient right ealdriht *(n)* LAW
and and, ond
anew edneowe TIM
angel engel *(m)* CHU
Angeln Angel *(f)* STR
anger ierre *(f)* MIN
angle hwemm *(m)* ART
Angles Angelcynn *(n)* STR
  Engle *(mpl)*
angry ierremōd MIN
  wrāð
animal dēor *(m)* ANI
ankle anclēow *(f)* BOD
anniversary gemynddæg *(m)* TIM
announce (ā)bēodan *2* SAY
  bodian *w*
annoyance æfðonca *(m)* MIN
annul āīdligan *w* FAI, LAW
another ōðer
answer andswaru *(f)* ASK, SAY
  oncweðan *5*
  ondswerian *6*
  ondwyrdan *w*
  ondwyrde *(n)*
ant æmette *(f)* ANI
anthill æmetbedd *(n)* ANI
anticipate forecuman *4* GO, TIM
anticlockwise wiðersȳnes GO
antirrhinum hundeshēafod *(n)* PLA
anus earsgang *(m)* BOD
  setl *(n)*
  ūtgang *(m)*
anxiety ymbhoga *(m)* MIN
any ænig

anyone (ge)hwā
  nāthwilc
  sum
anything āwuht
  ōht
  wiht
anywhere āhwǣr POS
apart (on)sundor POS
ape apa *(m)* ANI
apostate apostata *(m)* CHU
apostle apostol *(m)* CHU
  ærendwrecca *(m)*
apparel gegyrela *(m)* CLO
appear wrongly misðyncan *w* SEE
appearance ansīen *(f,n)* ART, LOV
  hīw *(n)* COL
  wlite *(m)*
apple æppel *(m)* EAT
apple-tree apulder *(m,f)* PLA
apply oneself befēolan *3* MIN, THI
apply oneself to gefeallan *7* PFM
appoint betǣcan *w* LAW
  lagian *w*
  stihtan *w*
appoint a day āndagian *w* LAW
appointed day āndaga *(m)* TIM
approach gegangan *7* GO
  (ge)nēalǣcan *w*
  nēosian *w*
appropriate cyn GD
  gelimplic
April Eastermōnað *(m)* TIM
apron bearmclāð *(n)* CLO
aquatic monster brimwylf *(f)* MON
  meredēor *(n)*
  nicor *(m)*
  wæteregesa *(m)*
arbitration sōm *(f)* AGR
arch boga *(m)* HSE
archangelica blindenetele *(f)* PLA
archbishop ærcebiscop *(m)* CHU
archbishopric arcebisceoprīce *(n)* CHU
  ærcestōl *(m)*
ardour hātheortnes *(f)* LOV
  wylm *(m)*

arena pleghūs *(n)* REC
  wæferhūs *(n)*
argument beadurūn *(f)* WAR
  geflit *(n)* AGR
  mǣl *(f)* SAY
arise wæcnan 6 GO
arithmetic rīmcræft *(m)* KNO
ark earc *(f)* CHU
arm earm *(m)* BOD
  syrwan *w* WAR, WPN
  wǣpnian *w*
arm's length fæðm *(m)* MEA
  fæðmrīm *(n)*
armed attack ecgðracu *(f)* EVL
armour herewǣde *(n)* PRO, WPN
armour, in shining scīrham LRD
armpit ōcusta *(m)* BOD
  ōxn *(f)*
army fierd *(f)* WAR
  folc *(n)*
  getrum *(n)*
  getruma *(m)*
  prass *(m)*
army division fierdstemn *(m)* WAR
  gefylce *(n)*
army of spearmen æschere *(m)* WAR
aroma stenc *(m)* EAT
around embe POS
  onbūtan
  ymb(e)
arouse āweccan *w* SLP
arrange stihtian *w* LRD
arrangement gesetednes *(f)* HSE
array trymian *w* LRD
arrival (tō)cyme *(m)* GO
arrive becuman 4 GO
arrogance gielp *(m,n)* MIN
  ofermōdignes *(f)*
arrow flān *(m,f)* WPN
  strǣl *(m,f)*
arse ears *(m)* BOD
arson in a house hūsbryne *(m)* FIR
arson in a wood
  wudubærnett *(n)* FIR
art cræft *(m)* ART
  wrǣtt *(f)*

as ealswā
  swā
  swilc
as.....as swā.....swā
as if swilce
as necessary tō ðearfe NEE
ascension ūpāstignes *(f)* GO
ash axe *(f)* FIR
  æsce *(f)*
  æsc *(m)* PLA
ashamed scōmig BLM
ashamed, be
  (ge)scomian *w* MIN, THI
ask ācsian *w* ASK
  āhsian *w*
  āscian *w*
ask for (ā)biddan 5 ASK
asking ācsung *(f)* ASK
asleep, be fast swodrian *w* SLP
asleep, half- healfslæpende SLP
asparagus eorðnafola *(m)* PLA
aspen æspe *(f)* PLA
aspire to fundian *w* LOV, MIN
ass esol *(m)* ANI
  esole *(f)*
assail gestandan 6 WAR
  onsittan 5 EVL
assemble (ge)somnian *w* ASK, BRI
assembly gemōt *(n)* BRI
  gesomnung *(f)*
assent geðafung *(f)* ASK
assess dēman *w* THI, WEA
  geeahtian *w*
assist fultumian *w* WAR
  helpan 3
assistance fultum *(m)* GD
  fylst *(m)*
  help *(m,f)*
assistance, be of on stale bēon *a*
associate geðēodian *w* GO
association geðēodnes *(f)* GD
asthma angbrēost *(n)* AIL
  nyrwett *(n)*
astronomy tungolǣ *(f)* KNO
  tungolcræft *(m)*

at æt
   tō
at home innanbordes HSE
at last sīð ond late TIM
   æt niehstan
at leisure ǣmettig MIN
at once ǣdre TIM
   instæpe
   sōna
at one time ... at another
   hwīlum ... hwīlum TIM
at the moment on ondweardnesse TIM
at times tīdlīc TIM
   hwīlum
at will on lyste LOV
atom mot *(n)* MAT
atone for gebētan *w* LAW
atrophy smalung *(f)* AIL
attack gesēcan *w* WAR
   gestandan *6*
   onrǣs *(m)*
   onscyte *(m)*
attack beacon herebēacen *(n)* LAN
attacking onsǣge WAR
attempt fandian *w* PFM
   tilian *w*
attend andweardian *w* POS
   ætwesan *a*
attract getēon *2* ASK, LOV
   spanan *6*
augur hālsiend *(m)* KNO
   hwata *(m)*
August Rugern *(m)* TIM
   Wēodmōnað *(m)*
aunt (maternal) mōdrige *(f)* KIN
aunt (paternal) faðe *(f)* KIN
authority hlāforddōm *(m)* LRD
   onweald *(m)*
autumn hærfest *(m)* TIM
avail behealdan *7* GD
   dugan *a*
avarice gītsung *(f)* ASK, EVL
avaricious feohgīfre EVL
avenge (ge)wrecan *5* EVL, LAW
avenger wrecend *(m)* FOE

avoid bebūgan *2* GO
   forbūgan *2*
   forsittan *5* EVL
   onscunian *w*
avow gebēotian *w* SAY
await ābīdan *1* POS
awake onwæcnan *w* SLP
awake early ǣrwacol TIM
aware gemyndig MIN
awareness gewitnes *(f)* MIN
away āweg, onweg GO
   forþ
   fram
awe ege *(m)* MIN
awkward ambyre EVL
   earfoðlic
awl æl *(m)* TOO
axe æcs *(f)* TOO, WPN
axle eax *(f)* DRI, TOO

B

baby bearn *(n)* KIN
   (cradol)cild *(n)*
bachelor ānhaga *(m)* KIN
   hægsteald *(m)*
back eft
   oferbæc
   underbæc
   bæc *(m)* BOD
   hrycg *(m)*
backwards earsling
   eft
   on bæcling
back-to-back bæcling POS
bacon spic *(n)* EAT
bad yfel EVL
bad news lāðspell *(n)* SAY
bad weather unweder *(n)* SKY
bad-tempered gedreht MIN
   hrēohmōd
badger brocc *(m)* ANI
bag pocca *(m)* CLO
   pusa *(m)*

bail borg *(m)* LAW, WEA
bailiff wīcgerēfa *(m)* WOR
bait ǣs *(n)* EAT
bake (ā)bacan *6* EAT
baker bæcere *(m)* EAT, WOR
 bæcestre *(f)*
bald blerig BOD
 calu
balefire bǣl *(n)* DIE
baleful bealoful EVL
balista stæfliðere *(f)* WAR
ball clīewen *(n)* TOO
 ðōðor *(m)*
balk bælc *(m)* HSE
Baltic Sea Ōstsǣ *(f)* STR
band gedryht *(f)* WAR
 gesīðmægen *(n)*
 hlōð *(f)*
 þrēat *(m)*
bandage onwrīðung *(f)* AIL
 wrīðan *1*
bandit ūtlaga *(m)* FOE
 wulfeshēafod *(n)*
bane bana *(m)* FOE
banish ādrīfan *1* DRI
 geūtian *w*
 āhwettan *w* LAW
banner segen *(m,n)* WPN
banquet swæsende *(npl)* EAT
 symbel *(n)*
baptism fulluht *(n)* CHU
bar scyttels *(m)* TOO
barbican burhgeat *(n)* HSE
bare bær CLO
barefoot bærfōt CLO
bargain bycgan *w* WEA
 nǣming *(f)*
bark beorcan *2* ANI
 rind *(f)* PLA
barking beorc *(f)* ANI
barley bēow *(n)* EAT, PLA
 bere *(m)*
barley crop berewæstm *(m)* PLA
barm beorma *(m)* EAT
barmaid tæppestre *(f)* WOR

barman tæppere *(m)* WOR
barn ærn *(n)* HSE
 bæren *(n)*
barque flota *(m)* WAT
 naca *(m)*
barrel byden *(f)* EAT
 byrla *(m)* TOO
 tunne *(f)* WAT
barren gǣsne AIL
 unwǣstmbǣre LAN
 wēste
barrier clūstor *(n)* LAN, PRO
 eodor *(m)*
barrow beorg *(f)* DIE
barter cēap *(m)* WEA
 cēapian *w*
base hēanlīc EVL
bashful forhtful MIN
basil mistel *(m)* PLA
basket spyrte *(f)* TOO
 windel *(m)*
bast bæst *(m)* PLA
bastard bastard *(m)* KIN
 cifesboren
 hornungsunu *(m)*
bat hrēaðmūs *(m)* ANI
batch gebæc *(n)* EAT
bath bæð *(n)* HSE, WAT
bathe baðian *w* WAT
bathhouse bæðern *(n)* WAT
bathing ðwēal *(n)* WAT
bathing place bæðstede *(m)* WAT
battle beadu *(f)* WAR
 (ge)camp *(n)*
 camphād *(m)*
 getoht *(n)*
 gūð *(f)*
 hild *(f)*
 lāc *(n,f)*
 wīg *(n)*
 wīgrǣden *(f)*
battlefield campstede *(m)* LAN, WAR
 folcstede *(m)*
 wælfeld *(m)*
 wælstōw *(f)*

Bavarians Bǣgwære *(mpl)* STR
be wesan *a*
  bēon *a*
be able cunnan *a* KNO
  magan *a* PFM
be addicted to
  underðēodan *w* MIN
be amazed wāfian *w* MIN
be ashamed
  (ge)scomian *w* MIN, THI
be at rest restan *w* POS
  sittan *5*
  standan *6*
  wunian *w*
be born wæcnan *6* KIN
be convenient onhagian *w* GD
be empowered to onhagian *w* PFM
be enough genōgian *w* GD
  genihtsumian *w*
be envious æfestian *w* MIN
be exempt scīran *w* LAW
be fast asleep swodrian *w* SLP
be fitting behōfian *w* GD
  gerīsan *1*
be in the habit of gewunian *w* MIN
be intent hīgian *w* MIN, THI
be lost losian *w* FAI
  oðstandan *6*
be merciful to gemiltsian *w* MIN
be moist fūhtian *w* WAT
be necessary nēodian *w* NEE
be obliged sculan *a*
be occupied ābisgian *w* THI
be of assistance on stale bēon *a* GD
be of use dugan *a* GD, TOO
be permitted mōtan *a*
be pleasing to gelīcian *w* LOV
be possible onhagian *w* BEC
be present ætwesan *a* POS
be prone (to) forðlūtan *2*
be ruined forweorðan *3* EVL
be sad sorgian *w* MIN
  sweorcan *3*
be sane tela witan *a* MIN
be shipwrecked forlīðan *1* GO

be sick ādlian *w* AIL
  sīclian *w*
  spiwian *w*
be tired tēorian *w* SLP
be troubled (ge)sweorcan *3* MIN
  swincan *3*
be wary of warian *w* MIN
be weary ātēorian *w* SLP
be willing willan *a*
beach strand *(m)* LAN, WAT
beacon (ge)bēacn *(n)* LAN
  forebēacn *(n)* FIR
beak bile *(f)* BOD
  neb *(n)*
beam of light bēam *(m)* FIR
beam of wood bēam *(m)* HSE
bean bēan *(f)* EAT, PLA
bear (ā)cennan *w* KIN
  (ge)beran *4* BRI
  wegan *5*
  beorn *(m)* ANI
  bera *(m)*
bear away āberan *4* BRI
  oðberan *4*
  oðferian *w*
bear children cennan *w* BRI
bear in mind beðencan *w* THI
  gemunan *w* MIN
  gemyndian *w*
bear skin, made of beren CLO
bear to ætberan *4* BRI
beard beard *(m)* BOD
beast dēor *(m)* ANI
beat bēatan *7* BRK
beat down bēatan *7* WAR
  cnyssan *w*
beaten geðrūen TOO
  gefliemed WAR
  sigelēas PFM
beautiful ælfscīenu LOV
  beorht
  blāchlēor
  cȳmlīc
  deall
  fæger

hīwbeorht
hwīt
leoht
scīene
scīr
smicer
wlitig ART
wrǣst(līc)
beautify geglengan *w* ART
(ge)gyrwan *w*
wlitigian *w*
beauty blēoh *(n)*, LOV
glǣm *(m)*
lēoma *(m)*
mægwlite *(m)* GD
scīma *(m)*
torht *(n)*
wlite *(m)* ART
beaver befor *(m)* ANI
because ðȳ
forðǣm (þe)
forðȳ
become (ge)weorðan *3* BEC
become better gōdian *w* BEC
become bigger weaxan *7* BEC
ȳcan *w*
become cold cōlian *w* BEC
become dark (ge)nīpan *1* BEC, TIM
sweorcan *3*
become day dagian *w* BEC, TIM
become divided gedǣlan *w* BEC
tōtwǣman *w*
become drunk oferdrencan *w* BEC
become hard hyrdan *w* BEC
stīðian *w*
become heavy hefigian *w* BEC
become known gecȳðan *w* BEC
geopenian *w*
become larger ēacnian *w* BEC
become less sweðrian *w* BEC
(ge)wanian *w*
become loose tōslūpan *2* BEC
wagian *w*
become lost losian *w* BEC
become molten gemeltan *w* BEC

become new ednīwian *w* BEC
become pimply pypelian *w* AIL, BEC
become poisonous
gehwelian *w* AIL, BEC
become red ārēodian *w* BEC
become remiss dwellan *w* BEC
wandian *w*
become ruined forweorðan *3* BEC
become sick ādlian *w* BEC
sīclian *w*
become small dwīnan *1* BEC
lȳtlian *w*
become soft lissan *w* BEC
become strong elnian *w* BEC
become tired tēorian *w* BEC
become warm wyrman *w* BEC
become weak onwǣcan *w* BEC
sweðrian *w*
wācian *w* FAI
become wealthy gestrȳnan *w* BEC
spēdan *w*
become weary mēðian *w* BEC
become winter winterlǣcan *w* BEC
become worse wyrsian *w* BEC
yfelian *w*
become yellow geolwian *w* BEC
bed bedd *(n)* HSE
bedrest *(f)*
ræst *(f)* SLP
bed of flowers wyrtbedd *(n)* PLA
bedfellow gebedda *(m)* SLP
gemæecca *(m)*
hǣmere *(m)*
Bedfordshire
Bedanfordscīr *(f)* STR
bedridden person beddridda *(m)* AIL
bedroom slǣpern *(n)* SLP
bee bēo *(f)* ANI
beech bōc *(f)* PLA
beekeeper bēoceorl *(m)* ANI
bēocere *(m)*
beer bēor *(n)* EAT
beer-feast (ge)bēorscipe *(m)* EAT
beestings bēost *(m)* EAT
bīesting *(f)*

beetle budda *(m)* ANI
 wifel *(m)*
beetroot bēte *(f)* PLA
befall gebyrian *w* BEC
 getīmian *w*
befit (ge)dafenian *w* GD
before ǣr TIM
 ætforan
 beforan
 foran
 fore
 on foran
 tōforan
beg biddan *5* ASK
 giernan *w*
beget cennan *w* KIN
 strȳnan *w*
beggar ælmesmann *(m)* ASK, WEA
 wǣdla *(m)*
begin āginnan *3* STA
 beginnan *3*
 onginnan *3*
 onstellan *w*
beginning fruma *(m)* STA
 ord *(m)*
behave drohtnian *w* WOR
 gebǣran *w* MIN, PFM
behaviour gebǣru *(npl)* PFM
behead
 behēafdian *w* BOD, EVL, LAW, WAR
behest hǣs *(f)* ASK
behind æthindan POS
 behindan
 on lāst
behold gesēon *5* SEE
 lōcian *w*
behold! lōc nū!
behove behōfian *w* NEE
bejewelled sinchroden ART
belie ālēogan *2* SAY
belief gelēafa *(m)* THI
believe gelīefan *w* THI
believing gelēafful CHU
bell belle *(f)* CHU

 clucge *(f)* REC
bellows blǣstbelg *(m)* TOO
 bylig *(m)*
belong belimpan *3* WEA
beloved fǣle LOV
 lēof
 luflīc
 swǣs
beloved companion
 wilgesīð *(m)* LOV
 wilgeðofta *(m)*
below(-mentioned) hērbeæftan POS
belt belt *(m)* CLO
 fetels *(m)*
 gyrdel *(m)*
bemoan besorgian *w* MIN
 murnan *3*
bench benc *(f)* HSE
 scamol *(m)*
benchmate gebēor *(m)* EAT
bend būgan *2* GO
 gebīgan *w*
 hnīgan *1*
bend down (on)hyldan *w* GO
beneath (be)neoðan POS
 under
benefactor (in wealth)
 bēahgifa *(m)* LRD
benefit ār *(f)* MIN
 feorm *(f)* WEA
 bōt *(f)* GD
 fremfulnes *(f)*
 gedīgan *w*
 gōd *(n)*
benevolent ruler winedrihten *(m)* LRD
bent wōh BRK
bequeath
 (be-)cweðan *5* DIE, SAY, WEA
 (ge-)cweðan *5*
bequest lāf *(f)* KIN
bereave belēosan *2* DIE, NEE
bereft berēafod NEE
 benumen
 sceard

Berkshire Bearrucscīr *(f)* STR
Bernician (people)
  Beornice *(mpl)* STR
berry berge *(f)* PLA
beside andlang
  be
  tōemnes
besides ēac
  furðum
  tōēacan ðǣm
besiege besittan *5* WAR
besmirch besmītan *1* EVL
bespatter bedrīfan *1* EVL
best betst
  selest
bestow forgiefan *5* LAW**bestow
honour upon** ārian *w* GD
  inwyrcan *w* LRD
  weorðian *w*
betoken tācnian *w* MIN
betony betonice *(f)* PLA
  brūnwyrt *(f)*
betray beswīcan *1* EVL
  forrǣdan *w*
  forrǣdan of līfe *w* WAR
betrayer beswīcend *(m)* FOE
better betera
  selra
better, become gōdian *w* BEC
between betwēonum POS
  betwuh (betwux)
bewail cwiðan *w* SAY
beware of warnian *w* THI
beyond begeondan POS
  ofer
Biarmians (White Sea people)
  Beormas *(mpl)* STR
bible biblioðece *(f)* WRI
  cȳðnes *(f)*
bide (ge)bīdan *1* POS
bier bǣr *(f)* DIE
big grēat MEA
  micel
bigger, become weaxan *7* BEC
  ȳcan *w*

big-hearted rūmheort MIN
bill (beak) bile *(m)* ANI
  neb *(n)*
bin binne *(f)* HSE
bind (ge)bindan *3* EVL
  cnyttan *w*
  hæftan *w*
  rǣpan *w*
  sǣlan *w*
bind a salve to forlecgan *w* AIL
bind up bindan *3* HSE
bind (tie in) bendan *w* HSE
binder bindere *(m)* WOR
binding bindere *(m)* HSE
  byndelle *(f)*
  gebind *(n)* EVL
bindweed wiðowinde *(f)* PLA
birch berc *(f)* PLA
bird fugol *(m)* ANI
birdcatcher fuglere *(m)* WOR
birth ācennednes *(f)* KIN, LRD
  (ge)byrd *(f)*
bishop biscop *(m)* CHU
bishopship biscophād *(m)* CHU
bitch bicce *(f)* ANI
  tife *(f)*
bite bītan *1* EAT
bite into ābītan *1* EAT
bitter biter EVL, MIN
  wrāð
bittern hæferblǣte *(f)* ANI
bitumen eorðtyrewe *(f)* MAT
black blæc FIR
  sweart COL
  wonn
blackberry bremel *(m)* PLA
blackthorn slāhþorn *(m)* PLA
bladder blǣdre *(f)* BOD
  tyncen *(n)*
blade ecg *(f)* WPN
  īren *(n)* TOO
blain blegen *(f)* AIL
blame leahtrian *w* BLM
  oncunnan *w*
  tǣlan *w*
  (æt)wītan *1* SAY

blameless bilewit BLM, GD
  orleahtre
  ungyltig
  unscende
blanket hwītel *(m)* SLP
blast blǣst *(m)* SKY
  fnǣst *(m)*
bleary-eyed sīwenēge SLP
bleed blēdan *w* AIL
blend blendan *3* BRI
bless bletsian *w* CHU, GD
blessed ēadig GD
  gesǣlig
  hālig
blessing bletsung *(f)* CHU, GD
blind āblendan *w* EVL
  blind AIL, BOD, SEE
bliss bliss *(f)* GD
  blīðnes *(f)*
  drēam *(m)*
  ēadignes *(f)*
block forfaran *6* EVL
  forstandan *6*
blond(e) fæger COL
blood blōd *(n)* BOD
  heolfor *(m,n)*
  stēam *(m)*
  swāt *(m)*
blood-stained drēorig WPN
  swātfāg BOD
bloodshed blōdgyte *(m)* WAR
bloodthirsty wælhrēow EVL
bloody drēorig BOD
bloom blōma *(m)* MAT
  blōstma *(m)* PLA
  blōwan *7*
blossom blōstma *(m)* PLA
  blōwan *7*
blow drepe *(m)* EVL
  dynt *(m)*
  slege *(m)* WAR
  swinge*(f)*
  blāwan *7* SKY
  wāwan *7*
blow against ondhweorfan *3* SKY

blow round bewāwan *7* SKY
blow to the ear ēarslege *(m)* EVL
blowfly smegawyrm *(m)* ANI
blue hǣwe
  hǣwen COL
blush rudu *(f)* BOD
  blyscan *w* LOV
boar bār *(m)* ANI
  eofor *(m)*
board bord *(n)* HSE
boarspear eoforspere *(n)* WPN
  eoforsprēot *(n)*
boast (ge)bēot *(n)* SAY
  (ge)bēotian *w*
  gielp *(m,n)*
  gielpword *(n)*
  gielpan *w* MIN
  hrēman *w*
boat bāt *(m)* WAT
  naca *(m)*
boatkeeper bātweard *(m)* WAT
bodily līchomlīc BOD
body bodig *(n)* BOD
  feorhbold *(n)*
  feorhhord *(n)*
  feorhhūs *(n)*
  flǣsc *(n)*
  līc *(n)*
  līcfæt *(n)*
  līchoma *(m)*
body of water lagu *(f)* WAT
  wæterscipe *(m)*
bodyguards werod *(n)* WAR
bogmyrtle gagel *(m)* PLA
Bohemians Bǣme *(mpl)* STR
  Bēhēmas *(mpl)*
boil blegen *(f)* AIL
  gesēoðan *2* WAT
  āwiellan *w* EAT
  weallan *7*
boil, head of a dott *(m)* AIL
boiled vegetables
  gesodene wyrta *(fpl)* EAT
boiled, lightly- hrēre EAT

bold beald MIN, WAR
  cāf
  collenferhð
  dǣdcēne
  dēor
  dyrstig
  fram
  mōdelīc
boldness gebyld *(f)* MIN
bolster bolster *(m)* SLP
  heafodbolster *(n)*
  cweornbill *(n)* TOO
bolt scyttels *(m)* TOO
bond clomm *(m)* EVL
  racente *(f)*
  bend *(m,f)* HSE
bondsman ðēowmon *(m)* WOR
  hæft *(m)* EVL
bondswoman ðēowen *(f)* WOR
  wȳln *(f)*
bone bān *(n)* BOD
bone, made of bǣnen MAT
bonemarrow mearg *(m)* BOD
bonfire bǣl *(n)* FIR
book bōc *(f)* WRI
book of instruction lārbōc *(f)* WRI
bookcase bōcfōdder *(m)* WRI
booth sceoppa *(m)* HSE
booty lāc *(n,f)* WAR
border efes *(f)* CLO
  biwindla *(m)* LAN
  haga *(m)*
  mǣre *(n)*
  mearc *(f)*
  ōra *(m)*
bore into borian *w* BRK, TOO
  ðurhdrīfan *1*
boredom ǣðrytnes *(f)* MIN
born ācenned KIN
  geboren
born, be wæcnan *6* KIN
borrow (ā)borgian *w* WEA
bosom bearm *(m)* BOD
  bōsm *(m)*
  fæðm *(m)*

both bā
  begen
  bū
both ... and ǣgðer ge...ge
  (ǣghwæðer) ge...ge
bottle cylle *(m)* EAT, WAT
  flaxe *(f)*
  pinne *(f)*
bottle (made of leather)
  buteric *(m)* EAT
  higdifæt *(n)*
bottom botm *(m)* BOD, WAT
boundary gemǣre *(n)* LAN
  londgemǣre *(n)*
  mearc *(f)*
bountiful gifol EAT
  rōp WEA
bounty blǣd *(m)* WEA
  bōt *(f)*
bow ābūgan *2* GO
  (ge)būgan *2*
  hnīgan *1*
  (on)lūtan *2*
  bȳgan *w* AIL
  boga *(m)* WPN
bowel innoð *(m,f)* BOD
bower būr *(f)* SLP, HSE
bowl blēd *(f)* EAT
  bolla *(m)*
box cist *(f)* BRI
  teag *(f)*
boxer bēatere *(m)* WOR
box tree box *(m)* PLA
  boxtrēow *(n)*
boxwood, made of byxen MAT
boy cnapa *(m)* KIN
bracelet bēag *(m)* ART, WEA
  būl *(m)*
  dalc *(m)*
braided-haired wundenlocc BOD
brain brægen *(n)* BOD
  hærn *(m)*
bramble brember *(m)* PLA
  brēmel *(m)*
bran sifeða *(m)* EAT

branch blēd *(f)* PLA
  bōg *(m)*
  telga *(m)*
brand mearcian *w* ANI
branding iron ceorfingīsen *(n)* TOO
brandish ācweccan *w* LRD
  bregdan *3*
brass ār *(n)* MAT
  mæstling *(n)*
brass, made of æren MAT
bravado ellen *(m)* MIN
  wlencu *(f)*
brave dēor MIN
  rōf
  stīðmōd
  unhēanlīc
  felamōdig WAR
brave deed ellendǣd *(f)* WAR
brazen æren MAT
breach bryce *(m)* BRK
breach of a fast fæstenbryce *(m)* EAT
breach of a festival
  frēolsbryce *(m)* CHU
breach of bail borgbryce *(m)* LAW
breach of holy law æswice *(m)* CHU
breach of law lahbryce *(m)* LAW
breach of promise wedbryce *(m)* LAW
breach of surety
  borgbryce *(m)* EVL
bread hlāf *(m)* EAT
breadmaker dǣge *(f)* WOR
break brecan *4* BRK
  clēofan *2*
  tōberstan *3* EVL
break apart bebrecan *4* BRK
break away (æt)berstan *3* BRK
break into ābrecan *4* BRK
break to pieces bebrecan *4* BRK
break up ābrēotan *2* BRK
  tōberstan *3*
  tōbrecan *4*
breakfast morgenmete *(m)* EAT
breast bōsm *(m)* BOD
  brēost *(m,n,f)*
  titt *(m)*

breath ǣþm *(m)* LIV
  blǣd *(m)*
breathing ǣðung *(f)* BOD, LIV
breathing difficulty hrēoung *(f)* AIL
breeches brēc *(fpl)* CLO
  brēchrægl *(n)*
breed tyddrian *w* KIN
brew brēowan *2* EAT
brick tigele *(f)* HSE
bride brȳd *(f)* KIN
bridesmaid hādswǣpe *(f)* LOV
bridesman hādswǣpa *(m)* LOV
bridge brycg *(f)* HSE
bridge over brycgian *w* HSE
bridle brīdel *(m)* ANI
bright beorht FIR
  blāc
  lēoht
  brūn COL
  scīr WAT
bright-edged brūnecg WPN
brightness beorhtnes *(f)* FIR
brine-stained wārig WAT
bring (ge)brengan *w* BRI
  bringan *3*
  (ge)feccan *w*
  ferian *w* DRI
  (ge)lǣdan *w*
  tōgelǣdan *w*
bring about (ge)fremman *w* PFM
  geweorcan *w*
bring forth ācennan *w* KIN
bring together gegaderian *w* BRI
  mengan *w*
bring up gebringan *3* KIN
  tēon *2*
brisk snell GO
bristle byrst *(f)* ANI
Britain Bryten *(f)* STR
British Bryttisc STR
  Wylisc
Britons (Bret)wēalas *(mpl)* STR
  Wēalcynn *(n)*
brittle brēað BRK
broad brād LAN

broadcast tōbrǣdan *w* SAY
wīdmǣrsian *w*
broad-bosomed sīdfæðme BOD
broken (limb) forod BOD, BRK, EVL
gebrocen
broken-legged scancforod BOD
brooch dalc *(m)* ART, WEA
prēon *(m)* CLO
sigil *(n)*
brood brōd *(f)* KIN
brook brōc *(m)* WAT
brook lime hleomoce *(f)* PLA
broom besma *(m)* TOO
brōm *(m)* PLA
broth broð *(n)* EAT
brothel forligerhūs *(n)* HSE
brother brōðor *(m)* KIN
brothers gebrōðor *(mpl)* KIN
brow brū *(fpl)* BOD
ēagbrǣw *(m)*
brown brūn COL
dunn
bruise lǣl *(f)* AIL
tōbrȳsan *w*
brutish stunt MIN
bryony hymele *(f)* PLA
buck bucca *(m)* ANI
buckbean glæppe *(f)* EAT, PLA
bucket byden *(f)* TOO
Buckinghamshire
Buccingahāmscīr *(f)* STR
buckle oferfeng *(m)* CLO
sigil *(n)*
buckthorn ðȳfeðorn *(m)* PLA
bucktoothed twiseltōþ BOD
bugle ðunorclǣfre *(f)* PLA
build beweorcan *w* WOR
bytlian *w* HSE
scyppan *6*
(ā-, ge-)timbrian *w*
weorcan *w*
wyrcean *w*
build up bewyrcean *w* HSE
building bold *(n)* HSE
botl *(n)*

bytling *(f)*
getimbre *(n)*
timber *(n)*
Bulgarians Pulgare *(fpl)* STR
bull fearr *(m)* ANI
hriðer *(n)*
bumblebee dora *(m)* ANI
bun healstān *(m)* EAT
bunch of berries lēactrēog *(m)* PLA
bundle bindele *(f)* BRI
burbot ǣlepūte *(f)* ANI
burden bȳrðen *(f)* EVL
burdock clāte *(f)* PLA
clifwyrt *(f)*
ēawyrt *(f)*
Burgundians Burgendan *(mpl)* STR
burn (ge)bærnan *w* FIR
byrnan *3*
burn away forbærnan *w* FIR
burn up forbyrnan *3* FIR
burning bærnet *(n)* FIR
brond *(m)*
bryne *(m)*
burr clāte *(f)* PLA
burst tōberstan *3* EVL
burst out (æt)berstan *3* GO
bury bebyrgan *w* DIE
bedelfan *3*
bush ðȳfel *(m)* PLA
wrid *(m)*
bushel mydd *(n)* MEA, TOO
business bisgu *(f)* WOR
busy bisig WOR
but ac
hwæðre
butcher flǣscmangere *(m)* EAT
butter butere *(f)* EAT
buttercup clufwyrt *(f)* PLA
buttercurd butergeðwēor *(n)* EAT
butterfly buterflēoge *(f)* ANI
fifalde *(f)*
buy (ge)bycgan *w* WEA
gecēapian *w*
buy off forgieldan *3* FOE
buzzard mūshafoc *(n)* ANI

by be
   bī
   fram
   þurh
by means of fram
   mid
   þurh
byway orwegstīg *(f)* LAN

C

cabbage cawel *(m)* PLA
cake cicel *(m)* EAT
   foca *(m)*
   healstān *(m)*
calamity heardsǣlð *(f)* NEE
   ðrēa *(m)*
calf cealf *(n)* ANI
call hātan *7* CAL
call on (ge)cīgan *w* CAL
   nemn(i)an *w*
call out (announce) ceallian *w* CAL
   hrīeman *w*
call out (summon) āweccan *w* CAL
call up (ā)bannan *7* CAL
calm smylte MIN
   stille GD
   stillnes *(f)*
calm down (ge)sweðrian *(m)* MIN
calumny hōl *(n)* SAY
   onscyte *(m)* EVL
Cambridgeshire
   Grantabrycgscīr *(f)* STR
camel olfend(a) *(m)* ANI
camp gewīcian *w* LIV
   set *(n)* LAN
camp out gewīcian *w* HSE
camp protected by water
   wæterfæsten *(n)* LAN
camp protected by woods
   wudufæsten *(n)* LAN
campaign campian *w* WAR
   fierd *(f)*
   fierdian *w*
   fyrding *(f)*

can cunnan *a*
   magan *a*
canal wæterweg *(m)* WAT
candelabrum
   candeltrēow *(n)* FIR, HSE
candle candel *(f)* FIR, HSE
   tapor *(m)*
candlestick candelsticca *(m)* FIR, HSE
canine tooth tūx *(m)* BOD
canker cancor *(m)* AIL
cannabis hænep *(m)* PLA
canon canon *(m)* CHU
capital hēaburg *(f)* LAN
   hēafodburg *(f)*
capital offence dēaðscyld *(f)* LAW
captive hæft *(m)* EVL, WOR
captivity hæfting *(f)* EVL
   hæftnung *(f)*
   hæftnȳd *(f)*
capture cēpan *w* BRI
   gelæccan *w*
care cearu *(f)* EVL, LOV, MIN
   gīeman *(f)*
   gīeming *(f)*
   murnan *3*
   ymbhoga *(m)*
   ymbhygd *(f)*
   gedrēfednes *(f)* NEE
   heord *(f)* LRD
care for begongan *7* LOV
   gīeman *w* WOR
   rēcan *w*
   reccan *w*
careful behȳdig MIN, THI
   hohful
careless mōdlēas MIN
   wanhȳdig
careworn earmcearig MIN
Carinthia Carendre *(f)* STR
carline thistle eoforðrotu *(f)* PLA
carnage wæl *(n)* DIE
carpenter trēowyrhta *(m)* WOR
carrion ǣs *(n)* EAT
carrot more *(f)* EAT, PLA

carry (ge)beran *4* BRI
  (ge)ferian *w*
  wegan *5*
carry a message
  geǣrendian *w* ASK, WRI
carry off ætferian *w* BRI, EVL, WAR
  gefeccan *w*
  (for)niman *4*
  offerian *w*
  onberan *4*
carry on ðurhtēon *2* PFM
carry on (an activity) begongan *7* PFM
carry out begān *a* PFM
  (ge)dōn *7*
  (ge)forðian *w*
  gefremman *w*
  gehēgan *w*
  (ge)lǣstan *w*
  ðurhtēon *2*
carrying lād *(f)* BRI
cart cræt *(n)* DRI
  (cræt)wægen *(m)*
cartload fōðor *(n)* MEA
carve āgrafan *6* WRI
  ceorfan *3*
case (in law) spǣc *(f)* LAW
cast weorpan *3* POS
cat catt *(m)* ANI
  catte *(f)*
catarrh brǣc *(n)* AIL
  mǣldropa *(m)*
catch gefōn *7* BRI
catch birds fuglian *w* ANI, WOR
catch red-handed āparian *w* LAW
caterpillar cawelwyrm *(m)* ANI
  lēafwyrm *(m)*
  mǣlsceafa *(m)*
catmint nepte *(f)* PLA
cattle cēap *(m)* ANI, WEA
  feoh *(n)*
  nēat *(n)*
  nȳten *(n)*
  orf *(n)*
cattle disease orfcwealm *(m)* AIL, ANI
cattleshed scipen *(f)* ANI, HSE
cauldron citel *(m)* TOO

  fæt *(n)*
  hwer *(m)*
cause intinga *(m)* AGR, ASK,
  MIN, THI, WRI
cause for complaint inca *(m)* AGR
☐**cavalryman** rīdwiga *(m)* WAR
cavern eorðscræf *(n)* LAN
  hol *(n)*
cease linnan *3* FAI
  swiðrian *w*
cedar ceder *(m?)* PLA
celebrate mǣran *w* LOV
  frēolsian *w* MIN, REC
  rǣran *w*
cellar cleafa *(m)* HSE
censer storfæt *(n)* CHU
centaury curmelle *(f)* PLA
certain cūðlīc KNO
  gewiss
  wīslīc
  witodlīc
certainty gewiss *(n)* KNO
chaff egenu *(f)* PLA
chaffinch ceaffinc *(m)* ANI
chain racente *(f)* TOO
  racentēag *(f)*
  clomm *(m)* EVL
chair stōl *(m)* HSE
chalice calic *(m)* EAT
chalk cealc *(m)* MAT
challenge orettan *w* CAL
challenger oretta *(m)* FIG
chamber būr *(m)* HSE
chamberlain būrðegn *(m)* HSE, SLP
champion (sige)cempa *(m)* FIG
chancellor canceler *(m)* WOR
change āwendan *w* BEC
  onwendan *w*
  gebregd *(n)* GO
  (ge)hweorfan *w*
  edhwyrft *(m)* TIM
  edwenden *(f)*
change of colour brigd *(n)* COL
channel flōde *(f)* WAT
  sund *(n)*

chaos gedwolma *(m)*
chapterhouse capitelhūs *(n)* CHU
charlock cedelc *(f?)* PLA
charm ōlǣcung *(f)* AGR, LOV
  begalan 6 CHU
  besingan 3
  galdor *(n)* REC
charter (lond)bōc *(f)* WEA, WRI
charter-land bōcland *(n)* LAN, WRI
chaste clǣne GD
  sȳferlic
cheap undēore WEA
cheek heagospind *(n)* BOD
  hlēor *(n)*
  wange *(n)*
cheekpiece hlēorberg *(f)* WAR
cheerful rōtlīc MIN
cheese cīese *(m)* EAT
cheesecurd cīesgerunn *(n)* EAT
cherish clyppan *w* LOV, MIN, PRO
  friðian *w*
  tyddrian *w*
cherry cerse *(f)* EAT
chervil cerfille *(f)* PLA
Cheshire Cestrescīr *(f)* STR
  Legeceasterscīr *(f)*
chest brēost *(npl)* BOD
  brēostcofa *(m)*
  hreðer *(n)*
chestnut tree cystel *(f)* PLA
chew the cud eodorcan *w* ANI, EAT
chewing gum hwētcwudu *(m)* EAT
chicken cicen *(n)* ANI
chickweed cicena mēte *(m)* PLA
chide (ge)cīdan *w* AGR
chief ǣðeling *(m)* LRD
  ealdor *(m)*
  frēa *(m)*
  lēod *(m)*
  ðēoden *(m)*
chief thane ealdorðegn *(m)* LRD, WOR
child bearn *(n)* KIN
  (cradol)cild *(n)*
  eafora *(m)*
  lytling *(m)*

chill cyle *(m)* SKY
chillblain ǣcelma *(m)* AIL
Chiltern (Hills) Ciltern *(m)* STR
chin cinn *(n)* BOD
chinbone cinbān *(n)* BOD
chipping sceafoða *(m)* MAT
chisel brǣdīsen *(n)* TOO
chisel for stone cweornbill *(n)* TOO
choice (best) cyst *(m,f)* GD, LOV
choice (choosing) cyre *(m)* GD
choose (ge)cēosan 2 LOV, THI
chopping block onhēaw *(m)* TOO
chough cēo *(m)* ANI
Christendom Crīstendōm *(m)* CHU
Christian Crīsten CHU
Christmas Eve Mōdraniht *(f)* TIM
chronic ungewendendlīc AIL
church cirice *(f)* CHU
churn cyrn *(f)* EAT
cider ǣppelwīn *(n)* EAT
  līð *(n)*
circle ymbhwyrft *(m)* HSE
circular sinewealt ART
circular tower windelstān *(m)* HSE
circumference ymbgong *(m)* HSE
citizens ceasterware *(fpl)* LAN
city burgstede *(m)* LAN
  ceaster *(f)*
claimant onspecend *(m)* ASK
clamour cirm *(m)* CAL
clan mǣgð *(f)* KIN
clang swēging *(f)* WOR
claret hluttordrenc *(m)* EAT
clash (of opponents)
  cumbolgehnāst *(n)* WAR
clasp gespong *(n)* TOO
  grāp *(f)* EVL
claw clēa *(m)* BOD
clay clǣg *(m)* LAN
clean clǣne WAT
cleanness clǣnnes *(f)* WAT
cleanse (ge)clǣnsian *w* AIL, WAT
  fǣlsian *w*
clear hlūtor REC, SAY
  swutol
  scīr WAT

clear, make swutelian *w* SAY
clear one's throat hrǣcca *(m)* AIL
clearly known undierne KNO
cleave clēofan *2* BRK
cleavers clāte *(f)* PLA
clever snotor MIN
cliff clif *(n)* LAN
climb climban *3* GO
cloak bratt *(m)* CLO
  hacele *(f)*
  hedeclāþ *(m)*
  sciccels *(m)*
  wǣfels *(m,n)*
clockwise sunganges GO
cloister clauster *(n)* CHU
close betȳnan *w* STA
  getenge POS
  nēah
close ancestors
  nēahfædras *(mpl)* KIN
close kinsman hēafodmǣg *(m)* KIN
close off beclȳsan *w* STA
  tȳnan *w*
close together getenge POS
  getenglīc
close up belūcan *2* STA
clot clott *(m)* AIL
cloth clāð *(m)* CLO
  godwebb *(n)*
  hrægel *(n)*
  scīte *(f)*
  twīn *(n)*
cloth shears hræglscēara *(fpl)* TOO
clothe bewǣfan *w* CLO
  gewǣdian *w*
  gierelian *w*
  (ge)scrȳdan *w*
clothes keeper hrægelðegn *(m)* CLO
clothing gewǣde *(n)* CLO
  gierela *(m)*
  hrægel *(n)*
  scrūd *(n)*
  wǣd *(f)*
cloud genip *(n)* SKY
  wolcen *(n)*

clover clǣfre *(f)* PLA
club casebill *(n)* WPN
clump clympre *(m)* LAN
clutch grāp *(f)* EVL
co-habit hǣman *w* LOV
coal col *(n)* MAT
  glēde *(f)* FIR
coast sǣrima *(m)* LAN, WAT
coastal defence sǣweall *(m)* WAT
coastguard londweard *(m)* WAT
coat tunece *(f)* CLO
cock cocc *(m)* ANI
cockchafer (eorð)ceafor *(m)* ANI
cockle sǣcocc *(m)* ANI
cockspur grass āttorlāðe *(f)* PLA
coerce geðȳn *w* AGR, ASK, LRD
coffin cist *(f)* DIE
  ðrūh *(f)*
coin sceatt *(m)* WEA
coitus (wīf)gemāna *(m)* LOV
  wīfþing *(n)*
cold ceald
  cyld *(f)* EVL
  cyle *(m)*
  cyldu *(f)* SKY
cold, become cōlian *w* BEC
cold with frost hrīmceald SKY
cole cāwel *(m)* PLA
collar bēag *(m)* ART
collarbone wiðobān *(m)* BOD
collect gaderian *w* BRI
  (ge)somnian *w*
colour blēo *(n)* ART, COL
  dēag *(f)*
  hīw *(n)*
  hīwian *w*
coloured fāg ART, COL
comb camb *(m)* TOO
  cemban *w* WOR
combine fēgan *w* POS
  gesamodlǣcan *w*
come (be)cuman *4* GO
  gegān *a*
come alive cwician *w* LIV

come upon becuman *4* SEE
comely cȳmlīc LOV
comfort ēðnes *(f)* GD
  (ge)frēfran *w* MIN
  frōfor *(f)*
  gefrēfrian *w* LOV
comfrey galluc *(m)* PLA
comic song scēawendwīse *(f)* REC
coming (tō)cyme *(m)* GO
command
  (be)bēodan *2* ASK, CAL, LRD, SAY
  bebod *(n)*
  diht *(m)*
  hǣs *(f)*
  hātan *7*
commandment gebodscipe *(m)* LRD
common law folclagu *(f)* LAW
  folcriht *(n)*
common property gemāna *(m)* WEA
commotion styrenes *(f)* MIN
  unstilnes *(f)*
community gegaderung *(f)* BRI
companion gefēra *(m)* GO
  gesīð *(m)*
companion in misfortune
  wēagesīð *(m)* EVL
company flocc *(m)* WAR
  gefērscipe *(m)* LOV
  geðēodnes *(f)* GD
  hēap *(m)* BRI
  hwearf *(m)*
compare (ge)ānlīcian *w* THI
comparison wiðmetennes *(f)* THI
compassion efensārgung *(f)* MIN
compel bǣdan *w* ASK, EVL, LRD, NEE
  fornȳdan *w*
  (tō)genȳdan *w*
  geðyn *w*
  nīedan *w*
compensate gebētan *w* WEA
compensation bōt *(f)* LAW
compete gesacan *6* WAR
  winnan *3*
complain besprecan *5* SAY
  gecīdan *w* AGR
  mǣnan *w* THI

complain of mǣnan *w* SAY
complete fullfremman *w* PFM, STA
  fullgān *a*
  (ge)fyllan *w*
  geendian *w*
completely fullfremedlīce MEA
  tō wissum
compline nihtsang *(m)* CHU
compose (ge)settan *w* WRI
computer circolwyrde *(m)* WOR
comrade gefēra *(m)* LOV
  geselda *(m)*
  genēat *(m)* LRD
comrade-in-arms gedryhta *(m)* WAR
conceive geēacnian *w* KIN
concern ontimber *(n)* AGR, SAY
concerning be
  ymb(e)
concord geðwǣrnes *(f)* AGR
  sibsumnes *(f)*
condemn fordēman *w* THI
  niðerian *w* BLM
condensation īsenswāt *(m)* MAT
condition hād *(m)* BEC
  ðing *(n)*
  gerǣden *(f)* THI
  wīse *(f)* MIN
condition that, on wið ðǣm ðe
conduct gebǣre *(n)* MIN
  ðēaw *(m)*
confess (ge)andettan *w* SAY
confessor scrift *(m)* CHU
confidence gebyld *(f)* MIN
confident ðrīste MIN
  unearg
confine gebindan *3* EVL
  (be)lūcan *2*
confirm fæstnian *w* SAY
conflict geflit *(n)* WAR
  gemōt *(n)*
  sacu *(f)*
congenital geæðele KIN
conjunction fēging *(f)* WRI
  gefēgnys *(f)*
  geþēodnys *(f)*

conscience ingeðanc *(m,n)* MIN
consecrate (ge)hāligan *w* CHU
  hālgian *w*
consent ðafung *(f)* ASK
  geðafian *w*
  geðafung *(f)* AGR
consent to ðafian *w* AGR
consenter geðafa *(m)* AGR
consequence finta *(m)* BEC
consider behycgan *w* MIN
  behealdan *7* THI
  bescēawian *w*
  beðencan w
  eahtian *w*
  geðencan *w*
  smēagan *w*
  ymbðencan *w*
consideration smēa(g)ung *(f)* THI
consolation frōfor *(f)* GD, MIN
console frēfran *w* LOV
consort gemæcca *(m)* LOV
constellation tungol *(n)* SKY
constipated fæst AIL
constipation gebind *(n)* AIL
  heardnys *(f)*
consume notian *w* LRD
contain (a disease) ablendan *w* AIL
contemplate geondðencan *w* THI
contempt forhogdnes *(f)* EVL, MIN, THI
  forsewennes *(f)*
  oll *(n)*
contend fettian *w* SAY
  flītan *1* AGR, WAR
  gehnǣstan *w*
  winnan *3*
contented person geðafa *(m)* ASK
contest geflit *(n)* WAR
continually simble TIM
  singallīc
continue ðurhwunian *w* POS
contrary ambyre FOE, MIN
control geweald *(n)* LRD
  (ge)wealdan *7*
  wieldan *w*

convenient gehæp GD
  gelimpful
convenient, be onhagian *w* GD
convent (nunnan)mynster *(n)* CHU
  stōw *(f)*
conversation gewosa *(m)* SAY
  sprǣc *(f)*
convict oferreccan *w* LAW
cook cōc *(m)* WOR
cooking vessel ālfæt *(n)* TOO
cool cōl WAT
  cōlian *w* AIL
copper ār *(n)* MAT
coppersmith ārsmið *(m)* WOR
copse bearu *(m)* LAN
  hyrst *(m)*
copy onhyrian *w* PFM
copy down āwrītan *1* WRI
copy out bewrītan *1* WRI
coriander celendre *(f)* PLA
cormorant scræb *(m)* ANI
corn corn *(n)* EAT
  spelt *(m)* PLA
corncockle coccel *(m)* PLA
corner hyrne *(f)* HSE
  wincel *(m)*
Cornish (people)
  Cornwēalas *(mpl)* STR
Cornwall Cornwēalas *(mpl)* STR
  Triconscīr *(f)*
corporal flǣsclic BOD
  līchomlīc
corpse dēað *(m)* DIE
  hrā *(m)*
  hrǣw *(m,n)*
correct riht LAW
correct account rihtracu *(f)* SAY
correct law rihtlagu *(f)* LAW
correct word wordriht *(n)* SAY
correction ðrēal *(f)* LAW
corresponding tōgeanes ASK
corrode ābītan *1* MAT
  forrotian *w*
corrupt gewemmodlīc EVL, WRI

corruption brosnung *(f)* AIL
cot cradol *(m)* SLP **couch grass** cwice
(m,f) PLA
cough cohhetan *w* AIL
hrǣcan *w*
coughing gebrǣceo *(f)* AIL
hrāca *(m)*
coulter culter *(m)* LAN, TOO
counsel geðeaht *(n,f)* THI
(ge)ðeahtung *(f)*
rǣdan *w* KNO
counsel, lacking rǣdlēas MIN
counsellor geðeahtere *(m)* THI
rǣdbora *(m)* WOR
wita *(m)*
counsellor, high hēahwita *(m)* LRD
count (ā)rīman *w* MEA
talian *w*
tellan *w*
counting by thousands
ðūsendgerīm *(n)* MEA
countless number un(ge)rīm *(n)* MEA
country land *(n)* LAN
courage ellen *(n)* MIN
mōd *(m)*
courageous ellenrōf MIN
course gegang *(m)* GO
ryne *(m)*
course of a meal sand *(f)* EAT
course of events wyrd *(f)* BEC
court hof *(n)* HSE
courthouse gerēfærn *(n)* LAW
cousin fæderansunu *(m)* KIN
modrigensunu *(m)*
swēor *(m)*
covenant ānnes *(f)* LAW
wǣr *(f)*
cover beðeccan *w* HSE
behelian *w* SEE
helm *(m)* PRO
ðeccan *w*
(be)wrēon *1*
cover of darkness nihthelm *(f)* SLP
cover up behrēosan *2* SEE
covering wǣfels *(m,n)* CLO

ðecen *(f)* HSE
cow cū *(n)* ANI
hriðer *(f)*
cow parsley wuducerfille *(f)* PLA
cowardice yrhðu *(f)* MIN
cowardly earg MIN
cowl cugele *(f)* CLO
cowslip cūslyppe *(f)* PLA
crab crabba *(m)* ANI
hæfern *(m)*
crackle brastlian *w* FIR
cradle cradol *(m)* SLP
craft cræft *(m)* ART, WOR
craftiness sierwung *(f)* MIN
cramp fortogennys *(f)* AIL
hramma *(m)*
swiung *(f)*
crane cran *(m)* ANI
crashing gebræc *(n)* BRK
crave crafian *w* LOV
giernan *w*
cream flīete *(f)* EAT
rēam *(m)*
create (ge)scyppan *6* HSE
tēon *w* ART
creation frumsceaft *(f)* STA
gesceaft *(f)* LAN
creator metod *(m)* CHU
scyppend *(m)*
creature gesceaft *(f)* ANI
gesceap *(n)*
wiht *(f,n)*
credible gelēaflēc SAY
creel spyrte *(f)* TOO
cress cærse *(f)* PLA
crime māndǣd *(f)* EVL
cripple bȳgan *w* AIL
crēopere *(m)*
crocus croh *(m)* PLA
crooked on wōh EVL
tō wōge
wōh HSE
crookedness wōh *(n)* EVL, HSE
wōnes *(f)*
crop failure unwæstm *(m)* LAN

cross oferfaran 6 GO
 oferfēran w
 ofergān a
 rōd (f) CHU
cross oneself segnian w CHU
crossing oferfæreld (n) GO
crossmember eaxlgespan (n) HSE
 lōhsceaft (m)
crosswort wrætte (m) PLA
crow crāwe (f) ANI
crowd hēap (m,f) GO
 flocc (m)
 þrēat (m)
crown corenbēg (m) CLO, LRD
 corōna (m)
 cynehelm (m)
crozier hæcce (f,n) CHU
cruel heard MIN
 slīðen EVL
 ðearl
 wrāð
cruelty wælhrēownes (f) EVL
crumb brēad (n) EAT
 cruma (m)
crumble wōrian w FAI, HSE
crumpet crompeht (f) EAT
crust hierstinghlāf (m) EAT
cry cirm (m) CAL
 grētan w EVL
 rēotan 2
 wēpan 7
 hlēoðrian w REC
cry out cirman w CAL
 cliopian w
 giellan 3
crystal cristalla (m) MAT
 ðurhscȳnestān (m)
cuckoo gēac (m) ANI
cucumber eorðæppel (m) PLA
 hwerhwette (f)
cudgel cycgel (m) WPN
 sāgol (m)
 steng (m)
cuff handstocc (n) CLO
cultivate būan w LAN, WOR

 tilian w
cultivated bȳne LAN
Cumberland Cumbraland (n) STR
Cumbrians Cumbras (mpl) STR
cummin cymen (n) PLA
cunning list (m,f) MIN
 lytig
 onglǣwlīc
 orðonc
 prættig
 searugrim
 sierwung (f)
cup bune (f) EAT
 dryncfæt (n)
 full (n)
 fyll (f)
curds cealer (m) EAT
cure gebētan w AIL
curiosity fyrwit (n) ASK, MIN
 fyrwitnes (f)
curious frymdig MIN
 searolīc
curl (ge)wealcian w GO
curlew hwilpe (f) ANI
curling tongs wealcspinl (f) TOO
current (brim)strēam (m) WAT
curse āwyrgan w EVL
 āwyrgednes (f)
 werhð (f) SAY
 wyrgðu (f)
 forswerian 5 CHU
cursed cīs EVI
curtain wāgrift (n) SLP
curve-prowed ship
 hringedstefna (m) WAT
custody gehealdsumnes (f) LAW
 hæftnoð (m)
 hæftnīed (f)
 heord (f) LRD
custom gewuna (m) LAW, MIN
 sidu (f)
 ðēaw (m)
customary geðȳwe MIN
 gewuna

cut down (ā-, ge-)hēawan 7 WAR
cut one's hair efsian w BOD
cut to pieces forhēawan 7 WAR
cuttlefish wāsescite (f) ANI
cyclamen slite (m,f) PLA

D

Dacia Datia (f) STR
dagger (hand)seax (n) WPN
daily dæghwāmlīc TIM
  on dæg
dairy woman
  smeremangestre (f) WOR
dais stīg (m,f) HSE
daisy dæges ēage PLA
Dalaments (Polish people)
  Dalamentsan (mpl) STR
dale cumb (m) LAN
  dæl (n)
dalliance with a woman
  wīfcȳððu (f) LOV
damage æfwyrdla (m) EVL
  demm (m)
  hearm (m)
damn fordēman w MIN, THI
damnation wyrgðu (f) CHU
damp ðān WAT
  wǣt
dance intrepettan w REC
dancer tumbere (m) REC, WOR
dandelion ǣgwyrt (f) PLA
Danelaw Denelagu (f) STR
Danes Dene (mpl) STR
danger fær (m) EVL
  frēc(ed)nes (f)
  pliht (m)
dangerous frēcne EVL
  plihtlīc
Danish Denisc STR
Danube Dōnua (f) STR
dare durran a MIN
  genēðan w
  geðristian w
  gedyrstlǣcan w THI

daring dyrstig MIN
  ðrȳste
dark blæc FIR
  mirce
  deorc SLP
  dimm SEE
  heolstor
  ðēostre
  sweart COL
  wonn
dark, become nīpan 1 BEC
  sweorcan 3
dark-haired dox BOD
dark red brūnbasu COL
dark room heolstorcofa (m) HSE
dark-coated salo(wig)pād
darkness dimnes (f) SKY, SLP
  genip (n) TIM
  heolstor (f)
  ðēostru (f)
darling dēorling (m) LOV
dart gescēotan 2 GO
  daroð (m) WPN
  scytel (m)
dash to pieces tōðerscan 3 BRK
date datārum (m) TIM
daughter dohtor (f) KIN
dawn ǣrnemergen (f) TIM
  dagian w
  dægrǣd (m)
  ūhta (m)
dawn raider ūhtsceaða (m) FOE
day dæg (m) TIM
  dōgor (n)
day, become dagian w BEC
day, in the on dæg TIM
day's work dægeweorc (n) WOR
daybreak dægrǣd (n) TIM
deacon dīacon (m) CHU
deaconship dīaconhād (m) CHU
dead dēad DIE
  gǣsne
  orsāwle
  unlifigend
dead bodies hrǣw (n,m) DIE
  wæl (n)

dead man dēað *(m)* CHU
hrēaw *(m)*
deadly bealoful EVL
deadly nightshade ælfðone *(f)* PLA
deaf dēaf AIL
deal unfairly
forhealdan 7 EVL, LAW
dear dēore LOV, WEA
lēof
luflīc
fæle
weorð
dear kinsman winemæg *(m)* KIN
death cwalu *(f)* DIE
dēað *(m)*
ealdorbealu *(n)*
forðfōr *(f)*
forðsīð *(m)*
fyll *(f)*
geendung *(f)*
hinsīð *(m)*
swylt *(m)*
unlīf *(n)*
death song fūslēoð *(n)* DIE, REC
deathbed nēobedd *(n)* DIE
debate mōtian *w* AGR, SAY
ðingian *w*
☐**decay** brosnian *w* FAI
forrotian *w*
deceit fācen *(n)* EVL
deceitful fācenful EVL
hindergēap
swicol
deceive bedydrian *w* EVL, SAY
bepæcan *w* THI
besyrwan *w* MIN
beswīcan *1*
dwelian *w*
gelēogan *2*
swician *w*
deceiver beswīcend *(m)* FOE
December ærra Gēola *(m)* TIM
Gēol *(n)*
Gēolmōnað *(m)*
deception lot *(n)* LAW

swicdōm *(m)* MIN
wrenc *(m)*
deceptive gedwimorlīc SEE
decide gecēosan *2* THI
gerædan *w*
gereccan *w* SAY
deciduous hrurul PLA
deck cēolðel *(n)* WAT
declare āreccean *w* SAY
āsecgan *w*
benemnan *w*
bodian *w*
(ā)cȳðan *w*
gecweðan *5*
gereccan *w*
onbēodan *2*
swutelian *w*
hātan *7* CAL
declare forfeited ætreccan *w* LAW
declension declīnung *(f)*
gebīgednys *(f)*
decline (to meet) forbūgan *2* FAI, GO
decompose fūlian *w* EAT
decorate glengan *w* ART
mearcian *w*
decorated fāg ART
gehyrsted
decorated cross mæl *(n)* CHU
decorated item mæl *(n)* ART
decorous ænlīc GD
rihtwīs
decrease lȳtlian *w* BEC, FAI
decree ārædan *7* SAY
āstihtan *w*
gereccan *w*
scyrian *w*
word *(n)*
bebod *(n)* LRD
deed dæd *(f)* PFM, WOR
gewyrht *(n)*
deed of evil bealu *(n)* EVL
māndæd *(f)*
undæd *(f)*
yfeldæd *(f)*

deed of violence firendǣd *(f)* EVL
deep bront WAT
  dēop
  hēah
  neowol MIN
  nīwol
  stēap LAN
deep pool wǣl *(m)* LAN
deep water dēop *(n)* WAT
deer hēorot *(m)* ANI
defeat gewinnan *3* FIG
  oferflītan *1*
  oferwinnan *3*
defecate gedrītan *1* BOD
  scītan *1*
defecation astyrung *(f)* BOD
defence of one's home
  wīcfreoðu *(f)* PRO
defenceless griðlēas PRO
defend werian *w* PRO
defiled gewemmed EVL
  womful
defilement gewemming *(f)* EVL
  womm *(m,n)*
defy wiðerian *w* WAR
Deiran (people) Dēre *(mpl)* STR
delay elcian *w* GO, TIM
  elcung *(f)*
  slacian *w*
delay, without unaswundenlīc TIM
deliberate smēagan *w* THI
deliberately willes THI
delicacy ēst *(f)* EAT, GD
delicious food wilþegu *(f)* EAT
delight gecwēmednes *(f)* LOV
  wynn *(f)*
  wynsumnes *(f)*
delightful wynsum LOV
delude bepǣcan *w* THI
delusion dyderung *(f)* MIN, THI
den denn *(n)* ANI, SLP
dene dene *(m)* LAN
  denu *(f)*
Denmark Denamearc *(f)* STR
deny ǣtsacan *6* ASK
  forsacan *6* SAY, THI

  wiðsacan *6*
depart gewītan *1* GO
  losian *w*
  sīðian *w*
departure gewitennes *(f)* GO
dependant cyrelīf *(n)* KIN, LAW
depending on gelang æt
depilatory cream pillsāpe *(f)* AIL
depression unmōd *(n)* MIN
deprive bedǣlan *w* EVL
  bedrēosan *2* NEE
  belīðan *1*
  benǣman *w*
  beniman *4*
  bescyrian *w*
  onwendan *w*
deprived of beliden NEE
  gǣsne ASK
  lēas
  sceard
depth dēopnes *(f)* WAT
deputy ðegn *(m)* WOR
Derbyshire Deorbyscīr *(f)* STR
deride bismrian *w* BLM, EVL
  hospettan *w*
  hyrwan *w*
derision bismrung *(f)* EVL
  hōcor *(m)*
derisive hōcorwyrde EVL
descendant eafora *(m)* KIN
describe āmearcian *w* WRI
desert ānæd *(n)* LAN
  wēsten *(m)*
deserted ǣmenne LAN
  wēste
deserve geearnian *w* PFM
desirable giernendlīc LOV
  wilsumlīc
desire fundian *w* LOV
  giernan *w* ASK
  lust *(m)*
  willa *(m)*
  willan *a*
  (ge)wilnian *w*
  wilnung *(f)*
  wyscan *w*

desirous frymdig, fyrmdig ASK
desist geswīcan *1* FAI
  linnan *3*
despairing ormōd MIN
desperate love sorglufu *(f)* LOV
despise forhogian *w* EVL, THI
  forsēon *5* SEE
  hyrwan *w*
despised forsewen EVL
  hēan
despiser oferhoga *(m)* EVL
despite þēah þe
destitute fēasceaft EVL
  wǣdla *(m)*
destroy ādīlegian *w* EVL
  āgētan *w*
  āwyrdan *w*
  fordōn *7*
  forgrindan *3*
  forniman *4*
  gewyrdan *w*
  (for)spillan *w*
destruction cwalu *(f)* EVL
  forspillednes *(f)*
  forwyrd *(f)*
destructive foray
  forhergung *(f)* WAR
determine gerǣdan *w* THI
  mearcian *w* LAN
determined ārǣd MIN
devil dēofol *(m,n)* CHU, MON
devilish dēoflīc CHU
  dēofolcund
device orðanc *(m,n)* THI
devise āsmēagan *w* THI
Devonish (people) Defnas *(mpl)* STR
Devonshire Defnascīr *(f)* STR
devotion wilsumnes *(f)* LOV
devour fretan *5* EAT
  frettan *w*
devout ǣfæst CHU
  ēstful
dew dēaw *(m,n)* WAT
diabolical dēoflīc CHU, EVL
  dēofolcund

diagonally across ðwȳres GO, POS
diaphragm midhriðre *(n)* BOD
diarrhoea unryne *(m)* AIL
  ūtsiht *(f)*
dibble spitel *(m)* TOO
dice tæflstān *(m)* TOO
die ācwelan *3* DIE
  cringan *3* WAR
  forðfaran *6*
  forðfēran *w*
  forðgelēoran *w*
  forð(ge)wītan *1*
  geendian *w*
  gefaran *6*
  sweltan *3*
difference gescād *(n)* MIN
difficult earfoðlīc EVL
difficulty earfoðnes *(f)* EVL
  nearu *(f)* NEE
  nīed *(f)*
  nīedðearf *(f)*
difficulty, with earfoðlīce EVL
  unsōfte
dig delfan *3* HSE
  grafan *6*
dignity geðyncðu *(f)* GD, MIN
  weorðscipe *(m)*
diligence gīeman *(f)* MIN
  gīeming *(f)*
diligent nēodlīc THI
dill dile *(m)* PLA
dim dimm SEE, SLP
dimness dimnes *(f)* SEE, SLP
din dynian *w* WAT
dining hall bēodærn *(n)* EAT
diocese biscoprīce *(n)* CHU
  biscopsetl *(n)*
  biscopstōl *(m)*
dip dyppan *w* WAT
dire atol EVL
  grimm
  ðroht
dire enemy feondsceaða *(m)* EVL

direct gerade GO
  gerec
  riht
direction diht *(m)* LRD, SAY
dirt gor *(n)* WAT
  meox *(n)*
disability ālēfednes *(f)* AIL
disable sārgian *w* AIL
disagree wiðcweðan *5* AGR
☐**disappointed** getrucod MIN
discoloration ǣhīwnys *(f)* COL
discourse mǣl *(f)* AGR, SAY
discover fandian *w* ASK, KNO
discretion gescēadwīsnes *(f)* THI
discuss maðelian *w* SAY
  wordum wrixlan *w*
discussion gesprec *(n)* SAY
disdain forhogdnes *(f)* EVL, THI
disease ādl *(f)* AIL
  broc *(n)*
  (un)coðu *(f)*
  unhǣlu *(f)*
diseased ādlīg AIL
  ongeflogen
disgrace bismer *(n,m,f)* FOE
  bismerian *w* SAY
  edwītscipe *(m)* EVL
  scomu *(f)* MIN
disgrace, public woroldscamu *(f)* BLM
disgraced ǣwiscmōd BLM, EVL
disgraced person nīðing *(m)* BLM
disgraceful earhlīc EVL
  scandlīc BLM
disgusting fūl EAT
  lāð
dish disc *(m)* EAT
dish of food sufel *(n)* EAT
dishearten yrgan *w* MIN
disheartened werigferhð MIN
dishonorable ārlēas EVL
dishonour, without unforcūð LRD
disinclination unðonc *(m)* MIN
disloyal flāh FAI
  unhold
dismayed ācol MIN

dismiss tōwurpan *3* BLM
disobey forgīemelēasian *w* PFM
  forgȳman *w*
  mishȳran *w*
disperse tōfaran *6* BRK
  tōhweorfan *3*
display oðȳwan *w* SEE
displease mislīcian *w* EVL
  ofðyncan *w* THI
dispose fadian *w* SAY
  stihtian *w* LRD
dispute fettian *w* AGR, ASK, SAY
  geflit *(n)*
  ☐ wiþcweþan *5*
dispute over inheritance
  yrfegeflit *(n)* LAW
dissemble lytegian *w* SAY
dissuade belēan *6* SAY
distance fyrlu *(f)* MEA
distant feorr LAN, STR
  fyrlen
distant land feorweg *(m)* STR
distinct ānlīpig SAY
  swutol
  ānlic
distress angsumnes *(f)* MIN
  gedrēfednes *(f)*
  nearunes *(f)* NEE
  swencan *w* EVL
distressing nearufāh FOE
distributor brytta *(m)* LRD
district scīr *(f)* LAN
ditch dīc *(m,f)* LAN
dive dūfan *2* WAT
dive through ðurhdūfan *2* WAT
divide bryttian *w* BRK
  gedǣlan *w*
  scēadan *7*
  tōtwǣman *w*
  tōlicgan *5* POS
divided, become gedǣlan *w* BEC
divine godcund CHU
  ūplīc
divine law ǣ *(f)* LAW
division dǣl *(m)* BRK
  scīr *(f)*

dizziness swīma *(m)* AIL, MIN
do dōn *a* PFM
do away with ādīlegian *w* EVL
  fordōn *a*
dock (wudu)docce *(f)* PLA
  hyð *(f)* WAT
dock-keeper hyðweard *(m)* WOR
doctor lǣce *(m)* AIL, WOR
document gewrit *(n)* WRI
dog hund *(m)* ANI
dog collar hoppe *(f)* ANI
dog rose hēopbrēmel *(m)* PLA
  wudurose *(f)*
dolphin mereswīn *(n)* ANI
domain gefeald *(n)* LAN
  rīce *(n)*
Don (river) Danais *(f)* STR
doomed (slege)fǣge DIE
doomed spirit gēosceaftgāst *(m)* MON
door duru *(f)* HSE
door jamb gedyre *(n)* HSE
doorman duruðegn *(m)* WOR
dormitory slǣpærn *(n)* SLP
dormouse sisemūs *(m)* ANI
Dorset Dornsǣtan *(mpl)* STR
dot prica *(m)* WRI
  pīc *(m)*
double twīfeald MEA
doubt twēo *(m)* THI
  twēogan *w*
  twēonian *w*
dough dāg *(m)* EAT
doughty dyhtig WAR
dove culfre *(f)* ANI
down dūn *(f)* LAN
  neoþan
  niþer
  ofdūne
down ,get līhtan *w* GO
downfall hryre *(m)* FAI
downward niðerweard POS
dowry brȳdgifu *(f)* WEA
  wituma *(m)*
doze hnappung *(f)* SLP
drag dragan *6* BRI
  tēon *2*

dragon draca *(m)* ANI, MON
  līgdraca *(m)*
  nīðdraca *(m)*
  wyrm *(m)*
drain drē(a)hnian *w* WAT
drake ened *(m)* ANI
draught drync *(m)* EAT
  scenc *(m)*
  drōht *(m?)* HSE
draw (ge)tēon *2* BRI, LOV
  ātīefran *w* ART
draw a sword
  (ā)bregdan *3* LRD, WPN
  ūtātēon *1,2*
draw away oftēon *2* EVL
draw out (for)teon *2* BRI
draw up stihtan *w* LRD
  trymian *w*
draw water hlādan *6* WAT
dread ondrǣdan *7* MIN
dream swefn *(n)* SLP
dregs drōs *(m)* EAT
drench begēotan *2* WAT
dress gierela *(m)* CLO
  hrægel *(n)*
  rēaf *(n)*
  (be)scrȳdan *w*
dried fig ciseræppel *(m)* EAT
drill bor *(m)* TOO
  ðurhdrīfan *1*
drink drenc *(m)* EAT
  drinca *(m)*
  drincan *3*
  drync *(m)*
  scenc *(m)*
drinking gedrync *(m)* EAT
drip drȳpan *w* EAT, WAT
dripping smeoru *(f)* EAT
drive ādrīfan *1* DRI
  ðȳn *w*
  ðȳwan *w*
drive along wegan *5* DRI
drive apart tōdrīfan *1* DRI

drive away ādrīfan *1* DRI
 flīeman *w*
 fȳsan *w*
 oðehtian *w*
drive off āflīgan *w* DRI
 āfȳsan *w*
 dræfan *w*
 (ā-, ge-)flīeman *w*
drive out (for)wrecan *5* DRI
 geūtian *w*
drive through (pierce)
 ðurhdrīfan *1* DRI
drop dropa *(m)* EAT, WAT
droppings tyrdelu *(npl)* ANI
drove drāf *(f)* ANI, DRI
drown ādrincan *3* DIE
 drencan *w*
drowsiness hnappung *(f)* AIL, SLP
drug lybb *(n)* PLA
drug-taking lyblāc *(m,n)* AIL, MIN
drum bydenbotm *(m)* REC
 tunnebotm *(m)*
drummer-girl
 glīwbydenestre *(f)* REC
drunk with beer ealugāl EAT
drunk with mead meodugāl EAT
drunk with wine wīngāl EAT
drunk, become ,get
 druncnian *w* BEC, EAT
 oferdrencan *w*
drunkard wēsa *(m)* EAT
drunken druncen EAT
dry drȳgan *w* WAT
 drȳge
 sīere
dub dubbian *w* WAR
dubbing gedrēog *(n)* MAT
duck dūce *(f)* ANI
 ened *(f)*
 dūfan *2* GO
due gerihte *(n)* LAW
 riht(līc)
due east ēastrihte POS
dull dwǣs MIN
dumb dumb AIL

dung gor *(n)* BOD, WAT
 meox *(n)*
 scearn *(n)*
 scytel *(m)*
 tord *(n)*
 tyrdelu *(npl)*
 ðost *(m)*
dung beetle tordwifel *(m)* ANI
dunghill myxen *(f)* HSE
duration hwīl *(f)* TIM
 ðrāg *(f)*
during mid þām þe
 ðenden
 þā hwīle þe
 under
dusky dox COL
 dungrǣg
dusky brown fealu COL
dust dūst *(n)* MAT
dust, pound to gecnūwian *w* BRK
 gnīdan *1*
duties gerisenu *(npl)* GD
duty ðegnung *(f)* WOR
 gerihte *(n)* LAW
 nytt *(f)* LRD
dwarf dweorg *(m)* MON, STR
dwarf elder līðwyrt *(f)* PLA
dwell būan *w* LIV
 (on)eardian *w* HSE, LAN
 onwunian *w*
 (ge)wīcian *w*
 (ge)wunian *w*
dweller on earth eorðbūend *(m)* LAN
 woroldbūend *(m)*
dwelling bold *(n)* HSE
 botl *(n)*
 cotlīf *(n)* LAN, LIV
 eardung *(f)*
 hof *(n)*
 inn *(n)*
 setl *(n)*
 stoc *(n)*
 wīc *(n)*
 (on)wunung *(f)*
dwelling-place stoclīf *(n)* LIV
 stocwīc *(n)*

dwindle wanian *w* FAI
dye dēagian *w* COL
dyed twice twiblēo CLO

E

each (one) gehwilc
each (of two) gehwæðer
eager cēne MIN
  georn(ful) ASK
  fūs LOV
eager for glory dōmgeorn MIN
eagerness ellenwōdnes *(f)* MIN
  georn(ful)nes *(f)* ASK
eagle earn *(m)* ANI
ear eare *(n)* BOD
earl ealdorman *(m)* LRD
  eorl *(m)*
earliest ǣrest MEA, TIM
  forma
early awake ǣrwacol SLP, TIM
early morning ǣrnemergen *(m)* TIM
  ūhta *(m)*
earn āwyrcan *w* WOR
  (ge)earnian *w* GD, PFM
earn a living drohtnian *w* LIV, WOR
  tilian *w*
earn infamy
  word gespringan *3* BLM
earnestness earnost *(f)* MIN
earring ēarhring *(m)* ART
earth eardgeard *(m)* LAN
  eorðe *(f)*
  folde *(f)*
  grund *(m)*
  hruse *(f)*
  middangeard *(m)*
  molde *(f)*
earthquake eorðstyren *(f)* LAN
earthworm angeltwicce *(m,f)* ANI
  regnwyrm *(m)*
earwax drōs *(f)* WAT
earwig ēarwicga *(m)* ANI
ease ēðnes *(f)* GD
easily īeð PFM

īeðelīce
east ēast POS
East Angles Ēastengle *(mpl)* STR
East Franks Ēastfrancan *(mpl)* STR
East Kent Ēastcentingas *(mpl)* STR
East Saxons Ēastseaxe *(mpl)* STR
Easter Sunday Ēasterdæg *(m)* TIM
eastern region ēastdǣl *(m)* LAN
  ēastende *(m)*
  ēasthealf *(f)*
Eastertide Ēastertīd *(f)* TIM
easy īeðe(līc) PFM
eat etan *5* EAT
  mēsan *w*
  ðicgan *5*
eat as much as efenetan *5* EAT
eat like an animal fretan *5* ANI
eaves efes *(f)* HSE
ebb (ā)ebbian *w* WAT
ebbtide ebba *(m)* WAT
ecclesiastical ciriclīc CHU
ecclesiastical measure
  ciricmitta *(m)* MEA
echo onscillan *w*,
  dweorg *(m)* MIN
ecstasy elhygd *(f)* LOV, MIN
edge ecg *(f)* WPN
  efes *(f)* CLO, LAN
  ōra *(m)*
eel ǣl(fix) *(m)* ANI
effective fremful AIL, GD
effeminate blēað EVI
effeminate man bǣddel
egg ǣg *(n)* EAT
Egyptian Egiptisc STR
Egyptians Ægypte *(mpl)* STR
eight eahta
eighteen eahtatīene
eighteenth eahtatēoða
eighth eahtoða
eightieth eahtatigoða
eighty hundeahtatig
either...or oððe...oððe
Elbe (river) Ælf *(f)* STR

Elbing (river) Ilfing *(m)* STR
elbow elnboga *(m)* BOD
elder ealdor *(m)* KIN, LRD
  ealdorman *(m)*
  ellen *(n)* PLA
elder ashtree ellenahse *(f)* PLA
elegant smicer LOV
elephant elpend *(m)* ANI
eleven endleofon
eleventh endlufoða
elk eolh *(m)* ANI
ell eln *(f)* MEA
eloquence getingnes *(f)* AGR, SAY
□**eloquent** cwedol AGR
else elles STR
  elleshwæt
elsewhere ellor STR
embankment dīc *(m,f)* LAN
  geweorc *(n)*
embark āstīgan *1* GO, WAT
  scipian *w*
emblem of victory sigesceorp *(n)* ART
embrace (ymb)clyppan *w* LOV
  fæðm *(m)* PRO
embroidery borda *(m)* CLO, WOR
  tæpped *(n)*
embryo beorðor *(m)* KIN
emperor cāsere *(m)* LRD
employ bisgian *w* WOR
empowered to, be onhagian *w* PFM
empress cāsern *(f)* LRD
empty æmtig MEA
  tōm
emulate gelǣcan *w* PFM
  onhyrian *w*
encamp wīcian *w* LIV
encampment wīcstōw *(f)* LIV
enchant begalan *6* CHU
  besingan *3*
enchanter lyblǣca *(m)* CHU
enchantress galdricge *(f)* CHU
  lybbestre *(f)*
encircle ymbgān *a* GO
  ymbwindan *3*
  ymbgyrdan *w*

enclosure tūn *(m)* LAN
enclosure by water worðig *(m)* HSE
encompass ymbhwearfan *3* POS
  ymblicgan *5*
encourage byldan *w* WAR
  ehtian *w* MIN
  hyrdan *w*
encouragement forbylding *(f)* MIN
end edwenden *(f)* TIM
  ende *(m)* LAN, STA
  endian *w*
end up geendian *w* DIE
ending geendung *(f)* DIE, STA
endless endelēas TIM
endure ādrēogan *2* STA
  ðolian *w*
enemy feond *(m)* FOE
  genīðla *(m)*
  groma *(m)*
  hettend *(m)*
  inwitt *(m)*
  lāð *(m)*
  lāðgenīðla *(m)*
  feondscaða *(m)* EVL
  flīema *(m)*
enemy, public ðēodscaða *(m)* FOE
enemy fleet unfriðflota *(m)* WAR
enemy troops unfriðhere *(m)* WAR
enfold befealden *7* LOV
engagement winetrēow *(f)* LOV
England Englalond *(n)* STR
English Englisc STR
English language
  Englisc *(n)* SAY, WRI
  Engliscgereord *(n)*
English Nation Angelcynn *(n)* STR
  Angelþēod *(f)*
  Engle *(mpl)*
engrave āgrāfan *6* WOR, WRI
engraving tool græfseax *(n)* TOO
enjoy brūcan *2* GD
  nēotan *2* LRD
enjoy to the full ðurhbrūcan *2* LOV
enjoyment brȳce *(m)* GD
  notu *(f)*

enough genōg MEA
enough, be genōgian *w* GD
  genihtsumian *w*
enquire befrīnan *1* ASK
  frignan *3*
enrich gōdian *w* GD
  geweligian *w* WEA
enslave ðēowian *w* WOR
enslavement monsylen *(f)* EVL
ensnare begrynian *w* EVL
  beswīcan *1*
  sierwan *w*
enter fēolan *3* GO
  ingān *a*
  innian *w*
enterprise onginn *(n)* STA
entertainer trūð *(m)* REC
entertainment feorm *(f)* EAT, GD
entice (ā)spanan *6* ASK, LOV
  getihtan *w*
entire anwealh MEA
entrance ingang *(m)* HSE
entrap betræppan *w* EVL
entreat biddan *5* ASK
  healsian *w*
entreaty ācsung *(f)* ASK
  healsung *(f)*
entrenchment set *(n)* LAN
entrust befæstan *w* AGR, THI
  betǣcan *w*
envelop ymbwindan *3* GO
  forðylman *w* STA
envious æfestful MIN
  æfestig
envious, be æfestian *w* MIN
envy anda *(m)* EVL, FOE, MIN
  nīð *(m)*
ephod mæssegierela *(m)* CHU
  mæssehrægl *(n)*
epilepsy fyllewærc *(m)* AIL
epilogue endespǣc *(f)* WRI
Epiphany Bæðdæg *(m)* TIM
equal gelīca *(m)* AGR
  gemæcc
equinox efniht, emniht *(f)* TIM

equip scyrpan *w* TOO
  syrwan *w* WAR
erelong nīehst TIM
  sōna
  ungēara
errand ærende *(n)* ASK
error gedwild *(n)* THI
  gedwola *(m)*
  wōh *(n)* EVL
  wōnes *(f)*
escape æthlēapan *7* GO
  bebūgan *2*
  (æt)berstan *3*
  forflēon *2*
  gedīgan *w*
  oðwindan *3*
especially swīþost MEA
espy scēawian *w* SEE
Essex Ēast Seaxe *(mpl)* STR
establish gestaðolian *w* HSE
  onstellan *w*
  settan *w*
estate hām *(m)* HSE, LAN
  tūn *(m)*
esteem prōfian *w* THI
estimate (ge)eahtian *w* THI
Estonia Estland *(n)* STR
Estonians Este *(mpl)* STR
eternal ēce TIM
eternal cold sincaldu *(f)* SKY
eternity ēcnes *(f)* TIM
Ethiopian Sigelhearwa *(m)* STR
eucharist hūsl *(n)* CHU
eunuch cwēnhirde *(m)* WOR
  hwasta *(m)*
eve niht *(f)* TIM
even furðum
  efn LAN
  filde
evening ǣfen *(m,n)* TIM
  ǣfentīd *(f)*
evening meal ǣfenmete *(m)* EAT
evening twilight cwildseten *(f)* TIM
evening's rest ǣfenræst *(f)* SLP
evensong ǣfensong *(m)* CHU

event gelimp *(n)* BEC
 wend *(m)*
 wyrd *(f)*
ever ā TIM
 æfre
everyday dæghwæmlīc TIM
everyone æghwā
 gehwā
everywhere æghwær POS
 gehwær
evidence gewitennes *(f)* LAW
evil bealu *(n)* EVL
 forsyngod
 mānful
 misdæd *(f)*
 nīð *(m)*
 yfel *(n)*
evil custom uncræft *(m)* EVL
 unsidu *(f)*
evil tidings lāðspell *(n)* SAY
evildoer lāðgetēona *(m)* MON
 mānfremmend *(m)* EVL
ewe ēowu *(f)* ANI
exaction manung *(f)* WEA
examine smēagan *w* THI
example bīsen *(f)* WRI
excavation gedelf *(n)* LAN
exceed oferstīgan *l* PFM
excellent æltæwe GD
 til
 ðrȳðlīc
except (for) būton
except (that) būton ðæm (ðe)
exchange gehwearf *(n)* WEA
 gewrixl *(n)*
exchange, in tō gehwearfe ASK
exchange for, in wiþ
exchange hostages gīslian *w* LAW
excite hwettan *w* MIN
 onbryrdan *w*
exciting hrōr MIN
excommunicate āmānsemian *w* CHU
excrement þost *(m)* BOD
excuse belādung *(f)* LAW, SAY
 lād *(f)* AGR
 talu *(f)*

exempt, be scīran *w* LAW
exert oneself strūtian *w* WOR
exhort byldan *w* WAR
 monian *w* MIN
 trymian *w*
 rædan *w* AGR
exile āflīeman *w* LAW
 forwrecan *5* DRI
 flīema *(m)* EVL
 wræc *(n)*
exodus ūtgong *(m)* GO
expect onbīdan *l* POS
expectation wēn *(f)* MIN
 wēna *(m)*
expedient nytlic MIN
 rædlīc
expedition fyrding *(f)* WAR
experience drēogan *2* NEE
 gefaran *6*
 onfundelnys *(f)* KNO, LIV
experienced frōd MIN
explain (ge)reccean *w* SAY, THI
 trahtian *w* WRI
exploration scēawung *(f)* SEE
explore fandian *w* LAN
 rāsian *w*
express (ā)cweðan *5* SAY
extend licgan *5* POS
 rȳman *w* LAN
extent ymbhwyrft *(m)* HSE
extinguish ādwæscan *w* FIR
 (ā)cwencan *w*
exult behliehhan *6* MIN, THI
 hrēman *w* SAY
 mōdigian *w*
exultant hrēmig MIN
 sigehrēðig PFM
eye ēage *(n)* BOD
eyebright ēagwyrt *(f)* PLA
eyesocket ēahhring *(m)* BOD

F

face nebb *(n)* BOD
 ondwlita *(m)*
 onsīen *(f)*

face powder nebsealf *(f)* AIL
face-to-face nebb wið nebb POS
fade brosnian *w* COL, FAI
fail ābrēoðan *2* FAI
  ālicgan *w*
  drēosan *2*
  forberstan *3*
  geswīcan *1*
fain gefægen MIN
fainted geswogen AIL
fair fæger LAW, LOV
  gemēde
fair of face blāchlēor LOV
  wlitescīene
fairspoken swǣswyrde SAY
faith gelēafa *(m)* CHU
  trēow *(f)* SAY
faithful getrȳwlīc GD
  hold
faithfulness getrȳwð *(f)* GD
fall fyll *(m)* DIE
  feallan *7* GO
fall asleep onslǣpan *w* SLP
fall dead cringan *3* DIE
  feallan *7*
fall in battle (ge)cringan *3* DIE, WAR
fall in ruins drēosan *2* FAI, HSE
fall to (an action) gefeallan *7* PFM
fallow fealu COL
false lēas EVL
  swicol
false god gedwolgod *(n)* CHU
falter wācian *w* FAI
  wandian *w* MIN
fame dōm *(m)* THI
  mǣrðu *(f)* GD
familiar hīwcūþ KNO
  welcūþ
family cynn *(n)* KIN
  cynren *(n)*
  hēored *(m)*
  hīred *(m)*
  hīwisc *(n)*
  mǣgð *(f)*
family land ēðel *(m,n)* KIN

family members hīwan *(mpl)* KIN
family wartroop sibgedriht *(f)* KIN
famine hungor *(m)* NEE
famous blǣdfæst GD
  brēme
  mǣre
fan fann *(f)* TOO
far off feorr LAN, STR
  fyrlen
far-travelled wīdgongel GO
fare gefaran *6* GO
farmer gebūr *(m)* LAN
fast, make fæstan *w* PRO
  sǣlan *w*
fasted for a night nihtnistig EAT
fasten gefæstnian *w* EVL, HSE,POS
  sǣlan *w* PRO
fastening gespong *(n)* TOO
  ðwang *(m,f)*
fastidious cīs MIN
fasting fæsten *(n)* EAT
fat fǣtt EAT
  rysle *(m)*
  smeru *(n)*
fat-legged spærlīred BOD
fate gesceaft *(m,n,f)* BEC
  gesceap *(n)*
  orlæg *(n)*
  wyrd *(f)*
father fæder *(m)* KIN
father's brother fædera *(m)* KIN
father's sister faðe *(f)* KIN
fatherland eard *(m)* KIN
  ēðel *(m)*
fatherly fæderlīc KIN
fault lǣst *(f)* FAI
  unfulfremming *(f)*
favour ēst *(f)* GD
  forspǣc *(f)* AGR
  fremsumnes *(f)* LOV, MIN
  hyldu *(f)* PRO
  liss *(f)* ASK
fear forhtian *w* MIN
  ege *(m)* EVL

fearful ācol MIN
egelic
forht
feast sendan *(w)* EAT
swæsende *(npl)*
symbel *(n)*
feasting gebēorscipe *(m)* EAT
feat dǣd *(f)* PFM, WOR
feather feðer *(n)* ANI
February Solmōnað *(m)* TIM
feed (ā)fēdan *w* EAT, KIN
feel drēogan *2* THI
ongietan *5*
feel pity ofhrēowan *2* MIN
feign līcettan *w* SEE
fell fyllan *w* PFM
gehnǣgan *w*
fellow feaster gebēor *(m)* EAT
fellow traveller gesīð *(m)* GO
felon māndǣda *(m)* FOE
wearg *(m)*
female pupil lǣringmǣden *(n)* WOR
female side of the family
spinelhealf *(f)* KIN
wīfhand *(f)*
female spirit āglǣcwīf *(n)* MON
fen fenn *(n)* LAN
mersc *(m)*
fencing tīning *(f)* LAN
fencing wood tīning *(f)* HSE
fennel finol *(m)* PLA
fern fearn *(n)* PLA
fervent mōdig MIN
onǣled
fervour wylm *(m)* LOV
festival mæssedæg *(m)* CHU
fetch (ge)feccan *w* BRI
(ge)fetian *w*
fetter clomm *(m)* EVL
cosp *(m)*
cospan *w*
fetor *(f)*
fōtcops *(m)*
grindel *(m)*
hæftan *w*
wrīðan *1*

feud fǣhðu *(f)* EVL
fever fefor *(m)* AIL
feverfew feferfuge *(f)* PLA
few fēa MEA
fey fǣge DIE
fiddle fiðele *(f)* REC
fiddler fiðelere *(m)* REC
fiðelestre *(f)*
field æcer *(m)* LAN
wong *(m)*
fierce āfor EVL, MIN
grimm
hrēoh
hrēðe
fierce spirit heoruwearg *(m)* MON
fiery-haired fȳrfeaxen BOD
fifteen fīftīene
fifteenth fīftēoða
fifth fifta
fiftieth fīftigoða
fifty fīftig
fight (ge)feohtan *3* WAR
feohte *(f)*
gefeoht *(n)*
fight on foot fēðewīg *(m)* WAR
file fēol *(f)* TOO
file-hardened fēolheard TOO
filigree wīr *(m)* ART
wundengold *(n)*
filings gesweorf *(n)* MAT
fill fyllan *w* BRI
filth horh *(m,n)* WAT
filthy horig WAT
unclǣne
fin finn *(m)* ANI
find out fandian *w* KNO
geascian *w* ASK
gewitan *w*
onfindan *3*
fine gōdlīc GD
smæl MEA
fine cloth godwebb *(n)* CLO, MAT
fine flour grytt *(n)* EAT

fine for fighting fihtewīte *(n)* LAW
fine for illegal dealing
  wōhcēapung *(f)* LAW
fine sieve hērsyfe *(f)* TOO
  tæmespīle *(f)*
  temse *(f)*
finely ground smæl BRK
finger finger *(m)* BOD
finger, index scytefinger *(m)* BOD
finger, little ēarclǽnsend *(m)* BOD
finger, middle hālettend *(m)* BOD
finger joint fingerlið *(m)* BOD
finish (ge)endian *w* FAI, STA
finned finiht ANI
fir-tree furhwudu *(m)* PLA
fire ǽled *(m)* FIR
  bǽl *(n)*
  brond *(m)*
  bryne *(m)*
  fȳr *(n)*
  līg *(m)*
firedog brandīren *(n)* FIR, TOO
firewood wudu *(m)* HSE
firewood, stack of scīdhrēac *(m)* FIR
firm (stede)fæst MIN
  stīð(līc) GD
  stronglīc
  trum
firm, make gestaðolian *w* HSE
firmness ānmōdnes *(f)* MIN
  fæstnes *(f)* BOD
first ǽrest TIM
  ǽrra
  forma MEA
first mass capitolmæsse *(f)* CHU
first place, in the æt ǽrestan TIM
fish fisc *(m)* ANI
  fiscian *w* WOR
  laguswimmend *(m)*
fish-hook angil *(m)* ANI, TOO
fish-trap hæcwer *(m)* TOO
  sprincel *(m)* WAT
fishbait ǽs *(n)* ANI
fisherman fiscere *(m)* ANI, WOR
fishing fiscoð *(m)* ANI

fist fȳst *(f)* BOD
fit fyllewærc *(m)* AIL
  gehæp GD
fitting behēfe GD
  cyn
  gedafenlīc
  gedēfe
  gelimplic
  gerisenlīc
  gerisne
fitting, be gerīsan *1* GD
five fīf
fix fæstnian *w* HSE
fix a day āndagian *w* TIM
flag fana *(m)* ART
flame līg *(m)* FIR
  sweoðol *(m?)*
flask cylle *(m)* WAT
  flaxe *(f)* EAT
  pinne *(f)*
  wīnhorn *(m)*
flat efn LAN
  filde
  smēðe
flat-fish fag *(f)* ANI
flatter ōlǽcan *w* AGR, ASK, LOV
flattery ōlǽcung *(f)* AGR
flautist hrēodpipere *(m)* REC, WOR
  hwistlere *(m)*
flavour smæc *(m)* EAT
  swæc *(m)*
flax fleax *(n)* PLA
flea flēa *(m)* ANI
fledgling bridd *(n)* ANI
flee (for-, oð-)flēon *2* GO
  forbūgan *2*
flee, make geflīeman *w* DRI
fleece flīes *(n)* ANI
fleeing flēam *(m)* GO
fleet flota *(m)* WAT
  scipfierd *(f)*
  sciplið *(n)*
fleeting lǽne TIM
flesh flǽsc *(n)* BOD
  flǽscmete *(m)* EAT

flight flyht *(m)* GO
flinch wācian *w* FAI
flint flint *(m)* MAT
flitch flicce *(n)* EAT
float flēotan 2 GO, WAT
flock heord *(f)* ANI, DRI
flog beswingan 3 EVL
flood bestēman *w* WAT
  faroð *(m)*
  flōd *(m)*
  wæd *(n)*
flood, in flēde WAT
floodwave flōdȳð *(f)* WAT
floor flet *(n)* HSE
  flōr *(f,m)*
flounder flōc *(n)* ANI
flour melu *(n)* EAT
flow dennian *w* WAT
  flōwan 7
  iernan 3 GO
  weallan 7
flow away tōflōwan 7 WAT
  tōrinnan 3
flow under underflōwan 7 WAT
flower blōstma *(m)* PLA
  cropp *(m)*
flower-bed wyrtbedd *(n)*
flower festival blōstmfrēols *(m)* PLA
fluke (fish) flōc *(n)* ANI
fluke (worm) liferwyrm *(m)* ANI
flute hwistle *(f)* REC
flux flēwsa *(m)* WAT
fly flēogan 3 GO
  flēoge *(f)* ANI
fly-net flēohnet *(n)* ANI, HSE
foal fola *(m)* ANI
foam fām *(m)* WAT
foamy-necked fāmigheals WAT
fodder foddor *(n)* EAT
foetus brōd *(m)* KIN
fog mist *(m)* SKY
folding stool fyldestōl *(m)* HSE
folk folc *(n)* STR
follow æfterhyrgan *w* GO, TIM
  æfterspyrian *w* ASK

(æfter)fylgian *w*
  gelǣstan *w* WOR
following folgað *(m)* WOR
  hērbeæftan POS
folly dysignes *(f)* MIN
  gāl *(n)* EVL, LOV
  gālnes *(f)*
  hygelēast *(f)*
  unrǣd *(m)*
foment beðian *w* EAT
food ǣt *(m)* EAT
  bīleofa *(m)*
  fōðor *(n)*
  mete *(m)*
  mōs *(n)*
  sand *(f)*
  wist *(f)*
food, provide with metsian *w* EAT
foolish dol(gilp) THI
  dwǣs MIN
  dwollīc
  dysig
  stunt
foot fōt *(m)* BOD
  fōtmǣl *(n)* MEA
foot-track fēðelāst *(m)* GO
  swæð *(n)*
footman fōtsetla *(m)* WOR
footpath ānpæð *(m)* LAN
  fōtlāst *(m)*
  swaðu *(f)*
  swæð *(n)*
footsoldier fēða *(m)* WAR
footstep fōtswæð *(n)* BOD
footstool fōtscamol *(m)* HSE
footwear fōtgewǣde *(n)* CLO
  scō *(m)*
for for
  forðǣm ðe
  tō
forbid forbēodan 2 EVL, SAY
force geðȳn *w* AGR, LRD
  ðrēa *(m)*
  ðrēat *(m)*
forced tribute nīedbād *(f)* LRD

forceps hæferbite *(m)* TOO
ford ford *(m)* LAN
  wæd *(n)*
forearm eln *(f)* BOD
forefinger scytefinger *(m)* BOD
forehead hnifel *(m)* BOD
foreign elðēodig STR
  feorcund
  feorrancumen
  fremde
  ofersǣwisc
  ūtancumen
foreign army ūthere *(m)* WAR
foreign land uncȳð ðu *(f)* STR
forementioned foresǣd SAY
forename fulwihtnama *(m)* SAY
foreshore ȳðlāf *(f)* WAT
forest weald *(m)* LAN
  wudu *(m)*
foretell foresecgan *w* SAY
  forewītegian *w*
forever ā TIM
  ā on ēcnesse
  ǣfre
  tō worulde
forfeit forwyrcan *w* LAW
forge slēan 6 WOR
forged geðrūen TOO
forget forgietan 5 PFM, THI
  ofergietan 5
  ofergitolian *w*
forgetfulness ofergitolnys *(f)* MIN, THI
fork forca *(m)* TOO
former days ǣrdagas *(mpl)* TIM
formerly gēara TIM
  gefyrn
  gēo
fornicate firenian *w* LOV
  forlecgan *w*
fornication forliger *(n)* LOV
  wōhhǣmed *(n)*
forsake forlǣtan 7 EVL, FAI, GO
forswear forswerian 6 EVL, SAY
fort burg *(f)* WAR
  ceaster *(f)*
  fæsten *(n)*

forthwith āninga TIM
  ǣdre
  instæpe
  lungre
  semninga
  sōna
fortieth fēowertigoða
fortified place burg *(f)* PRO
  burghlīð *(n)* LAN
  ceaster *(f)*
fortress burg *(f)* HSE
  fæsten *(n)*
  geweorc *(n)* LAN
forty fēowertig
forward fram MIN
forwardly unforwandigendlīce GO
forwards forð GO
fostering fōstor *(n)* KIN
foul fūl EAT, EVL
foul-smelling fūlstincend EVL
foundation staðol *(m)* HSE
four fēower
fourlegged fiðerfēte ANI
fourteen fēowertīene
fourteenth fēowertēoða
fourth fēowerða
fowler fuglere *(m)* WOR
fox fox *(m)* ANI
France Francland *(n)* STR
fracture tōclēofan 2 BRK
fracture a bone brecan 2 AIL
  tōclēofan 2
fractured skull hēafodbryce *(m)* AIL
fragrance stenc *(m)* PLA
fragrant welstincend PLA
frame gesteal *(n)* HSE
frankincense stōr *(m)* WEA
Franks Francan *(mpl)* STR
fraternity gefērscipe *(m)* LOV
fraud swicdōm *(m)* FAI, LAW
freckle cyrnel *(n)* BOD
free frēo GD
  frīg
free, set frēogan *w* LOV, GD

free from sorrow sorglēas MIN
free kinsman frēomǣg *(m)* KIN
freedom frēodōm *(m)* GD
  frēols *(m)*
  frēot *(m)* LAW
freehold ēleð *(m)* HSE
freeman ceorl *(m)* WOR
  frēomann *(m)*
freeze frēosan 2 SKY, WAT
freight hlæst *(m)* WAT
French Frencisc STR
  Gallisc STR
Frenchmen Galwalas *(mpl)* STR
frequent gelōmlic LIV, TIM
  gewunian *w*
frequently gelōmlīce TIM
fresh fersc EAT, WAT
Friday Frigedæg *(m)* TIM
fried elebacen EAT
friend frēond *(m)* LOV
  wine *(m)*
friendless frēondlēas EVL
  winelēas LOV
  wineðearfend
friendly blīðe LOV
  blīðmōd
  frēondlīc
  welwillende
friendship cȳððu *(f)* LOV
  frēod *(f)* GD
  frēondrǣden *(f)*
  frēondscipe *(m)*
  sibb *(f)*
fright fyrhto *(f)* EVL
fringe ðrǣs *(f)* CLO
Frisches Haff Estmere *(m)* STR
Frisia Frīsland *(n)* STR
Frisian Frysisc STR
Frisian (man) Frīesa *(m)* STR
frivolous dysig MIN
  gālsmǣre
  oferblīþe
frog fenȳce *(f)* ANI
  frogga *(m)*

frosc *(m)*
tosca *(m)*
ȳce *(m)*
from fram
  of
from above ūfan
from afar feorran STR
from behind æftan POS
  hindan
from beneath neðan POS
from every direction ǣghwonan POS
from now on heonanforð TIM
from overseas ofersǣwisc STR
front, in foran(tō) POS
  forne
  onforan
front of, in tōgēanes
frost forst *(m)* SKY
  hrīm *(m)*
frosty frēorig SKY
  hrīmceald
froth gist *(m)* EAT
frozen frēorig SKY
frozen over oferfroren WAT
fruit blēd *(f)* PLA
  ofett *(n)*
  wæstm *(m)* EAT
frying pan hierstepanne *(f)* TOO
fuel tynder *(f)* FIR
fulfill fyllan *w* PFM
full moon mōnaðfylen *(f)* TIM
fullness fyllu *(f)* GD
fully-armed fullwēpnod WAR
furlong furhlang *(n)* LAN, MEA
furrow furh *(f)* LAN
further furðor
  ufor
further (an aim) (ge)forðian *w* PFM
  fremian *w*
  (ge)fremman *w*
furze gors *(m)* PLA
future forðgesceaft *(f)* TIM
  tōweard
future, in forð TIM

G

gadfly bēaw *(m)* ANI
gain earnian *w* GD, WOR
  gedīgan *w*
  gewinnan *3*
  rǣd *(m)*
  gestrȳnan *w* WEA
gain strength elnian *w* BOD, GD
gainful nytt GD
  nytwyrðe
gall gealla *(m)* BOD
game gamen *(n)* MIN, REC
  huntung *(f)* ANI
  lāc *(n)* PFM
  plega *(m)*
gander gandra *(m)* ANI
garden wyrtgeard *(m)* PLA
gardener ediscweard *(m)* PLA, WOR
  wyrtweard *(m)*
garland wīþig *(m)* CLO
garlic gārlēac *(n)* PLA
  hramsa *(m)*
  hramse *(f)*
garment gegyrela *(m)* CLO
  rēaf *(n)*
  scēat *(m)*
  scrūd *(n)*
garter hosebend *(m)* CLO
  mēoning *(m)*
gasp orðian *w* SAY
gateway geat *(n)* HSE
gather gaderian *w* BRI
gathering gesomnung *(f)* BRI
gaze hāwian *w* SEE
  wlītan *1*
gemstone gimm *(m)* ART, WEA
  gimstān *(m)*
generous ginfæst MIN
  rūmheort
genitals gecyndelīcu *(npl)* BOD
  gesceapu *(npl)*
genitals (male) geweald *(n)* BOD
  ðēohgeweald *(npl)*
gentian feldwyrt *(f)* PLA

gentle bilewit GD, MIN
  līðe LOV
geometry eorðcræft *(m)* KNO
gestures gebǣru *(npl)* PFM
get (be)gietan *5* WEA
get down līhtan *w* GO
get drunk druncnian *w* BEC, EAT
  oferdrencan *w*
get lost losian *w* GO
ghost dēað *(m)* CHU, DIE
  gāst *(m)* MIN
  gǣst *(m)*
  scīma *(m)*
  scinngedwola *(m)* MON
giant ent *(m)* MON
  fifel *(n)*
  ðyrs *(m)*
giddiness swinglung *(f)* AIL
gift gifu *(f)* GD
  selen *(f)* ASK
gift of money feohgift *(f)* WEA
gill pægel *(m)* MEA
gills cīan *(mpl?)* BOD
gird (be)gyrdan *w* CLO
gird on begyrdan *w* WPN
girl mǣden *(n)* KIN
  wencel *(n)*
give giefan *5* WEA
  sellan *w*
give up būgan *2* FAI
  gieldan *3*
give way before būgan *2* FAI
glad (ge)fægen GD, LOV, MIN
  glæd
  lustlīc
gladden blissian *w* GD, LOV
glance of the eye bryhtm *(m)* BOD
glass glæs *(n)* MAT
glass, made of glæsen MAT
glide glīdan *1* GO
glide away tōglīdan *1* GO
gloomy ðēostre SLP
  galgmōd MIN
  sweorcendferhð
  mirce SKY

glorify mǣrsian *w* GD
  wuldrian *w*
glorious torhtmōd MIN
  foremǣre GD
  tīrfæst
  ðrymful
  ðrymfæst
  weorðful
  wuldorful
  wuldorlīc
glory ār *(f)* MIN
  blǣd *(m)* GD
  dōm *(m)*
  mǣrðu *(f)*
  tīr *(m)*
  ðrymm *(m)*
  weorðmynd *(m,f,n)*
  wuldor *(n)*
Gloucestershire
  Gleawcestrescīr *(f)* STR
glove glofu *(f)* CLO
glue līm *(m)* TOO
  lēag *(f)*
glutton swelgere *(m)* EAT
gluttonous waxgeorn EAT
gluttony oferfylle *(f)* EAT
gnash one's teeth gristbitian *w* BOD
gnat gnæt *(m)* ANI
go (ge)faran *6* GO
  fēran *w*
  (ge)gān *a*
  (ge)gangan *7*
  gedīgan *w*
  lendan *w*
  lēoran *w*
  līðan *1*
  scacan *6*
  sīðian *w*
  wadan *6*
go away āgān *a* GO
  gewītan *1*
go back āswāmian *w* GO
go back on one's word ālēogan *2* FAI
go before foregangan *7* GO
  forestæppan *6*
go down sīgan *1* GO

go head first snyðian *w* GO
go in fēolan *3* GO
go mad wēdan *w* MIN
go on board gestīgan *1* WAT
go out forðgān *a* GO
  forðgangan *7*
go round befaran *6* GO
go to gesēcan *w* GO
go up ārīsan *1* GO
  āstīgan *1*
go with gefēran *w* GO
go without forðolian *w* NEE
go wrong mislimpan *3* BEC
  mistīmian *w*
  tōsǣlan *w*
goad gād *(m)* TOO
  gādīsen *(n)*
goat gāt *(m)* ANI
goblin nihtgenga *(m)* MON
  pūca *(m)*
  pūcel *(m)*
god god *(m,n)* CHU
God Dryhten *(m)* CHU
  God *(m)*
  Metod *(m)*
god-fearing ǣfæst CHU
  godfyrht
godchild godbearn *(n)* KIN
goddess gyden *(f)* CHU
godfather cumpæder *(m)* KIN
godparent godsibb *(n)* KIN
godson godsunu *(m)* KIN
going faru *(f)* GO
  sīð *(m)*
  sīðfæt *(n)*
gold gold *(n)* COL, MAT
gold, made of gylden MAT
gold-covered eallgylden COL
gold-studded fǣted ART
golden gylden COL, MAT
goldsmith goldsmið *(m)* WOR
good gōd GD
  riht
  rihtlīc
  rihtwīs
  til

good (thing) gōd *(n)* GD
good enough medemlīc GD
  weorð
good fortune gesǣlð *(f)* GD
  rǣd *(m)*
. sǣl *(m,f)*
good, make
  (ge)bētan *w* CLO, GD, HSE, PRO
  geinnian *w*
goodness fremu *(f)* GD
  gōd *(n)*
  gōdnes *(f)*
  rǣd *(m)*
goods gōd *(npl)* GD
goodwill frēod *(f)* GD
  welwillendnes *(f)*
goose gōs *(f)* ANI
gore heolfor *(m,n)* BOD
  wældrēor *(m,n)* WAR
gorse gors *(m)* PLA
gospel godspel *(n)* CHU
gospel commentary
  godspeltraht *(m)* CHU
Goths Gotan *(mpl)* STR
gourd cucurbite *(f)* MEA, WAT
gout fōtādl *(f)* AIL
govern stȳran *w* LRD
  wieldan *w*
gown serc *(m)* CLO
grace ēst *(f)* GD
  gifu *(f)*
  liss *(f)*
graceful ēstful GD
gracious ārfæst MIN
  glæd
  brēme GD
  fremsum
  hold
grammar stæfcræft *(m)* WRI
granddaughter nefene *(f)* KIN
  nift *(f)*
grandfather ealdfæder *(m)* KIN
  yldrafæder *(m)*
grandmother ealdmōdor *(f)* KIN
grandson nefa *(m)* KIN

grant ālȳfan *w* LAW
  forgiefan 5
  gescēawian *w* ASK
  geunnan *w*
  lēon *w*
  selen *(f)*
grant a tithe getīðian *w* ASK
grant by charter
  (ge)bōcian *w* LAN, WRI
granted gifeðe ASK
granter geðafa *(m)* ASK
grape wīnberge *(f)* EAT
grappling with ætgrǣpe WAR
grass gærs *(n)* PLA
grasshopper hyllehāma *(m)* ANI
  staða *(m)*
grassland græsmolde *(f)* LAN
  græswang *(m)*
grateful ðoncful ASK
gratis būtan cēape *(m)* WEA
gratitude ðoncung *(f)* ASK, THI
grave byrgen *(f)* DIE
  dēaðreced *(n)*
  wælrest *(f)*
gravel ceosol *(m)* LAN
graveyard līctūn *(m)* DIE
graze ettan *w* ANI, EAT
grease smeru *(n)* EAT
great ēacen WAR
  grēat LRD, MEA
  micel
great grandfather
  ðriddafæder *(m)* KIN
great grandmother
  ðriddemōdor *(f)* KIN
great grandson ðriddasunu *(m)* KIN
greatly miclum, micle MEA
greatness dōm *(m)* LRD
  grēatnes *(f)*
greave bānbeorge *(f)* WAR
greed gīfernes *(f)* ASK
  gītsung *(f)* EVL

greediness gīfernes *(f)* EVL
greedy frec EAT
  grǣdig
  waxgeorn
  gīfre ASK, EVL
Greek (people) Crēcas *(mpl)* STR
green grēne COL
  hǣwen
greet hālettan *w* LOV, SAY
  (ge)grētan *w*
grey grǣg COL
  hasu
  hǣwe
grey-coated hasupād ANI, COL
grey-eyed glæsenēage BOD
grey-haired blondenfeax BOD, COL
  hār
griddle brandrād *(f)* TOO
grief brēostwylm *(m)* MIN
  cearu *(f)* EVL
  hrēow *(f)*
  mōdcearu *(f)*
  sorg *(f)*
grieve ofðyncan *w* THI
grieving hrēowigferhð MIN
  hrēowigmōd
  sorgende
grievous hefigtȳme EVL
  ðroht
  swār NEE
  swǣr
grim āfor EVL
  grimm
  heard
grin grennian *w* LOV
grind (ge)grindan *3* BRK, EAT
grind up gegrindan *3* EVL
grip grāp *(f)* EVL
  gripe *(m)*
grit grēot *(m)* LAN
groin scearu *(f)* BOD
ground folde *(f)* LAN
  grund *(m)*
  hruse *(f)*
  molde *(f)*

ground-rent londfeoh *(n)* WEA
groundsel grundswylige *(f)* PLA
group of spears æscholt *(n)* WPN
grove bearu *(m)* LAN
  grāf *(n,m)*
  wuduholt *(n)*
grow weaxan *7* BEC
grow cold cōlian *w* EAT
grow dark
  (ge)nīpan *1* SKY, SLP
  (ge)sweorcan *3*
grow wintry winterlǣcan *w* SKY
grudge æfðonca *(m)* MIN
  inca *(m)*
grumble grēotan *2* SAY
  missprecan *5*
grumbling ceorung *(f)* SAY
grunt grymetian *w* ANI
guard warian *w* PRO
  weard *(m)* WOR
  werian *w*
guardian of a country
  londweard *(m)* PRO
guest bencsittend *(m)* HSE
  cuma *(m)* STR
  fletsittend *(m)*
  giest *(m)* LOV
guest house gesthūs *(n)* HSE
  giestærn *(n)*
guidance lātēowdōm *(m)* SAY
  stēor *(f)*
  wissung *(f)*
guide lātteow *(m)* WOR
  stīeran *w*
  weard *(m)*
  (ge)wīsian *w*
  (ge)wissian *w*
guild gesomnung *(f)* WOR
guildsman gegilda *(m)* WOR
guile fācn *(n)* EVL
  lēasung *(f)*
guilt gylt *(m)* LAW
guiltless unscyldig LAW
guilty forsyngod CHU, EVL
  scyldig LAW

gull mǣw *(m)* ANI
gullet edroc *(m)* BOD
gum gōma *(m)* BOD
gums tōþreōman *(mpl)* BOD
gut guttas *(mpl)* BOD
　ðearm *(m)*
guyrope stæg *(n)* TOO
gymnasium bæðstede *(m)* HSE, REC
gypsum spærstān *(m)* MAT

H

habit ðēaw *(m)* MIN
habit of, be in the gewunian *w* MIN
habitation cotlīf *(n)* HSE
　eardung *(f)* LIV
hail hālettan *w* LOV, SAY
　hagol *(m)* SKY
　hægl *(m)*
hail! welgā!
　wes ðū hāl!
hailstorm hæglfaru *(f)* SKY
hair feax *(m)* BOD
　hǣr *(n)*
hair, lock of windelocc *(m)* BOD
hairpin hǣrnǣdl *(f)* TOO
half healf *(f)* MEA
half, in emtwā
half dead sōmcucu DIE
half-asleep healfslæpende SLP
half-boiled healfsoden WAT
half-built samworht HSE
half-grown healfeald KIN
hall flet *(n)* HSE
　flōr *(f,m)*
　heall *(f)*
　reced *(n)*
　seld *(n)*
　sele *(m)*
hall-governor selerǣdend *(m)* LRD
hallow hālgian *w* CHU
halter hælfter *(f)* ANI
hammer homer *(m)* TOO
　slecg *(f)*
Hampshire Hāmtūnscīr *(f)* STR

hand folm *(f)* BOD
　hand *(f)*
　mund *(f)*
hand-to-hand handlinga WAR
handbasin mundlēow *(f)* WAT
handcart bearwe *(f)* BRI
handful handfull *(f)* MEA
　grīpa *(m)*
handle gripe *(m)* WPN
　hylfe *(n)* TOO
hang hōn 7 POS
　hongian *w*
happen gebyrian *w* BEC
　gegān *a*
　gelimpan *3*
　(ge)sǣlan *w*
　weorðan *3*
happiness ēadignes *(f)* GD
　gesǣlignes *(f)* MIN
　gesǣlð *(f)*
happy blīðemod GD, LOV
　ēadig
　fægen
　gesǣlig
harangue mǣlan *w* AGR, BLM, SAY
harass dreccan *w* EVL
　wǣgan *w*
harbour hȳð *(f)* WAT
　port *(m)* LAN
hard heard BRK
　stīð
hard, become hyrdan *w* BEC
　stīðian *w*
hard skin wearr *(m)* BOD
hard to count earfoðrīme MEA
hard-edged heardecg WPN
hardness heardnes *(f)* MAT
　stīðnes *(f)*
hardship earfoð *(n)* EVL
　gewinn *(n)* NEE
hare hara *(m)* ANI
hare-lip hærsceard *(n)* AIL, BOD
harlot hōre *(f)* LOV
　firenhicge *(f)*
harlot's dress forlīsgleng *(m,f)* CLO

harm daru *(f)* FOE
  derian *w*
  hearm *(m)*
  lāð *(n)*
  (ge)sceððan *6* EVL
harmer sceaða *(m)* FOE, EVL
harming by sympathetic magic
  stacung *(f)* CHU
harmless bilewit GD
  unsceððig
harmonious gesībsum LOV
  geðwǣre
harp glīwbēam *(m)* REC
  hearpe *(f)*
harp, play the hearpian *w* REC
harpstring hearpestreng *(m)* REC
harrow egðe *(f)* TOO
harry (for)hergian *w* WAR
  (for-, ge-)hergian *w* EVL
harrying hergoð *(m)* EVL
harsh grimm EVL
  horsc
  unswǣslīc
hart heort *(m)* ANI
harvest hærfest *(m)* EAT, LAN
  rīp *(n)* WOR
harvest time onrīptīd *(f)* TIM
hasp grindel *(m)* EVL
hassock cassuc *(m)* PLA
haste ofost *(f)* GO
haste, in ofstum GO
  on ofste
hasten crūdan *2* GO
  efstan *w*
  fundian *w* MIN
  onettan *w*
  rǣsan *w*
  scacan *6*
  scyndan *w*
  snyrian *w*
hasty ofostlīc GO
  recen TIM
hasty in speech hrædwyrde SAY
hat hæt *(m)* CLO
hatchet wudubil *(m)* TOO

hate gefēogan *w* EVL
  hatian *w*
hated lāð EVL
hateful fāh EVL
  fūl
  hetelīc
  heteðoncol
  hetol
  lāðlīc
hatred anda *(m)* FOE, MIN
  æfest *(m,f)*
  feondscipe *(m)* EVL
  hete *(m)*
  nīð *(m)*
  synn *(f)*
  wlǣtta *(m)*
haughty ofermōdig EVL
  ranc
haul dragan *6* BRI
  tēon *2*
have āgan *w* WEA
  habban *w*
have mercy on
  (ge)miltsian *w* GD, THI
haven hæfen *(f)* WAT
  hȳð *(f)*
hawk hafoc *(m)* ANI
hawthorn ðȳfeðorn *(m)* PLA
hay hīg *(n)* EAT
haystack hrēac *(m)* LAN
hazel hæsel *(m)* PLA
he hē *(nom.)*
head hafela *(m)* BOD
  heafod *(n)*
head cold gepos *(n)* AIL
head for mynian *w* GO
head of a boil dott *(m)* AIL
head officer
  ealdorðegn *(m)* LRD, WOR
headband binda *(m)* CLO
  heafodbend *(n)*
headland næss *(m)* LAN
headscarf wimpel *(m)* CLO
heal batian *w* AIL
  ge)hǣlan *w*
  hālian *w*

healing hālwende AIL
healing herb lǣcewyrt *(f)* PLA
health gesundfulnes *(f)* AIL
  gesyntu *(f)*
  hǣl(u) *(f)* GD
healthy gesund AIL
  (ge)hāl
  onsund
hear gehlȳstan *w* SAY
  (ge)hīeran *w*
hear about geāscian *w* ASK
hearing gehȳrnes *(f)* REC, SAY
  hlȳst *(f)*
hearse līcrest *(f)* DIE
heart ferhð *(m,n)* BOD, MIN
  geðonc *(m,n)* THI
  gewitloca *(m)*
  heorte *(f)*
  hreðer *(n)*
  mōd *(m)*
  mōdgeðonc *(m,n)*
  (mōd)sefa *(m)*
heart's ease bānwyrt *(f)* PLA
heartburn heortēce *(m)* AIL
heartfelt love ferhðlufu *(f)* LOV
  mōdlufu *(f)*
hearth heorð *(m)* FIR, HSE
heat (on)hǣtan *w* EAT, FIR, SKY
  hǣtu *(f)*
  hǣða *(m)*
heathen hǣðen CHU
heather hǣþ *(m,n)* PLA
heave hebban *6* HSE
heaven heofon *(m,f)* CHU
  swegl *(n)*
  ūpheofon *(m)*
heavenly heofonlīc CHU
  ūplīc
heavy hefig MEA
  swār NEE
  swǣr
heavy, become hefigian *w* BEC
Hebrew Ēbraisc STR
Hebrews Ēbrēas *(mpl)* STR
  Israhēla folc *(n)*

hedge bewindla *(m)* LAN, PLA
  haga *(m)*
  hege *(m)*
hedgehog hattefagol *(m?)* ANI
  hǣrenfagol *(m?)*
  īgel *(m)*
heed gīeman *w* LOV, MIN, WOR
heedless gīemelēas MIN
heel hēla *(m)* BOD
  hōh(fōt) *(m)*
  spure *(f)*
height hēanes *(f)* LAN
  hēhðu *(f)*
  leng *(f)* BOD, HSE
heir yrfeweard *(m)* LAW
heirloom (yrfe)lāf *(f)* KIN, LAW
hell hel *(f)* CHU
hellfire hellebryne *(m)* CHU
hellish spirit hellegāst *(m)* MON
  helsceaða *(m)*
hellish torment cwicsūsl *(n)* CHU
helmet helm *(m)* WPN
help fultum *(m)* GD
  (ge)fultumian *w*
  gēoc *(f)*
  (ge)helpan *3*
  wraðu *(f)*
  fylstan *w* PRO
  help *(f)*
  gelǣstan *w* WOR
help out fultumian *w* WAR
helve hylfe *(n)* TOO
hem ðrǣs *(f)* CLO
hemisphere healftryndel *(n)* HSE
hemlock hymlic *(m)* PLA
  hymlice *(f)*
hemp hænep *(m)* PLA
hen hænn *(f)* ANI
  henfugol *(m)*
henbane belene *(f)* PLA
hence hēonan
henceforth heonanforð TIM
her hīe *(acc.)*
  hire *(gen. dat.)*

herald ār *(m)* SAY, WRI
ǣrendraca *(m)*
boda *(m)*
herb wyrt *(f)* AIL
lēac *(n)*
herbal infusion wyrtdrenc *(m)* AIL
herd drāf *(f)* ANI, DRI
heord *(f)*
herdsman hyrde *(m)* WOR
swān *(m)*
here hēr
here and there ongemang ðissum TIM
Herefordshire Herefordscīr *(f)* STR
heresy gedwild *(n)* CHU
gedwola *(m)*
hermaphrodite bǣddel *(m)* KIN, BOD
hermithood ancerlīf *(n)* CHU
hero beorn *(m)* WAR
brego *(m)*
guma *(m)*
hæleð *(m)*
herring hǣring *(m)* ANI
Hertfordshire Heortfordscīr *(f)* STR
hesitate (for)wandian *w*
FAI, MIN, PFM, SAY, THI
twēogan *w*
twēonian *w*
hey! hīg
hū
hwæt
hiccup ælfsogoða *(m)* AIL
gicða *(m)*
sūgan *2*
hide bedīglian *w* SEE
behelian *w*
behȳdan *w*
bewrēon *1*
(ge)hȳdan *w*
mīðan *1*
fell *(n)* ANI
hȳd *(f)* MAT
hide of land hīd *(f)* LAN, MEA
hide unlawfully forhelan *4* LAW
high hēah LAN
stēap

high counsellor hēahwita *(m)* LRD
high price dēop cēap *(m)* WEA
high priest ealdorbiscop *(m)* CHU
high reeve hēahgerēfa *(m)* WOR
high seas hēahsǣ *(f)* WAT
sǣlīce dǣlas *(mpl)*
high-born æðele KIN, LRD
byrde
high-ranking hēahðungen LRD
hill beorg *(m)* LAN
dūn *(f)*
hlīð *(n)*
munt *(m)*
hilt gripe *(m)* WPN
hilt *(m,n)*
him hine *(acc.)*
him *(dat.)*
hinder hindrian *w* EVL
(ge)lettan *w*
oðstandan *6* FAI
hip hēopbrēmel *(m)* PLA
hēope *(f)*
hype *(f)* BOD
his his *(gen.)*
hiss hwinsian *w* SAY
hwistlian *w*
historian wyrdwrītere *(m)* WRI
historical wyrdelīc WRI
historical narrative
spellcwide *(m)* WRI
history spell *(n)* SAY
stǣr *(n)*
hit bēatan *7* EVL
cnucian *w*
cnyssan *w*
gerǣcan *w*
hither hider
hive hȳf *(f)* ANI
hoard hord *(n,m)* WEA
hoarhound hūne *(f)* PLA
hoarse hās SAY
hoe tyrfhaga *(m)* TOO
hog fearh *(m)* ANI
hold gehendan *w* EVL
grīpan *1*
healdan *7*

hold (safe) warian *w* PRO
   weardian *w*
hold back gehealdan *7* EVL
hole ðȳrel *(n)* BRK
   pytt *(m)* LAN
   sēað *(m)*
hollow out holian *w* HSE, WOR
holly hole(g)n *(m)* PLA
holocaust ealloffrung *(f)* EVL
holy hālig CHU
holy orders hād *(m)* CHU
holy orders, in gehādod CHU
holy water hāligwæter *(n)* CHU
home hām *(m)* HSE
home forces fierd *(f)* WAR
   innhere *(m)*
home happiness seledrēam *(m)* HSE
homecoming hāmcyne *(m)* GO
homeland eard *(m)* LAN
   ēðel *(m)*
honest eornost *(f)* MIN
honey hunig *(n)* EAT
honeycomb bēobrēad *(n)* EAT
honour ār *(f)* GD, MIN
   ārian *w*
   inwyrcan *w*
   mærnes *(f)*
honoured welðungen GD
   weorð
hood cugele *(f)* CLO
   hōd *(m)*
   snōd *(f)*
hoof hōf *(m)* BOD
hook ancgil *(m)* TOO
   hōc *(m)*
hop hoppan *w* GO
hop plant hymele *(f)* PLA
hope gehyhtan *w* MIN, THI
   hopian *w*
   hyht *(m)*
   tōhopa *(m)*
horizon lyftedor *(m)* SKY
horn horn *(m)* ANI, MAT
   sweglhorn *(m)* REC
hornet hyrnetu *(f)* ANI

horrible egeslic EVL
   unhīere
horse ēoh *(m)* ANI
   hors *(n)*
   mearh *(m)*
   wicg *(n)*
horse thief stōdðēof *(m)* LAW
horse-handler horsðegn *(m)* WOR
   horswealh *(m)*
horseback, on gehorsod GO
horseback bōg *(m)* ANI
horselitter horsbær *(f)* BRI
horseman ēoredman *(m)* GO
horses, provide with horsian *w* WOR
hose hosa *(m)* CLO
hospitable giestlīðe LOV
host ǣtgiefa *(m)* EAT
hostage foregīsl *(m)* EVL, LAW
   gīsel *(m)*
hostile fāg FOE
hostile encounter ætsteall *(m)* WAR
   wǣpengewrixl *(n)*
hostility fǣhðu *(f)* EVL
   feondscipe *(m)*
   unfrið *(m)* WAR
hot hāt FIR, SKY
hot coal glēd *(f)* FIR
hot meal panmete *(m)* EAT
hour stund *(f)* TIM
   tīd *(f)*
hour of winter winterstund *(f)* TIM
house hām *(m)* HSE
   hūs *(n)*
   reced *(n)*
   seld *(n)*
house-burning hūsbryne *(m)* FIR
household hēored, hīred *(m)* HSE
household goods inierfe *(n)* HSE
   inorf *(n)*
householder boldāgend *(m)* HSE, WEA
houseleek ðunorwyrt *(f)* PLA
how? hū
   hūmeta
however hūru
   swāðēah
   hwæðre

howl ðēotan *2* ANI
howling wōma *(m)* MIN
hub nafeða *(m)* TOO
  nafu *(f)*
hue dēag *(f)* COL
hug ymbclyppan *w* LOV
huge ormǣte MEA
human mennisc KIN
human joy mondrēam *(m)* MIN
humanity menniscnes *(f)* KIN
humble ēaðmōd GD, MIN
  geēaðmēdan *w* EVL
  hīenan *w*
humiliate forbīgan *w* EVL
  hīenan *w*
humiliation hȳnðu *(f)* BLM, EVL
humility ēaðmēdu *(n)* MIN
  ēaðmētto *(f)*
  ēaðmōdnes *(f)*
hump hofor *(m)* BOD
hump-backed gehoferod AIL
hundred hund
  hundtēontig
hundred and ten hundendlufontig
hundred and twenty hundtwelftig
  hundtwentig
hundredth hundtēontigoða
hunger hungor *(m)* EAT, NEE
hungry hungrig EAT
hunt huntian *w* REC, WOR
hunt with a bow ofscēotan *2* ANI
hunter hunta *(m)* REC, WOR
  huntere *(m)*
hunting huntoð *(m)* REC, WOR
  wāð *(f)*
Huntingdonshire
  Huntadūnscīr *(f)* STR
hurry gescēotan *2* GO
  snyrian *w*
hurt hearm *(m)* EVL
husband ceorl *(m)* KIN
  wer *(m)*
husband's brother tācor *(m)* KIN
hut cȳte *(f)* HSE
  stocwīc *(n)*

hyacinth iācinctus *(m)* PLA
hymnal hymnere *(m)* WRI
hypocrisy līcetung *(f)* MIN

I

I ic *(nom.)*
ibex firgenbucca *(m)* ANI
ice īs *(n)* SKY, WAT
icicle cylegicel *(m)* WAT
  wǣlrāp *(m)*
icy īsig SKY, WAT
idea geðōht *(m,n)* THI
idleness āsolcennes *(f)* EVL, MIN
  īdel *(n)* WOR
  īdelnes *(f)*
idol gedwolgod *(n)* CHU
idolatry dēofolgield *(n)* CHU
if gif
  ðǣr
ignite onǣlan *w* FIR
ignorant ungelǣred KNO
ignore forsuwian *w* SAY, WRI
  forswigian *w*
ill ādlig AIL
  sēoc
ill-treat tāwian *w* EVL
  tūcian *w*
illness, lying-in leger *(n)* AIL
illumine geondlȳhtan *w* FIR
  onlīhtan *w*
illusion dyderung *(f)* SEE
illusory gedwimorlīc SEE
imagine wēnan *w* THI
imitate æfterhyrgan *w* MIN
  gelǣcan *w*
immediately sōna TIM
impede āmyrran *w* EVL
impel fordrīfan *1* DRI
impending onsǣge WAR
  tōweard TIM
imperfect unfulfremed GD
impetuous forðgeorn MIN
  ungefōglīc

impossibility unmihtilicnys *(f)* BEC
impoverish foryrman *w* EVL, WEA
imprison gehæftan *w* LAW
improve gōdian *w* GD
  gebētan *w* AIL
impure unclǣnlic EVL
  unsȳfre
impurity wīdl *(m,n)* AIL
impute gestælan *w* THI
in in
  on
in addition on ðǣrtō MEA
in addition to tōēacan
in any way on ǣnigum MEA
in detail smēaðanclīce KNO
in exchange tō gehwearfe ASK
in exchange for wiþ
in flood flēde WAT
in front foran(tō) POS
  forne
  onforan
in front of tōgēanes
in future forð TIM
in half emtwā
in haste ofstum GO
  on ofste
in holy orders gehādod CHU
in need ðearfendlīc NEE
  wǣdligend
in order that tō þǣm þæt
  tō þæs þe
in place of for
in reply tōgeanes ASK
in shining armour scīrham LRD, WPN
in succession æfter POS
in the day on dæg TIM
in the first place æt ǣrestan TIM
in the lower part neoðeweard POS
in the meantime betwēnan TIM
  betweoh ðon
  ongemang ðissum
  ðendan
in the middle middeweard POS
  onmiddan
  tō middes

in truth sōðe SAY
  tō sōðe
in two parts emtwā
in time sīðlīc TIM
in turn ðurh endebyrdnesse TIM
in vain hōlunga FAI
inactive blēaþ PFM
inappropriate ungedēfe EVL
incantation onsang *(m)* REC
incarnation menniscnes *(f)* CHU
incautiously unforscēawodlīc KNO
incense rēcels *(m)* CHU, FIR
incest sibbleger *(n)* EVL
inch ince *(m)* MEA
incite getyhtan *w* SAY
  stihtian *w*
incite desire lystan *w* LOV
incline gebūgan *2* GO
  hyldan *w*
  gelīðian *w* MIN
income ār *(f)* LAW, WEA
  demn *(m)*
incomplete ungeendod FAI
inconvenience ungerisene *(n)* EVL
incredible ungelīefedlīc THI
incurable unhālwendlīc AIL
indeed hūru
indescribable unāsecgendlīc SAY
index finger scytefinger *(m)* BOD
Indian Syndonisc STR
Indians Indie *(mpl)* STR
indiction year gebonngēar *(n)* CHU
indigestion hrēa *(m)* AIL
indolent īdelgeorn MIN
indoors inne HSE, POS
inexorable ārǣd MIN
infant cradolcild *(n)* KIN
infantryman fēða *(m)* WAR
infirmity mettrumnes *(f)* AIL
  untrymnes *(f)*
inflame hǣtan *w* FIR
  onǣlan *w*
inflict on onbelǣdan *w* AIL, EVL
informer melda *(m)* LAW, SAY

infringe woman *w* EVL
inhabit būan *w* LAN, LIV
  onwunian *w*
  warian *w* HSE
inhabitant bīgenga *(m)* LAN, LIV
inhabited bȳne LAN
inheritance ierfe *(n)* WEA
inheritance, without ierfelēas WEA
inherited home yrfestōl *(m)* HSE
inimical wiðerweardlīc FOE
initiate onstellan *w* STA
injure derian *w* FOE, EVL
  gewyrdan *w*
  oðwyrcean *w*
  (ge)sceððan 6
injury byrst *(m)* EVL
  daru *(f)*
  demn *(m)*
  lāð *(n)*
  synn *(f)*
  tēona *(m)*
injustice unlagu *(f)* LAW
  unriht *(n)* MIN
ink blæc *(n)* WRI
inkwell blæchorn *(m)* WRI
inn gesthūs *(n)* HSE
  inn *(n)*
  tēcērhēs *(n)*
innards innoð *(m,f)* BOD
innkeeper wīnbrytta *(m)* WOR
innocence bilewitnes *(f)* GD, MIN
innocent bilewit GD, MIN
  unforwyrht LAW
  unsynnig
innumerable unārīmed MEA
inquisitive frymdig, fyrmdig ASK
inquisitiveness fyrwitnes *(f)* ASK
insect wyrm *(m)* ANI
insert borian *w* TOO
insolence bismrung *(f)* EVL
insomnia slæplēast *(f)* AIL, SLP
inspector inscēawere *(m)* WOR
inspiration inbryrdnes *(f)* MIN
inspire onbærnan *w* THI
  onbryrdan *w*

instability unstæðelfæstnes *(f)* HSE
inside innan
  inne
install onstellan *w* STA
instantly bearhtme TIM
  sōna
instead on his lōh POS
instep fōtwylm *(m)* BOD
institution gesetednes *(f)* LAW
instruct behwyrfan *w* SAY
  tēon 2
  (ge)tȳn *w*
instruction lārcwide *(m)* SAY
insult bismer *(m,n,f)* EVL, FOE, SAY
  bismerian *w*
  bismrung *(f)*
  hearm *(m)*
  hosp *(m)*
  misgrētan *w*
insulting bismerlīc EVL, SAY
intellect gewit *(n)* MIN
  mōd *(n)* KNO, THI
  ondgit *(n)* SAY
  ongitennes *(f)*
intelligible ondgitfullīc SAY
intend hogian *w* MIN
  hycgan *w* THI
  mynian *w*
  teohhian *w*
  ðencan *w*
  willan *w*
intent behygdig MIN
  gemyndig
intent, be hīgian *w* MIN, THI
intercede geðingian *w* ASK, SAY
intercede with prayer ðingian *w* CHU
intercept foran tō scēotan 2 GO
  forrīdan 1
intercession ðingung *(f)* SAY
interlace ornament wyrmlīc *(n)* ART
internal incund BOD
  innanweard POS
interpret (ge)reccean *w* SAY, THI
  trahtian *w*
interpretation gereccennes *(f)* THI

intervene swīfan on *1* PFM
intestine rop *(m)* BOD
intimate friend wilgehleða *(m)* LOV
into in
   on
invader ingenga *(m)* FOE
invading force flocrād *(f)* WAR
invention finding *(f)* MIN
investigate fandian *w* ASK
   fricgan *5*
   gecunnian *w* KNO
invisible ungesewenlīc SEE
invite (ge)laðian *w* ASK, SAY
invoke gecīgan *w* CAL
inward incund AIL
Ireland Īraland *(n)* STR
iris glædene *(f)* PLA
iris illyrica hwatend *(m)* PLA
Irish Īrisc STR
Irishmen Scottas *(mpl)* STR
iron īren *(n)* MAT
   īsern *(n)*
iron, made of īsern MAT
irritable ēaðbylige MIN
island ēalond *(n)* LAN, WAT
   īeg *(f)*
   īggað *(m)*
   īgland *(n)*
Isle of Man Mǣnīg *(f)* STR
Isle of Wight Wihtland *(n)* STR
issue geðinge *(n)* AGR, SAY
   intinga *(m)*
   ðing *(n)*
it hit *(nom. acc.)*
   him *(dat.)*
it occurs to me beirnð mē on mōde THI
Italians Eotolware *(mpl)* STR
itch cleweða *(m)* AIL
   giccan *w*
itinerant wīdgongel GO
its his *(gen.)*
ivory elpendbān *(m)* MAT
   elpendtōð *(m)*
   ylpesbān *(n)*
ivory, made of elpendbǣnen MAT
ivy īfig *(n)* PLA

J

jackdaw ceahhe *(f)* ANI
jacket pād *(m)* CLO
jail carcern *(n)* LAW
   cweartern *(n)*
January æfterra Gēola *(m)* TIM
jaundice gealādl *(f)* AIL
javelin daroð *(m)* WPN
   franca *(m)*
   pǣl *(m)*
jaw cēace *(f)* BOD
   cinbān *(n)*
jay higera *(m)* ANI
jealous andig EVL
   æfestig
jesting gegafsprǣc *(f)* SAY
   hygelēast *(f)*
jeweller gimwyrhta *(m)* WOR
jewellery frætwa *(fpl)* ART
jewels frætwa *(fpl)* WEA
Jews Ēbreas *(mpl)* STR
join fēgan *w* GO
   geðēodan *w*
join in marriage beǣwnian *w* CHU
joint līþ *(m,n,)* BOD
jointly-owned land gedālland *(n)* LAN
joke glēowian *w* SAY
Jordan (river) Iordānen *(f)* STR
journey faru *(f)* GO
   fær *(n)*
   færeld *(n)*
   lād *(f)*
   rād *(f)*
   sīð *(m)*
   sund *(n)* WAT
journey in exile wrǣclast *(m)* GO
   wræcsīð *(m)*
journey south sūðfōr *(f)* GO
jowl gēagl *(m,n)* BOD
joy blīðnes *(f)* LOV
   wynn *(f)*
   drēam *(m)* GD
   gefēa *(m)* MIN
   glīwstæf *(m)*
   gomen *(n)*
   mondrēam *(m)*

joy of mead drinking
  meodudrēam *(m)* EAT
joyful blīðe LOV
  lustlīc
  wynlīc
  blīðemōd GD
  gelustful MIN
joyous lustbǣre LOV
judge dēma *(m)* LAW, THI, WOR
  dēman *w*
  dēmend *(m)*
judgement dōm *(m)* LAW, THI
judgement seat dōmsetl *(n)* LAW
jug cēac *(m)* EAT
juice sēaw *(n)* EAT
  wōs *(n)*
juice of a plant wōs *(n)* PLA
July æfterra Līða *(m)* TIM
jump hlēapan 7 GO
June ǣrra Līða *(m)* TIM
  Midsumermōnað *(m)*
  Sēremōnað *(m)*
juniper cwīcbēam *(m)* PLA
just riht GD
  rihtlīc
  rihtwīs
just about efnswā
just as much efnlīce MEA
justice folcriht *(n)* LAW
  riht *(n)*
Jutes Ēote *(mpl)* STR
Jutish Ēotisc STR

K

kalend cālend *(m)* TIM
keen cēne MIN
  fram
  georn(ful)
  hwæt PFM
keep gehabban *a* PRO
  healdan 7
  weardian *w*

keep peace with friðian *w* LOV, MIN
keeper hyrde *(m)* PRO
  weard *(m)*
keeping wǣr *(f)* PRO
keeping of a service geheald *(n)* CHU
Kent Cent *(f)* STR
Kentish (people) Cantware *(fpl)* STR
  Centingas *(mpl)*
kernel cyrnel *(m)* EAT
kettle cytel *(m)* EAT
key cǣg *(f)* TOO
kick spurnan 3 WAR
kid ticcen *(n)* ANI
kidnapper monðēof *(m)* EVL
kidney lundlaga *(m)* BOD
kill ācwellan *w* WAR
  āfyllan *w*
  forniman 4
  forwegan 5
  gecwylman *w*
  (ā)swebban *w*
killer with a sword ecgbana *(m)* FOE
kin cynn *(n)* KIN
kind ārfæst MIN
  bilewit GD
  glæd
  mildelīc
  hold
kindle onǣlan *w* FIR
  onbærnan *w*
kindness ār *(f)* WEA
  fremsumnes *(f)* GD, LOV, MIN
kindred cynn *(n)* KIN
  cynren *(n)*
king cyng *(m)* LRD
  cyning *(m)*
king over a nation
  ðēodcyning *(m)* LRD
king's wife or daughter cwēn *(f)* KIN
kingdom cynedōm *(m)* LAN, LRD
  (cyne)rīce *(n)*

kingship cynehād *(m)* LRD
kinship mǣgrǣden *(f)* KIN
  sibb *(f)*
kinsman gesibb *(m,f)* KIN
  magu *(m)*
  mǣg *(m)*
kinsman, dear winemǣg *(m)* KIN
kinsman-retainer
  maguðegn *(m)* WOR
kinsmen cnēomagas *(mpl)* KIN
kirtle cyrtele *(f)* CLO
kiss (ge)cyssan *w* LOV
kitchen cycene *(f)* HSE, EAT
kite glida *(m)* ANI
knead gecnedan *5* EAT
knee cnēow *(n)* BOD
kneecap hweorfbān *(n)* BOD
kneel cnēow(l)ian *w* POS
knell cnyll *(m)* CHU
knife seax *(n)* TOO
knock cnossian *w* ASK
  gecnucian *w*
  gecnycc *(n)* BRI
knoll cnoll *(m)* LAN
knot brēdan *3* EVL
  cnotta *(m)*
  cnyttan *w*
knot in wood ōst *(m)* MAT
know (on)cnāwan *7* KNO
  cunnan *a*
  gecnāwan *7*
  ongietan *5*
  witan *a*
know in advance forewitan *a* KNO
knowledge cȳððu *(f)* KNO
  gewitnes *(f)* MIN
  leornung *(f)*
  ongietennes *(f)*
known cūð KNO
  gēanwyrde
  yppe
known, become gecȳðan *w* BEC
known, make
  cȳððan *w* KNO, SAY, SEE

L

labour deorfan *3* PFM
  earfoð *(n)* WOR
  gedeorf *(n)*
  winnan *3*
lack forðolian *w* ASK, NEE
  gād *(n)*
  onsȳn *(f)*
  wana *(m)*
lack of food metelīest *(f)* NEE
lacking gewana NEE
  orfeorme
lacking counsel rǣdlēas MIN
ladder hlǣder *(f)* TOO
ladle hlǣdel *(m)* EAT, TOO
lady hlǣfdige *(f)* LRD
  ides *(f)*
lake mere *(m)* LAN
  wæterscipe *(m)* WAT
lamb lamb *(n)* ANI
lame healt AIL, GO
lament geōmrung *(f)* MIN
  mǣnan *w* THI
  seofian *w* SAY
  sorglēoð *(n)* REC
lamenting wōpig MIN
Lammas Hlāfmæsse *(f)* CHU
lamp blǣcern *(n)* FIR
  blǣse *(f)*
  lēohtfæt *(n)*
lamprey lamprede *(f)* ANI
lance gār *(m)* WPN
land eard *(m)* LAN
  grund *(m)*
  land *(n)*
landed wealth londār *(f)* WEA
landing ūpganga *(m)* GO
landmark gebēacen *(n)* LAN
lane lanu *(f)* DRI
language gereord *(n)* MIN, SAY
  geðēode *(n)*
lap bearm *(m)* BOD

Lappish Finnisc STR
Lapps Finnas *(mpl)* STR
larboard bæcbord *(n)* WAT
lard rysle *(m)* EAT
large grēat MEA
  micel
  ormǣte
larger, become ēacnian *w* BEC
larynx ðrotbolla *(m)* BOD
last night tōniht TIM
late læt TIM
  sīð
later æfterra TIM
lather fām *(n)* WAT
Latin Lædengereord *(n)* WRI
  Lædengeðēode *(n)*
Latin, literary bōclæden *(n)* WRI
Latins (people) Lædenware *(fpl)* STR
laugh hlihhan *6* GD, LOV
laugh over behliehhan *6* THI
laughter breahtm *(m)* LOV
  hleahtor *(m)*
laurel lawertrēow *(n)* PLA
law ǣ *(f)* LAW
  gemet *(n)*
  lagu *(f)*
  riht *(n)*
  regol *(f)* LRD
lawful lahlīc LAW
  regollīc LRD
lawful slave rihtðēowa *(m)* WOR
lawless man wearg *(m)* FOE
lawsuit spǣc *(f)* LAW
lawyer lahwita *(m)* LAW
lax earg MIN
  slāw
lay lǣwede CHU
  (ā)lecgan *w* POS
lay waste āwēstan *w* EVL
  ȳðan *w*
lazy īdelgeorn MIN
lead (ge)lǣdan *w* BRI
  ferian *w* DRI
  hweorfan *3* GO
  lēad *(n)* MAT

lead away ālǣdan *w* BRI
  oðlǣdan *w*
leadline sundrāp *(m)* TOO
leader brego *(m)* LRD
  ealdor *(m)*
  heretoga *(m)* WAR
leaderless hlāfordlēas LRD
leaf lēaf *(n)* PLA
lean hlinian *w* POS
leap onto (ge)hlēapan *7* GO
learn geāscian *w* ASK
  gefrignan *3*
  geleornian *w*
  hīeran *w* SAY
learned gelǣred MIN
leasehold land lǣn *(f)* LAN
least lǣst MEA
leather leðer *(n)* CLO
leather breeches leðerhosu *(f)* CLO
leatherworker scōwyrhta *(m)* WOR
leave ālǣtan *7* GO
  (ā)faran *6*
  gewītan *1*
  (of)lǣfan *w*
  sceacan *6*
leave on an ebb-tide beebbian *w* WAT
leek lēac *(n)* PLA
left hand side wynstra BOD, POS
  wynstre *(f)*
leg bān *(n)* BOD
  scanca *(m)*
leg-band wyning *(m)* CLO
legal ǣwlic LAW
  lahlic
Leicestershire
  Lægreceastrescīr *(f)* STR
leisure ǣmetta, ēmta *(m)* MIN
lend (on)lǣnan *w* WEA
length langnys *(f)* MEA
lengthy longsum TIM
Lent Lencten *(m)* TIM
leper hrēofla *(m)* AIL
less lǣssa MEA
less, become sweðrian *w* BEC
  (ge)wanian *w*

lessening wanung *(f)* BEC
lest þȳ lǣs þe
let go ālīesan *w* GO
letter ǣrendgewrit *(n)* SAY
letter of the alphabet stæf *(m)* WRI
lettuce lactuce *(f)* EAT, PLA
level efn LAN
level out efnan *w* LAN
liar lēogere *(m)* SAY
liberate frēogan *w* GD
library bibliođēce *(f)* WRI
   bōchord *(n)*
   bōchūs *(n)*
lichen ragu *(f)* PLA
lick liccian *w* EAT
lid hlid *(n)* TOO
lie (ā)lēogan *2* SAY
   forlēogan *2* LAW
   licgan *5* POS
lie between tōlicgan *5* POS
lie dead licgan *5* DIE
   swefan *5*
lie round ymblicgan *5* POS
lie supine upweard licgan *w* POS
life blǣd *(m)* LIV
   ealdor *(n)*
   feorh *(m,n)*
   līf *(n)*
life, spend one's drohtnian *w* LIV
life, way of drohtnung *(f)* LIV, WOR
lifeless belifd WAR
   orsāwle DIE
   unlifigend
lift āhebban *6* GO
light līht COL, MEA
   lēoht *(n)* FIR
light-hearted lēohtmōd MIN
lightly-boiled hrēre EAT
lightning līget *(n,m)* SKY
   līgetu *(f)*
   onǣlet i(n)
lightning flash līgræsc *(m)* SKY
like gelīc LOV
   līcian *w*
likeness gelīcnes *(f)* ART

   onlīcnes *(f)*
lily of the valley glofwyrt *(f)* PLA
limb lið *(n)* BOD
lime līm *(m)* MAT
lime (whitewash)
   hwītingmelu *(n)* MAT
limestone cealcstān *(m)* MAT
limit mearc *(f)* LAN
limp lemphealt AIL
Lincolnshire Lincolnescīr *(f)* STR
lindenwood, made of linden MAT
Lindisfarne Lindisfarnēa *(f)* STR
Lindisfarne (people)
   Lindisfaran *(mpl)* STR
Lindsey Lindesīg *(f)* STR
Lindsey (people) Lindisse *(mpl)* STR
line līne *(f)* TOO
linen līn *(n)* CLO
   twīn *(n)*
linen, made of līnen MAT
linen cloth scīte *(f)* CLO
linseed līnsǣd *(n)* PLA
lintel oferdyre *(n)* HSE
lion lēo *(m,f)* ANI
lip smǣr *(m)* BOD
   weler *(m,f)*
liquid wǣta *(m)* WAT
lisp wlips *(m?)*, wlisp *(m?)* SAY
listen gehlȳstan *w* SAY
   hlosnian *w* REC
listen! hwæt
listen for hlosnian *w* SAY
litany lētanīa *(m)* CHU
literary composition
   gesetednes *(f)* WRI
literary Latin bōclǣden *(n)* WRI
literature bōccræft *(m)* WRI
   stafas *(mpl)*
little lytel MEA
little by little dǣlmǣlum MEA
little finger ēarclǣnsend *(m)* BOD
live libban *w* LIV
   lifian *w*
live on ālibban *w* LIV
livelihood bigleofa *(m)* LIV

liver lifer *(f)* BOD
living bīleofa *(m)* LIV
  ealdor *(n)*
Livonia Sermende *(mpl)* STR
lizard āðexe *(f)* ANI
lo! efne
  lā
  ono
lo & behold! ono hwæt
load hlæst *(m)* WAT
  hlæstan *w*
  scipian *w*
  lād *(f)* BRI
loaf hlāf *(m)* EAT
loan gelænan *w* WEA
loathe lāðian *w* EVL
loathesome lāð(līc) EVL
loathing wlætta *(m)* EVL
lobster lopystre *(f)* ANI
locality eorðweard *(m)* LAN
  stōw *(f)*
location stede *(m)* LAN
lock lūcan *2* POS
lock of hair windelocc *(m)* BOD
locker hwicce *(f)* HSE
lodgings tēcērhēs *(n)* HSE
log bēam *(m)* PLA
  stocc *(m)*
logic flitcræft *(m)* SAY
  wordloc *(n)*
loins lendenu *(npl)* BOD
Lombards (people)
  Langbeardan *(mpl)* STR
Lombardy Langbeardnarīce *(n)* STR
lone-dweller ānhoga *(m)* LIV
long lang MEA
long ago gefyrn TIM
long-haired feaxed BOD
longing fūs LOV, MIN
  longað *(m)*
  lustbǣre
  mynela *(m)* LOV
look besēon *5* SEE
  hāwian *w*
  lōcian *w*

(ge)scēawian *w*
  wlātian *w*
look after begongan *7* LOV
  gīeman *w* WOR
look down on forsēon *5* SEE
look forward to cēpnian *w* THI
look (out) for wlātian *w* ASK, SEE
loom webbēam *(m)* CLO
loose unfæst HSE, POS
loose, become tōslūpan *2* BEC
  wagian *w*
loosen onlætan *7* EVL
  onlȳsan *w*
loquacious cwidol SAY
lord dryhten *(m)* LRD
  ealdor *(m)*
  frēa *(m)*
  hearra *(m)*
  hlāford *(m)*
  mondryhten *(m)*
lordless ealdorlēas LRD
  hlāfordlēas
lordly protector eodor *(m)* PRO
lordly wealth eorlgestrēon *(n)* WEA
lordship hlāforddōm *(m)* LRD
lore gefræge *(n)* KNO
  gefreoge *(n)*
lose forlēosan *2* EVL
loss æfwyrdla *(m)* EVL
  byrst *(m)*
  losing *(f)* FAI
  lyre *(m)*
lost, be oðstandan *6* FAI
  losian *w*
lost, become losian *w*
lot hlot *(n)* BEC
lot(s) fela MEA
  monig
  worn
lot-casting hlytm *(m)* CHU
loud hlūd REC, SAY
louse lūs *(f)* ANI
louse-eggs hnitu *(f)* ANI
lovage lubastice *(f)* PLA

love frēogan *w* GD, LOV
    frīge *(fpl)*
    lufian *w*
    lufu *(f)*
love, with frēondlīc LOV
love-making restgemāna *(m)* LOV
loved one drūt *(f)* LOV
lovely cȳmlīc LOV
    lufiendlīc
lover frēond *(m)* LOV
    hǣmedwīf *(n)*
    hǣmend *(m)*
    hǣmere *(m)*
    lufestre *(f)*
    lufiend *(m)*
    wine *(m)*
loving lufiendlīc LOV
    luflīc
low lāh POS
    niðerlīc
    hlōwan 7 ANI
low-born unǣðele LRD
lower niðera POS
lower leg fōtscanca *(m)* BOD
lower part, in the neoðeweard POS
lowly hēanlīc EVL
loyal hold GD
loyalty hyldu *(f)* GD
    trēow *(f)* THI
loyalty to a friend winetrēow *(f)* GD
luck gesǣlignes *(f)* MIN
    gesǣlð *(f)* GD
    rǣd *(m)*
    sǣl *(m,f)*
lukewarm wlæc WAT
lump blōma *(m)* LAN, MAT
    clympre *(m)*
    wecg *(m)*
    wolcen *(m,n)*
lung lungen *(f)* BOD
lupin elehtre *(f)* PLA
lurk lūtian *w* POS
lust gāl *(n)* EVL, LOV, MIN
    gālnes *(f)*
    lust *(m)*

lustful gālferhð LOV, MIN
    gālmōd
    wrǣne EVL
luxuriant geþūf PLA
luxurious furðumlīc GD
    oferranc
lye lēah *(f)* WAT
    lēag *(f)* TOO
lying lēasung *(f)* SAY
lying down leger *(n)* SLP
lynx lox *(m)* ANI
lyre hearpe *(f)* REC

M

machine searu *(n)* TOO
mad gemād MIN
    wōd
madder mædere *(f)* PLA
made of beechwood bēcen MAT
made of bone bǣnen MAT
made of boxwood byxen MAT
made of brass ǣren MAT
made of glass glæsen MAT
made of gold gylden MAT
made of iron īsern MAT
made of ivory elpendbǣnen MAT
made of lindenwood linden MAT
made of linen līnen MAT
made of otterskin yteren MAT
made of planks breden HSE, MAT
made of roses gerōsod PLA
made of silk seolcen MAT
made of stone stǣnen MAT
made of wheat hwǣten EAT, MAT
made of wood trēowen MAT
made of wool wullen MAT
madness wōdnes *(f)* MIN
maggot maða *(m)* ANI
    flǣscwyrm *(m)* EAT
magic drȳcræft *(m)* CHU
magic word galdorword *(n)* CHU, SAY
magical drȳlīc CHU
magically skilled drȳcræftig CHU
magician drȳmann *(m)* CHU
magnificent micellic SKY
    sweglwered

maiden fǣmne *(f)* KIN
  mǣden *(n)*
  mǣgð *(f)*
  mēowle *(f)*
maidenhead mǣgðhād *(f)* LOV
maidenhood mǣgðhād LOV
mailcoat beadohrægl *(n)* WPN
  byrne *(f)*
  byrnhoma *(m)*
  hringloca *(m)*
  hringnett *(n)*
main dwelling hēafodbotl *(n)* HSE
maintain gehealdan 7 PRO
  gelǣstan *w*
majesty mægenðrymm *(m)* GD
make āsmiðian *w* WOR
  dōn *a*
  gewyrcan *w*
  macian *w*
make a powder cnucian *w* AIL
  cnuwian *w*
make clear swutelian *w* SAY
make fast fæstan *w* PRO
  sǣlan *w*
make firm gestaðolian *w* HSE
make flee geflīeman *w* DRI
make good
  (ge)bētan *w* CLO, GD, HSE, PRO
  geinnian *w*
make known
  (ge)cȳðan *w* KNO, SAY, SEE
make love with cnēowian *w* LOV
make manifest geswutelian *w* SEE
make pregnant geēacnian *w* KIN
make ready fȳsan *w* PFM
  gearwian *w*
make room gerȳman *w* GO
make useless āīdligan *w* FAI
make verses
  wordum wrixlan *w* REC
maker smið *(m)* WOR
  wyrhta *(m)*
male side of the family
  sperehealf *(f)* KIN
  wæpnedhand *(f)*
  wæpnedhealf *(f)*

malevolent heteðoncol EVL
  inwit
  yfelwille
malice anda *(m)* EVL, MIN
malicious heteðancol MIN
malicious wound
  inwiddhlem *(m)* EVL
mallet slic *(n)* TOO
mallow hocc *(m)* PLA
  hoclēaf *(n)*
malt mealt *(n)* EAT
maltreat misbēodan 2 EVL
man (adult human) mon *(m)* KIN
  monna *(m)*
man (adult human male)
  secg *(m)* KIN
  wǣpnedmann *(m)*
  wer *(m)*
manage gedōn 7 PFM
  manian *w*
  stihtan *w*
manager fadiend *(m)* WOR
mane manu *(f)* BOD
manger binn *(f)* EAT, HSE
manifest, make geswutelian *w* SEE
manifold monigfeald MEA
maniple handlīn *(n)* CLO
mankind moncynn *(n)* KIN
manner gemet *(n)* LAW
  wīse *(f)* MIN
manor hām *(m)* LAN
mantle orel *(n)* CLO
mantle of goat skin hrēða *(m)* CLO
manual sign hondseten *(f)* SAY
many fela MEA
  manig
  worn
maple tree hlin *(m)* PLA
  mapuldor *(m)*
mar āmyrran *w* EVL
marauding army stælhere *(m)* EVL
marble marmastān *(m)* MAT
march faran 6 GO
  fær *(n)*
  stæppan 6
  wadan 6

March Hlȳda *(m)* TIM
  Hrēðmōnað *(m)*
mare mȳre *(f)* ANI
margin efes *(f)* LAN
  ōra *(m)*
marigold sigelhweorfa *(m)* PLA
marine sǣlīc WAT
maritime sǣlīc WAT
mark mǣl *(n)* ART
marketplace cēapstōw *(f)* WEA
marriage ǣwnung *(f)* LOV
  hǣmed *(m)*
  legertēam *(m)*
married couple sinhīwan *(mpl)* KIN
marsh mersc *(m)* LAN
marshmallow merscmealuwe *(f)* PLA
marshy land ēalond *(n)* WAT
  fenn *(n,m)*
  mōr *(m)*
marten mearð *(m)* ANI
martyrology martirlogium *(n)* WRI
marvel wundor *(n)* GD
mask grima *(m)* CLO
mason stāncræftiga *(m)* WOR
mass mæsse *(f)* CHU
mass against ðrēatian *w* WAR
mast mæst *(m)* WAT
master frēa *(m)* LRD
  hearra *(m)*
  hlāford *(m)*
mastic hwētcwudu *(m)* EAT
mastiff ryðða *(m)* ANI
mat meatt *(f)* HSE
mate gemæcca *(m)* LOV
materials ontimber *(n)* HSE
matins ūhtsang *(m)* CHU
matter geðinge *(n)* AGR, SAY
  ontimber *(n)*
  ðing *(n)*
  intinga *(m)* ASK, MIN, THI, WRI
  ondweorc *(n)*
mattock becca *(m)* TOO
may mōtan *a*
May Ðrīmeolce *(n)* TIM
  Ðrīmilcemōnað *(m)*

me mē *(acc. dat.)*
  mec *(acc.)*
mead meodu *(f)* EAT
meadow gærstūn *(m)* LAN
  mǣd *(f)*
  wongturf *(f)*
meadowsweet medowyrt *(f)* PLA
meal gereorde *(f)* EAT
  gereording *(f)*
meal (flour) melu *(n)* EAT
mealtime mǣl *(n)* EAT
mean behealdan *7* GD
  forstandan *6* SAY, WRI
  tācnian *w* MIN
  wyrslīc EVL
meaning ondgit *(n)* SAY
means ār *(f)* LAW
  æht *(f)*
  feoh *(n)*
meantime, in the betwēnan TIM
  betweoh ðon
  ongemang ðissum
  ðendan
measure gemet *(n)* MEA
  mǣð *(f)*
  metan *5*
  mitta *(m)*
  trȳm *(n)*
measure (amphora)
  amber *(m,f,n)* EAT
measure by weight wæge *(f)* MEA
measure of bulk sester *(m)* MEA
measure of corn sesðlar *(n)* MEA
measuring cup cuppe *(f)* MEA
meat flǣscmete *(m)* EAT
meat pudding mearhæccel *(n)* EAT
  mearhgehæcc *(n)*
mechanics weorccræft *(m)* WOR
medicine lācnung *(f)* AIL
Mediterranean Sea
  Wendelsǣ *(f)* STR
medlar æpening *(m)* EAT, PLA
  openears *(m)*

meet gemētan *w* SEE
meeting gemāna *(m)* SAY
  ðing *(n)*
  gemēting *(f)* SEE
  gemitting *(f)*
  gemōt *(n)*
meeting day mēting *(f)* TIM
meeting place meðelstede *(m)* AGR
melody hlēoðor *(n)* REC
  swinn *(m)*
  swinsung *(f)*
melt meltan *3* FIR, WAT
melt away gemeltan *3* SKY
member of a guild gegilda *(m)* WOR
memory gemynd *(f,n)* MIN, THI
men beornas *(mpl)* KIN
  fīras *(mpl)*
  men *(mpl)*
  ylde *(mpl)*
mend bētan *w* GD
  geeftgian *w*
menstruation mōnaðādl *(f)* AIL
mental aberration
  onweggewit *(n)* MIN
mention secgan *w* SAY
merchandise cēap *(m)* LAW
merchant cȳpmann *(m)* WEA, WOR
Mercia Mierce *(mpl)* STR
Mercian Miercisc STR
Mercians (people) Mierce *(mpl)* STR
merciful milde MIN
merciful to, be gemiltsian *w* MIN
mercy mildheortnes *(f)* GD
  milts *(f)*
merit (ge)earnung *(f)* GD, PFM, WOR
merry blīðe MIN
  hlagol
  myrge
message ǣrende *(n)* ASK, SAY
  lāc *(n,f)*
  spell *(n)*
  ǣrendgewrit *(n)* WRI
message, spoken ǣrendsprǣc *(f)* SAY
messenger ār *(m)* CAL, WRI
  ǣrendwreca *(m)* SAY

  boda *(m)*
metre gemet *(n)* MEA
midday middæg *(m)* TIM
midday meal nōn mete *(m)* EAT
middle midde *(f)* POS
  middel *(n)*
middle, in the middeweard POS
  onmiddan
  tō middes
middle-age midfeorh *(m,n)* LIV
middle finger hālettend *(m)* BOD
Middlesex Middelseaxan *(mpl)* STR
midge gnæt *(m)* ANI
  micg *(m)*
midnight middeniht *(f)* TIM
midriff midrif *(n)* BOD
midsummer middansumer *(m)* TIM
midway midd POS
midwife byrþþīnen *(f)* WOR
midwinter middanwinter *(m)* TIM
might mægen *(n)* GD
mighty ðearlmōd MIN
  ēacen WAR
  felameahtig
  mihtig(līc) GD
  rīce LRD
  þyhtig
  wielde
mild līðe LOV
  milde MIN
  rōw
  smolt
  smylte
mile mīl *(f)* MEA
military punishment
  fierdwīte *(n)* WAR
militia londfyrde *(f)* WAR
milk meolcan *3* ANI
  meolc *(f)* EAT
mill mylen *(f)* HSE
millet hers *(f)* PLA
millstone cweornstān *(m)* HSE
millstream hwēolrīðig *(n)* LAN, WAT

mind ferhð *(m,n)* MIN
  geðonc *(m,n)* THI
  gewitloca *(m)*
  hordcofa *(m)*
  hyge *(f)*
  mōd *(m)*
  mōdgeðonc *(m,n)*
  (mōd)sefa *(m)*
mindful gemyndig MIN
  hohful THI
minnow myne *(m)* ANI
minstrel glīwmon *(m)* REC
minstrelsy glīwdrēam *(m)* REC
mint minte *(f)* PLA
miracle working
  wundorcræft *(m)* GD
mirror scēawere *(m)* SEE
mirth bearhtm *(m)* LOV
  blīðnes *(f)* REC
  drēam *(m)* GD
  glīwstæf *(m)*
  myrhð *(f)* MIN
miscarry mislimpan *3* BEC
  tōsǣlan *w*
miserable earm EVL, NEE
  unlǣde
miserliness gītsung *(f)* EVL
misery broc *(n)* EVL
  iermðu *(f)* MIN
  wēa *(m)*
  wracu *(f)*
  wræc *(n)*
misfortune ungesǣlð *(f)* NEE
  ungelimp *(n,m)* EVL
  unsīð *(m)*
mislead bedydran *w* SAY
  dwelian *w* MIN
  forsponan *6* BRI, LOV
  misðyncan *w* SEE
miss missan *w* FAI
missile scotung *(f)* WPN
missing ofhende FAI
mist mist *(m)* SKY
mistake misfēran *w* MIN
  misfōn *7* THI
  misðyncan *w* SEE

mistletoe mistel *(m)* PLA
  mistiltān *(m)*
mistreat forhealdan *7* LAW
  mistūcian *w*
mix blandan *7* BRI
  mengan *w*
  miscian *w*
moan cwiðan *w* SAY
mock bismerian *w* EVL
  cancettan *w*
moderation gemetfæstnes *(f)* GD
  gemetgung *(f)*
  syfernys *(f)* MIN
modest cūsc GD
  scomfæst MIN
moist, be fūhtian *w* WAT
moisten wǣtan *w* WAT
molar wongtōð *(m)* BOD
mole moldeweorpere *(m)* ANI
  māl *(n)* BOD
molten, become gemeltan *w* BEC
moment bearhtmhwæt *(f)* TIM
  prēowthwīl *(f)*
monastery mynster *(n)* CHU
monastic mynsterlīc CHU
monastic building
  mynsterstede *(m)* CHU
monastic life munuclīf *(n)* CHU
monastic orders munuchād *(f)* CHU
Monday Mōnandæg *(m)* TIM
money feoh *(n)* WEA
  sceat *(m)*
money, without feohlēas WEA
moneyer mynetere *(m)* WOR
monk munuc *(m)* CHU
  mynstermonn *(m)*
monk's hood cugele *(f)* CHU
monster āglǣca *(m)* MON
  egesa *(m)*
monstrous unhȳre STR
month mōnað *(m)* TIM
monument gebēacen *(n)* HSE
  gemyndstōw *(f)* LAN
mood hyge *(m)* MIN
  mōd *(m)*

moon mōna *(m)* SKY
moor mōr *(m)* LAN
moorhen wōrhenn *(f)* ANI
morality sidu *(f)* LAW
Moravians (people)
  Marware *(fpl)* STR
more mā MEA
  māra
morning dægredlīc TIM
  mergen *(m)*
  mergenlīc
  morgentīd *(f)*
morning light morgenlēoht *(n)* FIR
mortar (bowl) mortere *(m)* TOO
mosquito micg *(m)* ANI
moss ragu *(f)* PLA
  mēos *(m)* LAN
most mæst MEA
moth moððe *(f)* ANI
moth-eaten moðfreten CLO
mother mōdor *(f)* KIN
mother's brother ēam *(m)* KIN
moulder brosnian *w* EVL
  (ge)molsnian *w*
mound beorg *(f)* DIE
  cnoll *(m)* LAN
  hlæw *(m)*
mount gehlēapan *7* ANI, GO
mountain beorg *(m)* LAN
  dūn *(f)*
  munt *(m)*
mountain cave dūnscræf *(n)* LAN
mountain slope beorghlīð *(n)* LAN
mountain stream
  firgenstrēam *(m)* LAN
mounted man onstīgend *(m)* GO
mounted troop ēored *(n)* WAR
  ēoredcyst *(m)*
  rǣdehere *(m)*
mourn cwiðan *w* SAY
  mǣnan *w* THI
  gnornian *w* MIN
  hrēowan *2*
  murnan *3*
mourning gnornung *(f)* EVL, MIN

mouse mūs ANI
mouse's squeaking hwicung *(f)* ANI
mousetrap mūsfealle *(f)* TOO
moustache cenep *(m)* BOD
mouth mūð *(m)* BOD
mouthful snæd *(m)* EAT
move āstyrian *w* MIN
  hrēran *w* GO
  glīdan *6*
  sceacan *6*
movement fōr *(f)* GO
  gebregd *(n)* BEC
movement, power of faru *(f)* GO
  fēðe *(n)*
mow māwan *7* WOR
much grēat MEA
  micel
  worn fela
mucus mældropa *(m)* AIL
  snofl *(m)*
  snot *(m)*
mud horh *(m,n)* LAN
mugwort mucgwyrt *(f)* PLA
mulberry byrigberge *(f)* EAT, PLA
mule mūl *(m)* ANI
mulled wine morað *(n)* EAT
mullet hacod *(m)* ANI
multiply gemænigfealdian *w* MEA
multitude menigu *(f)* MEA
munificence cystignes *(f)* GD
murder monslyht *(m)* WAR
  morðdæd *(f)*
  morðor *(n)*
murderous wælgīefre EVL
muscle (biceps) mūs *(f)* BOD
mushroom swamm *(m)* EAT
music sōncræft *(m)* REC
  swēg *(m)*
musical skill swēgcræft *(m)* REC
musical sound orgeldrēam *(m)* REC
musician trūð *(m)* REC
mussel musle *(f)* ANI
must sculan *a*
mustard
  (gerenod) senep *(m)* EAT, PLA

muzzle cāma *(m)* TOO
my mīn *(gen.)*
myrtle wīr *(m)* PLA
mystery dīgelnes *(f)* KNO
rūn *(f)*
mystic rȳnemann *(m)* CHU
mystical gerȳnelīc CHU

N

nail nægl *(m)* BOD
næglian *w* HSE
scēað *(f)* TOO
nailtrimmer næglseax *(n)* TOO
naked nacod BOD, CLO
ungegearwod
name nama *(m)* CAL
(ge)nemnan *w*
nemnian *w*
benemnan *w* SAY
napkin scēat *(m)* EAT
narcissus halswyrt *(f)* PLA
narcotic substance lybb *(n)* PLA
narrative gerecennes *(f)* SAY
narrow enge LAN
nearu
narrow place nearu *(f)* LAN
nasturtium lēaccærse *(f)* PLA
nation folc *(n)* WAR
geðēode *(m)* LRD
lēod *(f)*
lēode *(mpl)*
ðēod *(f)*
ðēodscipe *(m)*
national treasure
ðēodgestrēon *(n)* ART
native land cȳððu *(f)* KIN, LAN, STR
eard *(m)*
ēðel *(m,n)*
native people londlēod *(f)* LAN
londwaru *(f)*
natural geæðele KIN
gecynde
nature gecynd *(n)* BOD, MIN
swelcnes *(f)* ART

nausea snoffa *(m)* AIL
spiwe *(m)*
wlætta *(m)*
nauseous wealg AIL
naval expedition scipfyrding *(f)* WAT
naval force scipfyrd *(f)* WAT
sciphere *(m)*
navel nafela *(m)* BOD
near genēalæcan *w* GO
nēah POS
near to gehende LAN
nearly æthwōn MEA
fulnēah
welnēah
neat gesmicerod GD
trum
necessary nīedbehefe NEE
nīedbeðearf
nīedðearflīc
necessary, be nēodian *w* NEE
necessity nīed *(f)* NEE
nīedðearf *(f)*
ðearf *(f)*
necessity for a task ondweorc *(n)* NEE
neck heals *(m)* BOD
swēora *(m)*
need behōfian *w* NEE
gād *(n)*
nīed *(f)*
nīedðearf *(f)*
ðurfan *a*
need, in ðearfendlīc NEE
wædligend
needful nīedbehefe NEE
nīedbeðearf
nīedðearflīc
ðearf
needle nædl *(f)* TOO
neglect forgiefan *5* THI
oferhebban *6* FAI
forgīemelēasian *w* PFM
forgietan *5*
forgȳman *w*
āgīemelēasian *w* EVL, POS
forsittan *5*
wandian *w* MIN

negro ælmyrca *(m)* STR
neigh hnægan *w* ANI
neighbour nēahgebūr *(m)* LIV
  nīehsta *(m)* LAN
neighbourhood efenehð *(f)* LAN
  nēawest *(m,f)*
neither. . . nor ne. . . ne
nephew nefa *(m)* KIN
nerve sinu *(f)* BOD
ness næss *(m)* LAN
  nōse *(f)*
nest nest *(n)* ANI
net max *(n)* TOO
  nett *(n)*
nether neðera POS
nettle netle *(f)* PLA
never nā TIM
  næfre
nevertheless hwæðre
  nō þȳ læs
  þēahwæðre
new nīw TIM
new, become ednīwian *w*
newt efeta *(m)* ANI
next æfterra TIM
next to be
next year ōðergēara TIM
nib græf *(n)* WRI
niece nefene *(f)* KIN
  nift *(f)*
nigh nēah POS
night niht *(f)* TIM
night, by nihterne TIM
night creature nihtgenga *(m)* MON
  nihtscūa *(m)*
nightclothes bedrēaf *(f)* CLO
  nihtwaru *(f)*
nightingale nihtegala *(m)* ANI
nightlong nihtlong TIM
nightmare ælfsiden *(f)* SLP
nine nigon
nineteen nigontīene
nineteenth nigontēoða
ninetieth nigontigoða
ninety hundnigontig

ninth nigoða
nipple delu *(f)* BOD
  titstricel *(m)*
nit hnitu *(f)* ANI
no! nā
  nese
nobility (of birth)
  æðelborennes *(f)* KIN, LRD
noble æðele KIN
  byrde
  indryhten LRD
  torhtmōd MIN
noble family æðelu *(f)* KIN, LRD
nocturns ūhtsang *(m)* CHU
noise bearhtm *(m)* LOV
  hrēam *(m)* CAL, SAY
  swēg *(m)*
  wōp *(m)* REC
none nān MEA
  nænig
Nones (3pm) nōn *(f)* TIM
noose ðelma *(m)* TOO
nor ne
Norfolk Norðfolc *(n)* STR
normal gewuna MIN
Normandy Ricardesrīce *(n)* STR
north norð POS
Northamptonshire
  (Norþ)Hāmtūnscīr *(f)* STR
Northumberland
  Norðhymbre *(mpl)* STR
Norway Norðweg *(m)* STR
Norwegian Norðmannisc STR
Norwegians (people)
  Norðmenn *(mpl)* STR
nose nebb *(n)* BOD
  nosu *(f)*
nostril nosþyrl *(n)* BOD
not ne
not at all nælles
  næs
  nō
not doomed unfæge DIE
not fully grown unweaxen KIN

not only...but also
   nā þæt ān (þæt). . .ac swylce
nota bene! lōc nū! WRI
nothing nāht
   ōwiht
notice onfindan *3* THI
   ongietan *5*
notorious forcūð EVL
Nottinghamshire
   Snotingahāmscīr *(f)* STR
noun nama *(m)* WRI
nourish (ā)fēdan *w* EAT, KIN
November Blōtmōnað *(m)* TIM
now nū TIM
   nūða
nowhere nāhwǣr POS
number gerīm *(n)* MEA
   getæl *(n)*
   worn *(m)*
nun mynecen *(f)* CHU
nurse gelācnian *w* AIL
nurture fēdan *w* KIN
   fōstrian *w*
nut hnutu *(m)* EAT, PLA

O

O! ēalā
oak āc *(m)* PLA
oakum ācumba *(m)* MAT
oar ār *(f)* WAT
oars gerēðru *(npl)* WAT
oath āð *(m)* SAY
oathbreaking āðbryce *(m)* EVL
oats ǣtan *(mpl)* EAT
obedience
   (ge)hīersumnes *(f)* LRD, WOR
obedient gehīersum WOR
   ðēowlīc
obey (ge)hīeran *w* LRD, SAY
   (ge)hīersumian *w* WOR
   gīeman *w* MIN
object of desire willa *(m)* LOV
obliged, be sculan *a*
obliging gehīersum WOR

oblivion ofergeatu *(f)* MIN
Obodrites (Baltic people)
   Afdrede *(mpl)* STR
observe ofersēon *5* SEE
   (ge)scēawian *w*
observation of a service
   geheald *(n)* CHU
obstacle earfoðnes *(f)* EVL
obstruct forfaran *6* EVL
obtain begietan *5* WEA
   gefōn *7*
obvious ēaðfynde SEE
   ēaðgesyne
   sweotol
occasion byre *(m)* TIM
   cirr *(m)*
   sīð *(m)*
   tīma *(m)*
occult art gedwolcræft *(m)* CHU
occupation bisgu *(f)* WOR
occupied bisig WOR
occupied, be ābisgian *w* THI
occupy bisgian *w* WOR
   weardian *w* LIV
   wīcian *w*
occurence gelimp *(n)* BEC
occurs to me, it
   beirnð mē on mōde THI
ocean brim *(n)* WAT
   ēar *(m)*
   gārsecg *(m)*
   geofon *(n)*
   hēahsǣ *(f)*
   holm *(m)*
October Winterfyllēð *(m)* TIM
odd number ofertæl *(n)* MEA
odour stenc *(m)* BOD, PLA
of fram
   of
of this country ūrelendisc STR
off fram
   of
offer bēodan *2* ASK, SAY
office hād *(m)* WOR
   notu *(f)*
   ðegnung *(f)*

officer ambyhtscealc *(m)* WOR
  gerēfa *(m)* LRD
official gerēfa *(m)* WOR
often gelōmlīce TIM
  oft(rǣdlīc)
  oftsōna
oil ele *(m)* EAT
oil press wringe *(f)* TOO
ointment sealf *(f)* AIL
  smyrung *(f)*
Oland (Baltic island)
  Ēowland *(n)* STR
old eald TIM
olive eleberge *(f)* EAT
omen hwatu *(f)* KNO
omit oferhebban *6* FAI, THI
on in
  on
on condition that wið ðǣm ðe
on the way tōgēanes GO
on this side behionan POS
once gēara TIM
  gēo
  on ǣnne sīð
  on ǣnre tīde
one ān
one's own beloved swǣs LOV
onion (hwīt)lēac *(n)* PLA
only āna *(m)*
  āne *(f,n)*
onto in
  on
  uppan
onwards forð GO
ooze sīpian *w* LAN, WAT
  wāse *(f)*
open gerýman *w* GO
  onhlīdan *1* SEE
  ontýnan *w*
  openian *w* STA
open land feld *(f)* LAN
open sea ūtermere *(m)* WAT
  wīdsǣ *(m,f)*
open up geopenian *w* STA
opponent of the church

cirichata *(m)* FOE
opportunity byre *(m)* TIM
  sǣl *(m,f)*
opposed ambyre FOE, POS
  andweard
opposite wiþ
oppress dreccan *w* EVL
  nīedan *w*
  ðryccan *w*
oppressive tintreglīc EVL
oppressive weight byrðen *(f)* EVL
option cyre *(m)* THI
or oððe
orange ǣppelfealu COL
  (geolu)rēad
oratory gebedhūs *(n)* ASK, CHU
orchard ortgeard *(m)* LAN
ordain hādian *w* CHU
  lagian *w* LAW
  scyrian *w* SAY
order bebod *(n)* ASK
  diht *(m)* LRD, SAY
  fadian *w*
  hātan *7*
  endebyrdnes *(f)* TIM
ordination hādung *(f)* CHU
ore ār *(m)* MAT
organ organa *(m)* REC
organist organestre *(f)* REC
  swegesweard *(m)*
origin fruma *(m)* STA
  frymð *(m,f)*
  ord *(m)*
original position frumstaðol *(m)* STA
Orion Eoforðring *(m)* SKY
ornament hyrst *(f)* ART
  wrǣtt *(f)*
ornamented gehroden ART
ornaments glenge *(m)* ART
orthodox rihtgelēafful CHU
other ōþer
otherwise elcor STR
  elles
otter ottor *(m)* ANI

otterskin, made of yteren MAT
ounce yndse *(f)* MEA
our ūre *(gen.)*
  ūser *(gen.)*
  uncer *(gen.)*
out ūt
out of doors onūtan POS
outing ȳting *(f)* GO
outlaw flīema *(m)* EVL
  ūtlaga *(m)*
outlawed fāg LAW
  wrǣclic
outlive oferbīdan *1* LIV
outside ūte POS
  būtan
  ūtan
  wiðūtan
outsider unmǣg *(m)* STR
outstanding ǣrgōd GD, MIN
outwit lytegian *w* SAY
ouzle ōsle *(f)* ANI
oven ofen *(m)* TOO
over ofer POS
overcoat hedeclāð *(m)* CLO
overcome beswīcan *1* PFM
  gehnǣgan *w*
  gereccan *w*
  ofercuman *4*
  oferdrīfan *1*
  oferflītan *1*
  oferwinnan *3*
overpower oferflītan *1* PFM
  oferswīðan *1*
  oferwīgan *1*
overrun gegān *a* EVL
  ofergān *a* WAR
overtake offaran *6* GO
overthrow tōbrecan *4* PFM
  tōweorpan *3*
owe āgan *w* NEE
  sculan *a*
owl ūle *(f)* ANI
own āgan *w* WEA
  agen
  swǣs

ox hriðer *(n)* ANI
  oxa *(m)*
oxeye gescādwyrt *(f)* PLA
Oxfordshire Oxnafordscīr *(f)* STR
oxgang (eighth of a hide)
  oxangang *(n)* MEA
oxherd oxanhyrde *(m)* WOR
oxslip oxanslyppe *(f)* PLA
oyster ostre *(f)* ANI, EAT

P

pace stæpe *(m)* MEA
pack-horse ealfara *(m)* ANI, BRI
page cine *(f)* WRI
  lēaf *(n)*
pail byden *(f)* TOO
  pægel *(m)*
  sā *(m)*
pain bite *(m)* AIL
  sār *(f)*
  wærc *(m)*
  sārnes *(f)* MIN
  sārwracu *(f)*
pain in the buttocks
  endewærc *(m)* AIL
painful biter EVL
  sār AIL
  smeart
  swǣre
painless unsār AIL, MIN
paint fǣgan *w* ART, COL
  mētan *w*
pair of shoes gescȳ *(n)* CLO
palace cynestōl *(m)* LRD
palate gōma *(m)* BOD
  mūðhrōf *(m)*
pale blāc FIR
  blāt
pale blue hǣwengrēne COL
pale yellow geoluhwīt COL
paleness ablǣcnys *(f)* AIL
pallium pæll *(m)* CLO
palm folm *(f)* BOD
  handbrēd *(n)*
  palmtrēow *(m)* PLA

palsy dropa *(m)* AIL
pan panne *(f)* TOO
pancake crompeht *(f)* EAT
paper carte *(f)* WRI
paradise neorxnawang *(f)* CHU
  paradīs *(m)*
paradisical neorxnawanglīc CHU
paralysis lyftēdl *(m)* AIL
paralytic eorðcryppel *(m)* AIL
parchment cine *(f)* WRI
pardon forgiefan *5* THI
parent ealdor *(m)* KIN
parents ieldran *(mpl)* KIN
parishioner hīeremonn *(m)* CHU
parsley petersilie *(f)* PLA
parsnip feldmoru *(f)* PLA
  more *(f)*
part dæl *(m)* MEA
  ende *(m)* POS, STA
partaking ðigen *(f)* EAT
participle dælnimend *(m)* WRI
partly be sumum dæle MEA
partner gemæcca *(m)* LOV
pass āgān *a* GO
pass by geweorpan *3* GO
pass in silence forsuwian *w* SAY, WRI
  forswīgan *1*
pass sentence scrīfan *1* LAW
pass through geondhweorfan *3* GO
passage geat *(n)* HSE
  nearu *(f)*
passing gewītend GO
  læne TIM
passing the mead cup round
  meodurǣden *(f)* EAT
passion ðrōwung *(f)* LOV, NEE
passionate hātheort LOV
past on ǣrdagum TIM
  on geardagum
  wyrd *(f,n)*
paste brīw *(m)* EAT
  clām *(m)*
  slypa *(m)* MAT
pasture hamm *(m)* LAN
  lǣs *(f)*

patch clāðflyhte *(m)* CLO
paten disc *(m)* CHU
paternal fæderlīc KIN
paternal kinsman
  fæderenmæg *(m)* KIN
path foldweg *(m)* LAN
  gegang *(m)* GO
patience geðyld *(f)* MIN
patient geðyldig MIN
patriarch hēahfæder *(m)* KIN
pavilion feldhūs *(n)* HSE
  (būrge)teld *(n)*
  træf *(n)*
pay gieldan *3* WEA
  mēd *(f)*
pay attention to onmunan *w* THI
pay for angieldan *3* WEA
  gebētan *w*
  (fore)gieldan *3*
payment gafol *(n)* LAW, WEA
  gescot *(n)*
pea pīse *(f)* EAT, PLA
peace frið *(m,n)* GD, LAW
  sibb *(f)*
  stillnes *(f)*
  grið *(n)* WAR
peace with, keep friðian *w* LOV, MIN
peace treaty frioðowǣr *(f)* LAW
peaceful geðwǣre LOV
  smolt MIN
peach persic *(m)* PLA
peacock pawa *(m)* ANI
Peak District Peācland *(n)* STR
pear peru *(f)* EAT
pearl meregreot *(n)* WAT
peasant ceorl *(m)* WOR
pebble papolstān *(m)* LAN
peg pinn *(n)* TOO
pelican dūfedoppa *(m)* ANI
pelisse pyleca *(m)* CLO
pen hrēod *(n)* WRI
  wrītingfeðer *(f)*
  wrītingīsen *(n)*
  writseax *(n)*

penalty bōt *(f)* LAW
   stēor *(f)*
   wīte *(n)*
penetrate fēolan *3* GO
   ðurhfaran *6*
   ðurhwadan *6*
penetrating glēaw MIN
penis pintel *(m)* BOD
   teors *(m)*
   wæpen *(n)*
penny peni(n)g *(m)* MEA, WEA
pennyroyal brōðerwyrt *(f)* PLA
   dweorgedrostel *(m)*
   hǣlwyrt *(f)*
   pollegie *(f)*
pennyweight peningwǣg *(f)* MEA
pennyworth sceat *(m)* WEA
peony peonie i(f) PLA
people ðēodscipe *(m)* LRD
   folc *(n)* STR
pepper piporian *w* EAT
   pipor *(m)* PLA
peppercorn piporcorn *(n)* EAT
perceive oncnāwan *7* KNO
   undergietan *5*
   ongietan *5* THI
   understandan *6*
   gesēon *5* SEE
perfect in sanctity eallhālig CHU
perfection fulfremednes *(f)* GD
perform begān *a* PFM
   gefremman *w*
   gelǣstan *w*
perfume stēran *w* MAT
   stōr *(m)*
perhaps ēaðe mæg
peril frēc(ed)nes *(f)* EVL
perilous frēcne EVL
period of service stemn *(m)* WAR
period of time fæc *(n)* TIM
   þrāg *(f)*
perish ābrēoðan *2* FAI
   ālicgan *w* DIE
   forweorðan *3*
   losian *w*

periwinkle pinewincla *(m)* ANI
perjure forlēogan *2* LAW, SAY
perjury āðbryce *(m)* LAW, SAY
permission lēaf *(f)* ASK
permit līefan *w* ASK
permitted, be mōtan *a*
perry perewōs *(n)* EAT
persecutor lēodhata *(m)* EVL
Persian Persisc STR
Persians (people) Perse *(mpl)* STR
persist ðurhwunian *w* POS
person mon *(m)* KIN
   monna *(m)*
persuade gelǣran *w* AGR, MIN
persuasion swǣp *(n?)* SAY
persuasive getinge AGR
perverse wiðerweardlīc MIN
perversion forliger *(n)* LOV
pestilence cwild *(m)* AIL, EVL
   moncwild *(m)*
   steorfa *(m)*
petition bēn *(f)* LAW
pewter tin *(n)* MAT
phantom scīnlāc *(n)* MON
pheasant wildhænn *(f)* ANI
   wōrhana *(m)* ANI
philosopher ūðwita *(m)* KNO
phlegm hrǣcung *(f)* AIL
Picts (people) Peohtas *(mpl)* STR
pierce ðurhdrīfan *1* DRI
   stician *w* EVL, WOR
   stingan *3*
pierced, holed ðurhholod BRK
   ðȳrel
piety ārfæstnes *(f)* CHU, GD, MIN
pig swīn *(n)* ANI
pigeon culfre *(f)* ANI
pike hacod *(m)* ANI
pilgrimage abroad
   elðīodignes *(f)* CHU, STR
pill posling *(m)* AIL
pillar bēam *(m)* HSE
   stapol *(m)*
   sȳl *(f)*
pillow bolster *(m)* SLP
   pyle *(m)*

pillow-down healsrefeðer *(f)* SLP
pimpernel brysewyrt *(f)* PLA
pimple nebcorn *(n)* AIL
pimply, become pypelian *w* AIL, BEC
pin pinn *(n)* TOO
  prēon *(m)*
pinch twengan *w* EVL
pinetree furhwudu *(m)* PLA
pious ǣwfæst CHU
  gelēafful
  godfyrht
piper pīpere *(m)* REC
pirate flotman *(m)* WAT
pit hol *(n)* LAN
  pytt *(m)*
  sēað *(m)*
pitch pic *(n)* MAT
pitchfork forcel *(m)* TOO
pitier gemiltsiend *(m)* GD
placate ōlǣcan *w* LOV
place stede *(m)* POS
  stōw *(f)*
place of, in for
plaice fag *(f)* ANI
plain efenehð *(f)* LAN
  feld *(f)*
  foldwong *(n)*
  græsmolde *(f)*
  wong *(m)*
  ānfeald ART
plain, unadorned unorne ART
plan gerǣdan *w* MIN, THI
  hogian *w*
  rǣd *(m)*
plane locor *(m)* TOO
  scafa *(m)*
plank bord *(n)* HSE
  bred *(n)*
  ræsn *(n)*
planks, made of breden HSE, MAT
plant þȳfel *(m)* PLA
  wyrt *(f)*
plant juice wōs *(n)* PLA
plaster plaster *(n)* AIL

play (be)lācan *7* WOR
  gomen, gamen *(n)* MIN, PFM, REC
  lāc *(n)*
  plega *(m)*
  plegian *w*
play the harp hearpian *w* REC
playful plegol LOV
playground plegstede *(m)* LAN
plead ðingian *w* ASK
  mōtian *w* SAY
pleasant gecwēmlīc LOV
  līðe
  myrge MIN
  wynsum
please gecwēman *w* LOV
  (ge)līcian *w*
  lystan *w*
pleasing ðoncwyrðe THI
pleasing to, be gelīcian *w* LOV
pleasure gecwēmednes *(f)* LOV
  lust *(m)*
  willa *(m)*
  wynsumnes *(f)*
pleasurecraft plegscip *(n)* WAT
plectrum hearpenægel *(m)* REC
pledge wedd *(n)* AGR
  wordbēotung *(f)* SAY
plough (ge)erian *w* LAN, WOR
  beswincan *3* PLA
  sulh *(f)* TOO
Plough Wǣnes Ðisla *(fpl)* SKY
ploughing equipment
  sulhgeteog *(n)* TOO
ploughman ierðling *(m)* WOR
  sȳla *(m)*
ploughshare scear *(m,n)* TOO
plum plyme *(f)* EAT
plumber lēadgota *(m)* WOR
plumbline weallþrǣd *(m)* TOO
plunder berēafian *w* EVL, WEA
  herehȳð *(f)*
  (for-, ge-)hergian *w*
  hīðan *w* WAR
plunder taken at sea sǣlāc *(n)* WAT
plundering hergoð *(m)* EVL

pock pocc *(m)* AIL
poem lēoð *(n)* REC
   lēoðsong *(m)*
poet scop *(m)* REC
   wōðbora *(m)* SAY
poetic language scopgereord *(n)* REC
poetic skill lēoðcræft *(m)* REC
point ord *(m)* WPN
point out (ge)wīsian *w* SAY
   wissian *w*
pointed tool pīl *(n)* TOO
poison ātor *(n)* EAT, EVL
poisoned ǣttren EAT, WPN
poisonous, become gehwilian *w* BEC
pole pāl *(m)* HSE
   post *(m)*
   steng *(m)*
Polish Wendisc STR
polishing feormung *(f)* WAT
pollute besmītan *1* EVL
   wīdlian *w*
polluted fūl WAT
   unclǣnlīc
pomegranate cornæppel *(n)* PLA
pool wǣl *(m)* WAT
poor ðearfendlīc NEE
   unspēdig
   earm(līc) WEA
poor man ðearfa *(m)* NEE
   wǣdla *(m)*
pope pāpa *(m)* CHU
populate gesettan *w* LAN
   gesittan *5*
pork sausage mearg *(m,n)* EAT
porpoise mereswīn *(n)* ANI
porridge brīw *(m)* EAT
port port *(m)* LAN
port-side bæcbord *(n)* WAT
portent wēatācn *(n)* KNO
portion dǣl *(m)* WEA
portrait gelīcnes *(f)* ART
position stede *(m)* POS
   stōw *(f)*
   till *(n)*
possession ǣht *(f)* LRD, WEA

possible, be onhagian *w* BEC
post post *(m)* HSE
pot fæt *(n)* EAT
   crocca *(m)* TOO
pot (with a handle) stelmēle *(m)* TOO
pot-bellied wæmbede BOD
pottage brīw *(m)* EAT
potter pottere *(m)* WOR
poultice clām *(m)* AIL
   onlegen *(f)*
poultry hāmhænn *(f)* ANI
pound pund *(n)* MEA
   pundwǣg *(f)*
pound to a powder
   cnucian *w* AIL, EAT
   cnūwian *w*
pound to dust gecnūwian *w* BRK
   gnīdan 1
pour (ā)gēotan *2* WAT
poverty ðearfednes *(f)* NEE
   wǣdl *(f)*
powder, pound to a
   cnucian *w* AIL, EAT
   cnūwian *w*
power ǣht *(f)* LRD
   geweald *(n)*
   onweald *(m)*
   rīccetere *(n)*
power of movement faru *(f)* GO
   fēðe *(n)*
power of protection
   mundcræft *(m)* PRO
powerful mihtig LRD
   rīce
powerful emotion
   brēostwylm *(m)* MIN
powerless unmihtig LRD
practice begān *a* PFM
praise dōm *(m)* GD
   herenes *(f)* SAY
   hering *(f)*
   lof *(f)*
praiseworthy dōmfæst GD
praiseworthy deed lofdǣd *(f)* GD
pray gebiddan *5* ASK, CHU

pray before forebiddan 5 CHU
prayer bēn (f) ASK
  gebed (n)
  bodung (f) CHU
  gebedrǣdan (f)
praying gebedrǣden (f) ASK
precarious tealt HSE
precede foregangan 7 TIM
precept lār (f) THI
precious dēor LOV, WEA
  weorð
  dēorweorðe ART
precious thing māððum (m) ART
  māððumǣht (f)
prefer bet lystan w LOV
  foreberan 4
  swīðor unnan a
pregnant ēacen KIN
pregnant, make geēacnian w KIN
prejudice fordēman w MIN, THI
prepare gearcian w PFM
  (ge)gearwian w AIL, EAT
  gierwan w
presence ondweardnes (f) POS
present andweard POS, TIM
present, be ætwesan a POS
presently eftsōna TIM
  sīðlīc
preserve beorgan 3 PRO
press ðringan 3 BRI, WAR
press on crūdan 2 GO
  ðȳn w DRI
pressed curds cealer (m) EAT
pretend līcettan w SEE
pretty blāchlēor LOV
  wlitescīene
prevail rīcsian w PFM
prevalent genge PFM
prevent forstandan 6 EVL, POS
  forwiernan w AGR, FAI, PFM
  forwyrcan w
  gelettan w
previous time ǣrdagas (mpl) TIM
prey huntung (f) ANI

price weorð (n) LAW
prickle pīl (m) AIL
pride bælc (m) EVL, MIN
  gāl (n)
  gālnes (f)
  hyge (f)
  (ofer)mōd (m)
  mōdignes (f)
  oferhygd (f,n)
  ofermettu (f)
  prȳte (f) THI
  ūpāhefednes (f)
  wlencu (f)
priest prēost (m) CHU
  sācerd (m)
prime (service) prīm (n) CHU
prince æðeling (m) LRD
  brego (m)
  ealdor (m)
  eodor (m)
  lēod (m)
  ðēoden (m)
princely treasure
  ðēodenmāðm (m) ART
prior prāfost (m) CHU
prison carcern (n) EVL, LAW
  cweartern (n)
  hengen (f)
private part scamlim (n) BOD
private property sundorfeoh (n) LAW
  (syndrig) ǣht (f) WEA
privy gangern (n) HSE
proclaim (ā)bēodan 2 SAY
  wīdmǣrsian w
produce ācennan w KIN
professed geanwyrde KNO, SAY
profit bryce (m) GD, WEA
  gedīgan w
  geðēon 1
  nytt (f) LRD
profound neowol MIN
  nīwol
prohibit forbēodan 2 EVL
promiscuity gālscipe (m) EVL

promise behātan 7 AGR, ASK, SAY
  gebēot *(n)*
  gehāt *(n)*
  gehātan 7
  wedd *(n)*
  weddian *w* LAW
prompt cāf TIM
  recen
  gearu MIN
prone neowol BOD, SLP
  nīwel
prone (to), be forðlūtan 2
pronoun bīnama *(m)* WRI
prop stuðansceaft *(m)* HSE
proper time tīma *(m)* TIM
property æht *(f)* LAW
  cēap *(m)*
  feoh *(n)*
prophesy forewītegian *w* SAY
prophet witega *(m)* CHU, KNO
propitiation ōlæcung *(f)* ASK
proposing forspæc *(f)* SAY
propriety gerisenu *(npl)* GD
  mæð *(f)* MIN
prosper geðēon *1* WEA
prosperity ēad *(n)* GD
  sæl *(m,f)*
  gesyntu *(f)* WEA
prosperous blædfæst GD, WEA
  spēdig
  welig
prostitute forlegnis *(f)* WOR
protect āwerian *w* PRO
  (ge)beorgan *3*
  (ge)ealgian *w*
  friðian *w* LOV
  griðian *w*
  healdan 7
protected place burg *(f)* HSE
protection fæðm *(m)* PRO
  gebeorg *(n)*
  gescyldnes *(f)*
  hlēow *(m)*
  hlēowð *(f)*
  hyldu *(f)*
  mund(byrd) *(f)*

  trēownes *(f)*
  wǣr *(f)*
protection, power of
  mundcræft *(m)* PRO
protective clothing
  hlēosceorp *(n)* CLO
protective kinsman/woman
  friðemæg *(m,f)* GD
protector helm *(m)* LRD
  eodor *(m)* PRO
  gehola *(m)*
  healdend *(m)*
  mundbora *(m)*
  weard *(m)*
proud mōdelīc MIN
  wlonc
  ranc EVL
prove āfandian *w* AGR
prove a claim geāgnian *w* LAW, WEA
proven geresp ASK, LAW
provide with food metsian *w* EAT
provide with horses horsian *w* WOR
providence forescēawung *(f)* MIN
province ealdordēm *(m)* LRD
provincial governor
  ealdormann *(m)* LRD
provision feorm *(f)* GD
provision for a journey
  wegnest *(n)* GO
provisions bīleofa *(m)* EAT
  feorm *(f)*
  metsung *(f)*
  wist *(f)*
provost profost *(m)* CHU
prow frumstemn *(m)* WAT
psalm sealm *(m)* CHU
psalm-singing sealmsong *(m)* CHU
psalter saltere *(m)* CHU
public openlīc LAW
public disgrace woroldscamu *(f)* BLM
public enemy ðēodscaða *(m)* FOE
public entertainer ealuscop *(m)* REC
pudendum mægðblæd *(n)* BOD
pull tēon 2 BRI

pull out apullian *w* BRI
pungent gestence PLA
punishment hearmscearu *(f)* LAW
  ðrēal *(f)*
  wīte *(n)* EVL
punishment, military
  fierdwīte *(n)* WAR
punitive tax ungylde *(n)* LAW
pupil of the eye sēo *(f)* BOD
purchase cēapian *w* WEA
pure clǣne WAT
  swutol
  unwemmed
pure white eallhwīt COL
purge afeormian *w* PLA
purify geclǣnsian *w* AIL, WAT
  merian *w*
purple basurēadan *w* COL
  hǣwen
  weolucbasu
purple dye purpure *(f)* COL
  wurma *(m)*
purpose gemynd *(f,n)* THI
  myndgian *w*
  teohhian *w*
pursue a craft begongan *w* WOR
pus dylsta *(m)* AIL
  geolstor *(n)*
  hora *(m)*
  lyswen *(n)*
push scūfan *2* BRI
put on begyrdan *w* CLO
  ondōn *a*
put right gerihtan *w* LAW
put to flight (ā)flīeman *w* GO
  (ā)flīgan *w*
  āfȳsan *w*
put to shame ofscamian *w* BLM
  scendan *w*
put to sleep āswebban *w* SLP
puzzle cnotta *(m)* THI
  rǣdels *(m,f)*
pyre ād *(m)* DIE, FIR
  bǣl *(n)*

Q

quail edischenn *(f)* ANI
Quains (Finnish people)
  Cwēnas *(mpl)* STR
quality ēst *(f)* GD
  gōdnes *(f)*
  swelcnes *(f)* ART, BOD
quarrel beadurūn *(f)* AGR, WAR
  cīdan *w*
  geflit *(n)*
quarter feorðandǣl *(m)* MEA
quay hȳð *(f)* WAT
queen cwēn *(f)* LRD
queen bee bēomōder *(f)* ANI
quench ācwencan *2* WAT
quick arod GO
  recen
  snel
  snūde
  swift
  cāf TIM
quick (at dice) hrædtæfle REC
quick-witted horsc MIN
quickly hraðe TIM
  recene
quickness snelnes *(f)* GO
quicksand cwecesand *(m)* LAN
quiet stille GD
  swīge SAY
quill fiðer *(f)* WRI
quince coddæppel *(m)* EAT
quite lythwōn MEA
  sumes
quiver bifian *w* GO
  bogefōdder *(m)* WEA

R

radiant sweglwered SKY
  torht FIR
radish ontre *(f)* EAT
radius (bone) hrēsel *(f)* BOD
raid forhergung *(f)* EVL
  hergoð *(m)*
  rād *(f)* GO

raiding force here *(m)* WAR
rain regn *(m)* SKY
  rīnan *w*
rainbow heofonlic boga *(m)* SKY
raise fēdan *w* KIN
  rǣran *w*
rake egðe *(f)* TOO
rally against ðrēatian *w* WAR
ram weðer *(m)* ANI
rancour inca *(m)* MIN
rank gebyrd *(f)* KIN, LRD
  hād *(m)* WOR
ransom wliteweorð *(n)* LAW
rapeseed nǣpsǣd *(n)* PLA
rare seldcūð STR
  seldsīene
rash firenlīc EVL
  hātheort MIN
  hrēofl *(f)* AIL
raspberry hindberge *(f)* PLA
rather hraðor LOV
  swīðor
ratify fæstnian *w* LAW
rattlestick clædersticca *(m)* REC
rattlewort hrætelwyrt *(f)* PLA
ravage forhergian *w* EVL
rave wēdan *w* SAY
  woffian *w*
raven crāwe *(f)* ANI
  hræfn *(m)*
  hremn *(m)*
raw (vegetable) grēne EAT
  hrēaw
raw material ondweorc *(n)* TOO
  ontimber *(n)*
ray scīma *(m)* FIR
ray fish ruhha *(m)* ANI
ray of light (bryne)lēoma *(m)* FIR
razor scearseax *(n)* TOO
reach gerǣcan *w* GO
  gesēcan *w*
reach out rǣcan *w* GO
read rǣdan *w* WRI
read out ārǣdan *7* WRI
read through oferrǣdan *w* WRI

reader rǣdere *(m)* WRI
reading bēcrǣde *(f)* WRI
  (bēc)rǣding *(f)*
ready fūs LOV, MIN
  gearu
  gegearwod TIM
  recen
ready, make fȳsan *w* PFM
  gearwian *w*
ready to start ūtfūs STA
real sōð KNO
reality swelcnes *(f)* BEC
reap (ge)rīpan *1* WOR
reaping rīp *(n)* WOR
rear rǣran *w* KIN
  endemǣst MEA
rebuke lēanian *w* BLM
receiving the eucharist
  hūslgong *(m)* CHU
recently nīwan TIM
reckless reccelēas MIN
reckon rīman *w* MEA, THI
recognise gecnāwan *7* KNO
recompense forgieldan *3* LAW
reconcile gesēman *w* AGR
rectify gerihtlǣcan *w* LAW
rectum bæcþearm *(m)* BOD
red rēad COL
red, become ārēodian *w* BEC
red colouring rudu *(f)* COL
red lead tēafor *(n)* MAT
redden ārēodian *w* COL
redeem ālīesan *w* CHU, PRO
redeemer ālīesend *(m)* CHU
redemption ālȳsednes *(f)* LAW
reed hrēod *(n)* PLA
reek rēocan *2* BOD
reel gearnwinde *(f)* TOO
  hrēol *(m)*
reeve gerēfa *(m)* LRD, WOR
refined smǣte MAT
refined flour smedma *(m)* EAT
reflect behycgan *w* MIN, THI
  smēagan *w*

refuse forsacan *6* AGR, SAY, THI
(for)wiernan *w* FAI, PFM
ðreax *(m)* MAT
refuse with contempt
forhogian *w* AGR
regard behealdan *7* THI
region londscipe *(m)* LAN
regular regollīc LRD
regulate besīdian *w* LAW, LRD
fadian *w* SAY
reign rīxian *w* LRD
reindeer hrān *(m)* ANI
reinforcements ēaca *(m)* WAR
fultum *(m)*
reins brīdelðwang *(m)* ANI
reject wiðercēosan *2* EVL
rejoice (ge)blissian *w* GD, LOV
gefēon *5* MIN
rejoice together efenblissian *w* GD
related gesibb KIN
release onlǣtan *7* EVL
onlȳsan *w*
release from taxes gefrēogan *w* LAW
relief līþung *(f)* AIL
relieve gelīþigian *w* AIL
religion ǣfæstnes *(f)* CHU
hālignes *(f)*
religious ǣfæst CHU
godcund
religious observance gerihte *(n)* CHU
relish for bread syfling *(f)* EAT
rely on getrūwian *w* THI
remain (ā)wunian *w* LIV, POS
(ge)bīdan *1*
seomian *w*
remedy bōt *(f)* AIL, GD, LAW
lǣcedōm *(m)*
remember gemunan *w* MIN, THI
gemyndian *w*
geðencan *w*
remembrance mynegung *(f)* MIN
remind gemonian *w* MIN, SAY, THI
mynian *w*
remiss, become dwellan *w* BEC
wandian *w*

remote dīgel SEE
fyrlen POS
remove āfyrran *w* GO
ofdōn *a* POS
renew (ge)ednīwan *w* HSE
renewed edneowe TIM
rennet cīeslybb *(n)* EAT
renounce ānforlǣtan *7* CHU
wiðsacan *6* SAY
renown mǣrnes *(f)* GD
renowned gefrǣge KNO
rent feorm *(f)* WEA
rent-payer gafolgielda *(m)* LAW
repair ednīwian *w* CLO, HSE, PRO
gebētan *w*
repay gebētan *w* LAW
repayment ǣgift *(m,n)* WEA
repeatedly eftsōna TIM
on oftsīðas
repent gescomian *w* MIN, THI
hrēowan *2*
reply, in tōgeanes ASK
report gesǣgen *(f)* SAY
repose (ge)restan *w* SLP
repress ofðryscan *w* EVL
reproach hosp *(m)* SAY
reprobate ābroðen FOE
reproductive organ
gecyndlim *(n)* BOD
reptile slincend *(m)* ANI
repudiate āwǣgan *w* AGR, DRI
request bēn *(f)* ASK, LAW
biddan *5*
healsian *w*
require beðurfan *a* NEE
biddan *5* ASK
require of bǣdan *w* NEE
requite forgieldan *3* LAW
rescue āhreddan *w* PRO
resin eolhsand *(n)* MAT
glǣr *(m)*
resist wiðstandan *6* POS
resistance wiðre *(n)* WAR
resolute ānrǣd MIN
rǣdfæst
stīðmōd

resolution ānrǣdnes *(f)* MIN
resolve gecweðan *5* THI
  gescēadan *7*
resound hlynnan *w* SKY, WAT
  ðunian *w*
respond andswerian *w* SAY
rest hlinian *w* SLP
  leger *(n)*
  rǣst *(f)*
  (ge)restan *w*
  seomian *w* POS
rest, be at restan *w* POS
  sittan *5*
  standan *6*
  wunian *w*
resting place strēowen *(f)* POS
restless unstille MIN
  ūtfūs
restoration eftnīwung *(f)* HSE
restore (ge)ednīwian *w* HSE
restore the sight onlīhtan *w* AIL
restrain belēan *6* DRI, EVL
  gestȳran *w*
  (ge)healdan *7*
  gehaþerian *w* LRD
result finta *(m)* BEC
resume gedyrstlǣcan *w* THI
retainer ðēningman *(m)* WOR
retch hrǣcan *w* AIL
retreat mylma *(m)* WAR
return æthweorfan *3* GO
  cirran *w*
  gewendan *w*
return journey eftsīð *(m)* GO
reveal cȳðan *w* SEE
  onhlīdan *1*
  ontȳnan *w*
  yppan *w*
revenge wrecan *5* BLM
reverence ārwyrðnes *(f)* GD
  mǣð *(f)* MIN
reversal edhwyrft *(m)* TIM
  edwenden *(f)*
revile leahtrian *w* BLM

revolve cirran *w* GO
  hweorfan *3*
  hweorfian *w*
reward (ed)lēan *(n)* ASK
  lēanian *w*
  (ge)earnung *(f)* GD, PFM, WEA, WOR
  mēd *(f)*
Rhaetia Rētie *(f)* STR
Rhine (river) Rīn STR
rib ribb *(n)* BOD
ribwort ribbe *(f)* PLA
rich welig WEA
riches blǣd *(m)* WEA
  gestrēon *(n)*
rick hrēac *(m)* LAN
rid ālīesan *w* WEA
  geryddan *w* FAI
ride rīdan *1* GO
ride before forrīdan *1* GO
ride over gerīdan *1* GO
ride round berīdan *1* GO
rider ridda *(m)* GO
ridge hrycg *(m)* LAN
riding the waves sundplega *(m)* WAT
rigging mǣstrāp *(m)* WAT
right riht *(n)* LAW
  riht(līc)
right hand rihthand *(f)* BOD
right hand side swīðra BOD, POS
right to alms
  ælmesriht *(n)* ASK, CHU, WEA
right to take fines sōcn *(f)* LAW
righteous rihtwīs *(f)* GD
righteousness rihtwīsnes *(f)* GD
rightly āriht MIN
rights of a freeman frēoriht *(n)* LAW
rime hrīm *(m)* SKY
rind rind *(f)* EAT
ring bēah *(m)* ART, WEA
  hring *(m)*
  wealte *(f)*
ring-giver bēahgifa *(m)* LRD
ringworm rengwyrm *(m)* AIL
  teter *(m)*

ripe rīpe PLA
ripen gerīpian *w* EAT, PLA
rise āstīgan *1* GO
  uppian *w*
rising ūpgong *(m)* GO
risk (ge)nēðan *w* MIN, THI
  pliht *(m)* EVL
risky plihtlīc EVL
rite gerihte *(n)* CHU
river ēa *(f)* WAT
riverbank ēastæð *(n)* LAN
  stæð *(m,n)* WAT
  strand *(n)*
rivermouth mūða *(m)* LAN, WAT
road strǣt *(f)* GO, LAN
roam wandrian *w* GO
  wǣðan *w*
roar rȳn *w* ANI
  swēging *(f)* WOR
roast brǣdan *w* EAT
rob ongerēafian *w* EVL
  (be)rēafian *w* WEA
  (be)rȳpan *w*
robber rēafere *(m)* EVL
  . rȳpere *(m)*
robbery rēaflāc *(n)* EVL
robin ruddoc *(m)* ANI
rock clūd *(m)* LAN
  stān *(m)*
rocky cliff stānclif *(n)* LAN
rocky slope stānhlið *(n)* LAN
rod gyrd *(f)* MEA, TOO
  stæf *(m)*
roedeer rā *(m)* ANI
  rǣge *(f)*
rogation days gangdagas *(mpl)* CHU
roll wealwian *w* GO
  windan *3*
rolling waves gewealc *(n)* WAT
Roman Rēmisc STR
  Rōmānisc
Romans (people)
  Lǣdenware *(fpl)* STR
  Rōmāne *(fpl)*
  Rōmwēalas *(mpl)*

Rome Rōm *(f)* STR
  Rōmeburg *(f)*
roof hrōf *(m)* HSE
  ðaca *(m)*
roof over beðeccan *w* HSE
roof timber hrēstbēag *(m)* HSE
room inn *(n)* HSE
  rȳmet *(n)* LAN
room, make gerȳman *w* GO
roomy rūm HSE
root more *(f)* PLA
  moru *(f)*
  wyrtruma *(m)*
rope līne *(f)* TOO
  rāp *(m)*
  sāl *(m)*
rope for prisoners wealsāda *(m)* TOO
rope-walker rāpgenga *(m)* REC
rose rōse *(f)* PLA
rosehip hēope *(f)* PLA
rosemary boðen *(m,n)* PLA
  feldmædere *(f)*
roses, made of gerōsod PLA
rosy rōsen PLA
rot brosnian *w* EAT
  forrotian *w*
  fūlian *w*
rough unsmēðe EVL
rough shoe hemming *(m)* CLO
round sinetrundel ART
  sinewealt
roundabout onbūtan POS
  ymbūtan
rouse āwacan *6* MIN
  onhrēran *w*
rout flīeman *w* WAR
  flīgan *w*
row rōwan *7* WAT
row around berōwan *7* GO, WAT
row away oðrōwan *7* WAT
rowing rēwet *(n)* WAT
rowlock hā *(m)* WAT
royal cynelīc LRD
royal dwelling cynestōl *(m)* LAN
royal family cynecynn *(n)* LRD

royal hall dryhtsele *(m)* HSE
rubbish geswǣpa *(fpl)* WAT
  ðreax *(m?)*
rubbishy dræstig FAI
rue rūde *(f)* PLA
  hrēowan *2* BLM, MIN
ruin fordōn *a* EVL
  forwyrcan *w*
ruined, be forweorðan *3* EVL
ruined, become forweorðan *3* BEC
ruination firenðearf *(f)* EVL
rule rǣdan *w* LRD
  regol *(f)*
  rīce *(n)*
  rīxian *w*
  wealdan *7*
  wieldan *w*
rulebook regol *(m)* WRI
ruler anwealda *(m)* CHU
  weard *(m)* LRD
  reogol *(m)* WRI
ruler, benevolent
  winedrihten *(m)* LRD
ruler of a district londfruma *(m)* LRD
rumour hlīsa *(m)* SAY
run ærnan *w* GO
  (ge)iernan *3*
run aground āsittan *5* WAT
run round beirnan *3* GO
rune rūn *(f)* WRI
  rūnstæf *(m)*
rung hrung *(f)* HSE
ruptured healede AIL
rush iernan *3* GO
  (ā)rǣsan *w*
rush up ūpirnan *3* GO
rust ābītan *1* MAT
  ōm *(m)*
rusty ōmig MAT
Rutland Roteland *(n)* STR

S

sabre seax *(n)* WPN
sacred office godcundnes *(f)* CHU

sacrifice lāc *(n,f)* CHU
sacrist ciriceweard *(m)* CHU
sad geōmor MIN
  hrēoh
  hrēowigferhð
  hrēowigmōd
  mēðe
  unrōt
sad, be sorgian *w* MIN
  sweorcan *3*
sad at heart frēorigferð MIN
  mōdcearig
  sārigferð
sad-faced drēorighlēor BOD
sad-spirited galgmōd MIN
  wintercearig
saddle sadol *(m)* DRI
safe gebeorglīc PRO
  gesund
  hæghāl
  unplēolīc
safe keeping gedrēog *(n)* PRO
safe quarters friðstōl *(m)* PRO
saffron croh *(m)* PLA
sage ūðwita *(m)* KNO
  salfie *(f)* PLA
sail faran *6* WAT
  segl *(m,n)*
  seglian *w*
  siglan *w*
sail, set lagu drēfan *w* WAT
sail to geseglian *w* WAT
  gesiglan *w*
sailor flotman *(m)* WAT
saint halga *(m)* CHU
  halge *(f)*
  sanct *(m)*
  sancte *(f)*
salad grēne wyrte *(fpl)* EAT
salmon leax *(m)* ANI
salt sealt *(m)* EAT
saltmaker sealtere *(m)* WOR
salty sealt EAT
salute hālettan *w* SAY
salutory hālwende AIL

salvation gesyntu *(f)* PRO
salve sealf *(f)* AIL
same ilca *(m)*
    ilce *(f,n)*
sample ābyrian *w* EAT
    onbyrgan *w*
    swæc *(m)*
sanctuary ciricgrið *(n)* CHU
    generstede *(m)*
sand ceosol *(m)* LAN
    grēot *(m)*
    sond *(n)*
sandmartin stæðswealwe *(f)* ANI
sandy beach sondlond *(n)* LAN
sane gewittig MIN
sane, be tela witan *a* MIN
sanity gewit *(n)* MIN
sap sæp *(n)* PLA
sardine smelt *(m)* ANI
sated sæd MIN
sated with wine wīnsǣd EAT
satisfaction bliss *(f)* MIN
satisfied with gehealden on ASK, THI
Saturday Sæternesdæg *(m)* TIM
saucepan stelmēle *(m)* TOO
sauna stofbæð *(n)* WAT
sausage gehæcca *(m)* EAT
savage grim EVL
    hrēowmōd
save āhreddan *w* PRO
    ālīesan *w*
    beorgan *3*
    (ge)nerian *w*
saviour hǣlend *(m)* PRO
    nergend *(m)* CHU
savoury sæðerige *(f)* PLA
    sealt EAT
saw sagu *(f)* TOO
saxifrage sundcorn *(n)* PLA
Saxon Seaxisc STR
Saxons Seaxe *(mpl)* STR
Saxons (Continental)
    Ealdseaxe *(mpl)* STR
say āsecgan *w* SAY
    cweðan *5*
    (ge)secgan *w*

saying cwide *(m)* SAY
    sagu *(f)*
scab hrȳfing *(f)* AIL
    sceab *(m)*
scaffold gealga *(m)* LAW
    līchanga *(m)*
scale-bowl scealu *(f)* MEA
scalpel ceorfsæx *(n)* TOO
scaly scurfed AIL
scan geondscēawian *w* SEE
Scandinavia Scedenīg *(f)* STR
    Scōnēg *(f)*
scapulary scapulare *(m)* CHU
scar dolh *(m)* AIL
scarce seldsīene SEE
scare āfyrhtan *w* EVL
scarlet dye derodine *(m)* CLO, COL
scatter (for)scēadan *7* BRK
    tōbrǣdan *w*
Schleswig Sīlende STR
scholar bōcere *(m)* WOR
    leornere *(m)*
    ūðwita *(m)* KNO
sciatica hypebānece *(m)* AIL
scissors scēarra *(fpl)* TOO
scorch ǣlan *w* FIR
scornful hōcorwyrde EVL
scot (tax) gescot *(n)* WEA
Scotland Scottaland *(n)* STR
Scots (people) Scottas *(mpl)* STR
Scottish Scyttisc STR
scourger swingere *(m)* EVL
scratch gesceorpan *w* EVL
scream scriccettan *w* EVL
scrip pusa *(m)* CLO
scroll ymele *(f)* WRI
scrotum codd *(m)* BOD
    herþbylg *(m)*
sculpture græft *(m,n,f)* ART
scurf scurf *(m)* AIL
Scythia Sciððiu *(f)* STR
Scythians Scyððie *(mpl)* STR

sea brim *(n)* WAT
 flot *(n)*
 gārsecg *(m)*
 geofon *(n)*
 holm *(m)*
 lagu *(f)*
 mere(flōd) *(m)*
 sǣ *(m,f)*
 seolhbæð *(n)*
 sund *(n)*
sea journey yðfaru *(f)* WAT
sea-bird brimfugol *(m)* ANI, WAT
sea-going vessel
 sǣgenga *(m)* WAT
seabed (sǣ)grund *(m)* WAT
seaboard sǣrima *(m)* LAN, WAT
seafarer sǣlida *(m)* WAT
 sǣmon *(m)*
 sǣrinc *(m)*
 scipflota *(m)*
seal geinseglian *w* WRI
 insigle *(n)* ART
 seolh *(m)* ANI
sealskin flīes *(n)* ANI
seam sēam *(m)* CLO
seaman brimlīðend *(m)* WAT
 brimman *(m)*
 lidmonn *(m)*
 merefara *(m)*
search (ge)sēcan *w* SEE
season sǣl *(m,f)* TIM
seasoned gesufel EAT
seat geset *(n)* HSE, POS
 setl *(n)*
 stōl *(m)*
seat cover setrægl *(n)* HSE
seawall sǣweall *(m)* LAN, WAT
seaweed sǣwār *(n)* PLA
 wāroð *(n)* WAT
second æfterra TIM
 ōðer
secrecy dīgolnes *(f)* SEE
secret dīgel SEE
 dyrne
 rūn *(f)* KNO
secretly dearnunge EVL

sector ende *(m)* LAN
 londscipe *(m)*
 scēat *(m)*
secular eorðlīc CHU
 lǣwede
 woruldcund
secular life woroldhād *(f)* CHU
secure fæst POS
 gefæstenian *w*
 sǣlan *w* PRO
secure from orsorg PRO
security borg *(f)* LAW
 fæstnung *(f)* GD
security for a loan
 anwedd *(n)* LAW, WEA
sedge dūðhamor *(m)* PLA
sedition stric *(n)* EVL
seduce costnian *w* ASK, BRI, EVL, LOV
 forsponan 6
see biscoprīce *(n)* CHU
 biscopsetl *(n)*
 biscopstōl *(m)*
 lōcian *w* SEE
 scēawian *w*
 (ge)sēon 5
see (something) through
 fullfremman *w* PFM
 gelǣstan *w*
seed cīð *(m)* PLA
 corn *(n)*
 sǣd *(n)*
seek sēcan *w* ASK
seek out (ge)sēcan *w* GO
seem sēon 5 SEE
 ðyncan *w*
seep sīpian *w* WAT
seethe (ge)sēoðan 2 WAT
seize befōn 7 GO
seldom seldan TIM
select cēosan 2 LOV
sell cȳpan *w* WEA
semen (gecyndelīc) sǣd *(n)* BOD
semi-vowel healfclypigend *(m)* SAY
semicircular healfsinewealt HSE
send sendan *w* DRI
send away āsendan *w* DRI

send forth onsendan *w* DRI
send greetings hǽlo bodian *w* LOV
sensible gewittig MIN
sentence fers *(n)* SAY, WRI
separate ānlīpig MEA
  āscēadan 7 BRK
  getwǽman *w*
  (on)sundor POS
separate dwelling
  sundorwīc *(n)* HSE, LIV
September Hāligmōnað *(m)* TIM
  Hærfestmōnað *(m)*
sepulchre moldærn *(n)* DIE
  ofergeweorc *(n)* HSE
serene smolt SKY
serenity smyltnes *(f)* SKY
series getæl *(n)* MEA
serious hefig(tȳme) EVL, MIN
servant ambyhtscealc *(m)* WOR
  esne *(m)*
  geongra *(m)*
  hæft *(m)*
  scealc *(m)*
  selesecg *(m)*
  ðēow(a) *(m)*
serve gehīersumian *w* WOR
  gelǽstan *w*
  ðegnian *w*
  ðēowan *w*
serve well tō gōdre āre cuman 4 WOR
service folgað *(m)* WOR
  ðegnscipe *(m)*
  ðegnung *(f)*
  ðēow(ot)dōm *(m)*
service, keeping of a geheald *(n)* CHU
service, period of stemn *(m)* WAR
serviceable stǽlwyrðe LRD
servile ðēow WOR
serving-man ðēningman *(m)* WOR
serving-woman ðīnen *(f)* WOR
set a day āndagian *w* TIM
set a limit gemǽrian *w* LAN
  mearcian *w*
set about fōn on 7 STA
set down settan *w* WRI

set free frēogan *w* GD, LOV
set on fire ātendan *w* FIR
  forswǽlan *w*
  onǽlan *w*
  ontendan *w*
set right gebētan *w* LAW
  rihtan *w*
set sail lagu drēfan *w* WAT
set up onstellan *w* HSE
settle ārǽdan 7 AGR, SAY, THI
  gecweðan 5
  sēman *w*
  ðingian *w*
  gesettan *w* LAN
  gesittan 5 POS
settler gebūr *(m)* LAN
seven seofon
seventeen seofontīene
seventeenth seofontēoða
seventh seofoða
seventieth hundseofontigoða
seventy hundseofontig
sever getwǽfan *w* BRK
several manigfeald MEA
severe ðearl EVL
  wrāðlīc
  hefig MIN
  hrēðe
  stearc
  stīð(līc) GD
  strong
  swīð PFM
severely ðearle MEA
sew sīwian *w* CLO
sex hǽmed *(m)* LOV
  liger *(n)*
  hād *(m)* KIN
sexual gecyndelīc BOD
sexual intercourse
  hǽmedlāc *(n)* LOV
sexual pleasure wynlust *(m)* LOV
shadow sceadu *(f)* FIR
  scua *(m)*
shaft sceaft *(m)* HSE

shake ācweccan *w* LRD
  (ā)scacan *6*
  beofian *w* GO
  onðringan *3*
shake off tōbregdan *3* LRD
shall sculan *w*
shallow undīop WAT
shame bismer *(m,n,f)* EVL, FOE, SAY
  bismerian *w*
  bismrung *(f)*
  edwītscipe *(m)*
  scomu *(f)* MIN
shameless nebwlātful EVL
shampooing hēafodbæð *(n)* WAT
shape hīw *(n)* ART, BOD
  scyppan *6* HSE
share gedǣlan *w* BRK
share out dǣlan *w* BRK, WEA
shared dwelling
  somodeard *(m)* LAN
sharp cēne MIN
  scearp WPN
sharpen scyrpan *w* TOO
sharpened (mechanically)
  mylenscearp WPN
shave besciran *4* BOD
shaven-headed homol BOD
she hēo *(nom.)*
she-wolf wylfen *(f)* ANI
shear bescieran *4*
  efsian *w*
sheath scēað *(f)* PRO, WPN
sheep scēap *(m)* ANI
sheer nīowol WAT
  scīr
sheet hopscȳte *(f)* SLP
  scēat *(m)*
  scīte *(f)*
sheet metal platung *(f)* MAT
shelf scylf *(m)* HSE
shell sciell *(f)* ANI
shellfish scilfisc *(m)* ANI
shelter hlēow *(m)* PRO
  hlēowð *(f)*
sheltered hlēowfæst PRO

shepherd (scēap)hyrde *(m)* WOR
shield bord *(n)* WPN
  lind *(f)*
  rond *(m)*
  scyld *(m)*
  (ge)scyldan *w* PRO
shield formation bordweall *(m)* WPN
  scyldburh *(f)*
shieldwall bordweall *(m)* WAR
  wīghaga *(m)*
shifty ðusenthīwe MIN
shilling scilling *(m)* MEA
shin scīa *(m)* BOD
shine līxan *w* FIR
  scīnan *1*
shine forth āscīnan *1* FIR
shingle ceosol *(m)* LAN
shining heavens sweglwundor *(n)* SKY
ship bāt *(f)* WAT
  brimwudu *(m)*
  bundenstefna *(m)*
  cēol *(m)*
  fær *(n)*
  flota *(m)*
  lid *(n)*
  (sǣ)naca *(m)*
  scip *(n)*
  sundwudu *(m)*
  wǣghengest *(m)*
  wæterðīsa *(m)*
  ȳðhengest *(m)*
ship, wooden bēam *(m)* WAT
ship's hold wranga *(m)* WAT
ship's rope sciprāp *(m)* WAT
ship's stem stefn *(m)* WAT
shipwreck forlidennes *(f)* EVL, WAT
shipwrecked, be forlīðan *1* EVL, GO
shire scīr *(f)* LAN
shirt hemeðe *(n)* CLO
shiver sprengan *w* BRK
shoe mēo *(m)* CLO
  scōh *(m)*
shoe polish gedrēog *(n)* CLO
shoemaker scēowyrhta *(m)* WOR
shoes, pair of gescȳ *(n)* CLO

shoot blēd *(f)* PLA
  cīð *(m)*
shoot down (of-, on-)scēotan *2* WAR
shore ōfer *(m)* WAT
  stæð *(m,n)* LAN
  strand *(n)*
short scort MEA
short of breath swōretendlīc AIL
shortly scortwyrplīc TIM
shortness sceortnes *(f)* MEA
shoulder bōg *(m)* BOD
  eaxl *(f)*
  sculdor *(m)*
shout ceallian *w* CAL
  hlēoðrian *w* REC
  hlūdan *w* SAY
  hlynnan *w*
  hrīeman *w*
shove scufan *2* DRI
shove off āscūfan *2* WAT
shovel scofl *(f)* TOO
show ætīewan *w* SEE
  gecȳðan *w*
  oðȳwan *w*
  tǣc(n)an *w* SAY
  wīsian *w*
  wissian *w*
shower scūr *(m)* WAT
shred (ge)scrēadian *w* BRK
shrew screwa *(m)* ANI
shrine scrīn *(n)* CHU
shrink scrincan *3* BEC
shrive scrīfan *1* CHU
Shropshire Scrobbesbyrigscīr *(f)* STR
shudder onðringan *3* GO
shun onscunian *w* EVL, GO
  (ge)scunian *w*
shut betȳnan *w* FAI
shy scēoh MIN
sick sēoc AIL
  untrum
sick, be ādlian *w* AIL
  sīclian *w*
  spiwian *w*
sick, become ādlian *w* BEC
  sīclian *w*

sickness mettrumnes *(f)* AIL
  sēocnes *(f)*
side healf *(f)* BOD
  sīde *(f)*
side, on this behionan POS
side of meat flicce *(n)* EAT
side-ache sīdece *(m)* AIL
  sīdwærc *(m)*
side-dish gabote *(f)* EAT
sieved flour āsift *(m)* EAT
sigh seofian *w* SAY
sigh over sīcan *1* LOV
sight gesihð *(f)* SEE
  wlitesēon *(f)*
sign gebēacen *(n)* LAN, SAY
  getācnung *(f)*
  segen *(m,n)* WPN
  tācn *(n)* MIN
sign of misfortune wēatācn *(n)* EVL
sign of the cross, make the
  gesegnian *w* CHU
signet insigle *(n)* ART
signify forstandan *6* SAY, WRI
  mǣnan *w*
silence swīgian *w* SAY
silk seolc *(m)* MAT
  sīde *(f)* CLO
silk, made of seolcen MAT
silver seolfor *(n)* MAT
silversmith seolforsmið *(m)* WOR
similar gelīc ART
  onlīc
similarity onlīcnes *(f)* ART
simple ānfeald MEA
simplicity of mind bilewitnes *(f)* MIN
sin gylt *(m)* CHU
  leahtor *(m)* EVL
  (ge)syngian *w*
  synn *(f)*
since siððan TIM
sincere bilewit MIN
  eornoste
sinew sinu *(f)* BOD
sinful firenful CHU, EVL
  forsȳngod
  synful

sing (ā)singan *3* REC
  (ge)giddian *w*
sing out (ā)galan *6* REC
singer scop *(m)* REC
single ānge MEA
  ānlīpig
singly ānlīpig TIM
sink besencean *w* WAT
  besincan *3*
  sīgan *1* GO
sip sūpan *2* EAT
sister sweostor *(f)* KIN
sister's husband āðum *(m)* KIN
sister's son swustersunu *(m)* KIN
sit sittan *5* POS
sit down gesittan *5* POS
sit round ymbsittan *5* POS
six sīex
sixteen sīextīene
sixteenth sīextēoða
sixth sīexta
sixtieth sīextigoða
sixty hundsīextig
size grēatnes *(f)* MEA
  micelnes *(f)*
skate (ge)glīdan *1* GO
skeleton bāncofa *(m)* BOD
skewer sticca *(m)* TOO
skilful gelǣred MIN
skill cræft *(m)* ART, WOR
  list *(m,f)* MIN
skilled craftsman
  smēawyrhta *(m)* WOR
skin fell *(n)* BOD
  hȳd *(f)*
skulk lūtian *w* POS
skull brægenpanne *(f)* BOD
  hēafodbolla *(m)*
  hēafodpanne *(f)*
sky heofon *(m,f)* SKY
  lyft *(f)*
  rodor *(m)*
  swegl *(n)*
slackness sleacnes *(f)* MIN
  yrhðu *(f)*

slander folclēasung *(f)* EVL
  forcweðan *5*
slaughter dēaðcwealm *(m)* EVL, WAR
  wæl *(n)* DIE
  wælsleaht *(m)*
  wīghryre *(m)*
slave ðēow(a) *(m)* WOR
  ðēowman *(m)*
slave, lawful rihtðēowa *(m)* WOR
slavery ðēowdōm *(m)* WOR
  ðēowot *(m)*
slay (for-, of-) slēan *6* WAR
slayer bana *(m)* EVL, FOE, WAR
sledgehammer slecg *(f)* TOO
sleep ræst *(f)* SLP
  (ge)restan *w*
  slǣp *(m)*
  slǣpan *7*
  slūma *(m)*
  swefan *5*
  sweofot *(n)*
sleeping chamber būr *(f)* SLP
sleepy slāpol SLP
  slǣpor
sleeve earmella *(m)* CLO
  earmstoc *(m)*
  slȳf *(f)*
sleeveless slȳflēas CLO
slender wāc BOD
slide slīdan *1* GO
slight gehwǣde MEA
slim þynn MEA
  wāc
sling stæfliðere *(f)* WAR
  ymbhringan *3* BRI
slip off bestelan *4* GO
slipper stæppescōh *(m)* CLO
  swyftlere *(m)*
slippery sliddor LAN
slit tōslītan *1* BRK
slither slingan *3* GO
sloe slā *(m)* EAT
slope hlinc *(m)* LAN
  hlīð *(n)*

sloping hwelmdragen HSE
sloth āsolcennes *(f)* MIN
 nytennes *(f)* EVL
slow læt GO
 longsum TIM
 slāw
slowworm slāwyrm *(m)* ANI
smack plætt *(m)* WAR
 plættan *w*
small lytel MEA
small, become dwīnan *1* BEC
 lȳtlian *w*
small ship cnearr *(m)* WAT
smash tōbēatan *7* BRK, EVL
smear clǣman *w* EAT
 smerian *w*
 smirwan *w*
 smītan *1*
 (ge)dēcan *w* BRI
smell stenc *(m)* BOD
smile smercian *w* BOD
smith smið *(m)* WOR
smithy smiððe *(f)* TOO
smoke rēc *(m)* FIR
 ðrosm *(m)*
smooth smēðe LAN
 smōð
snail snægl *(m)* ANI
snake snaca *(m)* ANI
 wyrm *(m)*
snapdragon hundeshēafod *(n)* PLA
snare begrynian *w* ANI, EAT
 grin *(n)*
snatch abrēdan *3* BRI
sneeze fnēsan *5* AIL
sniff stincan *3* BOD
snore fnǣrettan *w* SLP
snow snāw *(m)* SKY
 snīwan *w*
snowstorm hrīð *(f)* SKY
 snāwgebland *(n)*
 wintergeweorð *(n)*
 winterscūr *(m)*
so swā
 swāsame

soak socian *w* WAT
soap sāpe *(f)* WAT
society gefērscipe *(m)* LRD
sock socc *(m)* CLO
socket stæpe *(m)* POS
sod turf *(f)* LAN
soft hnesc BOD
soft, become lissan *w* BEC
soften lissan *w* GD, MIN
soil folde *(f)* LAN
 molde *(f)*
solace frōfor *(f)* GD, MIN
sole sole *(f)* BOD
solid gold eallgylden ART, MAT
solid iron eallīren MAT
some other thing elleshwæt STR
someone hwā
 sum
Somerset Sumersǣtan *(mpl)* STR
something (ā)wuht
sometimes hwīlum TIM
somewhat hwega MEA
 nāthwōn
 sumes
son bearn *(n)* KIN
 eafora *(m)*
 magu *(m)*
 sunu *(m)*
son's wife snoru *(f)* KIN
son-in-law āðum *(m)* KIN
song (cwide)giedd *(n)* REC
 (lēoð)song *(m)*
song of joy blissesang *(m)* CHU, REC
song of longing fūslēoð *(n)* REC
song of praise lofsang *(m)* REC
song of victory sigelēoð *(n)* REC
soon eftsōna TIM
 hraðe
soot hrūm *(m)* MAT
soothe (ge)smēðan *w* AIL
soothsayer hwata *(m)* SAY
sooty behrūmig FIR
soporific slǣpbǣre SLP
Sorbians (Baltic people)
 Surpe *(mpl)* STR

sorceress hægtesse *(f)* CHU
 lybbestre *(f)*
sorceror lyblǣca *(m)* CHU
sorcery drȳ *(m)* CHU
 drȳcræft *(m)*
 wiglung *(f)*
sore dolh *(n)* AIL
 sār *(f)*
sore throat hrǣcgebrǣc *(n)* AIL
sorrel sure *(f)* PLA
sorrow murcnung *(f)* MIN
 sārnes *(f)*
 (gnorn)sorg *(f)*
sorrow for gnornian *w* MIN
 (be)sorgian *w*
sorrowful sārig MIN
 sārlīc
 sorgcearig
 sorhful
sorry sārig MIN
 sārlīc
sort cynn *(n)* MAT
soul sāwol *(f)* CHU
sound (ge)hāl AIL
 gesund
 onsund
 hlēoðor *(n)* REC
 swēg *(m)*
soup broð *(n)* EAT
sour afor EAT
 sūr
sour milk sȳring *(f)* EAT
source æwielme *(m)* WAT
 wiella *(m)*
 wielle *(f)*
 ordfruma *(m)* STA
south sūð POS
south coast sūðrima *(m)* LAN
 sūðstæð *(n)*
southern side sūðhealf *(f)* POS
sow (ā)sāwan 7 PLA, WOR
 sū *(f)* ANI
 sugu *(f)*
sowthistle ðufeðistel *(m)* PLA

space rȳmet *(n)* LAN
space of time hwīl *(f)* TIM
 stund *(f)*
spacious rūm LAN
spade delfīsen *(n)* TOO
 spadu *(f)*
Spanish Spēonisc STR
spare (ge)sparian *w* LAW, WEA
sparing spær MEA
spark spearc *(m)* FIR
 (fȳr)spearca *(m)*
sparrow hrandsparwa *(m)* ANI
 spearwa *(m)*
 sugga *(m)*
spasm hramma *(m)* AIL
 swiung *(f)*
speak cweðan 5 SAY
 maðolian *w*
 (ge)mǣlan *w* AGR, BLM
 secgan *w*
 (ge)sprecan 5
speak about mǣnan *w* SAY
speak in verse hlēoðrian *w* REC
speak out (ā)cweðan 5 SAY
speaker reordberend *(m)* SAY
speaking a foreign language
 elreord SAY
spear æsc *(m)* WPN
 franca *(m)*
 gafeluc *(m)*
 gār *(m)*
 spere *(n)*
spearman æscmann *(m)* WAR
spearpoint ord *(m)* WPN
spearstrap sceaftlō *(m?)* WPN
special sundorlic GD
 synderlīpe
species of animal dēorcynn *(n)* ANI
speck mot *(n)* WAT
speckled cylu COL
spectacle wǣfersȳn *(f)* SEE
spectator hāwere *(m)* SEE
 scēawere *(m)*

speech cwide *(m)* SAY
  gereord *(n)*
  gesprec *(n)*
  mǣl *(f)* AGR
  sp(r)ǣc *(f)*
  word *(n)*
  wordcwide *(m)*
speed hrædnes *(f)* GO
speedwell hleomoce *(f)* PLA
spell gealdor *(n)* CHU, REC
spend (ā)spendan *w* WEA
spend one's life drohtnian *w* LIV
spend the winter oferwintrian *(w)* TIM
spew spīwan *1* EAT
spice wyrtgemang *(n)* EAT
spider āttorcoppe *(f)* ANI
  gongewæfre *(f)*
  hunta *(m)*
  lobbe *(f)*
spider's web renge *(f)* ANI
spike scēað *(f)* TOO
  spīcing *(m)*
spikenard nard *(m)* PLA
spill (ge)spillan *w* FAI
spin (ge)spinnan *3* GO
spindlewhorl hweorfa *(m)* TOO
spine gelodr *(f)* BOD
  hrycgbān *(m)*
spirit gāst *(m)* CHU, MIN
  gæst *(m)*
  sāwol *(f)*
spirited mōdig MIN
spiritual gāstlīc, gǣstlīc CHU
spit spittian *w* EAT
  spīwan *1* AIL
spit on gespeoftian *w* EVL
spite nīð *(m)* EVL
spleen mitte *(f)* BOD
splendid ǣnlic MIN
  wrǣtlīc ART
splendour scīma *(m)* FIR
  weorðnes *(f)* GD
splint spilc *(m)* AIL
splinter spōn *(m)* HSE
split āclēofan *2* BRK
  sprengan *w*

split up forlǣtan ūpp *7* BRK
  tōdǣlan *w*
  tōdrīfan *1*
spoke hrung *(f)* HSE
spoken message ǣrendsprǣc *(f)* SAY
spoliation strūdung *(f)* EVL
sponsor forespeca *(m)* LAW
spoon cuculer *(m)* TOO
spoon(ful) sticca *(m)* MEA, TOO
sport gomen *(n)* MIN
spout wæterðrūh *(f)* WAT
sprat sprott *(m)* ANI
spray sprengan *w* WAT
spread springan *3* GO
spread out brǣdan *w* LAN, BRK
spread over oferbrǣdan *w* BRK
spring lencten *(m)* TIM
  springan *3* GO
  æwielme *(m)* WAT
  wæteræddre *(f)*
  wiella *(m)*
  wielle *(f)*
spring up āspringan *3* WAT
springwater wiellewæter *(n)* WAT
sprinkle begēotan *2* WAT
sprout spryttan *w* PLA
spun twice twispunnen CLO
spur spura *(m)* CLO
spurn (ge)spurnan *3* EVL
spurstrap spurleðer *(n)* CLO
spy scēawere *(m)* SEE
squalour orfeormnes *(f)* EVL
squander forspendan *w* EVL, WEA
square fēowerscȳte ART
squeeze out āwringan *3* EAT
squinting sceolh SEE
squirrel ācweorna *(m)* ANI
stab stician *w* EVL
  stingan *3*
stab to death ofstician *w* WAR
  ofstingan *3*
stable horsern *(n)* ANI, HSE
  staðolfæst
  untealt
stack hrēac *(m)* LAN
stack of firewood scīdhrēac *(m)* FIR

staff cycgel *(m)* WPN
gyrd *(f)* MEA, TOO
stæf *(m)*
Staffordshire Stæffordscīr *(f)* STR
stag heort *(m)* ANI
stagga *(m)*
staidness gestæððignes *(f)* MIN
stairs stǣger *(m)* HSE
stake staca *(m)* TOO
stocc *(m)*
stalking stalcung *(f)* GO
stallion stēda *(m)* ANI
stōdhors *(n)*
stammer stam *(f?)* SAY
stamettan *w*
wlæffian *w* SAY
stamp stempan *w* WOR
stand (ge)standan *6* POS
stand by bestandan *6* POS
stand firm stemnettan *w* HSE, POS
stand for forstandan *6* WRI
stand in the way forstandan *6* POS
standard fana *(m)* WAR
standard-bearer
cumbolwiga *(m)* LRD, WAR
star steorra *(m)* SKY
(heofon)tungol *(n)* FIR
starboard stēorbord *(n)* WAT
stare starian *w* SEE
starling stær(ling) *(m)* ANI
start ōr *(n)* STA
ord *(m)*
starve hlǣnian *w* EAT
state ðing *(n)* BEC
state of affairs steall *(m)* BEC
statement (ge)sægen *(f)* SAY
statue onlīcnes *(f)* ART
stature leng *(f)* BOD
stay awake wæccan *w* SLP
stay away from forsittan *5* POS
stay behind lāst weardian *w* POS
steadfast ānhȳdig MIN
stedefæst
steadfastly unwāclīc PFM
steal stalian *w* GO, LAW

(for)stelan *4* WEA
steal away bestelan *4* GO
stealing stalu *(f)* LAW
stealthy sleac GO
steam stēam *(m)* WAT
steel stȳle *(n)* MAT
steep gewēsan *w* EAT
nēowol LAN
stēap
steer stȳran *w* LRD
stench stenc *(m)*
step (ge)stæppan *6* GO
stæpe *(m)*
stepchild stēopbearn *(n)* KIN
stepdaughter stēopdohtor *(f)* KIN
stepfather stēopfæder *(m)* KIN
stepmother stēopmōdor *(f)* KIN
stepping-stone cleac *(f)* GO
stepson stēopsunu *(m)* KIN
stern ðearlmōd MIN
hrēðe
sternum brēostbān *(n)* BOD
stew broð *(n)* EAT
stichwort æðelferðingwyrt *(f)* PLA
stick (ge)cleofian *w* POS
cycgel *(m)* WPN
stæf *(m)* TOO
sticky clibbor POS
stiff stīf POS
stīð
stile stigel *(f)* LAN
still forð TIM
(nū-, ðā-)gīen
(nū-, ðā-)gīet
hwæðre
stille GD
stillborn dēadboren DIE
stimulate scyrpan *w* MIN
sting stingan *3* EVL
stink (fūl)stincan *3* PLA
stipulation gerād *(f)* LAW
stir āstyrian *w* MIN
hrēran *w* GO
stir up drēfan *w* MIN
onhrēran *w*

stirring hrōr MIN
stitch stice *(m)* AIL
stock stocc *(m)* PLA
stocking hosa *(m)* CLO
stocks hengen *(f)* LAW
stole stola *(m)* CLO
stomach gehrif *(n)* BOD
   maga *(m)*
stomach-ache hriftēung *(f)* AIL
   hrifwerc *(m)*
stone stān *(m)* LAN, MAT
stone, made of stǣnen MAT
stone vessel stānfæt *(n)* EAT
stone wall stānweall *(m)* LAN
stool stōl *(m)* HSE
stoop stūpian *w* GO
stop forstoppian *w* FAI
storeroom hēddærn *(n)* HSE
storm storm *(m)* SKY
   styrman *w*
storm-beaten hrīðig SKY
storm-cloud wederwolcen *(n)* SKY
story racu *(f)* SAY
   spell *(n)*
stout fǣtt BOD, GD
   stīð(līc) MIN
stout-hearted stearcheort MIN
   stercedferhð
   stīðhycgend
   swīðmōd
stove cylen *(f)* EAT
   ofn *(m)*
   stofa *(m)*
straight gerād GO
   gerēc
   riht(līc) LAW
straight ahead gerihte *(n)* POS
straighten gerihtlǣcan *w* ART, LAW
strand strand *(n)* LAN, WAT
strange elelendisc STR
strange of speech elreord SAY
stranger gīest *(m)* STR
strangle smorian *w* DIE
strangury
   ðæs migðan earfoðlicnys *(f)* AIL

strap gewrið *(n)* CLO
   wriða *(m)*
straw healm *(m)* MAT
   strēaw *(n)* PLA
strawberry eorðberge *(f)* EAT
   strēaberge *(f)* PLA
stray losian *w* GO
   wandrian *w*
stream burna *(m)* LAN
   (ēa)strēam *(m)* WAT
   wiella *(m)*
   faroð *(m)*
   rīð *(m)*
   (lagu-)strēam *(m)*
street strǣt *(f)* GO
strength cræft *(m)* WOR
   eafoð *(n)* BOD
   ellen *(n)* MIN
   mægen *(f)* GD
   mægenðise *(f)*
   miht *(f)*
   strengu *(f)*
   ðrymm *(m)*
   ðrȳð *(f)*
strength, gain elnian *w* BOD, GD
strengthen gestrangian *w* AIL, GD
   getrymman *w* WAR
stress earfoð *(n)* EVL
stressful earfoðlīc EVL
stretch out gerǣcan *w* GO
stride strīdan *1* GO
strife geflit *(n)* WAR
   gewinn *(n)*
   sacu *(f)* EVL
   sæcc *(f)*
   wrōht *(m,f)*
strike bēatan *7* WAR
   beslēan *6*
   cnyssan *w*
   slēan *6* WOR
   swingan *3* EVL
strike against gespurnan *3* EVL
strike down forslēan *6* EVL, WAR
   gefyllan *w*
   offellan *w*
string streng *(m)* TOO

strip bestrīpan *w* CLO
  ongyrwan *w*
  unscrȳdan *w*
strip naked genacodian *w* CLO
striped stafod ART
strive sacan *6* EVL, PFM, WAR
  winnan *3* WOR
stroke drepe *(m)* EVL
  sweng *(m)*
  swingell *(f)*
  slege *(m)* WAR
  ðaccian *w* LOV
strong ðearl EVL
  dyhtig WAR
  fæst MIN
  mihtig(līc) GD
  stīð
  strong(līc)
  trum
  rōf PFM
  swīð
strong, become elnian *w* BEC
strong in mind ellenrōf MIN
strong-smelling gestence BOD
stronghold burg *(f)* WAR
  ceaster *(f)*
  fæsten *(n)*
structure gesteal *(n)* HSE
struggle through wrīgian *w* GO
stubble gedrif *(n)* PLA
  healm *(m)* MAT
stubborn fæst MIN
stud stuðansceaft *(m)* HSE
studded (shield) cellod WPN
studded (shoe) behammen CLO
study begengnes *(f)* MIN
  gecneordnes *(f)* KNO
  leornung *(f)*
stupid dysig THI
  inðicce
  medwīs
sturgeon styria *(m)* ANI
sty hlōse *(f)* HSE
stye stīgend *(m)* AIL
stylus græf *(n)* WRI
subdue gegān *a* EVL

  gereccan *w* PFM
  ofercuman *4*
  oferdrīfan *1*
  oferflītan *1*
  oferwinnan *3*
  lissan *w* MIN
subject gereccan *w* PFM
  geðinge *(n)* AGR
  ondweorc *(n)* THI
  underðēodan *7* LRD
submerge besincan *3* WAT
submit to gecierran *w* FAI
  underhnīgan *1* LRD
subside drūsian *w* AIL, FAI
succeed spēdan *w* PFM
  spōwan *7*
success spēd *(f)* PFM
successful spēdig PFM
succession, in æfter POS
successor
  æftergenga *(m)* GO, KIN, LRD
such ðylc
  swilc
suck sūcan *2* EAT
suckling diend *(m)* ANI
sudden færlīc TIM
sudden attack fær *(m)* WAR
sudden attacker færsceaða *(m)* FOE
sudden danger fær *(m)* EVL
suddenly færinga TIM
  semninga
suet cūself *(f)* EAT
  gelyndo *(f)*
suffer gefaran *6* NEE
  ðolian *w*
  ðrōwian *w* LOV
suffer shipwreck forlīðan *1* WAT
suffering ðrōwung *(f)* LOV
suffocate forþylman *w* AIL
Suffolk Sūðfolc *(n)* STR
suitable gecoren GD
  gedafenlīc
  gedēfe
  gelimplic
  gerisenlīc
  gerisne

sulfurwort cammoc *(m)* PLA
sully āfȳllan *w* EVL
sulphur swefel *(m)* MAT
summer sumor *(m)* TIM
summer expedition
  sumorlida *(m)* WAR
summit hēafod *(n)* LAN
  top *(m)*
summon (ā)bannan *7* ASK, CAL
  (ge)bannan *7* LRD
  bēodan *2*
  fetian *w*
sun sunne *(f)* SKY
sun, with the sunganges GO
sunbeam sunnbēam *(m)* SKY
Sunday Hāligdæg *(m)* TIM
  Sunnandæg *(m)*
sunder āsyndran *w* BRK
  getwæfan *w*
  tōslītan *1*
sundial dægmæl *(m,n)* TIM
  sōlmerca *(m)*
sunset setlgang *(m)* SKY
sunwise sunganges GO
superior to bet
  tōforan
superstructure ofergeweorc *(n)* HSE
supple līðig BOD
  swancor
supply geinnian *w* GD
  sellan *w*
supply of food onstāl *(m)* EAT
support ācuman *4* PRO
  fylstan *w*
  staðol *(m)* HSE
  gelæstan *w* GD
  wraðu *(f)*
  wrēðan *w*
suppose myntan *w* THI
  wēnan *w*
suppurate gehwelian *w* AIL
sure gewiss KNO
  sicor
surety borg *(f)* PRO, WEA

surface bred *(n)* HSE
surge wylm *(m)* WAT
surname cūðnoma *(m)* CAL
surpass oferstīgan *1* PFM
  oferðēon *1*
surprise besyrwan *w* EVL, MIN, THI
Surrey Sūðrige *(n)* STR
surround befōn *7* GO
  begān *a* WAR
  ymbsellan *w* POS
survey gehāwian *w* ASK
  geondscēawian *w* SEE
survive gedīgan *w* LIV
  oferlibban *w*
Sussex Sūð Seaxe *(mpl)* STR
sustenance bīleofa *(m)* EAT
Swabians (German people)
  Swǣfe *(mpl)* STR
swallow swealwe *(f)* ANI
  swelgan *3* EAT
swallow down forswelgan *3* EAT
swamp fenn *(n)* LAN
swan ilfetu *(f)* ANI
  swan *(m)*
swarm of bees bēogang *(m)* ANI
  sīgewīf *(n)*
sway geweald *(n)* LRD
swear (ge)swerian *6* SAY
sweat swāt *(m)* BOD
  swǣtan
Sweden Swēoland *(n)* STR
Swedes Swēon *(mpl)* STR
sweep swāpan *7* WAT
sweep away
  forswāpan *7* HSE, PFM, WOR
sweet swēte EAT
  swētlīc
  (ðurh-)werod
  līðe LOV
sweet-and-sour sūrmelsc EAT
sweeten geswētan *w* EAT
sweetness swētnes *(f)* EAT
swell ðindan *3* AIL
swelling swyle *(m)* AIL

swift hræd GO
 ofostlīc
 swift
swift ship scegð *(m)* WAT
swim swimman *3* GO, WAT
swimming sund *(n)* GO, WAT
swimming ability merestrengu *(f)* GO
swine swīn *(n)* ANI
swing swingan *3* GO
swollen gland cumul *(n)* AIL
swollen-eyed tornig AIL
swoon swīma *(m)* MIN
swooning geswōgung *(f)* AIL
sword bile *(m)* WPN
 bill *(n)*
 heoru *(f)*
 mēce *(f)*
 sweord *(n)*
sword-polisher sweordhwīta *(m)* WOR
syllable stæfgefēg *(n)* SAY, WRI
syllogism smēagelegen *(f)* KNO, WRI
symbol tācen *(n)* WRI
sympathize midðolian *w* THI

T

table bēod *(m)* HSE
 bord *(n)*
 mȳse *(f)*
tablecloth bēodclað *(m)* EAT
tableware bēodbolle *(f)* EAT
tail steort *(m)* ANI
 tægl *(m)*
tailor hrægelðegn *(m)* CLO
 sēamere *(m)* WOR
taint fūlian *w* EAT
take cēpan *w* BRI
 fōn *7*
 niman *4*
take a seat onsittan *5* POS
take care of rēcan *w* LOV
 reccan *w*
take note of gīeman *w* LOV, MIN
tale talu *(f)* SAY
talk gemaðel *(n)* SAY

 maðelian *w*
talkative specul SAY
 swīðsprecel
tall lang BOD
tambourine wīfhearpe *(f)* REC
tame tam ANI
 temian *w*
 temman *w*
tan dunn COL
 fealu
tankard orc *(m)* EAT
 wǣge *(n)*
tanner tannere *(m)* WOR
tansy helde *(f)* PLA
tap tæppa *(m)* WAT
taper taper *(m)* FIR
tapering plot of land gāra *(m)* LAN
tar eorðtyrewe *(f)* MAT
 teoru *(n)*
targe targa *(m)* WPN
taste ābyrian *w* EAT
 byrging *(f)*
 onbyrgan *w*
 swæcc *(m)*
taste-buds gōma *(m)* BOD
tax gescot *(n)* WEA
 nīedgyld *(n)* LAW
teach (ge)lǣran *w* MIN, SAY
 tǣcan *w*
tear hlēordropa *(m)* BOD
 teagor *(m)*
 tēar *(m)*
 wōpdropa *(m)*
 wōpeshring *(m)*
 slītan *1* EVL
 teran *4*
tearful tēargēotend MIN
teazel tǣsel *(f)* PLA
 wulfes camb *(m)*
tedium ǣleng *(f)* THI
tell gesecgan *w* SAY
 reccan *w*
 tellan *w*
 wīsian *w*
 wissian *w*

temper temprian *w* WOR
tempest stormsǣ *(m,f)* WAT
temple hearh *(m)* CHU
   herig *(m)*
   tempul *(n)*
   ðunwong *(f)* BOD
temporary hwīlen TIM
   lǣne
tempt costnian *w* EVL, LOV
temptation costnung *(f)* CHU
ten tīen
tenant gafolgielda *(m)* LAW
   genēat *(m)* WOR
tench slīw *(m)* ANI
tend begongan 7 LOV
   lǣstan *w*
tent feldhūs *(n)* HSE
   geteld *(n)*
   træf *(n)*
tenth tēoða
tern stearn *(m)* ANI
terrible angrislīc EVL
   atol
terrible distress firenðearf *(f)* NEE
terrify afǣran *w* EVL
terrifying noise wōma *(m)* EVL
terror broga *(m)* EVL
   ōga *(m)*
test cunnian *w* ASK, KNO
testament yrfegewrit *(n)* LAW
tested warriors duguð *(f)* WAR
testicles beallucas *(mpl)* BOD
   hearðan *(mpl)*
   sceallan *(mpl)*
testimony gewitennes *(f)* LAW
tetanus oferbæcgetēung*(f)* AIL
than ðonne
thane ðegn *(m)* WOR
thane, chief ealdorðegn *(m)* LRD, WOR
thank (ge)ðoncian *w* ASK, MIN, THI
thankful ðoncful ASK, THI
thankfulness ðoncung *(f)* ASK
thanks ðonc *(m)* ASK, MIN
thanksgiving ðoncung *(f)* THI
that se *(m)*

sēo *(f)*
þæt *(n)*
þe *(relative pronoun)*
that, in order tō þǣm þæt
   tō þæs þe
that which þætte
thatch healm *(n)* HSE
   ðæc *(n)*
   ðecen *(m)*
thaumaturgy wundorcræft *(m)* GD
thaw ðāwian *w* WAT
the se *(m)*
   sēo *(f)*
   þæt *(n)*
theft ðīefð *(f)* LAW
their heora *(gen.)*
them hīe *(acc.)*
   him *(dat.)*
then ðā TIM
   ðonne
thence þonan
there þǣr
therefore forðȳ
they hīe *(nom)*
thick ðicce BOD
thicket gewrid *(n)* PLA
thief ðēof *(m)* LAW
thigh ðēoh *(n)* BOD
thimble ðȳmel *(m)* TOO
thin ðynne BOD
thing ðing *(n)* SAY
think hogian *w* THI
   hycgan *w*
   myntan *w*
   (ge)ðencan *w*
think about behycgan *w* THI
think deeply geondðencan *w* THI
think of gehycgan *w* THI
   behycgan *w*
think out āðencan *w*
third ðridda
thirst ðyrstan *w* WAT
thirteen ðrīetīene
thirteenth ðrēotēoða

thirtieth ðrītigoða
thirty ðrītig
this þes *(m)*
  þēos *(f)*
  þis *(n)*
thistle ðistel *(m)* PLA
thither þider
thong gewrið *(n)* CLO
  ðwang *(m,f)*
  wriða *(m)*
thorn ðorn *(m)* PLA
thorn thicket ðorngrǣfe *(f)* PLA
though þēah (ðe)
  þēahwæðre
thought gehygd *(f)* MIN, THI
  geðeaht *(n,f)*
  geðeahtung *(f)*
  geðōht *(m)*
  ingeðonc *(m)*
  mōdgeðonc *(m,n)*
  mōdsefa *(m)*
  (ge)ðonc *(m,n)*
thousand ðusund
thrall ðrǣl *(m)* WOR
thrall's duty ðrǣlriht *(n)* WOR
thread ðrǣd *(m)* CLO
threadworm ficwyrm *(m)* ANI
threat bēot *(n)* SAY
threaten ðrēagan *w* SAY
threatening words ðēowracu *(f)* SAY
three ðrēo *(m)*
  ðrīe *(f,n)*
threefold ðrifeald MEA
thrice ðriwa MEA
thrive (ge)ðēon *1* AIL, GD, PFM
throat gōman *(mpl)* BOD
  ðrotu *(f)*
throb slecgettan *w* AIL
throne cynesetl *(n)* LRD
  giefstōl *(m)*
  setl *(n)* HSE, POS
throng ðringan *3* BRI, WAR
through þurh
  geond
throughout geond POS

throw weorpan *3* POS
thrush ðrostle *(f)* ANI
thrust scufan *2* DRI
thumb ðūma *(m)* BOD
thunder ðun(r)ian *w* SKY
  ðunor *(m)*
thunderclap ðunorrād *(f)* SKY
Thuringians (German people)
  Þyringas *(mpl)* STR
Thursday Ðunresdæg *(m)* TIM
  Ðursdæg *(m)*
thus swā
  þȳ
thyme boðen *(m)* PLA
  wuducūnelle *(f)*
tick ticia *(m)* ANI
tickling smeartung *(f)* LOV
tide faroð *(m)* WAT
  tīd *(f)* TIM
tide, with the æfter faroðe WAT
tidy gesmicerod GD
tie (ge)tīegan *w* BRI
tierce undernsong *(m)* CHU
  underntīd *(f)*
tiger tigris *(m)* ANI
tight nearu BOD
tile tigele *(f)* HSE
till beswincan *3* LAN, PLA
  erian *w*
tilt tealtian *w* GO
timber timber *(n)* HSE
time byre *(m)* TIM
  fierst *(m)*
  sǣl *(m,f)*
  tīma *(m)*
  tīd *(f)*
  ðrāg *(f)*
time, in sīðlīc TIM
time, period of fæc *(n)* TIM
  þrāg *(f)*
time, proper tīma *(m)* TIM
time of day mǣl *(n)* TIM
time of one's birth gebyrdtīd *(f)* TIM
timely tīdlīc TIM
  tōtīman

tin tin *(n)* MAT
tinder tynder *(f)* FIR
tire tēorian *w* SLP
tired, become tēorian *w* BEC
tired of sæd MIN
to æt
tō
toad tāde *(f)* ANI
tosca *(m)*
toadstool feldswamm *(m)* PLA
today tōdæg TIM
toe tā *(f)* BOD
together ongeador POS
somod BRI
tōgædre
tōsomne
toil deorfan *3* PFM
gedeorf *(n)* WOR
geswinc *(n)*
swincan *3*
wyrcan *w*
toilet gangern *(n)* HSE
rynatūn *(m)*
token getācnung *(f)* SAY
tācn *(n)* MIN
tomb beren *(m)* DIE
līcrest *(f)*
ðrūh *(f)*
wælrest *(f)*
tomorrow morgenlīca dæg *(m)* TIM
tōmergen
tongs (ge)tang *(fpl)* TOO
tongue tunge *(f)* BOD
tonic leohtdrenc *(m)* AIL
tonsure, give the
tō prēoste besciran *4* CHU
too ēac
too (much) forhwega MEA
tō
too often foroft TIM
too soon forhraðe TIM
forsōna
tool īren *(n)* TOO
tōl *(f)*
tooth tōð *(m)* BOD

toothpick tōðgār *(m)* EAT
top top *(m)* LAN
torch lēohtfæt *(n)* FIR
torment sūsl *(n)* EVL
tintreg *(n)*
torso lēap *(m)* BOD
tortoise byrdling *(m)* ANI
torture tintreg *(n)* EVL
torture implement wītesteng *(m)* TOO
touch hrepian *w* BOD
hreppan *w*
hrīnan *1*
touchstone cenningstān *(m)* KNO
tough tōh BOD
tow tōgian *w* BRI
towards ongēan GO
tōgēanes
wiþ
tower torr *(m)* HSE
wīghūs *(n)* WAR
tower up hlīfian *w* HSE, LAN
town burgstede *(m)* LAN
ceaster *(f)*
port *(m)*
town-reeve tūngerēfa *(m)* WOR
townhouse burgsæl *(n)* HSE, LAN
townsmen burgwaru *(f)* LAN
townwall burgweall *(m)* LAN
track lāst *(m)* GO
spor *(n)*
swaðu *(f)*
swæð *(n)* LAN
tracker spyremon *(m)* ASK, WOR
tract of land londscearu *(f)* LAN
trade cēapung *(f)* WEA
trader cīepemann *(m)* WOR
mangere *(m)*
tradition ealdgesegen *(f)* LAW
ealdriht *(n)*
gefreoge *(n)* KNO
traitor hlāfordswīca *(m)* FOE
wǣrloga *(m)* FAI
trample ātredan *5* GO
tranquil smylte MIN

transform forbrēdan *3* BEC
  forhwierfan *w*
  forscyppan *6*
transgress misdōn *a* EVL
  onwendan *w*
transient gewītend GO
  lǣne
translate āreccean *w* SAY
  āwendan *w*
  oferlǣdan *w*
translator wealhstōd *(m)* SAY, WRI
transport ferian *w* BRI
  tōgelǣdan *w*
trap trǣppe *(f)* ANI
trappings gerǣde *(n)* TOO
travel faran *6* GO, WAT
  fēran *w*
  sīðian *w*
tray bǣrdisc *(m)* TOO
treacherous flāh FAI, MIN
treachery fācen *(n)* EVL
  swicdōm *(m)* FAI
  hlāfordsearu *(f)* FOE
  hlāfordswice *(m)*
  searu *(n)* MIN
  searucræft *(m)*
tread (ā)tredan *5* GO
  wadan *6*
treasure frætwa *(fpl)* ART, WEA
  hord *(n,m)*
  gestrēon *(n)*
  māðm *(m)*
  sincfæt *(n)*
treasure-cave hordærn *(n)* WEA
treasurer hordere *(m)* WEA
treat (heal) lācnian *w* AIL
treat with contempt
  forhogian *w* EVL, THI
  forsēon *5*
tree bēam *(m)* PLA
  trēow *(n)*
trefoil ðrilēfe *(mpl)* PLA
tremble ācwacian *w* GO
  (ā)bifian *w*
trench dīc *(m,f)* LAN

triangular þrēohyrne ART
tribe geðēode *(n)* LRD
tribulation earfoðe *(n)* EVL
  gedrēfednes *(f)*
tribute gafol *(n)* LAW, WEA
trick besyrwan *w* EVL, MIN, THI
  lytegian *w* SAY
  wrenc *(m)*
trickster lēasbrēda *(m)* FOE
trinity ðrīnes *(f)* CHU
triple ðrifeald MEA
trivet trefet *(m)* TOO
Trojans Trōiāna *(mpl)* STR
troop flocc *(m)* GO, WAR
  gedryht *(f)*
  gemong *(n)*
  hlōð *(f)*
  ðrēat *(m)*
trophy myrcels *(m)* ART
troth winetrēow *(f)* LOV
trouble cearu *(f)* EVL, LOV, MIN
  ungesǣlð *(f)* NEE
troubled, be (ge)sweorcan *3* MIN
  swincan *3*
troubled waters ēargebland *(n)* WAT
troublesome earfoðlīc EVL
  ungedēfe
  unsōfte
trough trog *(m)* TOO
trousers brēc *(fpl)* CLO
trout sceota *(m)* ANI
truce grið *(n)* WAR
  trēownes *(f)* PRO
true sōð(līc) SAY
true to one's word wordfæst SAY
trumpet bȳmere *(m)* REC
  trūðhorn *(m)*
  tube *(f)*
trunk lēap *(m)* BOD
trust gehyhtan *w* MIN, THI
  gelȳfan *w*
  getrūwian *w*
trust in trīewan *w* THI
  trūwian *w*
trustworthy getrēowe GD

truth getrȳwð *(f)* GD
  sōð *(n)* SAY
  trēow *(f)* THI
truth, in sōðe SAY
  tō sōðe
try out cunnian *w* KNO
Tuesday Tīwesdæg *(m)* TIM
tug dragan *6* BRI
  tēon *2*
tunic cyrtele *(f)* CLO
  serc *(m)*
  syric *(m)*
turf turf *(f)* LAN
turn bewendan *w* GO
  būgan *2* GO
  ci(e)rran *w*
  gebīgan *w*
  gewendan *w*
  hweorfan *3*
  endebyrdnes *(f)* TIM
  gehwierfan *w* BEC
turn, in ðurh endebyrdnesse TIM
turn about ymbhweorfan *3* GO
turn against ondhweorfan *3* GO
turn aside gewendan *w* GO
turn to besēon *5* SEE
  gecierran *w* FAI
turnip næp *(m)* PLA
turret wīghūs *(n)* WAR
tusk tūx *(m)* ANI
twelfth twelfta
twelve twelf
twentieth twentigoða
twenty twentig
twice tū MEA
  twuwa
twig twig *(n)* PLA
twilight, evening cwildseten *(f)*
twin getwinn *(m)* KIN
  getwisa *(m)*
twine twīn *(n)* TOO
twinge twengan *w* AIL
twinkle twinclian *w* FIR
twinkling of an eye
  ēaganbryhtm *(m)* BOD

twist ðrāwan *7* GO
  windan *3*
two tū *(n)*
  twā *(f,n)*
  twegen *(m)*
two parts, in emtwā
two thirds twæde MEA
twofold twifeald MEA
two-edged twiecge(de) WAR
tyranny ofermægen *(f)* LRD
  rīccetere *(n)*
tyrant lēodhata *(m)* EVL

U

ugly unfæger BOD
ulcer dēadspring *(m)* AIL
  dolh *(n)*
unawares unforscēawodlīc KNO, MIN
  unwæres
unbind inbindan *3* EVL
  onbindan *3*
  untīgan *w*
unburnt unforbærned FIR
uncle (maternal) ēam *(m)* KIN
uncle (paternal) fædera *(m)* KIN
unclothe ongyrwan *w* CLO
  unscrȳdan *w*
uncompensated ægylde WEA
unconsecrated unhālgod CHU
uncontested unbefohten WAR
uncover onwrēon *1* SEE
undaunted ðyhtig MIN
  unearg
undefended fierdlēas PRO, WAR
  unwered
under (be)neoðan
  under
under the control of gewylde LRD
undermentioned hēræfter POS, WRI
  hērbeæftan
understand gecnāwan *7* KNO
  ongietan *5*
  understandan *6* THI

understanding andgiet *(n)* MIN
 ingehygd *(f)*
 (ge)wit *(n)*
 ondgit *(n)* KNO
 ongitennes *(f)*
undertake underfōn *7* STA
 underginnan *3*
undertaking anginn *(n)* WOR
underwear (tunic) hemeðe *(n)* CLO
undo undōn *a* PFM
unending ungeendod TIM
unfaithfulness ungetrȳwð *(f)* LOV
unfenced untȳned LAN
unfought unfohten WAR
ungrammatical gewemmodlīc WRI
unhappy unhȳðig MIN
 unrōt
uninhabited by yeomen ābūrod LAN
uninjured undered AIL
 unwemme
unintentionally ungewealdes LRD
unique ǣnlīc MIN
unity ānnes *(f)* AGR
unknown uncūð STR
unleavened bread þeorf *(n)* EAT
unless būton
 ðȳ lǣs ðe
unlike ungelīc ART
unlordly unæðele LRD
unloved frēondlēas EVL
unpaid unāgiefen WEA
 unlēanod
unprepared ungearu PFM
unrelated ungesibb KIN
unrighteous unrihtwīs CHU
unrighteousness unrihtwīsnes *(f)* CHU
unsalted ungesylt EAT
unsold unbeboht WEA
unspeakable unāsecgend SAY
unstable tealt HSE
 unstaðolfæst
unswayable ārǣd MIN
untaught ungelǣred KNO
untie untīgan *w* BRI
until oð(ðæt) POS
unwell ādlig AIL

unwind onwindan *3* GO
unyoke unscennan *w* ANI
up ūp
 uppe
up to oð(ðæt) POS
upon on POS
 onufan
 uppan
upper storey upflōr *(m)* HSE
uproar cierm *(m)* CAL, SAY
 hrēam *(m)*
upwards uppe
urge manian ASK
 ðȳwan *w* DRI, THI
urge on getyhtan *w* SAY
 stihtian *w*
urinate micgan *w* BOD, WAT
 (ge)mīgan *1*
urination astyrung *(f)* BOD
urine hland *(n)* WAT
 migoða *(m)*
Ursa Major Wǣnes Ðisla *(fpl)* SKY
us ūs *(acc. dat.)*
 ūsic *(acc.)*
 unc *(acc. dat.)*
 uncet *(acc.)*
use brūcan *2* GD, TOO
 brȳce *(m)*
 nēotan *2* LRD
 notian *w* WOR
 notu *(f)*
 nytnes *(f)*
 nytt *(n)*
useful behēfe GD, TOO
 nytt
 nytwyrðe
 til
usefulness fremfulnes *(f)* GD
 nytnes *(f)*
useless unnytt LRD
useless, make āīdligan *w* FAI
usual bewuna MIN
 wunelīc
utensils andlōman *(mpl)* TOO
utility nytnes *(f)* GD, TOO

utter gesprecan 5 SAY
wrecan 5
uvula hræctunge *(f)* BOD

V

vagina cwið *(m)* BOD
cwiðe *(m)*
wamba *(m)*
valley cumb *(m)* LAN
dal *(n)*
dene *(m)*
denu *(f)*
slæd *(n)*
valour dryhtscipe *(m)* MIN
ellen *(n)*
value weorð *(n)* LAW
geeahtian *w* WEA
Vandals Wendle *(mpl)* STR
vanguard warrior
ordfruma *(m)* WAR
vanish swiðrian *w* FAI
ungesewenlīc weorðan *4*
vanity īdel *(n)* EVL
īdelnes *(f)*
vapour æðm *(m)* WAT
variation missenlīcnes *(f)* COL
vary hweorfan *3*
vassal genēat *(m)* WOR
vault hwealf *(f)* CHU, HSE
vegetable wyrt *(f)* EAT
vehicle fering *(f)* DRI
vein ædre *(f)* BOD
venerable ārwyrðe GD
vengeance wracu *(f)* EVL
venom ātor *(n)* EVL
venomous ætrig ANI
venture nēðan *w* THI
verb word *(n)* WRI
verbal skill wōðcræft *(m)* SAY
verbose wordig SAY
verdigris ārsāpe *(f)* MAT
vermillion wealhbaso *(f)* COL
verse fers *(n)* REC
verses, make wordum wrixlan *w* REC

vertebra gelyndu *(npl)* BOD
vervain æscðrotu *(f)* PLA
very ful MEA
swīðe
wel
vespers æfen *(n)* CHU
vessel cylle *(m)* EAT, TOO
fæt *(n)*
fætels *(n)*
naca *(m)* WAT
sægenga *(m)*
vessel of nailed construction
nægledcnearr *(m)* WAT
vex dreccan *w* AIL, EVL
swencan *w*
vice leahtor *(m)* EVL
unðēaw *(m)*
victorious lord sigedrihten *(m)* PFM
victorious nation sigeðēod *(f)* PFM
victory sige *(m)* PFM
sigor *(m)*
view scēawian *w* SEE
vigil wæccen *(f)* SLP
vigorous felahrōr WAR
rōf PFM
vile lāð EVL
wyrslīc
vinegar eced *(m,n)* EAT
vineous wīnlīc EAT
violation æswice *(m)* LAW
violence firen *(n)* EVL
nīð *(m)*
ðracu *(f)*
violent firenlīc EVL
violet bānwyrt *(f)* PLA
symeringwyrt *(f)*
viper's bugloss haransprecel *(m)* PLA
virgin fæmne *(f)* KIN
mēowle *(f)*
virginity mægðhād *(f)* GD, LOV
virtue ār *(f)* GD
ārfæstnes *(f)* CHU, MIN
duguð *(f)*
viscera innoð *(m,f)* BOD
visible gesewenlīc SEE
gesīene

vision gesihð *(f)* SEE
visit nēosan *w* GO
  (ge)nēosian *w*
  sēcan *w*
visitation genēosung *(f)* GO
visor būc *(m)* WPN
vixen fyxe *(f)* ANI
voice reord *(n)* SAY
  stefn *(f)* BOD
voluntary agnes willan LAW
  wilsumlīc LOV
vomit spīwan *1* EAT, LOV
  spīwða *(m)* AIL
voracious ofergīfre EAT
voracity oferhrops *(f)* EAT
vow bēotian *w* SAY
  gebēot *(n)*
vulture earngēap *(f)* ANI
  glida *(m)*

W

wade wadan *6* GO
wage (war) ðurhtēon *2* PFM, WAR
  wīgian *w*
waggon cræt(wægen) *(m)* DRI
  wægen *(m)* GO
waist hrif *(n)* BOD
wait (on)bīdan *1* POS
wait for onbīdan *1* POS
wake weccan *w* SLP
waken āweccan *w* SLP
Wales Norðwalas *(mpl)* STR
walk gewadan *6* GO
  gongan *7*
  gong *(m)*
  hweorfan *3*
  stæppan *6*
walk across oferwadan *6* GO
wall wāg *(m)* LAN
  weall *(m)*
walnut frencisc hnutu *(f)* EAT
walrus horshwæl *(m)* ANI
wander āswǣman *w* GO
  wǣðan *w*

wanderer eardstapa *(m)* GO
wane wanian *w* FAI
want gād *(n)* NEE
  willan *a* LOV, MIN
wanting wana NEE
wanton gāl EVL
  wrǣne
wanton destroyer
  mānfordǣdla *(m)* EVL
wantonness firenlūst *(m)* EVL
  gālscipe *(m)*
war beadu *(f)* WAR
  gewinn *(n)*
  gūð *(f)*
  hild *(f)*
  wīg *(n)*
war fugitive hereflīema *(m)* PRO
war-gear heregeatu *(f)* WPN
war-leader bealdor *(m)* LRD
  folcāgend *(m)*
  folctoga *(m)*
  gūðweard *(m)*
  heretoga *(m)*
  wīgfruma *(m)*
war-spear wælspere *(n)* WPN
  wælsteng *(m)*
ward hyrde *(m)* PRO
warder rǣplingweard *(m)* WOR
wardrobe hrægelhūs *(n)* CLO
warfare beadu *(f)* WAR
warm wearm FIR
warm, become wyrman *w* BEC
warm through beðian *w* EAT
  wyrman *w*
warn (ge)warnian *w* MIN, SAY
warrior beorn *(m)* WAR
  cempa *(m)* FOE
  dreng *(m)*
  (dryht)guma *(m)*
  (gūð)rinc *(m)*
  secg *(m)*
  (byrn)wīga *(m)* WPN
  wīgend *(m)*
warriors, tested duguð *(f)* WAR
wart puduc *(m)* AIL
  wearte *(f)*

Warwickshire
Wǣringwīcscīr *(f)* STR
wary wær THI
wærlīc
wary of, be warian *w* MIN
wash ðwēan *6* WAT
wascan, waxan *6*
wash away ādwǣscan *w* WAT
washing ðwēal *(n)* WAT
wasp wæps *(m)* ANI
waste forspendan *w* EVL
spilling *(f)*
wēste LAN
wasteland ānæd *(n)* LAN
wēsten *(m,n)*
watch wacian *w* SEE
wæccan *w* SLP
watch over weardian *w* SEE
watchful behȳdig THI
wærlīc
water lagu *(f)* WAT
leccan *w*
wǣta *(m)*
wæter *(n)*
wæterian *w*
water lily ēadocce *(f)* PLA
fleoðe *(f)*
waterfall ðēote *(f)* WAT
watermeadow hamm *(m)* LAN
watersnake wæternǣddre *(f)* ANI
waterwheel hlædtrendel *(m)* TOO
wattle watel *(m)* HSE
wave waðum *(m)* WAT
wǣg *(m)*
ȳð *(f)*
wax weax *(n)* MAT
way fær *(n)* GO
fǣreld *(n)*
lād *(f)*
weg *(m)*
way, in any on ǣnigum MEA
way, on the tōgēanes GO
way forward forðweg *(m)* GO
way of life drohtnung *(f)* LIV, WOR
way up ūpweg *(m)* GO

waybread wegbrǣde *(f)* PLA
we wē *(nom.)*
wit *(nom.)*
weak unmihtig LRD
weak, become onwǣcan *w* BEC
sweðrian *w*
wācian *w* FAI
weakness lēwsa *(m)* FAI
untrumnes *(f)*
Weald, The Andrēdesweald *(n)* STR
wealth ǣht *(f)* WEA
cēap *(m)*
feoh *(n)*
spēd *(f)*
wela *(m)*
wealth, lordly eorlgestrēon *(n)* WEA
wealthy spēdig WEA
welig
wealthy, become gestrȳnan *w* BEC
spēdan *w*
wean gewenian *w* EAT
weapon wǣpn *(n)* WPN
wear (ā)werian *w* CLO
weary getēorod SLP
wērig
mēðe MIN
sæd
weary, be ātēorian *w* SLP
weary, become mēðian *w* BEC
weary-minded wērigferhð MIN
weasel weosule *(f)* ANI
weather gewider *(n)* SKY
weder *(n)*
weave brēdan *3* CLO
wefan *5*
weaver webba *(m)* WOR
web webb *(n)* ANI
wedded couple sinhīwan *(mpl)* KIN
wedding weddung *(f)* LOV
wedding gift (groom to bride)
morgengifu *(f)* LOV
wedlock hǣmedscipe *(m)* KIN
Wednesday Wōdnesdæg *(m)* TIM
weed wēod *(n)* PLA

week wucu *(f)* TIM
weep grēotan *2* LOV
  rēotan *2*
  tӯran *w*
  wēpan *7* BOD
weeping wōp *(m)* BOD, EVL
weevil wifel *(m)* ANI
weft ōweb *(n)* CLO, MAT
weight gewiht *(n)* MEA
  hefignes *(f)*
  wǣge *(f)*
welcome grēting *(f)* LOV
  lēof
welcome! wilcume
welcome guest wilcuma *(m)* LOV
welfare gesǣlð *(f)* GD
well tela
  wel
  pytt *(m)* LAN
  wiella *(m)* WAT
  wielle *(f)*
well up weallan *7* WAT
well-known cūð KNO, STR
  gefrǣge
wellspring wyllsprynge *(m)* WAT
Welsh Wylisc STR
Welsh (people) Norðwalas *(mpl)* STR
  Norðwēalcynn *(n)*
wen wenn *(f)* AIL
werewolf werwulf *(m)* MON
west west POS
west, from the westan POS
West Kent (people)
  Westcentingas *(mpl)* STR
West Saxons West Seaxe *(mpl)* STR
Westmorland
  Westmōringaland *(n)* STR
wet bestēman *w* WAT
  leccan *w*
  wǣt
  wǣtan *w*
wet nurse cildfēstre *(f)* WOR
wether weðer *(m)* ANI
whale hron(fix) *(m)* ANI
  hwæl *(m)*

wharf hwearf *(m)* WAT
what? hwæt
whatever swā hwæt swā
wheat hwǣte *(m)* EAT, PLA
wheat, made of hwǣten EAT, MAT
wheat for bread hlāfhwǣte *(m)* EAT
wheatcrop
  hwǣtewæstm *(m)* EAT, LAN
wheedle geswǣslǣcan *w* SAY
wheel hweohl, hwēol *(n)* DRI
whelk weoloc *(m)* ANI
whelp hwelp *(m)* ANI
when ðā (ðā)
  ðonne
  mid ðǣm ðe
when? hwonne
whence hwonan
whenever swā hwonne swā
where? hwǣr
wherever swā hwǣr swā
whether hwæþer
whether...or sam...sam
whetstone hwetstān *(m)* TOO
whey hwǣg *(n)* EAT
which (one)? hwilc
while hwīl *(f)* TIM
  þenden
whine hwīnan *1* SAY
whinge hwinsian *w* SAY
whip beswingan *3* EVL
  swipu *(f)* TOO
whisper hwisprian *w* SAY
whispering rēonung *(f)* SAY
whistle hwingian *w* REC
  hwistle *(f)*
  hwistlian *w*
  pīpe *(f)*
whistling hwistlung *(f)* REC
white hwīt COL
White Sea Cwēnsǣ *(f)* STR
whitewash hwītingmelu *(n)* MAT
whither? hwider
who? hwā
whoever swā hwā swā

whole ful MEA
  gesund AIL
  hāl
wholesome gehāl EAT
whore hōrcwene *(f)* WOR
  hōre *(f)*
whose? hwæs
whose-ever swā hwæs swā
why? forhwōn
  forhwȳ
  hwæt
  hwȳ
wick wēoce *(f)* FIR
wicked firenful EVL
  inwitt
  yfel
wickedness mān *(n)* EVL
  yfelnes *(f)*
widdershins wiðersȳnes GO
wide brād LAN
  sīd
  wīd
widely wīde MEA
widely known wīdcūð KNO
widespread rȳfe MEA
widow widewe *(f)* KIN
wield wealdan *7* LRD
  wieldan *w*
wife cwēn *(f)* KIN
wife's father swēor *(m)* KIN
wife's mother sweger *(f)* KIN
wild wilde ANI
wild animal dēor *(n)* ANI
  wilder, wildedēor *(n)*
wild thyme wuducūnelle *(f)* PLA
wile lot *(n)* MIN
  searu *(n)*
  searucræft *(m)*
will willan *a* .
  wyscan *w*
  cwide *(m)* LAW
  gesetednes *(f)*
  yrfegewrit *(n)*
willing (ge)fægen GD, LOV
  lustlīc
  gelustful MIN

willing, be willan *a*
willing companion wilgesīð *(m)* LOV
willow windeltrēow *(n)* PLA
  wīðig *(m)*
Wiltshire Wiltūnscīr *(f)* STR
wily searogrim MIN
win by exchange gewrixlan *w* PFM
win by fighting gefeohtan *3* PFM
  geslēan *6*
  gewinnan *3*
win by going gefēran *w* PFM
win by riding geærnan *w* PFM
winch wince *(f)* TOO
wind blǣst *(m)* SKY
  fnǣst *(m)*
  wind *(n)*
  windan *3* GO
wind instrument sweglhorn *(m)* REC
wind round bewindan *3* GO
wind-propelled lyftgeswenced SKY
window ēagðȳrel *(n)* HSE
windpipe þrotbolla *(m)* BOD
  windǣddre *(f)*
windy windig SKY
wine wīn *(n)* EAT
wine-drinking wīngedrinc *(n)* EAT
wine-drinking hall wīnsæl *(n)* EAT
wings feðerhoma *(m)* ANI
  fiðru *(npl)* BOD
wink wincian *w* SEE
winsome wynsum LOV
winsome female wynmǣg *(f)* LOV
winter winter *(m,n)* TIM
winter, become winterlǣcan *w* BEC
winter, spend the
  oferwintrian *(w)* TIM
winter shower winterscūr *(m)* SKY
winter's hour winterstund *(f)* SKY
wintertime wintertīd *(f)* TIM
wintry winterlīc SKY
wire wīr *(m)* TOO
wire fence eodorwīr *(m)* LAN
wisdom rǣd *(f)* AGR, KNO
  snyttru *(f)*
  wīsdōm *(m)*

wise frōd MIN
 glēaw
 snoterlīc KNO
 snottor
 wīs(līc)
 wītig
wise man wita *(m)* KNO
 witega *(m)*
wise of mind ferhōglēaw MIN
wish willan *a* LOV
 wȳscan *w* THI
wit witt *(n)* KNO, MIN
witch wicca *(m)* CHU
 wicce *(f)*
witchcraft lyblāc *(n,m)* CHU
with mid
 wiþ
with difficulty earfoðlīce EVL
 unsōfte
with love frēondlīc LOV
with one accord ānmōdlīc MIN
with the sun sunganges GO
with the tide æfter faroðe WAT
withhold gestȳran *w* EVL
 oðhealdan *7*
 oðwendan *w*
within (on-, in-, be-)innan POS
without būtan
without delay unaswundenlīc TIM
without dishonour unforcūð LRD
without inheritance ierfelēas WEA
without money feohlēas WEA
withstand wiðstondan *6* POS
withy wīþig *(m)* PLA
witness gewita *(m)* LAW
woad wurma *(m)* PLA
 wurme *(f)*
woe wēa *(m)* EVL, MIN
wolf wulf *(m)* ANI
wolfish wylfen ANI
woman cwēn *(f)* KIN
 mǣg *(f)*
 wīf *(n)*
 wīfmann *(m)*

womb cwiða *(m)* BOD
 hrif *(f)*
wonder wundor *(n)* GD
 wundrian *w*
wonderful wunderful GD
 wunderlīc
wondrous wrǣtlīc ART
wood bearu *(m)* LAN
 holt *(n)*
 holtwudu *(m)*
 hyrst *(m)*
 wuduholt *(n)*
wood for a house boldtimber *(n)* HSE
wood for an archway
 bōhtimber *(n)* HSE
wood, made of trēowen MAT
wood sorrel ðrilēfe *(mpl?)* PLA
woodbine wudubend *(m)* PLA
woodcock holthana *(m)* ANI
wooden trēowen MAT
wooden piece bēam *(m)* HSE
wooden ship bēam *(m)* WAT
woodland wudulond *(n)* LAN
woodpecker fīna *(m)* ANI
 higera *(m)*
woodruff wudurofe *(f)* PLA
woodsman wudere *(m)* WOR
woody nightshade ælfþone *(m)* PLA
wool wull *(f)* MAT
wool, made of wullen MAT
Worcestershire
 Wireceastrescīr *(f)* STR
word word *(n)* SAY
work āwyrcan *w* WOR
 beweorcan *w*
 geweorcan *w*
 gewinn *(n)*
 (ge)weorc *(n)*
 winnan *3*
 wyrcean *w*
work (take effect) fremman *w* AIL
workman bīgengere *(m)* WOR
 wyrhta *(m)*
workmanship geweorc *(n)* WOR
workshop oden *(f)* HSE, WOR

world eorðe *(f)* LAN
  gesceaft *(f)*
  middangeard *(m)*
  worold *(f)*
worldly eorðlīc CHU
worldly kingdom
  eorðrīce *(n)* CHU
worm wyrm *(m)* ANI
wormwood wermōd *(m)* PLA
worry caru *(f)* EVL, NEE
  gedrēfednes *(f)*
  ymbhoga *(m)*
worse wiersa
worse, become wyrsian *w* BEC, EVL
  yfelian *w*
worship begān *a* GD
  weorðung *(f)*
  begong *(m)* CHU
  gerihte *(n)*
worst wierst
worth weorð GD
worth remembering
  gemyndwyrðe THI
worthless fracod EVL, WEA
  unnyt
worthlessness īdel *(n)* EVL
  īdelnes *(f)*
worthy weorð WEA
wound āmyrran *w* EVL,
  benn *(f)* AIL, WAR
  dolh *(n)*
  sār *(f)*
  sārgian *w*
  tǣsan *w*
  wund *(f)*
  (ge)wundian *w*
wound in the eye ēagwund *(f)* AIL
wound in the tendon
  seonobenn *(f)* AIL
wound mortally
  forwundian *w* EVL, WAR
wounded wund AIL
wounded by swordstroke
  sweordwund AIL
woven twice twiðrāwen CLO

wrap (ge)wrēon *1* CLO
wreath wriða *(m)* CLO
wren wrenna *(m)* ANI
  wrenne *(f)*
wrest from beslēan *6* WAR
  gewinnan *3*
wrestler wrāxlere *(m)* WAR
  wrǣstliend *(m)*
wretched fēasceaft EVL
wright wyrhta *(m)* WOR
wring wringan *3* WAT
wrist wrist *(f)* BOD
write gesettan *w* WRI
  wrītan *1*
write out āwrītan *1* WRI
writer bōcere *(m)* WOR
  wrītere *(m)* WRI
writing bōccræft *(m)* WRI
  gewrit *(n)*
  stafas *(mpl)*
writing instrument græf *(n)* WRI
writing tablet weaxbred *(n)* WRI
wrong misdǣd *(f)* EVL
  on wōh
  tō wōge
  wrang
wrongful unriht LAW
  wrang
wrongful custom unsidu *(f)* LAW
wrongfully conceal
  forhelan *4* LAW, SEE
wrongthinking gedwild *(n)* THI
  gedwola *(m)*
wychelm wice *(m,f)* PLA

Y

yard geard *(m)* HSE
yardarm seglrōd *(f)* WAT
yarrow gearwe *(f)* PLA
yawn gīnan *w* SLP
year gēar *(n)* TIM
yearn for giernan *w* LOV
yearning longað *(m)* LOV

yeast beorma *(m)* EAT
  dærst *(f)*
  gist *(m)*
  hæf *(m)*
  ðæsma *(m)*
yell giellan *w* CAL
  gylian *w*
yellow fealu COL
  geolu
yellow, become geolwian *w* BEC
yeoman gebūr *(m)* LAN
yes! gīese
yesterday gierstandæg *(m)* TIM
  giestran
yet gīen TIM
  gīet
  hwæðre
  swāðēah
yew ēoh *(m)* PLA
  īw *(m)*
yield up gieldan *3* WEA
yoke iucian *w* ANI, WOR
yolk geoloca *(m)* EAT
Yorkshire Eoforwīcscīr *(f)* STR
you þū, git, gē *(nom.)*
  þē, inc, ēow *(acc. dat.)*
  þec, incet, ēowic *(acc.)*
young geong TIM
young bird bridd *(m)* ANI
young kinsman mǣgcild *(n)* KIN
young man cniht *(m)* KIN
  geoguð *(f)*
  hægsteald *(m)*
  hyse *(m)*
youngster cnapa *(m)* KIN
  cniht *(m)*
your þīn, incer, ēower *(gen.)*
youth geogoð *(f)* TIM
Yule Gēol *(n)* TIM

Z

zeal ellenwōdnes *(f)* MIN
  geornfulnes *(f)* ASK
zealous geornful ASK
  nēodful MIN

Thesaurus

Word Lists

Thesaurus - Word Lists

AGREE

acquiesce geþwǣrian *w*
underhnīgan *1*
advice mǣðel *(n)*
rǣd *(m)*
advise gelǣran *w*
rǣdan *w*
advocacy forspǣc *(f)*
agree gecweðan *5*
geðwǣrian *w*
ðingian *w*
agree to geðafian *w*
agree upon āstihtan *w*
agreement ānnes *(f)*
geðwǣrnes *(f)*
arbitration sōm *(f)*
argument geflit *(n)*
mǣl *(f)*
cause intinga *(m)*
cause for complaint inca *(m)*
charm ōlǣcung *(f)*
chide (ge)cīdan *w*
coerce geðȳn *w*
complain gecīdan *w*
concern ontimber *(n)*
concord geðwǣrnes *(f)*
sibsumnes *(f)*
consent geðafung *(f)*
ðafung *(f)*
consent to ðafian *w*
consenter geðafa *(m)*
contend flītan *1*
debate mōtian *w*
ðingian *w*
disagree wiðcweðan *5*
discourse mǣl *(f)*
dispute fettian *w*
geflit *(n)*
wiþcweþan *5*

eloquence getingnes *(f)*
eloquent cwedol
entrust befæstan *w*
equal gelīca *(m)*
gemǣcc
excuse lād *(f)*
exhort rǣdan *w*
favour forspǣc *(f)*
flatter ōlǣcan *w*
flattery ōlǣcung *(f)*
force geðȳn *w*
ðrēa *(m)*
ðrēat *(m)*
harangue mǣlan *w*
issue geðinge *(n)*
intinga *(m)*
ðing *(n)*
matter geðinge *(n)*
intinga *(m)*
ontimber *(n)*
meeting place meðelstede *(m)*
persuade gelǣran *w*
persuasive getinge
pledge wedd *(n)*
prevent forwiernan *w*
promise behātan *7*
wedd *(n)*
prove āfandian *w*
quarrel beadurūn *(f)*
cīdan *w*
geflit *(n)*
reconcile gesēman *w*
refuse forsacan *6*
(for)wiernan *w*
refuse with contempt forhogian *w*
repudiate āwǣgan *w*
settle ārǣdan *7*
gecweðan *5*
sēman *w*
ðingian *w*

speak mǣlan *w*
speech mǣl *(f)*
subject geðinge *(n)*
unity ānnes *(f)*
wisdom rǣd *(f)*

AIL

ache acan *6*
  ece *(m)*
  wærc *(m)*
addicted to gelenge
afflict dreccan *w*
afterbirth hala *(m)*
ail ādlian *w*
  yfelian *w*
asthma angbrēost *(n)*
  nyrwett *(n)*
atrophy smalung *(f)*
bandage onwrīðung *(f)*
  wrīðan *1*
barren gǣsne
be sick ādlian *w*
  sīclian *w*
  spiwian *w*
become pimply pypelian *w*
become poisonous gehwelian *w*
bedridden person beddridda *(m)*
bind a salve to forlecgan *w*
blain blegen *(f)*
bleed blēdan *w*
blind blind
boil blegen *(f)*
bow bȳgan *w*
breathing difficulty hrēoung *(f)*
bruise lǣl *(f)*
  tōbrȳsan *w*
canker cancor *(m)*

catarrh brǣc *(n)*
  mǣldropa i(m)
cattle disease orfcwealm *(m)*
chillblain æcelma *(m)*
chronic ungewendendlīc
cleanse geclǣnsian *w*
clear one's throat hrǣcca *(m)*
clot clott *(m)*
constipated fæst
constipation gebind *(n)*
  heardnys *(f)*
contain (a disease) ablendan *w*
cool (grow cold) cōlian *w*
corruption brosnung *(f)*
cough cohhetan *w*
  hrǣcan *w*
coughing gebrǣceo *(f)*
  hrāca *(m)*
cramp fortogennys *(f)*
  hramma *(m)*
  swiung *(f)*
cripple bȳgan *w*
  crēopere *(m)*
cure gebētan *w*
deaf dēaf
depilatory cream pillsāpe *(f)*
diarrhoea unryne *(m)*
  ūtsiht *(f)*
disability ālēfednes *(f)*
disable sārgian *w*
disease ādl *(f)*
  broc *(n)*
  (un)coðu *(f)*
  unhǣlu *(f)*
diseased ādlīg
  ongeflogen
dizziness swīma *(m)*
doctor lǣce *(m)*
drowsiness hnappung *(f)*
drug-taking lyblāc *(m,n)*
dumb dumb
effective fremful
epilepsy fyllewærc *(m)*
face powder nebsealf *(f)*
fainted geswogen

fever fefor *(m)*
fit fyllewærc *(m)*
fracture a bone brecan 2
  tōclēofan 2
fractured skull hēafodbryce *(m)*
giddiness swinglung *(f)*
gout fōtādl *(f)*
hare-lip hærsceard *(n)*
head cold gepos *(n)*
head of a boil dott *(m)*
heal batian *w*
  ge)hǣlan *w*
  hālian *w*
healing hālwende
health gesundfulnes *(f)*
  · gesyntu *(f)*
  hǣl(u) *(f)*
healthy gesund
  (ge)hāl
  onsund
heartburn heortēce *(m)*
herb lēac *(n)*
  wyrt *(f)*
herbal infusion wyrtdrenc *(m)*
hiccup ælfsogoða *(m)*
  gicða *(m)*
  sūgan 2
hump-backed gehoferod
ill ādlig
  sēoc
illness, lying-in leger *(n)*
improve gebētan *w*
impurity wīdl *(m,n)*
incurable unhālwendlīc
indigestion hrēa *(m)*
infirmity mettrumnes *(f)*
  untrymnes *(f)*
inflict on onbelǣdan *w*
insomnia slǣplēast *(f)*
inward incund
itch cleweða *(m)*
  giccan *w*
jaundice gealādl *(f)*
lame healt
leper hrēofla *(m)*

limp lemphealt
medicine lācnung *(f)*
menstruation mōnaðādl *(f)*
mucus mǣldropa *(m)*
  snofl *(m)*
  snot *(m)*
nausea snoffa *(m)*
  spiwe *(m)*
  wlǣtta *(m)*
nauseous wealg
nurse gelācnian *w*
ointment sealf *(f)*
  smyrung *(f)*
pain bite *(m)*
  sār *(f)*
  wærc *(m)*
pain in the buttocks endewærc *(m)*
painful sār
  smeart
  swǣre
painless unsār
paleness ablǣcnys *(f)*
palsy dropa *(m)*
paralysis lyftēdl *(m)*
paralytic eorðcryppel *(m)*
pestilence cwild *(m)*
  moncwild *(m)*
  steorfa *(m)*
phlegm hrǣcung *(f)*
pill posling *(m)*
pimple nebcorn *(n)*
plaster plaster *(n)*
pock pocc *(m)*
poultice clām *(m)*
  onlegen *(f)*
pound to a powder cnucian *w*
  cnuwian *w*
prepare gegearwian *w*
prickle pīl *(m)*
purify geclǣnsian *w*
pus dylsta *(m)*
  geolstor *(n)*
  hora *(m)*
  lyswen *(n)*
rash hrēofl *(f)*

relief līþung *(f)*
relieve gelīþigian *w*
remedy bōt *(f)*
  lǣcedōm *(m)*
restore the sight onlīhtan *w*
retch hrǣcan *w*
ringworm rengwyrm *(m)*
  teter *(m)*
ruptured healede
salutory hālwende
salve sealf *(f)*
scab hrȳfing *(f)*
  sceab *(m)*
scar dolh *(m)*
scaly scurfed
sciatica hypebānece *(m)*
scurf scurf *(m)*
short of breath swōretendlī
sick sēoc
  untrum
sickness mettrumnes *(f)*
  sēocnes *(f)*
side-ache sīdece *(m)*
  sīdwærc *(m)*
sneeze fnēsan *5*
soothe (ge)smēðan *w*
sore dolh *(n)*
  sār *(f)*
sore throat hrǣcgebrǣc *(n)*
sound (ge)hāl
  gesund
  onsund
spasm hramma *(m)*
  swiung *(f)*
spit spīwan *1*
splint spilc *(m)*
stitch stice *(m)*
stomach-ache hriftēung *(f)*
  hrifwerc *(m)*
strangury ðæs migðan earfoðlicnys *(f)*
strengthen gestrangian *w*
stye stīgend *(m)*
subside drūsian *w*
suffocate forþylman *w*
suppurate gehwelian *w*

swell ðindan *3*
swelling swyle *(m)*
swollen gland cumul *(n)*
swollen-eyed tornig
swooning geswōgung *(f)*
tetanus oferbæcgetēung *(f)*
thrive geðēon *1*
throb slecgettan *w*
tonic leohtdrenc *(m)*
treat, heal lācnian *w*
twinge twengan *w*
ulcer dēadspring *(m)*
  dolh *(n)*
uninjured undered
  unwemme
unwell ādlig
vex dreccan *w*
vomit spīwða *(m)*
wart puduc *(m)*
  wearte *(f)*
wen wenn *(f)*
whole gesund
  hāl
work, (take effect) fremman *w*
wound benn *(f)*
  sār *(f)*
  sārgian *w*
  wund *(f)*
wound in the eye ēagwund *(f)*
wound in the tendon seonobenn *(f)*
wounded wund
wounded by swordstroke sweordwund

ANIMAL

adder næddre *(f)*
animal dēor *(m)*
ant æmette *(f)*
anthill æmetbedd *(n)*
ape apa *(m)*
ass esol *(m)*
  esole *(f)*
badger brocc *(m)*
bark beorcan 2
barking beorc *(f)*
bat hrēaðmūs *(m)*
bear beorn *(m)*
  bera *(m)*
beast dēor *(m)*
beaver befor *(m)*
bee bēo *(f)*
beekeeper bēoceorl *(m)*
  bēocere *(m)*
beetle budda *(m)*
  wifel *(m)*
bill, beak bile *(m)*
  neb *(n)*
bird fugol *(m)*
bitch bicce *(f)*
  tife *(f)*
bittern hæferblǣte *(f)*
blowfly smegawyrm *(m)*
boar bār *(m)*
  eofor *(m)*
brand mearcian *w*
bridle brīdel *(m)*
bristle byrst *(f)*
buck bucca *(m)*
bull fearr *(m)*
  hriðer *(n)*
bumblebee dora *(m)*
burbot ǣlepūte *(f)*
butterfly buterflēoge *(f)*
  fifalde *(f)*
buzzard mūshafoc *(n)*
calf cealf *(n)*
camel olfend(a) *(m)*
cat catt *(m)*

catte *(f)*
catch birds fuglian *w*
caterpillar cawelwyrm *(m)*
  lēafwyrm *(m)*
  mǣlsceafa *(m)*
cattle cēap *(m)*
  feoh *(n)*
  nēat *(n)*
  nȳten *(n)*
  orf *(n)*
cattle disease orfcwealm *(m)*
cattleshed scipen *(f)*
chaffinch ceaffinc *(m)*
chew the cud eodorcan *w*
chicken cicen *(n)*
chough cēo *(m)*
cock cocc *(m)*
cockchafer (eorð)ceafor *(m)*
cockle sǣcocc *(m)*
cormorant scræb *(m)*
cow cū *(f)*
  hriðer *(n)*
crab crabba *(m)*
  hæfern *(m)*
crane cran *(m)*
creature gesceaft *(f)*
  gesceap *(n)*
  iht *(f,n)*
crow crāwe *(f)*
cuckoo gēac *(m)*
curlew hwilpe *(f)*
cuttlefish wāsescite *(f)*
dark-coated salo(wig)pād
deer hēorot *(m)*
den denn *(n)*
dog hund *(m)*
dog collar hoppe *(f)*
dolphin mereswīn *(n)*
dormouse sisemūs *(m)*
dove culfre *(f)*
dragon draca *(m)*
  līgdraca *(m)*
  wyrm *(m)*
drake ened *(m)*
droppings tyrdelu *(npl)*

drove, herd drāf *(f)*
duck dūce *(f)*
  ened *(f)*
dung beetle tordwifel *(m)*
eagle earn *(m)*
earthworm angeltwicce *(m,f)*
  regnwyrm *(m)*
earwig ēarwicga *(m)*
eat like an animal fretan *5*
eel ǣl(fix) *(m)*
elephant elpend *(m)*
elk eolh *(m)*
ewe ēowu *(f)*
feather feðer *(n)*
fin finn *(m)*
finned finiht
fish fisc *(m)*
  fiscian *w*
  laguswimmend *(m)*
fishbait ǣs *(n)*
fisherman fiscere *(m)*
fish-hook angil *(m)*
fishing fiscoð *(m)*
flat-fish fag *(f)*
flea flēa *(m)*
fledgling bridd *(n)*
fleece flīes *(n)*
flock heord *(f)*
flounder flōc *(n)*
fluke (fish) flōc *(n)*
fluke (worm) liferwyrm *(m)*
fly flēoge *(f)*
fly-net flēohnet *(n)*
foal fola *(m)*
fourlegged fiðerfēte
fox fox *(m)*
frog fenȳce *(f)*
  frogga *(m)*
  frosc *(m)*
  tosca *(m)*
  ȳce *(m)*
gadfly bēaw *(m)*
game huntung *(f)*
gander gandra *(m)*
gnat gnæt *(m)*

goat gāt *(m)*
goose gōs *(f)*
grasshopper hyllehāma *(m)*
  staða *(m)*
graze ettan *w*
grey-coated hasupād
grunt grymetian *w*
gull mǣw *(m)*
halter hælfter *(f)*
hare hara *(m)*
hart heort *(m)*
hawk hafoc *(m)*
hedgehog hattefagol *(m?)*
  hærenfagol *(m?)*
  īgel *(m)*
hen hænn *(f)*
  henfugol *(m)*
herd drāf *(f)*
  heord *(f)*
herring hǣring *(m)*
hide fell *(n)*
hive hȳf *(f)*
hog fearh *(m)*
horn horn *(m)*
hornet hyrnetu *(f)*
horse ēoh *(m)*
  hors *(n)*
  mearh *(m)*
  wicg *(n)*
horseback bōg *(m)*
howl ðēotan *2*
hunt with a bow ofscēotan *2*
ibex firgenbucca *(m)*
insect wyrm *(m)*
jackdaw ceahhe *(f)*
jay higera *(m)*
kid ticcen *(n)*
kite glida *(m)*
lamb lamb *(n)*
lamprey lamprede *(f)*
lion lēo *(m,f)*
lizard āðexe *(f)*
lobster lopystre *(f)*
louse lūs *(f)*
louse-eggs hnitu *(f)*

low hlōwan *7*
lynx lox *(m)*
maggot maða *(m)*
mare mȳre *(f)*
marten mearð *(m)*
mastiff ryðða *(m)*
midge gnæt *(m)*
  micg *(m)*
milk meolcan *3*
minnow myne *(m)*
mole moldeweorpere *(m)*
moorhen wōrhenn *(f)*
mosquito micg *(m)*
moth moððe *(f)*
mount gehlēapan *7*
mouse mūs *(m)*
mouse's squeaking hwicung *(f)*
mule mūl *(m)*
mullet hacod *(m)*
mussel musle *(f)*
neigh hnǣgan *w*
nest nest *(n)*
newt efeta *(m)*
nightingale nihtegala *(m)*
nit hnitu *(f)*
otter ottor *(m)*
ouzle ōsle *(f)*
owl ūle *(f)*
ox hriðer *(n)*
  oxa *(m)*
oyster ostre *(f)*
pack-horse ealfara *(m)*
peacock pawa *(m)*
pelican dūfedoppa *(m)*
periwinkle pinewincla *(m)*
pheasant wildhænn *(f)*
  wōrhana *(m)*
pig swīn *(n)*
pigeon culfre *(f)*
pike hacod *(m)*
plaice fag *(f)*
porpoise mereswīn *(n)*
poultry hāmhænn *(f)*
prey huntung *(f)*
quail edischenn *(f)*

queen bee bēomōder *(f)*
ram weðer *(m)*
raven crāwe *(f)*
  hræfn *(m)*
  hremn *(m)*
rayfish ruhha *(m)*
reindeer hrān *(m)*
reins brīdelðwang *(m)*
reptile slincend *(m)*
roar rȳn *w*
robin ruddoc *(m)*
roedeer rā *(m)*
  rǣge *(f)*
salmon leax *(m)*
sandmartin stæðswealwe *(f)*
sardine smelt *(m)*
seabird brimfugol *(m)*
seal seolh *(m)*
sealskin flīes *(n)*
she-wolf wylfen *(f)*
sheep scēap *(m)*
shell sciell *(f)*
shellfish scilfisc *(m)*
shrew screwa *(m)*
slowworm slāwyrm *(m)*
snail snægl *(m)*
snake snaca *(m)*
  wyrm *(m)*
snare begrynian *w*
  grin *(n)*
sow sū *(f)*
  sugu *(f)*
sparrow hrandsparwa *(m)*
  spearwa *(m)*
  sugga *(m)*
species of animal dēorcynn *(n)*
spider āttorcoppe *(f)*
  gongewæfre *(f)*
  hunta *(m)*
  lobbe *(f)*
spider's web renge *(f)*
sprat sprott *(m)*
squirrel ācweorna *(m)*
stable horsern *(n)*

stag heort *(m)*
  stagga *(m)*
stallion stēda *(m)*
  stōdhors *(n)*
starling stær(ling) *(m)*
sturgeon styria *(m)*
suckling diend *(m)*
swallow swealwe *(f)*
swan ilfetu *(f)*
  swan *(m)*
swarm of bees bēogang *(m)*
  sīgewīf *(n)*
swine swīn *(n)*
tail steort *(m)*
  tægl *(m)*
tame tam
  temian *w*
  temman *w*
tench slīw *(m)*
tern stearn *(m)*
threadworm ficwyrm *(m)*
thrush ðrostle *(f)*
tick ticia *(m)*
tiger tigris *(m)*
toad tāde *(f)*
  tosca *(m)*
tortoise byrdling *(m)*
trap træppe *(f)*
trout sceota *(m)*
tusk tūx *(m)*
unyoke unscennan *w*
venomous ætrig
vixen fyxe *(f)*
vulture earngēap *(f)*
  glida *(m)*
walrus horshwæl *(m)*
wasp wæps *(m)*
watersnake wæternǣddre *(f)*
weasel weosule *(f)*
web webb *(n)*
weevil wifel *(m)*
wether weðer *(m)*
whale hron(fix) *(m)*
  hwæl *(m)*
whelk weoloc *(m)*

whelp hwelp *(m)*
wild wilde
wild animal dēor *(n)*
  wilder, wildedēor *(n)*
wings feðerhoma *(m)*
wolf wulf *(m)*
wolfish wylfen
woodcock holthana *(m)*
woodpecker fīna *(m)*
  higera *(m)*
worm wyrm *(m)*
wren wrenna *(m)*
  wrenne *(f)*
yoke iucian *w*
young bird bridd *(m)*

ART

adorn gerēnian *w*
  (ge)glengan *w*
  (ge)gyrwan *w*
  hrēodan *2*
  tēon *w*
  weorðian *w*
adorned fāg
  gehroden
alike gelīc
  onlīc
angle hwemm *(m)*
appearance ansīen *(f,n)*
  hīw *(n)*
  wlite *(m)*
art cræft *(m)*
  wrǣtt *(f)*
beautiful wlitig
  wrǣst(lic)

beautify geglengan *w*
  (ge)gyrwan *w*
  wlitigian *w*
beauty wlite *(m)*
bejewelled sinchroden
bracelet bēag *(m)*
  būl *(m)*
  dalc *(m)*
brooch dalc *(m)*
circular sinewealt
collar bēag *(m)*
colour hīw *(n)*
coloured fāh
craft cræft *(m)*
create tēon *w*
decorate glengan *w*
  mearcian *w*
decorated fāg
  gehyrsted
decorated item mǣl *(n)*
draw ātīefran *w*
earring ēarhring *(m)*
emblem of victory sigesceorp *(n)*
filigree wīr *(m)*
  wundengold *(n)*
flag fana *(m)*
gemstone gimm *(m)*
  gimstān *(m)*
gold-studded fǣted
interlace ornament wyrmlīc *(n)*
jewellery frætwa *(fpl)*
likeness gelīcnes *(f)*
  onlīcnes *(f)*
mark mǣl *(n)*
national treasure ðēodgestrēon *(n)*
nature swelcnes *(f)*
ornament hyrst *(f)*
  wrǣtt *(f)*
ornamented gehroden
ornaments glenge *(m)*
paint fǣgan *w*
  mētan *w*
plain ānfeald
plain, unadorned unorne
portrait gelīcnes *(f)*

precious dēorweorðe
precious thing māððum *(m)*
  māððumǣht *(f)*
princely treasure ðēodenmāðm *(m)*
quality swelcnes *(f)*
ring bēah *(m)*
  hring *(m)*
  wealte *(f)*
round sinetrundel
  sinewealt
sculpture græft *(m,n,f)*
seal insigle *(n)*
shape hīw *(n)*
signet insigle *(n)*
similar gelīc
  onlīc
similarity onlīcnes *(f)*
skill cræft *(m)*
  list *(f)*
skillful gelǣred
solid gold eallgylden
splendid wrǣtlīc
square fēowerscȳte
statue onlīcnes *(f)*
straighten gerihtlǣcan *w*
striped stafod
treasure frætwa *(fpl)*
  māðm *(m)*
  sincfæt *(n)*
triangular þrēohyrne
trophy myrcels *(m)*
unlike ungelīc
wondrous wrǣtlīc

ASK

acceptable ðoncwyrðe
accepted folccūð
  freōndlic
accepted (as guilty) geresp
allure spanan 6
alms ælmesse (f)
answer andswaru (f)
  ondswerian 6
  ondwyrdan w
  ondwyrde (n)
ask ācsian w
  āhsian w
  āscian w
ask for (ā)biddan 5
asking ācsung (f)
assemble gesomnian w
assent geðafung (f)
attract spannan 6
avarice gītsung (f)
beg biddan 5
  giernan w
beggar ælmesmann (m)
  wǣdla (m)
behest hǣs (f)
carry a message geǣrendian w
cause intinga (m)
claimant onspecend (m)
coerce geðȳn w
command bebēodan 2
  diht (m)
  hātan 7
  hǣs (f)
compel bǣdan w
consent geðafian w
  ðafung (f)
contented person geðafa (m)
corresponding tōgeanes
curiosity fyrwit (n)
deny ætsacan 6
deprived of gǣsne
desire giernan w
desirous frymdig, fyrmdig
discover fandian w

dispute fettian w
eager georn(ful)
eagerness geornnes (f)
enquire befrīnan 1
  frignan 3
entice āspanan 6
entreat biddan 5
  healsian w
entreaty ācsung (f)
  healsung (f)
errand ǣrende (n)
favour liss (f)
find out geascian w
  gewitan w
  onfindan 3
flatter ōlǣcan w
follow æfterspyrian w
gift selen (f)
grant gescēawian w
  geunnan w
  lēon w
  selen (f)
grant a tithe getīðian w
granted gifeðe
granter geðafa (m)
grateful ðoncful
gratitude ðoncung (f)
greed gīfernes (f)
greedy gīfre
  grǣdig
hear about geāscian w
in exchange tō gehwearfe
in reply tōgeanes
inquisitive frymdig, fyrmdig
inquisitiveness fyrwitnes (f)
intercede geðingian w
investigate fandian w
  fricgan 5
  gecunnian w
invite laðian w
knock cnossian w
  gecnucian w
  gecnycc (n)
lack gād (n)

learn geāscian *w*
  gefrignan *3*
  geleornian *w*
look (out) for wlātian *w*
matter intinga *(m)*
message ǣrende *(n)*
offer bēodan *2*
oratory gebedhūs *(n)*
order bebod *(n)*
permission lēaf *(f)*
permit līefan *w*
plead ðingian *w*
pray gebiddan *5*
prayer bēn *(f)*
  gebed *(n)*
praying gebedrǣden *(f)*
promise behātan *7*
propitiation ōlǣcung *(f)*
proven geresp
request bēn *(f)*
  biddan *5*
  healsian *w*
require biddan *5*
reward (ed)lēan *(n)*
  lēanian *w*
right to alms ælmesriht *(n)*
satisfied with gehealden on
seduce forsponan *6*
seek sēcan *w*
summon (ā)bannan *7*
  bēodan *2*
survey gehāwian *w*
test cunnian *w*
thank geðoncian *w*
thankful ðoncful
thankfulness ðoncung *(f)*
thanks ðonc *(m)*
tracker spyremon *(m)*
urge manian
  ðȳwan *w*
zeal geornfulnes *(f)*
zealous geornful

BECOME

add ēacian *w*
be possible onhagian *w*
become (ge)weorðan *3*
become better gōdian *w*
become bigger weaxan *7*
  ȳcan *w*
become cold cōlian *w*
become dark nīpan *1*
  sweorcan *3*
become day dagian *w*
become divided gedǣlan *w*
  tōtwǣman *w*
become drunk oferdrencan *w*
become hard hyrdan *w*
  stīðian *w*
become heavy hefigian *w*
become known gecȳðan *w*
  geopenian *w*
become larger ēacnian *w*
become less sweðrian *w*
  (ge)wanian *w*
become loose tōslūpan *2*
  wagian *w*
become lost losian *w*
become molten gemeltan *w*
become new ednīwian *w*
become pimply pypelian *w*
become poisonous gehwilian *w*
become red ārēodian *w*
become remiss dwellan *w*
  wandian *w*
become ruined forweorðan *3*
become sick ādlian *w* BEC
  sīclian *w*

become small dwīnan *1*
  lȳtlian *w*
become soft lissan *w*
become strong elnian *w*
become tired tēorian *w*
become warm wyrman *w*
become weak onwǣcan *w*
  sweðrian *w*
become wealthy gestrȳnan *w*
  spēdan *w*
become weary mēðian *w*
  sweðrian *w*
become winter winterlǣcan *w*
become worse wyrsian *w*
  yfelian *w*
become yellow geolwian *w*
befall gebyrian *w*
  getīmian *w*
change āwendan *w*
  gebregd *(n)*
  (ge)hweorfan *w*
  onwendan *w*
condition hād *(m)*
  ðing *(n)*
consequence finta *(m)*
course of events wyrd *(f)*
decrease lȳtlian *(w)*
event gelimp *(n)*
  wend *(m)*
  wyrd *(f)*
fate gesceaft *(m,n,f)*
  gesceap *(n)*
  orlæg *(n)*
  wyrd *(f)*
get drunk druncnian *w*
go wrong mislimpan *3*
  mistīmian *w*
  tōsǣlan *w*
grow weaxan *7*
happen gebyrian *w*
  gegān *a*
  gelimpan *3*
  (ge)sǣlan *w*
  weorðan *3*
impossibility unmihtilicnys *(f)*

lessening wanung *(f)*
lot hlot *(n)*
miscarry mislimpan *3*
  tōsǣlan *w*
movement gebregd *(n)*
occurence gelimp *(n)*
reality swelcnes *(f)*
result finta *(m)*
shrink scrincan *3*
state ðing *(n)*
state of affairs steall *(m)*
transform forbrēdan *3*
  forhwierfan *w*
  forscyppan *6*
turn gehwierfan *w*
vary hweorfan *3*

BLAME

accuse oncunnan *w*
accuse wrongly forwrēgan *w*
accuser onspecend *(m)*
  tēond *(m)*
  wrēgend *(m)*
admonish monian *w*
  mynian *w*
  (æt)wītan *1*
ashamed scōmig
blame leahtrian *w*
  oncunnan *w*
  tǣlan *w*
  (æt)wītan *1*
blameless bilewit
  orleahtre
  ungyltig
condemn niðerian *w*
deride bismrian *w*
  hospettan *w*
  hyrwan *w*

disgraced ǣwiscmōd
disgraced person nīðing *(m)*
disgraceful scandlīc
dismiss tōwurpan *3*
earn infamy word gespringan *3*
harangue mǣlan *w*
humiliation hȳnðu *(f)*
public disgrace woroldscamu *(f)*
put to shame ofscamian *w*
   scendan *w*
rebuke lēanian *w*
revenge wrecan *5*
revile leahtrian *w*
rue hrēowan *2*
speak mǣlan *w*

BODY

ankle anclēow *(f)*
anus earsgang *(m)*
   setl *(n)*
   ūtgang *(m)*
arm earm *(m)*
armpit ōcusta *(m)*
   ōxn *(f)*
arse ears *(m)*
back bæc *(m)*
   hrycg *(m)*
bald blerig
   calu
beak bile *(f)*
   neb *(n)*
beard beard *(m)*
behead beheafdian *w*
bladder blǣdre *(f)*
   tyncen *(n)*
blind blind
blood blōd *(n)*

heolfor *(m,n)*
stēam *(m)*
swāt *(m)*
blood-stained swātfāg
bloody drēorig
blush rudu *(f)*
bodily līchomlīc
body bodig *(n)*
   feorhbold *(n)*
   feorhhord *(n)*
   feorhhūs *(n)*
   flǣsc *(n)*
   līc *(n)*
   līcfæt *(n)*
   līchoma *(m)*
bone bān *(n)*
bonemarrow mearg *(m)*
bosom bearm *(m)*
   bōsm *(m)*
   fæðm *(m)*
bottom botm *(m)*
bowel innoð *(m,f)*
braided-haired wundenlocc
brain brægen *(n)*
   hærn *(m)*
breast bōsm *(m)*
   brēost *(n)*
   titt *(m)*
breath ǣþm *(m)*
broad-bosomed sīdfæðme
broken (of a limb) forod
broken-legged scancforod
brow brū *(fpl)*
   ēagbrǣw *(m)*
bucktoothed twiseltōþ
canine tooth tūx *(m)*
cheek heagospind *(n)*
   hlēor *(n)*
   wange *(n)*
chest brēost *(npl)*
   brēostcofa *(m)*
   hreðer *(n)*
chin cinn *(n)*
chinbone cinbān *(n)*
claw clēa *(m)*

collarbone wiðobān *(m)*
corporal flæsclic
  līchomlīc
cut one's hair efsian *w*
dark-haired dox
defecate gedrītan *l*
  scītan *l*
defecation astyrung *(f)*
diaphragm midhriðre *(n)*
dung gor *(n)*
  meox *(n)*
ear eare *(n)*
elbow elnboga *(m)*
excrement þost *(m)*
eye ēage *(n)*
eyesocket ēahhring *(m)*
face nebb *(n)*
  ondwlita *(m)*
  onsīen *(f)*
fat-legged spærlīred
fiery-haired fȳrfeaxen
finger finger *(m)*
finger joint fingerlið *(m)*
firmness fæstnes *(f)*
fist fȳst *(f)*
flesh flǣsc *(n)*
foot fōt *(m)*
footstep fōtswæð *(n)*
forearm eln *(f)*
forefinger scytefinger *(m)*
forehead hnifel *(m)*
freckle cyrnel *(n)*
gain strength elnian *w*
gall gealla *(m)*
genitals gecyndelīcu *(npl)*
  gesceapu *(npl)*
genitals (male) geweald *(n)*
  ðēohgeweald *(npl)*
gills cīan *(mpl?)*
glance of the eye bryhtm *(m)*
gnash one's teeth gristbitian *w*
gore heolfor *(m,n)*
grey-eyed glæsenēage
grey-haired blondenfeax
  hār

groin scearu *(f)*
gullet edroc *(m)*
gum gōma *(m)*
gums tōþrēōman *(mpl)*
gut guttas *(mpl)*
  ðearm *(m)*
hair feax *(m)*
  hǣr *(n)*
hand folm *(f)*
  hand *(f)*
  mund *(f)*
hard skin wearr *(m)*
hare-lip hærsceard *(n)*
head hafela *(m)*
  heafod *(n)*
heart ferhð *(m,n)*
  heorte *(f)*
  hreðer *(n)*
heel hēla *(m)*
  hōh(fōt) *(m)*
  spure *(f)*
height leng *(f)*
hermaphrodite bǣddel *(m)*
hip hype *(f)*
hoof hōf *(m)*
hump hofor *(m)*
index finger scytefinger *(m)*
innards innoð *(m,f)*
instep fōtwylm *(m)*
internal incund
  innanweard
intestine rop *(m)*
jaw cēace *(f)*
  cinbān *(n)*
joint līð *(n,m)*
jowl gēagl *(m,n)*
kidney lundlaga *(m)*
knee cnēow *(n)*
kneecap hweorfbān *(n)*
lap bearm *(m)*
larynx ðrotbolla *(m)*
left hand side wynstra
  wynstre *(f)*
leg bān *(n)*
  scanca *(m)*

limb lið *(n)*
lip smǣr *(m)*
  weler *(m,f)*
little finger ēarclǣnsend *(m)*
liver lifer *(f)*
lock of hair windelocc *(m)*
loins lendenu *(npl)*
long-haired feaxed
lower leg fōtscanca *(m)*
lung lungen *(f)*
mane manu *(f)*
middle finger hālettend *(m)*
midriff midrif *(n)*
molar wongtōð *(m)*
mole māl *(n)*
moustache cenep *(m)*
mouth mūð *(m)*
muscle (biceps) mūs *(f)*
nail nægl *(m)*
naked nacod
  ungegearwod
nature gecynd *(n)*
  swelcnes *(f)*
navel nafela *(m)*
neck heals *(m)*
  swēora *(m)*
nerve sinu *(f)*
nipple delu *(f)*
  titstricel *(m)*
nose nebb *(n)*
  nosu *(f)*
nostril nosðyrl *(n)*
odour stenc *(m)*
palate gōma *(m)*
  mūðhrōf *(m)*
palm folm *(f)*
  handbrēd *(n)*
penis pintel *(m)*
  teors *(m)*
  wǣpen *(n)*
pot-bellied wæmbede
private part scamlim *(n)*
prone neowol
  nīwel
pudendum mægðblæd *(n)*

pupil of the eye sēo *(f)*
quality swelcnes *(f)*
radius (bone) hrēsel *(f)*
rectum bæcþearm *(m)*
reek rēocan 2
reproductive organ gecyndlim *(n)*
rib ribb *(n)*
right hand rihthand *(f)*
right hand side swīðra
sad-faced drēorighlēor
scrotum codd *(m)*
  herþbylg *(m)*
semen (gecyndelīc) sǣd *(n)*
sexual gecyndelīc
shape hīw *(n)*
shave besciran 4
shaven-headed homol
shin scīa *(m)*
shoulder bōg *(m)*
  eaxl *(f)*
  sculdor *(m)*
side healf *(f)*
  sīde *(f)*
sinew sinu *(f)*
skeleton bāncofa *(m)*
skin fell *(n)*
  hȳd *(f)*
skull brægenpanne *(f)*
  hēafodbolla *(m)*
  hēafodpanne *(f)*
slender wāc
smell stenc *(m)*
smile smercian *w*
sniff stincan 3
soft hnesc
sole sole *(f)*
spine gelodr *(f)*
  hrycgbān *(m)*
spleen mitte *(f)*
stature leng *(f)*
sternum brēostbān *(n)*
stomach gehrif *(n)*
  maga *(m)*
stout fǣtt
strength eafoð *(n)*

strong-smelling gestence
supple līðig
  swancor
sweat swāt *(m)*
  swǣtan
tall lang
taste-buds gōma *(m)*
tear hlēordropa *(m)*
  teagor *(m)*
  tēar *(m)*
  wōpdropa *(m)*
  wōpeshring *(m)*
temple ðunwong *(f)*
testicles beallucas *(mpl)*
  hearðan *(mpl)*
  sceallan *(mpl)*
thick ðicce
thigh ðēoh *(n)*
thin ðynne
throat gōman *(mpl)*
  ðrotu *(f)*
thumb ðūma *(m)*
tight nearu
toe tā *(f)*
tongue tunge *(f)*
tooth tōð *(m)*
torso lēap *(m)*
touch hrepian *w*
  hreppan *w*
  hrīnan *1*
tough tōh
trunk lēap *(m)*
twinkling of an eye ēaganbryhtm *(m)*
ugly unfæger
urinate micgan *w*
  gemīgan *1*
urination astyrung *(f)*
uvula hrǣctunge *(f)*
vagina cwið *(m))*
  cwiðe *(m)*
  wamba *(m*
vein ǣdre *(f)*
vertebra gelyndu *(npl)*
viscera innoð *(m,f)*
voice stefn *(f)*

waist hrif *(n)*
weep wēpan *7*
weeping wōp *(m)*
windpipe þrotbolla *(m)*
  windǣddre *(f)*
wings fiðru *(npl)*
womb cwiða *(m)*
  hrif *(f)*
wrist wrist *(f)*

BREAK

beat bēatan *7*
bent wōh
bore into borian *w*
  ðurhdrīfan *1*
breach bryce *(m)*
break brecan *4*
  clēofan *2*
break apart bebrecan *4*
break away (æt)berstan *3*
break into ābrecan *4*
break to pieces bebrecan *4*
break up ābrēotan *2*
  tōberstan *3*
  tōbrecan *4*
brittle brēað
broken (limb) forod
  gebrocen
cleave clēofan *2*
crashing gebræc *(n)*
dash to pieces tōðerscan *3*
disperse tōfaran *6*
  tōhweorfan *3*
divide bryttian *w*
  gedǣlan *w*
  scēadan *7*
  tōtwǣman *w*

division dæl *(m)*
  scīr *(f)*
finely ground smæl
fracture tōclēofan *2*
grind grindan *3*
hard heard
  stīð
hole ðȳrel *(n)*
pierced, holed ðurhholod
  ðȳrel
pound to dust gecnūwian *w*
  gnīdan *1*
scatter (for)scēadan *7*
  tōbrǣdan *w*
separate āscēadan *7*
  getwǣman *w*
sever getwǣfan *w*
share gedǣlan *w*
share out dǣlan *w*
shear bescieran *4*
  efsian *w*
shiver sprengan *w*
shred (ge)scrēadian *w*
slit tōslītan *1*
smash tōbēatan *7*
split āclēofan *2*
  sprengan *w*
split up forlǣtan ūpp *7*
  tōdǣlan *w*
  tōdrīfan *1*
spread out brǣdan *w*
spread over oferbrǣdan *w*
sunder āsyndran *w*
  getwǣfan *w*
  tōslītan *1*

BRING
assemble (ge)somnian *w*
assembly gemōt *(n)*
  gesomnung *(f)*
bear (ge)beran *4*
  wegan *5*
bear away āberan *4*
  oðberan *4*
  oðferian *w*
bear children cennan *w*
bear to ætberan *4*
blend blendan *3*
box cist *(f)*
  teag *(f)*
bring (ge)brengan *w*
  bringan *3*
  (ge)feccan *w*
  ferian *w*
  (ge)lǣdan *w*
  tōgelǣdan *w*
bring together gegaderian *w*
  mengan *w*
bundle bindele *(f)*
capture cēpan *w*
  gelæccan *w*
carry (ge)beran *4*
  (ge)ferian *w*
  wegan *5*
carry off ætferian *w*
  gefeccan *w*
  (for)niman *4*
  offerian *w*
  onberan *4*
carrying lād *(f)*
catch gefōn *7*
collect gaderian *w*
  (ge)somnian *w*
community gegaderung *(f)*
company hēap *(m)*
  hwearf *(m)*
drag dragan *6*
  tēon *2*
draw tēon *2*

draw out (for)teon *2*
fetch (ge)feccan *w*
  (ge)fetian *w*
fill fyllan *w*
gather gaderian *w*
gathering gesomnung *(f)*
handcart bearwe *(f)*
haul dragan *6*
  tēon *2*
horselitter horsbǣr *(f)*
knock gecnycc *(n)*
lead (ge)lǣdan *w*
lead away ālǣdan *w*
  oðlǣdan *w*
load lād *(f)*
mislead forsponan *6*
mix blandan *7*
  mengan *w*
  miscian *w*
pack-horse ealfara *(m)*
press ðringan *3*
pull tēon *2*
pull out apullian *w*
push scūfan *2*
seduce forsponan *6*
shred (ge)scrēadian *w*
sling ymbhringan *3*
smear (ge)dēcan *w*
snatch abrēdan *3*
take cēpan *w*
  fōn *7*
  niman *4*
throng ðringan *3*
tie (ge)tīegan *w*
together somod
  tōgædre
  tōsomne
tow tōgian *w*
transport ferian *w*
  tōgelǣdan *w*
tug dragan *6*
  tēon *2*
untie untīgan *w*

CALL

call hātan *7*
call on (ge)cīgan *w*
  nemn(i)an *w*
call out (announce) ceallian *w*
  hrīeman *w*
call out (summon) āweccan *w*
call up (ā)bannan *7*
challenge orettan *w*
clamour cirm *(m)*
command bebēodan *2*
cry cirm *(m)*
cry out cirman *w*
  cliopian *w*
  giellan *3*
declare hātan *7*
invoke gecīgan *w*
messenger ār *(m)*
name nama *(m)*
  (ge)nemnan *w*
  nemnian *w*
noise hrēam *(m)*
  swēg *(m)*
shout ceallian *w*
  hrīeman *w*
summon (ā)bannan *7*
  fetian *w*
surname cūðnoma *(m)*
uproar cierm *(m)*
  hrēam *(m)*
yell giellan *w*
  gylian *w*

CHURCH

abbess abbodisse *(f)*
abbot abbod *(m)*
abode of the dead dēaðwīc *(n)*
absolve scrīfan *1*
acolyte candelbora *(m)*
almighty alwealda *(m)*
alms ælmesse *(f)*
altar altare *(m)*
  wēofod *(n)*
  wīgbedd *(n)*
amulet lybesn *(f)*
angel engel *(m)*
apostate apostata *(m)*
apostle apostol *(m)*
  ærendwrecca *(m)*
archbishop ærcebiscop *(m)*
archbishopric arcebisceoprīce *(n)*
  ærcestōl *(m)*
ark earc *(f)*
baptism fulluht *(n)*
believing gelēafful
bell belle *(f)*
bishop biscop *(m)*
bishopship biscophād *(m)*
bless bletsian *w*
blessing bletsung *(f)*
breach of a festival frēolsbryce *(m)*
breach of holy law æswice *(m)*
canon canon *(m)*
censer storfæt *(n)*
chapter house capitelhūs *(n)*
charm galdor *(n)*
  begalan *6*
  besingan *3*
Christendom crīstendōm *(m)*
Christian Crīsten
church cirice *(f)*
cloister clauster *(n)*
compline nihtsang *(m)*
confessor scrift *(m)*
consecrate hālgian *w*
  (ge)hāligan *w*
convent (nunnan)mynster *(n)*

  stōw *(f)*
creator metod *(m)*
  scyppend *(m)*
cross rōd *(f)*
cross oneself segnian *w*
crozier hæcce *(f,n)*
curse forswerian *5*
damnation wyrgðu *(f)*
deacon dīacon *(m)*
deaconship dīaconhād *(m)*
dead man dēað *(m)*
  hrēaw *(m)*
decorated cross mǣl *(n)*
devil dēofol *(m,n)*
devilish dēoflīc
  dēofolcund
devout æfæst
  ēstful
diabolical dēoflīc
  dēofolcund
diocese biscoprīce *(n)*
  biscopsetl *(n)*
  biscopstōl *(m)*
divine godcund
  ūplīc
ecclesiastical ciriclīc
enchant begalan *6*
  besingan *3*
enchanter lyblæca *(m)*
enchantress galdricge *(f)*
  lybbestre *(f)*
ephod mæssegierela *(m)*
  mæssehrægl *(n)*
eucharist hūsl *(n)*
evensong æfensong *(m)*
excommunicate āmānsemian *w*
faith gelēafa *(m)*
false god gedwolgod *(n)*
festival mæssedæg *(m)*
first mass capitolmæsse *(f)*
ghost dēað *(m)*
God Dryhten *(m)*
  God *(m)*
  Metod *(m)*

god god *(m,n)*
god-fearing æfæst
  godfyrht
goddess gyden *(f)*
gospel godspel *(n)*
gospel commentary godspeltraht *(m)*
guilty forsyngod
hallow hālgian *w*
harming by sympathetic magic
  stacung *(f)*
heathen hǣðen
heaven heofon *(m,f)*
  swegl *(n)*
  ūpheofon *(m)*
heavenly heofonlīc
  ūplīc
hell hel *(f)*
hellfire hellebryne *(m)*
hellish torment cwicsūsl *(n)*
heresy gedwild *(n)*
  gedwola *(m)*
hermithood ancerlīf *(n)*
high priest ealdorbiscop *(m)*
holy hālig
holy orders hād *(m)*
holy water hāligwæter *(n)*
idol gedwolgod *(n)*
idolatry dēofolgield *(n)*
in holy orders gehādod
incarnation menniscnes *(f)*
incense rēcels *(m)*
indiction year gebonngēar *(n)*
intercede with prayer ðingian *w*
join in marriage beǣwnian *w*
keeping of a service geheald *(n)*
knell cnyll *(m)*
Lammas Hlāfmæsse *(f)*
lay lǣwede
litany lētanīa *(m)*
lot-casting hlytm *(m)*
magic drȳcræft *(m)*
magic word galdorword *(n)*
magical drȳlīc
magically skilled drȳcræftig
magician drȳmann *(m)*

mantle orel *(n)*
mass mæsse *(f)*
matins ūhtsang *(m)*
monastery mynster *(n)*
monastic mynsterlīc
monastic building mynsterstede *(m)*
monastic life munuclīf *(n)*
monastic orders munuchād *(f)*
monk munuc *(m)*
  mynstermonn *(m)*
monk's hood cugele *(f)*
mystic rȳnemann *(m)*
mystical gerȳnelīc
nocturns ūhtsang *(m)*
nun mynecen *(f)*
observation of a service geheald *(n)*
occult art gedwolcræft *(m)*
oratory gebedhūs *(n)*
ordain hādian *w*
ordination hādung *(f)*
orthodox rihtgelēafful
paradise neorxnawang *(f)*
  paradīs *(m)*
paradisical neorxnawanglīc
parishioner hīeremonn *(m)*
paten disc *(m)*
perfect in sanctity eallhālig
piety ārfæstnes *(f)*
pilgrimage elðēodignes *(f)*
pious ǣwfæst
  gelēafful
  godfyrht
pope pāpa *(m)*
pray gebiddan *5*
pray before forebiddan *5*
prayer bēn *(f)*
  bodung *(f)*
  gebed *(n)*
  gebeddrǣdan *(f)*
priest prēost *(m)*
  sācerd *(m)*
prime (service) prīm *(n)*
prior prāfost *(m)*
prophet witega *(m)*
provost profost *(m)*

psalm sealm *(m)*
psalm-singing sealmsong *(m)*
psalter saltere *(m)*
receiving the eucharist hūslgong *(m)*
redeem ālīesan *w*
redeemer ālīesend *(m)*
religion ǣfæstnes *(f)*
  hālignes *(f)*
religious ǣfæst
  godcund
religious observance gerihte *(n)*
renounce ānforlǣtan *7*
right to alms ælmesriht *(n)*
rite gerihte *(n)*
rogation days gangdagas *(mpl)*
ruler anwealda *(m)*
sacred office godcundnes *(f)*
sacrifice lāc *(n,f)*
sacrist ciriceweard *(m)*
saint halga *(m)*
  halge *(f)*
  sanct *(m)*
  sancte *(f)*
sanctuary ciricgrið *(n)*
  generstede *(m)*
saviour nergend *(m)*
scapulary scapulare *(m)*
secular eorðlīc
  lǣwede
  woruldcund
secular life woroldhād *(f)*
see biscoprīce *(n)*
  biscopsetl *(n)*
  biscopstōl *(m)*
shrine scrīn *(n)*
shrive scrīfan *1*
sign of the cross, make the
  gesegnian *w*
sin gesyngian *w*
  gylt *(m)*
sinful forsȳngod
song of joy blissesang *(m)*
sorceress hægtesse *(f)*
  lybbestre *(f)*
sorceror lyblǣca *(m)*

sorcery drȳ *(m)*
  drȳcræft *(m)*
  wiglung *(f)*
soul sāwol *(f)*
spell gealdor *(n)*
spirit gāst *(m)*
  gǣst *(m)*
  sāwol *(f)*
spiritual gāstlīc, gǣstlīc
temple hearh *(m)*
  herig *(m)*
  tempul *(n)*
temptation costnung *(f)*
tierce undernsong *(m)*
  underntīd *(f)*
tonsure, give the tō prēoste besciran *4*
trinity ðrīnes *(f)*
unconsecrated unhālgod
unrighteous unrihtwīs
unrighteousness unrihtwīsnes *(f)*
vault hwealf *(f)*
vespers ǣfen *(n)*
virtue ārfæstnes *(f)*
witch wicca *(m)*
  wicce *(f)*
witchcraft lyblāc *(n,m)*
worldly eorðlīc
worldly kingdom eorðrīce *(n)*
worship begong *(m)*
  gerihte *(n)*

CLOTHE

alb halba *(m)*
apparel gegyrela *(m)*
apron bearmclāð *(m)*
bag pocca *(m)*
  pusa *(m)*
bare bær
barefoot bærfōt

bear skin, made of beren
belt belt *(m)*
 fetels *(m)*
 gyrdel *(m)*
border efes *(f)*
breeches brēc *(fpl)*
 brēchrægl *(n)*
brooch prēon *(m)*
 sigil *(n)*
buckle oferfeng *(m)*
 sigil *(n)*
cloak bratt *(m)*
 hacele *(f)*
 hedeclāþ *(m)*
 sciccels *(m)*
 wǣfels *(m,n)*
cloth clāð *(m)*
 godwebb *(n)*
 hrægel *(n)*
 scīte *(f)*
 twīn *(n)*
clothe bewǣfan *w*
 gewǣdian *w*
 gierelian *w*
 (ge)scrȳdan *w*
clothes keeper hrægelðegn *(m)*
clothing gewǣde *(n)*
 gierela *(m)*
 hrægel *(n)*
 scrūd *(n)*
 wǣd *(f)*
coat tunece *(f)*
covering wǣfels *(m,n)*
cowl cugele *(f)*
crown corenbēg *(m)*
 corōna *(m)*
 cynehelm *(m)*
cuff handstocc *(n)*
dress gierela *(m)*
 hrægel *(n)*
 rēaf *(n)*
 (be)scrȳdan *w*
dyed twice twiblēo
edge efes *(f)*
embroidery borda *(m)*

 tæpped *(n)*
fine cloth godwebb *(n)*
footwear fōtgewǣde *(n)*
 scō *(m)*
fringe ðrǣs *(f)*
garland wīðig *(m)*
garment gegyrela *(m))*
 rēaf *(n)*
 scēat *(m)*
 scrūd *(n)*
garter hosebend *(m)*
 mēoning *(m)*
gird (be)gyrdan *w*
glove glofu *(f)*
gown serc *(m)*
harlot's dress forlīsgleng *(m,f)*
hat hæt *(m)*
headband binda *(m)*
 heafodbend *(n)*
headscarf wimpel *(m)*
hem ðræs *(f)*
hood cugele *(f)*
 hōd *(m)*
 snōd *(f)*
hose hosa *(m)*
jacket pād *(m)*
kirtle cyrtele *(f)*
leather leðer *(n)*
leather breeches leðerhosu *(f)*
legband wyning *(m)*
linen līn *(n)*
 twīn *(n)*
linen cloth scīte *(f)*
loom webbēam *(m)*
make good gebētan *w*
maniple handlīn *(n)*
mantle orel *(n)*
mantle of goat skin hrēða *(m)*
mask grima *(m)*
moth-eaten moðfreten
naked nacod
 ungegearwod
nightclothes bedrēaf *(f)*
 nihtwaru *(f)*
overcoat hedeclāð *(m)*

pair of shoes goscȳ *(n*
pallium pæll *(m)*
patch clāðflyhte *(m)*
pelisse pyleca *(m)*
protective clothing hlēosceorp *(n)*
put on begyrdan *w*
  ondōn *a*
repair ednīwian *w*
  gebētan *w*
rough shoe hemming *(m)*
scarlet dye derodine *(m)*
scrip pusa *(m)*
seam sēam *(m)*
sew sīwian *w*
shirt hemeðe *(n)*
shoe mēo *(m)*
  scōh *(m)*
shoe polish gedrēog *(n)*
shoes, pair of gescȳ *(n)*
silk sīde *(f)*
sleeve earmella *(m)*
  earmstoc *(m)*
  slȳf *(f)*
sleeveless slȳflēas
slipper stæppescōh *(m)*
  swyftlere *(m)*
sock socc *(m)*
spun twice twispunnen
spur spura *(m)*
spurstrap spurleðer *(n)*
stocking hosa *(m)*
stole stola *(m)*
strap gewrið *(n)*
  wriða *(m)*
strip bestrīpan *w*
  ongyrwan *w*
  unscrȳdan *w*
strip naked genacodian *w*
studded (shoe) behammen
tailor hrægelðegn *(m)*
thong gewrið *(n)*
  ðwang *(m,f)*
  wriða *(m)*
thread ðrǣd *(m)*
trousers brēc *(fpl)*

tunic cyrtele *(f)*
  serc *(m)*
  syric *(m)*
unclothe ongyrwan *w*
  unscrȳdan *w*
underwear (tunic) hemeðe *(n)*
wardrobe hrægelhūs *(n)*
wear (ā)werian *w*
weave brēdan *3*
  wefan *5*
weft ōweb *(n)*
woven twice twiðrāwen
wrap (ge)wrēon *1*
wreath wriða *(m)*

COLOUR

appearance hīw *(n)*
black sweart
  wonn
blond(e) fæger
blue hǣwe
  hǣwen
bright brūn
  scīr
brown brūn
  dunn
change of colour brigd *(n)*
colour blēo *(n)*
  dēag *(f)*
  hīw *(n)*
  hīwian *w*
coloured fāg
dark sweart
  wonn
dark red brūnbasu
discoloration ǣhīwnys *(f)*
dusky dox
  dungrǣg

dusky brown fealu
dye dēagian *w*
fade brosnian *w*
fallow fealu
gold gold *(n)*
gold-covered eallgylden
golden gylden
green grēne
  hæwen
grey græg
  hasu
  hæwe
grey-coated hasupād
grey-haired hār
hue dēag *(f)*
light līht
orange æppelfealu
  (geolu)rēad
paint fægan *w*
  mētan *w*
pale blue hæwengrēne
pale yellow geoluhwīt
pure white eallhwīt
purple basurēadan *w*
  hæwen
  weolucbasu
purple dye purpure *(f)*
  wurma *(m)*
red rēad
red colouring rudu *(f)*
redden ārēodian *w*
scarlet dye derodine *(m)*
speckled cylu
tan dunn
  fealu
variation missenlīcnes *(f)*
vermillion wealhbaso *(f)*
white hwīt
yellow fealu
  geolu

DIE

balefire bæl *(n)*
barrow beorg *(f)*
bequeath becweðan *5*
bereave belēosan *2*
bier bær *(f)*
bury bebyrgan *w*
  bedelfan *3*
carnage wæl *(n)*
coffin cist *(f)*
  ðrūh *(f)*
corpse dēað *(m)*
  hrā *(m)*
  hræw *(m,n)*
dead dēad
  gæsne
  orsāwle
  unlifigend
dead bodies hræw *(n,m)*
  wæl *(n)*
death cwalu *(f)*
  dēað *(m)*
  ealdorbealu *(n)*
  forðfōr *(f)*
  forðsīð *(m)*
  fyll *(f)*
  geendung *(f)*
  hinsīð *(m)*
  swylt *(m)*
  unlīf *(n)*
death song fūslēoð *(n)*
deathbed nēobedd *(n)*
die ācwelan *3*
  cringan *3*
  forðfaran *6*

forðfēran *w*
forðgelēoran *w*
forð(ge)wītan *1*
geendian *w*
gefaran *6*
sweltan *3*
doomed (slege)fǣge
drown ādrincan *3*
drencan *w*
end up geendian *w*
ending geendung *(f)*
fall fyll *(m)*
fall dead cringan *3*
feallan *7*
fall in battle gecringan *3*
fey fǣge
ghost dēað *(m)*
scīma *(m)*
grave byrgen *(f)*
dēaðreced *(n)*
wǣlrest *(f)*
graveyard līctūn *(m)*
half dead sōmcucu
hearse līcrest *(f)*
lie dead licgan *5*
swefan *5*
lifeless belifd
orsāwle
unlifigend
mound beorg *(f)*
not doomed unfǣge
perish abrēoðan *2*
ālicgan *w*
forweorðan *3*
losian *w*
pyre ād *(m)*
sepulchre moldærn *(n)*
slaughter wæl *(n)*
stillborn dēadboren
strangle smorian *w*
tomb beren *(m)*
līcrest *(f)*
ðrūh *(f)*
wǣlrest *(f)*

DRIVE

axle eax *(f)*
banish ādrīfan *1*
geūtian *w*
bring ferian *w*
cart cræt *(n)*
(cræt)wægen *(m)*
drive ādrīfan *1*
ðȳn *w*
ðȳwan *w*
drive along wegan *5*
drive apart tōdrīfan *1*
drive away ādrīfan *1*
flīeman *w*
fȳsan *w*
oðehtian *w*
drive off āflīgan *w*
āfȳsan *w*
drǣfan *w*
(ā-, ge-)flīeman *w*
drive out geūtian *w*
(for)wrecan *5*
drive through (pierce)
ðurhdrīfan *1*
drove drāf *(f)*
exile forwrecan *5*
flock heord *(f)*
herd drāf *(f)*
heord *(f)*
impel fordrīfan *1*
lane lanu *(f)*
lead ferian *w*
make flee geflīeman *w*
pierce ðurhdrīfan *1*
press on ðȳn *w*

repudiate āwǣgan *w*
restrain belēan *6*
saddle sadol *(m)*
send sendan *w*
send away āsendan *w*
send forth onsendan *w*
shove scufan *2*
thrust scufan *2*
urge ðȳwan *w*
vehicle fering *(f)*
waggon cræt(wægen) *(m)*
   wægen *(m)*
wheel hweohl, hwēol *(n)*

EAT

abstain forhabban *a*
abstemious mǣðlic
   sȳferǣte
ale ealoð *(n)*
   ealu *(n)*
almond amigdal *(m)*
apple æppel *(m)*
aroma stenc *(m)*
bacon spic *(n)*
bait ǣs *(n)*
bake (ā)bacan *6*
baker bæcere *(m)*
banquet swǣsende *(npl)*
   symbel *(n)*
barley bēow *(n)*
   bere *(m)*
barm beorma *(m)*
barrel byden *(f)*
batch gebæc *(n)*
bean bēan *(f)*
beer bēor *(n)*
beer-feast (ge)bēorscipe *(m)*

beestings bēost *(m)*
   bīesting *(f)*
benchmate gebēor *(m)*
bite bītan *1*
bite into ābītan *1*
boil āwiellan *w*
boiled vegetables gesodene wyrta *(fpl)*
bottle cylle *(m)*
   flaxe *(f)*
bottle (made of leather) buteric *(m)*
   higdifæt *(n)*
bountiful gifol
   rōp
bowl blēd *(f)*
   bolla *(m)*
bran sifeða *(m)*
breach of a fast fæstenbryce *(m)*
bread hlāf *(m)*
breakfast morgenmete *(m)*
brew brēowan *2*
broth broð *(n)*
buckbean glæppe *(f)*
bun healstān *(m)*
butcher flǣscmangere *(m)*
butter butere *(f)*
buttercurd butergeðwēor *(n)*
cake cicel *(m)*
   foca *(m)*
   healstān *(m)*
carrion ǣs *(n)*
carrot more *(f)*
chalice calic *(m)*
cheese cīese *(m)*
cheesecurd cīesgerunn *(n)*
cherry cerse *(f)*
chew the cud eodorcan *w*
chewing gum hwētcwudu *(m)*
churn cyrn *(f)*
cider æppelwīn *(n)*
   līð *(n)*
claret hluttordrenc *(m)*
corn corn *(n)*
course of a meal sand *(f)*
cream flīete *(f)*
   rēam *(m)*

crumb brēad *(n)*
  cruma *(m)*
crumpet crompeht *(f)*
crust hierstinghlāf *(m)*
cup bune *(f)*
  dryncfæt *(n)*
  full *(n)*
  fyll *(f)*
curds cealer *(m)*
decompose fūlian *w*
delicacy ēst *(f)*
delicious food wilðegu *(f)*
devour fretan *5*
  frettan *w*
dining hall bēodærn *(n)*
disgusting fūl
  lāð
dish disc *(m)*
dish of food sufel *(n)*
dough dāg *(m)*
draught drync *(m)*
  scenc *(m)*
dregs drōs *(m)*
dried fig ciseræppel *(m)*
drink drenc *(m)*
  drinca *(m)*
  drincan *3*
  drync *(m)*
  scenc *(m)*
drinking gedrync *(m)*
drip drȳpan *w*
dripping smeoru *(f)*
drop dropa *(m)*
drunk with beer ealugāl
drunk with mead meodugāl
drunk with wine wīngāl
drunkard wēsa *(m)*
drunken druncen
eat etan *5*
  mēsan *w*
  ðicgan *5*
eat as much as efenetan *5*
egg æg *(n)*
entertainment feorm *(f)*
evening meal æfenmete *(m)*

fasted for a night nihtnistig
fasting fæsten *(n)*
fat fætt
  rysle *(m)*
  smeru *(n)*
feast sendan *(w)*
  swæsende *(npl)*
  symbel *(n)*
feasting gebēorscipe *(m)*
feed (ā)fēdan *w*
fellow feaster gebēor *(m)*
fine flour grytt *(n)*
flask flaxe *(f)*
  pinne *(f)*
  wīnhorn *(m)*
flavour smæc *(m)*
  swæc *(m)*
flesh flæscmete *(m)*
flitch flicce *(n)*
flour melu *(n)*
fodder foddor *(n)*
foment beðian *w*
food æt *(m)*
  bīleofa *(m)*
  fōðor *(n)*
  mete *(m)*
  mōs *(n)*
  sand *(f)*
  wist *(f)*
foul fūl
fresh fersc
fried elebacen
froth gist *(m)*
fruit wæstm *(m)*
get drunk druncnian *w*
  oferdrencan *w*
glutton swelgere *(m)*
gluttonous waxgeorn
gluttony oferfylle *(f)*
grape wīnberge *(f)*
graze ettan *w*
grease smeru *(n)*
greedy frec
  grædig
  waxgeorn

grind gegrindan *3*
grow cold cōlian *w*
harvest hærfest *(m)*
hay hīg *(n)*
hazel hæsel *(m)*
heat hǣtan *w*
  hǣtu *(f)*
honey hunig *(n)*
honeycomb bēobrēad *(n)*
host ǣtgiefa *(m)*
hot meal panmete *(m)*
hunger hungor *(m)*
hungry hungrig
indigestion hrēa *(m)*
joy of mead drinking
  meodudrēam *(m)*
jug cēac *(m)*
juice sēaw *(n)*
  wōs *(n)*
kernel cyrnel *(m)*
kettle cytel *(m)*
kitchen cycene *(f)*
knead gecnedan *5*
ladle hlædel *(m)*
lard rysle *(m)*
lettuce lactuce *(f)*
lick liccian *w*
lightly-boiled hrēre
loaf hlāf *(m)*
made of wheat hwæten
maggot flǣscwyrm *(m)*
mastic hwētcwudu *(m)* EAT
malt mealt *(n)*
manger binn *(f)*
mead meodu *(f)*
meal gereorde *(f)*
  gereording *(f)*
meal (flour) melu *(n)*
mealtime mǣl *(n)*
measure (amphora) amber *(m,f,n)*
meat flǣscmete *(m)*
meat pudding mearhæccel *(n)*
  mearhgehæcc *(n)*
medlar æpening *(m)*
  openears *(m)*

midday meal nōn mete *(m)*
milk meolc *(f)*
mouthful snǣd *(m)*
mulberry byrigberge *(f)*
mulled wine moraδ *(n)*
mushroom swamm *(m)*
mustard (gerenod) senep *(m)*
napkin scēat *(m)*
nourish (ā)fēdan *w*
nut hnutu *(m)*
oats ǣtan *(mpl)*
oil ele *(m)*
olive eleberge *(f)*
oyster ostre *(f)*
pancake crompeht *(f)*
partaking δigen *(f)*
passing the mead cup round
  meodurǣden *(f)*
paste brīw *(m)*
  clam *(m)*
pea pīse *(f)*
pear peru *(f)*
pepper piporian *w*
peppercorn piporcorn *(n)*
perry perewōs *(n*
plum plyme *(f)*
poison ātor *(n)*
poisoned ǣttren
pork sausage mearg *(m,n)*
porridge brīw *(m)*
pot fæt *(n)*
pottage brīw *(m)*
pound to a powder cnucian *w*
  cnūwian *w*
prepare gegearwian *w*
pressed curds cealer *(m)*
provide with food metsian *w*
provisions bīleofa *(m)*
  feorm *(f)*
  metsung *(f)*
  wist *(f)*
quince coddæppel *(m)*
radish ontre *(f)*
raw (vegetable) grēne
  hrēaw

refined flour smedma *(m)*
relish for bread syfling *(f)*
rennet cīeslybb *(n)*
rind rind *(f)*
ripen gerīpian *w*
roast brǣdan *w*
rot brosnian *w*
  forrotian *w*
  fūlian *w*
salad grēne wyrta *(fpl)*
salt sealt *(m)*
salty sealt
sample ābyrian *w*
  onbyrgan *w*
  swæc *(m)*
sated with wine wīnsǣd
sausage gehæcca *(m)*
savoury sealt EAT
seasoned gesufel
side of meat flicce *(n)*
side-dish gabote *(f)*
sieved flour āsift *(m)*
sip sūpan *2*
sloe slā *(m)*
smear clǣman *w*
  smerian *w*
  smirwan *w*
  smītan *1*
snare begrynian *w*
soup broð *(n)*
sour afor
  sūr
sour milk sȳring *(f)*
spew spīwan *1*
spice wyrtgemang *(n)*
spit spittian *w*
squeeze out āwringan *3*
starve hlǣnian *w*
steep gewēsan *w*
stew broð *(n)*
stone vessel stānfæt *(n)*
stove cylen *(f)*
  ofn *(m)*
  stofa *(m)*
strawberry eorðberge *(f)*

suck sūcan *2*
suet cūself *(f)*
  gelyndo *(f)*
supply of food onstāl *(m)*
sustenance bīleofa *(m)*
swallow swelgan *3*
swallow down forswelgan *3*
sweet swēte
  swētlīc
  (ðurh-)werod
sweet-and-sour sūrmelsc
sweeten geswētan *w*
sweetness swētnes *(f)*
tablecloth bēodclað *(m)*
tableware bēodbolle *(f)*
taint fūlian *w*
tankard orc *(m)*
  wǣge *(n)*
taste ābyrian *w*
  byrging *(f)*
  onbyrgan *w*
  swæcc *(m)*
toothpick tōðgār *(m)*
unleavened bread þeorf *(n)*
unsalted ungesylt
vegetable wyrt *(f)*
vessel cylle *(m)*
  fæt *(n)*
  fætels *(n)*
vinegar eced *(m,n)*
vineous wīnlīc
vomit spīwan *1*
voracious ofergīfre
voracity oferhrops *(f)*
walnut frencisc hnutu *(f)*
warm through beðian *w*
  wyrman *w*
wean gewenian *w*
wheat hwǣte *(m)*
wheat for bread hlāfhwǣte *(m)*
wheatcrop hwǣtewæstm *(m)*
whey hwǣg *(n)*
wholesome gehāl
wine wīn *(n)*
wine-drinking wīngedrinc *(n)*

wine-drinking hall wīnsæl *(n)*
yeast beorma *(m)*
dærst *(f)*
gist *(m)*
hæf *(m)*
ðæsma *(m)*
yolk geoloca *(m)*

EVIL

abandon forlǣtan *7*
abase forbīgan *w*
abject hēan
accident belimp *(n)*
adversity broc *(n)*
afflict brocian *w*
(ge)dreccan *w*
geswencan *w*
hȳnan *w*
affliction hefignes *(f)*
armed attack ecgðracu *(f)*
assail onsittan *5*
avarice gītsung *(f)*
avaricious feohgīfre
avenge wrecan *5*
avoid forsittan *5*
onscunian *w*
awe ege *(m)*
awkward ambyre
earfoðlic
bad yfel
baleful bealoful
base hēanlīc
be ruined forweorðan *3*
become worse wyrsian *w*
yfelian *w*
behead behēafdian *w*
besmirch besmītan *1*
bespatter bedrīfan *1*

betray beswīcan *1*
forrǣdan *w*
bind (ge)bindan *3*
cnyttan *w*
hæftan *w*
rǣpan *w*
sǣlan *w*
binding gebind *(n)*
bitter biter
wrāð
blind āblendan *w*
block forfaran *6*
forstandan *6*
bloodthirsty wælhrēow
blow drepe *(m)*
dynt *(m)*
blow to the ear ēarslege *(m)*
bond clomm *(m)*
racente *(f)*
bondsman hæft *(m)*
breach of surety borgbryce *(m)*
break tōberstan *3*
broken (limb) forod
burden bȳrðen *(f)*
burst tōberstan *3*
calumny onscyte *(m)*
captive hæft *(m)*
captivity hæfting *(f)*
hæftnung *(f)*
hæftnȳd *(f)*
care cearu *(f)*
carry off forniman *4*
chain (fetter) clomm *(m)*
clasp grāp *(f)*
clutch grāp *(f)*
cold cyld *(f)*
cyle *(m)*
companion in misfortune
wēagesīð *(m)*
compel bǣdan *w*
confine gebindan *3*
(be)lūcan *2*
contempt forhogdnes *(f)*
forsewennes *(f)*
oll *(n)*

corrupt gewemmodlīc
crime māndǣd *(f)*
crooked on wōh
tō wōge
crookedness wōh *(n)*
wōnes *(f)*
cruel slīðen
ðearl
wrāð
cruelty wælhrēownes *(f)*
cry grētan *w*
rēotan *2*
wēpan *7*
curse āwyrgan *w*
āwyrgednes *(f)*
cursed cīs
damage æfwyrdla *(m)*
demm *(m)*
hearm *(m)*
danger fǣr *(m)*
frēc(ed)nes *(f)*
pliht *(m)*
dangerous frēcne
plihtlīc
deadly bealoful
deal unfairly forhealdan *7*
deceit fācen *(n)*
deceitful fācenful
hindergēap
swicol
deceive bedydrian *w*
swician *w*
deed of evil bealu *(n)*
māndǣd *(f)*
undǣd *(f)*
yfeldǣd *(f)*
deed of violence firendǣd *(f)*
defiled gewemmed
womful
defilement gewemming *(f)*
womm *(m,n)*
deprive bedǣlan *w*
bedrēosan *2*
onwendan *w*
deride bismrian *w*

hospettan *w*
hyrwan *w*
derision bismrung *(f)*
hōcor *(m)*
derisive hōcorwyrde
despise forhogian *w*
forsēon *5*
hyrwan *w*
despised forsewen
hēan
despiser oferhoga *(m)*
destitute fēasceaft
wǣdla *(m)*
destroy ādīlegian *w*
āgētan *w*
āwyrdan *w*
fordōn *7*
forgrindan *3*
forniman *4*
gewyrdan *w*
(for)spillan *w*
destruction cwalu *(f)*
forspillednes *(f)*
forwyrd *(f)*
diabolical dēoflīc
dēofolcund
difficult earfoðlīc
difficulty earfoðnes *(f)*
dire atol
grimm
ðroht
dire enemy feondsceaða *(m)*
disdain forhogdnes *(f)*
disgrace edwītscipe *(m)*
scomu *(f)*
disgraced ǣwiscmōd
disgraceful earhlīc
dishonorable ārlēas
displease mislīcian *w*
distress swencan *w*
do away with ādīlegian *w*
fordōn *a*
draw away oftēon *2*
effeminate blēað

enemy feond *(m)*
  feondscaða *(m)*
  flīema *(m)*
enslavement monsylen *(f)*
ensnare begrynian *w*
  beswīcan *1*
  sierwan *w*
entrap betræppan *w*
envy anda *(m)*
  nīð *(m)*
error wōh *(n)*
  wōnes *(f)*
evil bealu *(n)*
  forsyngod
  mānful
  misdǣd *(f)*
  nīð *(m)*
  yfel *(n)*
evil custom uncræft *(m)*
  unsidu *(f)*
evildoer mānfremmend *(m)*
exile flīema *(m)*
  wræc *(n)*
false lēas
  swicol
fasten gefæstenian *w*
fear ege *(m)*
fetter clomm *(m)*
  cosp *(m)*
  cospan *w*
  fetor *(f)*
  fōtcops *(m)*
  grindel *(m)*
  hæftan *w*
  wrīðan *1*
feud fæhðu *(f)*
fierce āfor
  grimm
flog beswingan *3*
folly gāl *(n)*
forbid forbēodan *2*
forsake forlǣtan *7*
forswear forswerian *6*
foul fūl
foul-smelling fūlstincend

friendless frēondlēas
fright fyrhto *(f)*
greed gītsung *(f)*
greediness gīfernes *(f)*
greedy gīfre
grief cearu *(f)*
  hrēow *(f)*
grievous hefigtȳme
  ðroht
grim āfor
  grimm
  heard
grind up gegrindan *3*
grip grāp *(f)*
  gripe *(m)*
guile fācn *(n)*
  lēasung *(f)*
guilty forsyngod
harass dreccan *w*
  wǣgan *w*
hardship earfoð *(n)*
harm daru *(f)*
  derian *w*
  hearm *(m)*
  lāð *(n)*
  (ge)sceððan *6*
harmer sceaða *(m)*
harry (for-, ge-)hergian *w*
harrying hergoð *(m)*
harsh grimm
  horsc
  unswǣslīc
hasp grindel *(m)*
hate gefēogan *w*
  hatian *w*
hated lāð
hateful fāh
  fūl
  hetelīc
  heteðoncol
  hetol
  lāðlīc
hatred anda *(m)*
  æfest *(m,f)*
  feondscipe *(m)*

hete *(m)*
nīð *(m)*
synn *(f)*
wlǣtta *(m)*
haughty ofermōdig
ranc
hinder hindrian *w*
(ge)lettan *w*
hit bēatan *7*
cnucian *w*
cnyssan *w*
gerǣcan *w*
hold gehendan *w*
grīpan *1*
healdan *7*
hold back gehealdan *7*
holocaust ealloffrung *(f)*
horrible egeslic
unhīere
hostage gīsl *(m)*
hostility fǣhðu *(f)*
feondscipe *(m)*
humble geēaðmēdan *w*
hīenan *w*
humiliate forbīgan *w*
hīenan *w*
humiliation hȳnðu *(f)*
hurt hearm *(m)*
idleness āsolcennes *(f)*
ill-treat tāwian *w*
tūcian *w*
impede āmyrran *w*
impoverish foryrman *w*
impure unclǣnlic
unsȳfre
inappropriate ungedēfe
incest sibbleger *(n)*
inconvenience ungerisene *(n)*
inflict on onbelǣdan *w*
infringe woman *w*
injure derian *w*
gewyrdan *w*
oðwyrcean *w*
(ge)sceððan *6*
injury byrst *(m)*

daru *(f)*
demn *(m)*
lāð *(n)*
synn *(f)*
tēona *(m)*
insolence bismrung *(f)*
insult bismer *(m,n,f)*
bismerian *w*
bismrung *(f)*
hearm *(m)*
insulting bismerlīc
jealous andig
æfestig
kidnapper monðēof *(m)*
knot brēdan *3*
cnotta *(m)*
cnyttan *w*
lay waste āwēstan *w*
ȳðan *w*
loathe lāðian *w*
loathesome lāð(līc)
loathing wlǣtta *(m)*
loosen onlǣtan *7*
onlȳsan *w*
lose forlēosan *2*
loss æfwyrdla *(m)*
byrst *(m)*
lowly hēanlīc
lust gāl *(n)*
lustful wrǣne
malevolent heteðoncol
inwit
yfelwille
malice anda *(m)*
malicious wound inwiddhlem *(m)*
maltreat misbēodan *2*
mar āmyrran *w*
marauding army stælhere *(m)*
mean wyrslīc
miserable earm
unlǣde
miserliness gītsung *(f)*
misery broc *(n)*
wēa *(m)*

misfortune ungelimp *(n,m)*
 unsīð *(m)*
mock bismerian *w*
 cancettan *w*
moulder brosnian *w*
 (ge)molsnian *w*
mourning gnornung *(f)*
murderous wælgīefre
neglect āgīemelēasian *w*
 forsittan *5*
notorious forcūð
oathbreaking āðbryce *(m)*
obstacle earfoðnes *(f)*
obstruct forfaran *6*
oppress dreccan *w*
 nīedan *w*
 ðryccan *w*
oppressive tintreglīc
oppressive weight byrðen *(f)*
outlaw flīema *(m)*
 ūtlaga *(m)*
overrun gegān *a*
painful biter
peril frēc(ed)nes *(f)*
perilous frēcne
persecutor lēodhata *(m)*
pestilence cwild *(m)*
pierce stician *w*
 stingan *3*
pinch twengan *w*
plunder berēafian *w*
 (for-, ge-)hergian *w*
plundering hergoð *(m)*
poison ātor *(n)*
pollute besmītan *1*
 wīdlian *w*
prevent forstandan *6*
 forwiernan *w*
 forwyrcan *w*
 gelettan *w*
pride bælc *(m)*
 gāl *(n)*
prison carcern *(n)*
 cweartern *(n)*
prohibit forbēodan *2*

promiscuity gālscipe *(m)*
proud ranc
punishment wīte *(n)*
raid forhergung *(f)*
 hergoð *(m)*
rash firenlīc
ravage forhergian *w*
reject wiðercēosan *2*
release onlǣtan *7*
 onlȳsan *w*
repress ofðryscan *w*
restrain belēan *6*
 gestȳran *w*
 (ge)healdan *7*
risk pliht *(m)*
risky plihtlīc
rob ongerēafian *w*
 (be)rēafian *w*
 (be)rȳpan *w*
robber rēafere *(m)*
 rȳpere *(m)*
robbery rēaflāc *(n)*
rough unsmēðe
ruin fordōn *a*
 forwyrcan *w*
ruination firenðearf *(f)*
savage grim
 hrēowmōd
scare āfyrhtan *w*
scornful hōcorwyrde
scourger swingere *(m)*
scratch gesceorpan *w*
scream scriccettan *w*
secretly dearnunge
sedition stric *(n)*
seduce costnian *w*
serious hefig(tȳme)
severe ðearl
 wrāðlīc
shame bismer *(m,n,f)*
 bismerian *w*
 bismrung *(f)*
 edwītscipe *(m)*
 scomu *(f)*
shameless nebwlātful

shipwreck forlidennes *(f)*
shipwrecked, be forlīðan *1*
shun onscunian *w*
 (ge)scunian *w*
sign of misfortune wēatācn *(n)*
sin leahtor *(m)*
 syngian *w*
 synn *(f)*
sinful firenful
 forsyngod
 synful
slander folclēasung *(f)*
 forcweðan *5*
slaughter dēaðcwealm *(m)*
 wæl *(n)*
slayer bana *(m)*
sloth nytennes *(f)*
smash tōbēatan *7*
spit on gespeoftian *w*
spite nīð *(m)*
spoliation strūdung *(f)*
spurn (ge)spurnan *3*
squalour orfeormnes *(f)*
squander forspendan *w*
stab stician *w*
 stingan *3*
stench stenc *(m)*
sting stingan *3*
stress earfoð *(n)*
stressful earfoðlīc
strife sacu *(f)*
 wrōht *(m,f)*
strike swingan *3*
strike against gespurnan *3*
strike down forslēan *6*
strive sacan *6*
stroke drepe *(m)*
 sweng *(m)*
 swingell *(f)*
strong ðearl
subdue gegān *a*
sudden danger fǣr *(m)*
sully āfȳllan *w*
surprise besyrwan *w*
tear slītan *1*

teran *4*
tempt costnian *w*
terrible angrislīc
 atol
terrify afǣran *w*
terrifying noise wōma *(m)*
terror broga *(m)*
 ōga *(m)*
torment sūsl *(n)*
 tintreg *(n)*
torture tintreg *(n)*
transgress misdōn *a*
 onwendan *w*
treachery fācen *(n)*
 swicdōm *(m)*
treat with contempt forhogian *w*
 forsēon *5*
tribulation earfoðe *(n)*
 gedrēfednes *(f)*
trick besyrwan *w*
trouble cearu *(f)*
troublesome earfoðlīc
 ungedēfe
 unsōfte
tyrant lēodhata *(m)*
unbind inbindan *3*
 onbindan *3*
 untīgan *w*
unloved frēondlēas
vanity īdel *(n)*
 īdelnes *(f)*
vengeance wracu *(f)*
venom ātor *(n)*
vex dreccan *w*
 swencan *w*
vice leahtor *(m)*
 unðēaw *(m)*
vile lāð
 wyrslīc
violence firen *(n)*
 nīð *(m)*
 ðracu *(f)*
violent firenlīc
wanton gāl
 wrǣne

wanton destroyer mānfordǣdla *(m)*
wantonness firenlūst *(m)* gālscipe *(m)*
waste forspendan *w*
  spilling *(f)*
weep tȳran *w*
weeping wōp *(m)*
whip beswingan *3*
wicked firenful
  inwitt
  yfel
wickedness mān *(n)*
  yfelnes *(f)*
with difficulty earfoðlīce
  unsōfte
withhold gestȳran *w*
  oðhealdan *7*
  oðwendan *w*
woe wēa *(m)*
worry caru *(f)*
  gedrēfednes *(f)*
  ymbhoga *(m)*
worthless fracod
worthlessness īdel *(n)*
  īdelnes *(f)*
wound āmyrran *w*
  benn *(f)*
  dolh *(n)*
  tǣsan *w*
  wund *(f)*
  (ge)wundian *w*
wound mortally forwundian *w*
wretched fēasceaft
wrong misdǣd *(f)*
  on wōh
  tō wōge
  wrang

FAIL
abate āswāmian *w*
  linnan *3*
  sweðrian *w*
annul āīdligan *w*
be lost losian *w*
  oðstandan *6*
become weak wācian *w*
cease linnan *3*
  swiðrian *w*
crumble wōrian *w*
decay brosnian *w*
  forrotian *w*
decline (to meet) forbūgan *2*
decrease lȳtlian *w*
desist geswīcan *1*
  linnan *3*
disloyal flāh
  unhold
downfall hryre *(m)*
dwindle wanian *w*
fade brosnian *w*
fail ābrēoðan *2*
  ālicgan *w*
  drēosan *2*
  forberstan *3*
  geswīcan *1*
fall in ruins drēosan *2*
falter wācian *w*
  wandian *w*
fault lǣst *(f)*
  unfulfremming *(f)*
finish endian *w*
flinch wācian *w*
forsake forlǣtan *7*
fraud swicdōm *(m)*
give up būgan *2*
  gieldan *3*
give way before būgan *2*
go back on one's word ālēogan *2*
hesitate wandian *w*
hinder oðstandan *6*
in vain hōlunga

incomplete ungeendod
loss losing *(f)*
  lyre *(m)*
make useless āīdligan *w*
miss missan *w*
missing ofhende
neglect oferhebban *6*
  wandian *w*
omit oferhebban *6*
perish ābrēoðan *2*
prevent forwiernan *w*
refuse forwiernan *w*
rid geryddan *w*
rubbishy dræstig
shut betȳnan *w*
spill (ge)spillan *w*
stop forstoppian *w*
submit to gecierran *w*
subside drūsian *w*
traitor wærloga *(m)*
treacherous flāh
treachery swicdōm *(m)*
turn to gecierran *w*
vanish swiðrian *w*
  ungesewenlic weorðan *4*
wane wanian *w*
weakness lēwsa *(m)*
  untrumnes *(f)*

FIRE

ablaze fȳren
alight fȳren
  onǣled
arson in a house hūsbryne *(m)*
arson in a wood wudubærnett *(n)*
ash axe *(f)*
  æsce *(f)*

beacon forebēacn *(n)*
beam of light bēam *(m)*
black blæc
bonfire bǣl *(n)*
bright beorht
  blāc
  lēoht
brightness beorhtnes *(f)*
burn (ge)bærnan *w*
  byrnan *3*
burn away forbærnan *w*
burn up forbyrnan *3*
burning bærnet *(n)*
  brond *(m)*
  bryne *(m)*
candelabrum candeltrēow *(n)*
candle candel *(f)*
  tapor *(m)*
candlestick candelsticca *(m)*
coal glēde *(f)*
crackle brastlian *w*
dark blæc
  mirce
extinguish ādwǣscan *w*
  (ā)cwencan *w*
fire ǣled *(m)*
  bǣl *(n)*
  brond *(m)*
  bryne *(m)*
  fȳr *(n)*
  līg *(m)*
firedog brandīren *(n)*
flame līg *(m)*
  sweoðol *(m?)*
fuel tynder *(f)*
hearth heorð *(m)*
heat (on)hǣtan *w*
  hǣtu *(f)*
  hæða *(m)*
hot hāt
hot coal glēd *(f)*
house-burning hūsbryne *(m)*
ignite onǣlan *w*
illumine geondlȳhtan *w*
  onlīhtan *w*

incense rēcels *(m)*
inflame hǣtan *w*
  onǣlan *w*
kindle onǣlan *w*
  onbærnan *w*
lamp blǣcern *(n)*
  blǣse *(f)*
  lēohtfæt *(n)*
light lēoht *(n)*
melt meltan *3*
morning light morgenloht *(n)*
pale blāc
  blāt
pyre ād *(m)*
  bǣl *(n)*
radiant torht
ray scīma *(m)*
ray of light (bryne)lēoma *(m)*
scorch ǣlan *w*
set on fire ātendan *w*
  forswǣlan *w*
  onǣlan *w*
  ontendan *w*
shadow sceadu *(f)*
  scua *(m)*
shine līxan *w*
  scīnan *1*
shine forth āscīnan *1*
smoke rēc *(m)*
  ðrosm *(m)*
sooty behrūmig
spark spearc *(m)*
  (fȳr)spearca *(m)*
splendour scīma *(m)*
stack of firewood scīdhrēac *(m)*
star heofontungol *(n)*
taper taper *(m)*
tinder tynder *(f)*
torch lēohtfæt *(n)*
twinkle twinclian *w*
unburnt unforbærned
warm wearm
wick wēoce *(f)*

FOE

adversary andsaca *(m)*
  wiðersaca *(m)*
  wiðerwinna *(m)*
ambusher fǣrsceaða *(m)*
avenger wrecend *(m)*
bandit ūtlaga *(m)*
  wulfeshēafod *(n)*
bane bana *(m)*
betrayer beswīcend *(m)*
buy off forgieldan *3*
contrary ambyre
dawn raider ūhtsceaða *(m)*
deceiver beswīcend *(m)*
disgrace bismer *(n,m,f)*
distressing nearufāh
enemy feond *(m)*
  genīðla *(m)*
  groma *(m)*
  hettend *(m)*
  inwitt *(m)*
  lāð *(m)*
  lāðgenīðla *(m)*
envy anda *(m)*
felon māndǣda *(m)*
  wearg *(m)*
harm derian *w*
harmer sceaða *(m)*
hatred anda *(m)*
hostile fāg
inimical wiðerweardlīc
injure derian *w*
insult bismer *(n,m,f)*
invader ingenga *(m)*

killer with a sword ecgbana *(m)*
lawless man wearg *(m)*
opponent of the church cirichata *(m)*
opposed ambyre
  andweard
public enemy ðēodscaða *(m)*
reprobate ābroðen
shame bismer *(n,m,f)*
slayer bana *(m)*
sudden attacker færsceaða *(m)*
traitor hlāfordswīca *(m)*
treachery hlāfordsearu *(f)*
  hlāfordswice *(m)*
trickster lēasbrēda *(m)*
warrior cempa *(m)*

GO

abandon forlætan *7*
abate āswāmian *w*
  linnan *3*
  sweðrian *w*
accessible gefēre
accompany midsīþian *w*
advance stæppan *6*
  wadan *6*
ahead forð
alight līhtan *w*
anti-clockwise wiðersȳnes
anticipate forecuman *4*
approach gegangan *7*
  (ge)nēalǣcan *w*
  nēosian *w*
arise wæcnan *6*
arrival (tō)cyme *(m)*
arrive becuman *4*
ascension ūpāstignes *(f)*
associate geðēodian *w*
avoid bebūgan *2*
  forbūgan *2*

onscunian *w*
away āweg, onweg
  forþ
  fram
be shipwrecked forlīðan *1*
bend būgan *2*
  gebīgan *w*
  hnīgan *1*
bend down (on)hyldan *w*
bow ābūgan *2*
  (ge)būgan *2*
  hnīgan *1*
  (on)lūtan *2*
brisk snell
burst out (æt)berstan *3*
change gebregd *(n)*
  hweorfan *w*
climb climban *3*
clockwise sunganges
come (be)cuman *4*
  gegān *a*
coming (tō)cyme *(m)*
companion gefēra *(m)*
  gesīð *(m)*
course gegang *(m)*
  ryne *(m)*
cross oferfaran *6*
  oferfēran *w*
  ofergān *a*
crossing oferfǣreld *(n)*
crowd hēap *(m,f)*
  flocc *(m)*
  þrēat *(m)*
curl (ge)wealcian *w*
dart gescēotan *2*
decline (to meet) forbūgan *2*
delay elcian *w*
depart gewītan *1*
  losian *w*
  sīðian *w*
departure gewitennes *(f)*
diagonally across ðwȳres
direct gerade
  gerec
  riht

duck dūfan 2 GO
embark āstīgan 1
  scipian w
encircle ymbgān a
  ymbwindan 3
  ymbgyrdan w
enter fēolan 3
  ingān a
  innian w
envelop ymbwindan 3
escape æthlēapan 7
  bebūgan 2
  (æt)berstan 3
  forflēon 2
  gedīgan w
  oðwindan 3
exodus ūtgong (m)
fall feallan 7
far-travelled wīdgongel
fare gefaran 6
fellow traveller gesīð (m)
flee (for-,oð-)flēon 2
  forbūgan 2
fleeing flēam (m)
flight flyht (m)
float flēotan 2
flow iernan 3
fly flēogan 3
follow æfterhyrgan w
  æfterspyrian w
  (æfter)fylgian w
foot-track fēðelāst (m)
  swæð (n)
forsake forlǣtan 7
forwardly unforwandigendlīce
forwards forð
get down līhtan w
get lost losian w
glide glīdan 1
glide away tōglīdan 1
go (ge)faran 6
  fēran w
  (ge)gān a
  (ge)gangan 7
  gedīgan w

  lendan w
  lēoran w
  līðan 1
  scacan 6
  sīðian w
  wadan 6
go away āgān a
  gewītan 1
go back āswāmian w
go before foregangan 7
  forestæppan 6
go down sīgan 1
go head first snyðian w
go in fēolan 3
go out forðgān a
  forðgangan 7
go round befaran 6
go to gesēcan w
go up ārīsan 1
  āstīgan 1
go with gefēran w
going faru (f)
  sīð (m)
  sīðfæt (n)
haste ofost (f)
hasten crūdan 2
  efstan w
  fundian w
  onettan w
  rǣsan w
  scacan 6
  scyndan w
  snyrian w
hasty ofostlīc
head for mynian w
homecoming hāmcyne (m)
hop hoppan w
horseback, on gehorsod
horseman ēoredman (m)
hurry gescēotan 2
  snyrian w
in haste ofstum
  on ofste
incline gebūgan 2
  hyldan w

intercept foran tō scēotan *2*
  forrīdan *1*
itinerant wīdgongel
join fēgan *w*
  geðēodan *w*
journey faru *(f)*
  fær *(n)*
  færeld *(n)*
  lād *(f)*
  rād *(f)*
  sīð *(m)*
journey in exile wræclast *(m)*
  wræcsīð *(m)*
journey south sūðfōr *(f)*
jump hlēapan *7*
lame healt
landing ūpganga *(m)*
lead hweorfan *3*
leap onto (ge)hlēapan *7*
leave ālǣtan *7*
  (ā)faran *6*
  gewītan *1*
  (of)lǣfan *w*
  sceacan *6*
let go ālīesan *w*
lift āhebban *6*
make room gerȳman *w*
march faran *6*
  fær *(n)*
  stæppan *6*
  wadan *6*
mount gehlēapan *7*
mounted man onstīgend *(m)*
move glīdan *6*
  hrēran *w*
  sceacan *6*
movement fōr *(f)*
  gebregd *(n)*
near genēalǣcan *w*
on the way tōgēanes
onwards forð
open gerȳman *w*
outing ȳting *(f)*
overtake offaran *6*
pass āgān *a*

pass by geweorpan *3*
pass through geondhweorfan *3*
passing gewītend
path gegang *(m)*
penetrate fēolan *3*
  ðurhfaran *6*
  ðurhwadan *6*
power of movement faru *(f)*
  fēðe *(n)*
press on crūdan *2*
provision for a journey wegnest *(n)*
put to flight āflīeman *w*
  āflīgan *w*
  āfȳsan *w*
quick arod
  recen
  snel
  snūde
  swift
quickness snelnes *(f)*
quiver bifian *w*
raid rād *(f)*
reach gerǣcan *w*
  gesēcan *w*
reach out rǣcan *w*
remove āfyrran *w*
return æthweorfan *3*
  cirran *w*
  gewendan *w*
return journey eftsīð *(m)*
revolve cirran *w*
  hweorfan *3*
  hweorfian *w*
ride rīdan *1*
ride before forrīdan *1*
ride over gerīdan *1*
ride round berīdan *1*
rider ridda *(m)*
rise āstīgan *1*
  uppian *w*
rising ūpgong *(m)*
road strǣt *(f)*
roam wandrian *w*
  wǣðan *w*

roll wealwian *w*
   windan *3*
row round berōwan *7*
run ærnan *w*
   (ge)iernan *3*
run round beirnan *3*
rush iernan *3*
   (ā)ræsan *w*
rush up ūpirnan *3*
seek out (ge)sēcan *w*
seize befōn *7*
shake beofian *w*
   onðringan *3*
shudder onðringan *3*
shun onscunian *w*
sink sīgan *1*
skate (ge)glīdan *1*
slide slīdan *1*
slip off bestelan *4*
slither slingan *3*
slow læt
   slāw
speed hrædnes *(f)*
spin (ge)spinnan *3*
spread springan *3*
spring springan *3*
stalking stalcung *(f)*
steal stalian *w*
steal away bestelan *4*
stealthy sleac
step (ge)stæppan *6*
   stæpe *(m)*
stepping-stone cleac *(f)*
stir hrēran *w*
stoop stūpian *w*
straight gerād
   gerēc
   riht
stray losian *w*
   wandrian *w*
street strǣt *(f)*
stretch out gerǣcan *w*
stride strīdan *1*
struggle through wrīgian *w*
successor æftergenga *(m)*

sunwise sunganges
surround befōn *7*
   begān *a*
swift hræd
   ofostlīc
   swift
swim swimman *3*
swimming sund *(n)*
swimming ability merestrengu *(f)*
swing swingan *3*
tilt tealtian *w*
towards tōgēanes
track lāst *(m)*
   spor *(n)*
trample ātredan *5*
transient gewītend
   lǣne
travel faran *6*
   fēran *w*
   sīðian *w*
tread (ā)tredan *5*
   wadan *6*
tremble ācwacian *w*
   (ā)bifian *w*
troop flocc *(m)*
turn bewendan *w*
   būgan *2*
   ci(e)rran *w*
   gebīgan *w*
   gehwierfan *w*
   gewendan *w*
   hweorfan *3*
turn about ymbhweorfan *3*
turn against ondhweorfan *3*
turn aside gewendan *w*
twist ðrāwan *7*
   windan *3*
unwind onwindan *3*
visit nēosan *w*
   (ge)nēosian *w*
   sēcan *w*
visitation genēosung *(f)*
wade wadan *6*
waggon wægen *(m)*

walk gewadan *6*
  gongan *7*
  gong *(m)*
  hweorfan *3*
  stæppan *6*
walk across oferwadan *6*
wander āswǣman *w*
  wǣðan *w*
wanderer eardstapa *(m)*
way fær *(n)*
  færeld *(n)*
  lād *(f)*
  weg *(m)*
way forward forðweg *(m)*
way up ūpweg *(m)*
widdershins wiðersȳnes
wind windan *3*
wind round bewindan *3*
with the sun sunganges

GOODNESS

abound genihtsumian *w*
abundance fyllu *(f)*
  nyhtsumnes *(f)*
advantage fremu *(f)*
aid (ge)fultumian *w*
  helpan *3*
appropriate cyn
  gelimplic
assistance fultum *(m)*
  fylst *(m)*
  help *(m,f)*
association geðēodnes *(f)*
avail behealdan *7*
  dugan *a*
be convenient onhagian *w*
be enough genōgian *w*
  genihtsumian *w*
be fitting behōfian *w*

  gerīsan *1*
be of assistance on stale bēon *a*
be of use dugan *a*
beauty mǣgwlite *(m)*
befit (ge)dafenian *w*
benefit bōt *(f)*
  fremfulnes *(f)*
  gedīgan *w*
  gōd *(n)*
bestow honour upon ārian *w*
  inwyrcan *w*
  weorðian *w*
blameless bilewit
  orleahtre
  ungyltig
  unscende
bless bletsian *w*
blessed ēadig
  gesǣlig
  hālig
blessing bletsung *(f)*
bliss bliss *(f)*
  blīðnes *(f)*
  drēam *(m)*
  ēadignes *(f)*
calm stille
  stillnes *(f)*
chaste clǣne
  sȳferlic
choice (best) cyst *(m,f)*
choice (choosing) cyre *(m)*
comfort ēðnes *(f)*
company geðēodnes *(f)*
consolation frōfor *(f)*
convenient gehæp
  gelimpful
decorous ǣnlīc
  rihtwīs
delicacy ēst *(f)*
dignity geðyncðu *(f)*
  weorðscipe *(m)*
duties gerisenu *(npl)*
earn earnian *w*
ease ēðnes *(f)*
effective fremful

enjoy brūcan *2*
enjoyment brȳce *(m)*
 notu *(f)*
enrich gōdian *w*
entertainment feorm *(f)*
excellent æltæwe
 til
 ðrȳðlīc
faithful getrȳwlīc
 hold
faithfulness getrȳwð *(f)*
fame mærðu *(f)*
famous blædfæst
 brēme
 mære
favour ēst *(f)*
 fremsumnes *(f)*
 hyldu *(f)*
 liss *(f)*
fine gōdlīc
firm stīð
 stronglīc
 trum
fit gehæp
fitting behēfe
 cyn
 gedafenlīc
 gedēfe
 gelimplic
 gerisenlīc
 gerisne
free frēo
 frīg
freedom frēodōm *(m)*
 frēols *(m)*
friendship frēod *(f)*
 sibb *(f)*
fullness fyllu *(f)*
gain earnian *w*
 gedīgan *w*
 ræd *(m)*
gain strength elnian *w*
gainful nytt
 nytwyrðe
gentle bilewit

gift gifu *(f)*
glad fægen
gladden blissian *w*
glorify mærsian *w*
 wuldrian *w*
glorious foremære
 tīrfæst
 ðrymful
 ðrymfæst
 weorðful
 wuldorful
 wuldorlīc
glory blæd *(m)*
 dōm *(m)*
 mærðu *(f)*
 tīr *(m)*
 ðrymm *(m)*
 weorðmynd *(m,f,n)*
 wuldor *(n)*
good gōd
 riht
 rihtlīc
 rihtwīs
 til
good (thing) gōd *(n)*
good enough medemlīc
 weorð
good fortune gesælð *(f)*
 ræd *(m)*
 sæl *(m,f)*
goodness fremu *(f)*
 gōd *(n)*
 gōdnes *(f)*
 ræd *(m)*
goods gōd *(npl)*
goodwill frēod *(f)*
 welwillendnes *(f)*
grace ēst *(f)*
 gifu *(f)*
 liss *(f)*
graceful ēstful
gracious brēme
 fremsum
 hold

happiness ēadignes *(f)*
  gesǣlignes *(f)*
  gesǣlð *(f)*
happy blīðemod
  ēadig
  fægen
  gesǣlig
harmless bilewit
  unsceððig
have mercy on (ge)miltsian *w*
health hǣlu *(f)*
help fultum *(m)*
  (ge)fultumian *w*
  gēoc *(f)*
  (ge)helpan *3*
  wraðu *(f)*
honour ār *(f)*
  ārian *w*
  inwyrcan *w*
  mǣrnes *(f)*
honoured welðungen
  weorð
humble ēaðmōd
imperfect unfulfremed
improve gōdian *w*
innocence bilewitnes *(f)*
innocent bilewit
joy drēam *(m)*
  gefēa *(m)*
  glīwstæf *(m)*
joyful blīðemōd
just riht
  rihtlīc
  rihtwīs
kind bilewit
  hold
kindness fremsumnes *(f)*
laugh hlihhan *6*
liberate frēogan *w*
love freogan *w*
  frige *(fpl)*
loyal hold
loyalty hyldu *(f)*
  trēow *(f)*
loyalty to a friend winetrēow *(f)*

luck gesǣlð *(f)*
  rǣd *(m)*
  sǣl *(m,f)*
luxurious furðumlīc
  oferranc
majesty mægenðrymm *(m)*
make good bētan *w*
  geinnian *w*
marvel wundor *(n)*
mean behealdan *7*
mend bētan *w*
  geeftgian *w*
mercy mildheortnes *(f)*
  milts *(f)*
merit earnung *(f)*
might mægen *(n)*
mighty mihtig(līc)
miracle working wundorcræft *(m)*
mirth drēam *(m)*
  glīwstæf *(m)*
moderation gemetfæstnes *(f)*
  gemetgung *(f)*
modest cūsc
munificence cystignes *(f)*
neat gesmicerod
  trum
outstanding ǣrgōd
peace frið *(m,n)*
  sibb *(f)*
  stillnes *(f)*
perfection fulfremednes *(f)*
piety ārfæstnes *(f)*
pitier gemiltsiend *(m)*
praise dōm *(m)*
  herenes *(f)*
  hering *(f)*
  lof *(f)*
praiseworthy dōmfæst
praiseworthy deed lofdǣd *(f)*
profit bryce *(m)*
  gedīgan *w*
  nytt *(f)*
propriety gerisenu *(npl)*
prosperity ēad *(n)*
  sǣl *(m,f)*

prosperous blædfæst
protective kinsman/woman
  friðemæg *(m,f)*
provision feorm *(f)*
quality ēst *(f)*
  gōdnes *(f)*
quiet stille
rejoice (ge)blissian *w*
  gefēon *5*
rejoice together efenblissian *w*
remedy bōt *(f)*
renown mǣrnes *(f)*
reverence ārwyrðnes *(f)*
reward earnung *(f)*
  mēd *(f)*
righteous rihtwīs *(f)*
righteousness rihtwīsnes *(f)*
security fæstnung *(f)*
set free freōgan *w*
severe stīð
  strong
soften lissan *w*
solace frōfor *(f)*
special sundorlic
  synderlīpe
splendour weorðnes *(f)*
still stille
stout fǣtt
  stīð
strength mægen *(f)*
  mægenðise *(f)*
  miht *(f)*
  strengu *(f)*
  ðrymm *(m)*
  ðrȳð *(f)*
strengthen gestrangian *w*
strong mihtig(līc)
  stīð
  strong(līc)
  trum
suitable gecoren
  gedafenlīc
  gedēfe
  gelimplic
  gerisenlīc

  gerisne
supply geinnian *w*
  sellan *w*
support gelǣstan *w*
  wraðu *(f)*
  wrēðan *w*
thaumaturgy wundorcræft *(m)*
thrive ðēon *1*
tidy gesmicerod
trustworthy getrēowe
truth getrȳwð *(f)*
  trēow *(f)*
use brūcan *2*
  brȳce *(m)*
  nytnes *(f)*
  nytt *(n)*
useful behēfe
  nytt
  nytwyrðe
  til
usefulness fremfulnes *(f)*
  nytnes *(f)*
utility nytnes *(f)*
venerable ārwyrðe
virginity mǣgðhād *(f)*
virtue ār *(f)*
  ārfæstnes *(f)*
  duguð *(f)*
welfare gesǣlð *(f)*
willing fægen
wonder wundor *(n)*
  wundrian *w*
wonderful wunderful
  wunderlīc
worship begān *a*
  weorðung *(f)*
worth weorð

HOUSE

abode hām *(m)*
  setl *(n)*
arch boga *(m)*
arrangement gesetednes *(f)*
at home innanbordes
balk bælc *(m)*
barbican burhgeat *(n)*
barn ærn *(n)*
  bæren *(n)*
bath bæð *(n)*
beam of wood bēam *(m)*
bed bedd *(n)*
  bedrest *(f)*
bench benc *(f)*
  scamol *(m)*
bin binne *(f)*
bind (tie in) bendan *w*
bind up bindan *3*
binding bindere *(m)*
  byndelle *(f)*
board bord *(n)*
bond bend *(m,f)*
booth sceoppa *(m)*
bower būr *(m)*
brick tigele *(f)*
bridge brycg *(f)*
bridge over brycgian *w*
brothel forligerhūs *(n)*
build bytlian *w*
  scyppan *6*
  (ā-, ge-)timbrian *w*
  weorcan *w*
  wyrcean *w*
build up bewyrcean *w*
building bold *(n)*
  botl *(n)*
  bytling *(f)*
  getimbre *(n)*
  timber *(n)*
camp out gewician *w*
candelabrum candeltrēow *(n)*
candle candel *(f)*
  tapor *(m)*

candlestick candelsticca *(m)*
cattleshed scipen *(f)*
cellar cleafa *(m)*
chair stōl *(m)*
chamber būr *(m)*
chamberlain būrðegn *(m)*
circle ymbhwyrft *(m)*
circular tower windelstān *(m)*
circumference ymbgong *(m)*
corner hyrne *(f)*
  wincel *(m)*
court hof *(n)*
cover beðeccan *w*
covering ðecen *(f)*
create (ge)scyppan *6*
crooked wōh
crookedness wōh *(n)*
crossmember eaxlgespan *(n)*
  lōhsceaft *(m)*
crumble wōrian *w*
dais stīg *(m,f)*
dark room heolstorcofa *(m)*
dig delfan *3*
  grafan *6*
door duru *(f)*
door jamb gedyre *(n)*
doorman duruðegn *(m)*
draught drōht *(m?)*
dunghill myxen *(f)*
dwell eardian *w*
  gewīcian *w*
dwelling bold *(n)*
  botl *(n)*
  cotlīf *(n)*
  hof *(n)*
  inn *(n)*
  setl *(n)*
  stoc *(n)*
eaves efes *(f)*
enclosure by water worðig *(m)*
entrance ingang *(m)*
establish gestaðolian *w*
  onstellan *w*
  settan *w*
estate hām *(m)*

extent ymbhwyrft *(m)*
fall in ruins drēosan *2*
fasten fæstnian *w*
fencing wood tīning *(f)*
firewood wudu *(m)*
fix fæstnian *w*
floor flet *(n)*
    flōr *(f,m)*
fly-net flēohnet *(n)*
folding stool fyldestōl *(m)*
footstool fōtscamol *(m)*
fortress burg *(f)*
    fæsten *(n)*
foundation staðol *(m)*
frame gesteal *(n)*
freehold ēleð *(m)*
gateway geat *(n)*
guest bencsittend *(m)*
guest house gesthūs *(n)*
    giestærn *(n)*
gymnasium bæðstede *(m)*
habitation cotlīf *(n)*
half-built samworht
hall flet *(n)*
    flōr *(f,m)*
    heall *(f)*
    reced *(n)*
    seld *(n)*
    sele *(m)*
hearth heorð *(m)*
heave hebban *6*
height leng *(f)*
hemisphere healftryndel *(n)*
hollow out holian *w*
home hām *(m)*
home happiness seledrēam *(m)*
house hām *(m)*
    hūs *(n)*
    reced *(n)*
    seld *(n)*
household hēored, hīred *(m)*
householder boldāgend *(m)*
household goods inierfe *(n)*
    inorf *(n)*
hut cȳte *(f)*

stocwīc *(n)*
indoors inne
inhabit warian *w*
inherited home yrfestōl *(m)*
inn gesthūs *(n)*
    inn *(n)*
    tēcērhēs *(n)*
instability unstæðelfæstnes *(f)*
kitchen cycene *(f)*
lintel oferdyre *(n)*
locker hwicce *(f)*
lodgings tēcērhēs *(n)*
loose unfæst
made of planks breden
main dwelling hēafodbotl *(n)*
make firm gestaðolian *w*
make good gebētan *w*
manger binn *(f)*
materials ontimber *(n)*
mat meatt *(f)*
mill mylen *(f)*
millstone cweornstān *(m)*
monument gebēacen *(n)*
nail næglian *w*
passage geat *(n)*
    nearu *(f)*
pavilion feldhūs *(n)*
    (būrge)teld *(n)*
    træf *(n)*
pillar bēam *(m)*
    stapol *(n)*
    sȳl *(f)*
plank bord *(n)*
    bred *(n)*
    ræsn *(n)*
pole pāl *(m)*
    post *(m)*
    steng *(m)*
post post *(m)*
pot crocca *(m)*
precarious tealt
privy gangern *(n)*
prop stuðansceaft *(m)*
protected place burg *(f)*
renew (ge)ednīwan *w*

repair ednīwian *w*
  gebētan *w*
restoration eftnīwung *(f)*
restore (ge)ednīwian *w*
roof hrōf *(m)*
  ðaca *(m)*
roof over beðeccan *w*
roof timber hrēstbēag *(m)*
room inn *(n)*
roomy rūm
royal hall dryhtsele *(m)*
rung hrung *(f)*
seat geset *(n)*
  setl *(n)*
  stōl *(m)*
seat cover setrægl *(n)*
semicircular healfsinewealt
separate dwelling sundorwīc *(n)*
sepulchre ofergeweorc *(n)*
set up onstellan *w*
shaft sceaft *(m)*
shape scyppan *6*
shelf scylf *(m)*
sloping hwelmdragen
splinter spōn *(m)*
spoke hrung *(f)*
stable horsern *(n)*
  staðolfæst
  untealt
stairs stǣger *(m)*
stand firm stemnettan *w*
stool stōl *(m)*
storeroom hēddærn *(n)*
structure gesteal *(n)*
stud stuðansceaft *(m)*
sty hlōse *(f)*
superstructure ofergeweorc *(n)*
support staðol *(m)*
surface bred *(n)*
sweep away forswāpan *7*
table bēod *(m)*
  bord *(n)*
  mȳse *(f)*
tent feldhūs *(n)*
  geteld *(n)*

  træf *(n)*
thatch healm *(n)*
  ðæc *(n)*
  ðecen *(m)*
throne cynesetl *(n)*
  setl *(n)*
tie (ge)tīegan *w*
tile tigele *(f)*
timber timber *(n)*
toilet gangern *(n)*
  rynatūn *(m)*
tower torr *(m)*
tower up hlīfian *w*
townhouse burgsæl *(n)*
unstable tealt
  unstaðolfæst
upper storey upflōr *(m)*
vault hwealf *(f)*
wattle watel *(m)*
window ēagðȳrel *(n)*
wood for an archway bōhtimber *(n)*
wood for a house boldtimber *(n)*
wooden piece bēam *(m)*
workshop oden *(f)*
yard geard *(m)*

KIN

adult fullðungen
  fullweaxen
  orped
affinity mægrǣden *(f)*
akin (ge)lenge
ancestor ealdfæder *(m)*
  foregenga *(m)*
  foregongel *(m)*

ancestors ieldran *(mpl)*
aunt (maternal) mōdrige *(f)*
aunt (paternal) faðe *(f)*
baby bearn *(n)*
  (cradol)cild *(n)*
bachelor ānhaga *(m)*
  hægsteald *(m)*
bastard bastard *(m)*
  cifesboren
  hornungsunu *(m)*
be born wæcnan *6*
bear (ā)cennan *w*
beget cennan *w*
  strȳnan *w*
bequest lāf *(f)*
birth ācennednes *(f)*
  (ge)byrd *(f)*
born ācenned
  geboren
boy cnapa *(m)*
breed tyddrian *w*
bride brȳd *(f)*
bring forth ācennan *w*
bring up gebringan *3*
  tēon *2*
brood brōd *(f)*
brother brōðor *(m)*
brothers gebrōðor *(mpl)*
child bearn *(n)*
  (cradol)cild *(n)*
  eafora *(m)*
  lytling *(m)*
clan mægð *(f)*
close ancestors nēahfædras *(mpl)*
close kinsman hēafodmæg *(m)*
conceive geēacnian *w*
congenital geæðele
cousin fæderansunu *(m)*
  modrigensunu *(m)*
  swēor *(m)*
daughter dohtor *(f)*
dear kinsman winemæg *(m)*
dependant cyrelīf *(n)*
descendant eafora *(m)*
effeminate man bæddel

elder ealdor *(m)*
embryo beorðor *(m)*
family cynn *(n)*
  cynren *(n)*
  hēored *(m)*
  hīred *(m)*
  hīwisc *(n)*
  mægð *(f)*
family land ēðel *(m,n)*
family members hīwan *(mpl)*
family wartroop sibgedriht *(f)*
father fæder *(m)*
father's brother fædera *(m)*
father's sister faðe *(f)*
fatherland eard *(m)*
  ēðel *(m)*
fatherly fæderlīc
feed fēdan *w*
female side of the family
  spinelhealf *(f)*
  wīfhand *(f)*
foetus brōd *(m)*
fostering fōstor *(n)*
free kinsman frēomæg *(m)*
girl mæden *(n)*
  wencel *(n)*
godchild godbearn *(n)*
godfather cumpæder *(m)*
godparent godsibb *(n)*
godson godsunu *(m)*
granddaughter nefene *(f)*
  nift *(f)*
grandfather ealdfæder *(m)*
  yldrafæder *(m)*
grandmother ealdmōdor *(f)*
grandson nefa *(m)*
great grandfather ðriddafæder *(m)*
great grandmother ðriddemōdor *(f)*
great grandson ðriddasunu *(m)*
half-grown healfeald
heirloom lāf *(f)*
hermaphrodite bæddel *(m)*
high-born æðele
  byrde
human mennisc

humanity menniscnes *(f)*
husband ceorl *(m)*
  wer *(m)*
husband's brother tācor *(m)*
infant cradolcild *(n)*
kin cynn *(n)*
kindred cynn *(n)*
  cynren *(n)*
king's wife or daughter cwēn *(f)*
kinship mǣgrǣden *(f)*
  sibb *(f)*
kinsman gesibb *(m,f)*
  magu *(m)*
  mǣg *(m)*
kinsmen cnēomagas *(mpl)*
maiden fǣmne *(f)*
  mǣden *(n)*
  mǣgð *(f)*
  mēowle *(f)*
make pregnant geēacnian *w*
male side of the family sperehealf *(f)*
  wǣpnedhand *(f)*
  wǣpnedhealf *(f)*
man (adult human) mon *(m)*
  monna *(m)*
man (adult human male) secg *(m)*
  wǣpnedmann *(m)*
  wer *(m)*
mankind moncynn *(n)*
married couple sinhīwan *(mpl)*
men beornas *(mpl)*
  fīras *(mpl)*
  men *(mpl)*
  ylde *(mpl)*
mother mōdor *(f)*
mother's brother ēam *(m)*
native land cȳððu *(f)*
  ēðel *(m,n)*
natural geæðele
  gecynde
nephew nefa *(m)*
niece nefene *(f)*
  nift *(f)*
nobility (of birth) æðelborennes *(f)*
noble æðele

byrde
noble family æðelu *(f)*
not fully grown unweaxen
nourish fēdan *w*
nurture fēdan *w*
  fōstrian *w*
parent ealdor *(m)*
parents ieldran *(mpl)*
paternal fæderlīc
paternal kinsman fæderenmæg *(m)*
patriarch hēahfæder *(m)*
person mon *(m)*
  monna *(m)*
pregnant ēacen
produce ācennan *w*
raise fēdan *w*
  rǣran *w*
rank gebyrd *(f)*
rear rǣran *w*
related gesibb
sex hād *(m)*
sister sweostor *(f)*
sister's husband āðum *(m)*
sister's son swustersunu *(m)*
son bearn *(n)*
  eafora *(m)*
  magu *(m)*
  sunu *(m)*
son's wife snoru *(f)*
son-in-law āðum *(m)*
stepchild stēopbearn *(n)*
stepdaughter stēopdohtor *(f)*
stepfather stēopfæder *(m)*
stepmother stēopmōdor *(f)*
stepson stēopsunu *(m)*
successor æftergenga *(m)*
twin getwinn *(m)*
  getwisa *(m)*
uncle (maternal) ēam *(m)*
uncle (paternal) fædera *(m)*
unrelated ungesibb
virgin fǣmne *(f)*
  mēowle *(f)*
wedded couple sinhīwan *(mpl)*
wedlock hǣmedscipe *(m)*

widow widewe *(f)*
wife cwēn *(f)*
wife's father swēor *(m)*
wife's mother sweger *(f)*
woman cwēn *(f)*
  mǣg *(f)*
  wīf *(n)*
  wīfmann *(m)*
young man cniht *(m)*
  geoguð *(f)*
  hægsteald *(m)*
  hyse *(m)*
young kinsman mǣgcild *(n)*
youngster cnapa *(m)*
  cniht *(m)*

KNOW

accomplishment cræft *(m)*
  gecneordnes *(f)*
acquaint cȳðan *w*
advise rǣdan *w*
arithmetic rīmcræft *(m)*
astronomy tungolǣ *(f)*
  tungolcræft *(m)*
augur hālsiend *(m)*
  hwata *(m)*
be able cunnan *a*
certain cūðlīc
  gewiss
  wīslīc
  witodlīc
certainty gewiss *(n)*
clearly known undierne
counsel rǣdan *w*
discover fandian *w*
experience onfundelnys *(f)*
familiar hīwcūþ

welcūþ
find out fandian *w*
geometry eorðcræft *(m)*
ignorant ungelǣred
in detail smēaðanclīce
incautiously unforscēawodlīc
intellect mōd *(n)*
  ondgit *(n)*
  ongitennes *(f)*
investigate gecunnian *w*
know (on)cnāwan *7*
  cunnan *a*
  gecnāwan *7*
  ongietan *5*
  witan *a*
know in advance forewitan *a*
knowledge cȳððu *(f)*
  leornung *(f)*
known cūð
  gēanwyrde
  yppe
lore gefrǣge *(n)*
  gefreoge *(n)*
make known cȳðan *w*
mystery dīgelnes *(f)*
  rūn *(f)*
omen hwatu *(f)*
perceive oncnāwan *7*
  undergietan *5*
philosopher ūðwita *(m)*
portent wēatācn *(n)*
professed gēanwyrde
prophet witega *(m)*
real sōð
recognise gecnāwan *7*
renowned gefrǣge
sage ūðwita *(m)*
scholar ūðwita *(m)*
secret rūn *(f)*
study gecneordnes *(f)*
  leornung *(f)*
sure gewiss
  sicor
syllogism smēagelegen *(f)*
test cunnian *w*

touchstone cenningstān *(m)*
tradition gefreoge *(n)*
try out cunnian *w*
unawares unforscēawodlīc
   unwǣres
understand gecnāwan *7*
   ongietan *5*
understanding ondgit *(n)*
   ongitennes *(f)*
untaught ungelǣred
well-known cūð
   gefrǣge
widely known wīdcūð
wisdom rǣd *(m)*
   snyttru *(f)*
   wīsdōm *(m)*
wise snoterlīc
   snottor
   wīs(līc)
   wītig
wise man wita *(m)*
   witega *(m)*
wit witt *(n)*

LAND

accessible gefēre
acre æcer *(m)*
agriculture eorðtilð *(f)*
attack beacon herebēacen *(n)*
barren unwǣstmbǣre
   wēste
barrier clūstor *(n)*
   eodor *(m)*
battlefield campstede *(m)*
   folcstede *(m)*
   wælfeld *(m)*
   wælstōw *(f)*
beach strand *(m)*
beacon (ge)bēacn *(n)*

border biwindla *(m)*
   efes *(f)*
   haga *(m)*
   mǣre *(n)*
   mearc *(f)*
   ōra *(m)*
boundary gemǣre *(n)*
   londgemǣre *(n)*
   mearc *(f)*
broad brād
byway orwegstīg *(f)*
camp set *(n)*
camp protected by water
   wæterfæsten *(n)*
camp protected by woods
   wudufæsten *(n)*
capital hēaburg *(f)*
   hēafodburg *(f)*
cavern eorðscræf *(n)*
   hol *(n)*
charter-land bōcland *(n)*
citizens ceasterware *(fpl)*
city burgstede *(m)*
   ceaster *(f)*
clay clǣg *(m)*
cliff clif *(n)*
clump clympre *(m)*
coast sǣrima *(m)*
copse bearu *(m)*
   hyrst *(m)*
coulter culter *(m)*
country land *(n)*
creation gesceaft *(f)*
crop failure unwæstm *(m)*
cultivate būan *w*
   tilian *w*
cultivated bȳne
dale cumb *(m)*
   dæl *(n)*
deep stēap
deep pool wǣl *(m)*
dene dene *(m)*
   denu *(f)*
desert ānæd *(n)*
   wēsten *(m)*

deserted ǣmenne
wēste
determine mearcian *w*
distant feorr
district scīr *(f)*
ditch dīc *(m,f)*
domain gefeald *(n)*
rīce *(n)*
down dūn *(f)*
dwell eardian *w*
dweller on earth eorðbūend *(m)*
woroldbūend *(m)*
dwelling cotlīf *(n)*
setl *(n)*
stoc *(n)*
wīc *(n)*
earth eardgeard *(m)*
eorðe *(f)*
folde *(f)*
grund *(m)*
hruse *(f)*
middangeard *(m)*
molde *(f)*
earthquake eorðstyren *(f)*
eastern region ēastdǣl *(m)*
ēastende *(m)*
ēasthealf *(f)*
edge efes *(f)*
ōra *(m)*
embankment dīc *(m,f)*
geweorc *(n)*
enclosure tūn *(m)*
end ende *(m)*
entrenchment set *(n)*
estate hām *(m)*
tūn *(m)*
even efn
filde
excavation gedelf *(n)*
explore fandian *w*
rāsian *w*
extend rȳman *w*
far off feorr
farmer gebūr *(m)*

fen fenn *(n)*
mersc *(m)*
fencing tīning *(f)*
field æcer *(m)*
wong *(m)*
flat efn
filde
smēðe
footpath ānpæð *(m)*
fōtlāst *(m)*
swaðu *(f)*
swæð *(n)*
ford ford *(m)*
wæd *(n)*
forest weald *(m)*
wudu *(m)*
fortified place burghlīð *(n)*
ceaster *(f)*
fortress geweorc *(n)*
furlong furhlang *(n)*
furrow furh *(f)*
grant by charter bōcian *w*
grassland græsmolde *(f)*
græswang *(m)*
gravel ceosol *(m)*
grit grēot *(m)*
ground folde *(f)*
grund *(m)*
hruse *(f)*
molde *(f)*
grove bearu *(m)*
grāf *(n,m)*
wuduholt *(n)*
harbour port *(m)*
harvest hærfest *(m)*
haystack hrēac *(m)*
headland næss *(m)*
hedge biwindla *(m)*
haga *(m)*
hege *(m)*
height hēanes *(f)*
hēhðu *(f)*
hide (land measure) hīd *(f)*
high hēah
stēap

hill beorg *(m)*
　dūn *(f)*
　hlīð *(n)*
　munt *(m)*
hole pytt *(m)*
　sēað *(m)*
homeland eard *(m)*
　ēðel *(m)*
inhabit būan *w*
inhabitant bīgenga *(m)*
inhabited bȳne
island ēalond *(n)*
　īeg *(f)*
　īggað *(m)*
　īgland *(n)*
jointly-owned land gedālland *(n)*
kingdom cynedōm *(m)*
　cynerīce *(n)*
knoll cnoll *(m)*
lake mere *(m)*
land eard *(m)*
　grund *(m)*
　land *(n)*
landmark gebēacen *(n)*
leasehold land lǣn *(f)*
level efn
level out efnan *w*
limit mearc *(f)*
locality eorðweard *(m)*
　stōw *(f)*
location stede *(m)*
lump clympre *(m)*
manor hām *(m)*
margin efes *(f)*
　ōra *(m)*
marsh mersc *(m)*
meadow gærstūn *(m)*
　mǣd *(f)*
　wongturf *(f)*
millstream hwēolrīðig *(n)*
monument gemyndstōw *(f)*
moor mōr *(m)*
moss mēos *(m)*
mound cnoll *(m)*
　hlǣw *(m)*

mountain beorg *(m)*
　dūn *(f)*
　munt *(m)*
mountain cave dūnscræf *(n)*
mountain slope beorghlīð *(n)*
mountain stream firgenstrēam *(m)*
mud horh *(m,n)*
narrow enge
　nearu
narrow place nearu *(f)*
native land cȳððu *(f)*
　eard *(m)*
　ēðel *(m,n)*
native people londlēod *(f)*
　londwaru *(f)*
near to gehende
neighbour nīehsta *(m)*
neighbourhood efenehð *(f)*
　nēawest *(m,f)*
ness næss *(m)*
　nōse *(f)*
ooze sīpian *w*
　wāse *(f)*
open land feld *(f)*
orchard ortgeard *(m)*
pasture hamm *(m)*
　lǣs *(f)*
path foldweg *(m)*
pebble papolstān *(m)*
pit hol *(n)*
　pytt *(m)*
　sēað *(m)*
plain efenehð *(f)*
　feld *(f)*
　foldwong *(n)*
　græsmolde *(f)*
　wong *(m)*
playground plegstede *(m)*
plough beswincan *3*
　(ge)erian *w*
populate gesettan *w*
　gesittan *5*
port port *(m)*
quicksand cwecesand *(m)*
region londscipe *(m)*

rick hrēac *(m)*
ridge hrycg *(m)*
riverbank ēastæð *(n)*
 stæð *(m,n)*
 strand *(n)*
rivermouth mūða *(m)*
road strǣt *(f)*
rock clūd *(m)*
 stān *(m)*
rocky cliff stānclif *(n)*
rocky slope stānhlið *(n)*
room rȳmet *(n)*
royal dwelling cynestōl *(m)*
sand ceosol *(m)*
 grēot *(m)*
 sond *(n)*
sandy beach sondlond *(n)*
seaboard sǣrima *(m)*
seawall sǣweall *(m)*
sector ende *(m)*
 londscipe *(m)*
 scēat *(m)*
set a limit gemǣrian *w*
 mearcian *w*
settle gesettan *w*
 gesittan *5*
settler gebūr *(m)*
shared dwelling somodeard *(m)*
shingle ceosol *(m)*
shire scīr *(f)*
shore stæð *(m,n)*
 strand *(n)*
sign gebēacen *(n)*
slippery sliddor
slope hlinc *(m)*
 hlīð *(n)*
smooth smēðe
 smōð
sod turf *(f)*
soil folde *(f)*
 molde *(f)*
south coast sūðrima *(m)*
 sūðstæð *(n)*
space rȳmet *(n)*
spacious rūm

spread out brǣdan *w*
stack hrēac *(m)*
steep nēowol
 stēap
stile stigel *(f)*
stone stān *(m)*
stone wall stānweall *(m)*
strand strand *(n)*
stream burna *(m)*
 strēam *(m)*
 wiella *(m)*
summit hēafod *(n)*
 top *(m)*
swamp fenn *(n)*
tapering plot of land gāra *(m)*
till beswincan *3*
 erian *w*
top top *(m)*
tower up hlīfian *w*
town burgstede *(m)*
 ceaster *(f)*
 port *(m)*
townhouse burgsæl *(n)*
townsmen burgwaru *(f)*
townwall burgweall *(m)*
track swaðu *(f)*
 swæð *(n)*
tract of land londscearu *(f)*
trench dīc *(m,f)*
turf turf *(f)*
unfenced untȳned
uninhabited by yeomen āfurod
valley cumb *(m)*
 dal *(n)*
 dene *(m)*
 denu *(f)*
 slǣd *(n)*
wall wāg *(m)*
 weall *(m)*
waste wēste
wasteland ānǣd *(n)*
 wēsten *(m,n)*
watermeadow hamm *(m)*
well pytt *(m)*
wheatcrop hwǣtewæstm *(m)*

wide brād
  sīd
  wīd
wire fence eodorwīr *(m)*
wood bearu *(m)*
  holt *(n)*
  holtwudu *(m)*
  hyrst *(m)*
  wuduholt *(n)*
woodland wudulond *(n)*
world eorðe *(f)*
  gesceaft *(f)*
  middangeard *(m)*
  worold *(f)*
yeoman gebūr *(m)*

LAW

accessory gewita *(m)*
adequate gemēde
  medemlic
adultery æwbryce *(m)*
advocate forespeca *(m)*
ancient duty ealdriht *(n)*
ancient right ealdriht *(n)*
annul āīdligan *w*
appoint betæcan *w*
  lagian *w*
  stihtan *w*
appoint a day āndagian *w*
atone for gebētan *w*
avenge gewrecan *5*
bail borg *(m)*
banish āhwettan *w*
be exempt scīran *w*
behead behēafdian *w*

bestow forgiefan *5*
breach of bail borgbryce *(m)*
breach of law lahbryce *(m)*
breach of promise wedbryce *(m)*
capital offence dēaðscyld *(f)*
case (in law) spæc *(f)*
catch red-handed āparian *w*
common law folclagu *(f)*
  folcriht *(n)*
compensation bōt *(f)*
convict oferreccan *w*
correct riht
correct law rihtlagu *(f)*
correction ðrēal *(f)*
courthouse gerēfærn *(n)*
covenant ānnes *(f)*
  wær *(f)*
custody gehealdsumnes *(f)*
  hæftnoð *(m)*
  hæftnīed *(f)*
custom gewuna *(m)*
  sidu *(f)*
deal unfairly forhealdan *7*
deception lot *(n)*
  swicdōm *(m)*
declare forfeited ætreccan *w*
dependant cyrelīf *(n)*
dispute over inheritance yrfegeflit *(n)*
divine law æ *(f)*
due gerihte *(n)*
  riht(līc)
duty gerihte *(n)*
evidence gewitennes *(f)*
exchange hostages gīslian *w*
excuse belādung *(f)*
exile āflīeman *w*
fair gemēde
fine for fighting fihtewīte *(n)*
fine for illegal dealing
  wōhcēapung *(f)*
forfeit forwyrcan *w*
fraud swicdōm *(m)*
freedom frēot *(m)*
grant ālȳfan *w*
  forgiefan *5*

guilt gylt *(m)*
guiltless unscyldig
guilty scyldig
heir yrfeweard *(m)*
heirloom yrfelāf *(f)*
hide unlawfully forhelan *4*
horse thief stōdðēof *(m)*
hostage foregīsl *(m)*
  gīsel *(m)*
imprison gehæftan *w*
income ār *(f)*
informer melda *(m)*
injustice unlagu *(f)*
  unriht *(n)*
innocent unforwyrht
  unsynnig
institution gesetednes *(f)*
jail carcern *(n)*
  cweartern *(n)*
judge dēma *(m)*
  dēmend *(m)*
judgement dōm *(m)*
judgement seat dōmsetl *(n)*
justice folcriht *(n)*
  riht *(n)*
law ǣ *(f)*
  gemet *(n)*
  lagu *(f)*
  riht *(n)*
lawful lahlīc
lawsuit spǣc *(f)*
lawyer lahwita *(m)*
legal ǣwlic
  lahlic
lie forlēogan *2*
manner gemet *(n)*
means ār *(f)*
  æht *(f)*
  feoh *(n)*
merchandise cēap *(m)*
mistreat forhealdan *7*
  mistūcian *w*
morality sidu *(f)*
ordain lagian *w*
outlawed fāg

wrǣclic
pass sentence scrīfan *1*
payment gafol *(n)*
peace frið *(m,n)*
peace treaty frioðowǣr *(f)*
penalty bōt *(f)*
  stēor *(f)*
  wīte *(n)*
perjure forlēogan *2*
perjury āðbryce *(m)*
petition bēn *(f)*
price weorð *(n)*
prison carcern *(n)*
  cweartern *(n)*
  hengen *(f)*
private property sundorfeoh *(n)*
promise weddian *w*
property ǣht *(f)*
  cēap *(m)*
  feoh *(n)*
prove a claim geāgnian *w*
proven geresp
public openlīc
punishment hearmscearu *(f)*
  ðrēal *(f)*
  wīte *(n)*
punitive tax ungylde *(n)*
put right gerihtan *w*
ransom wliteweorð *(n)*
ratify fæstnian *w*
recompense forgieldan *3*
rectify gerihtlǣcan *w*
redemption ālȳsednes *(f)*
regulate besīdian *w*
release from taxes gefrēogan *w*
remedy bōt *(f)*
rent-payer gafolgielda *(m)*
repay gebētan *w*
request bēn *(f)*
requite forgieldan *3*
right riht *(n)*
  riht(līc)
right to take fines sōcn *(f)*
rights of a freeman frēoriht *(n)*

scaffold gealga *(m)*
  līchanga *(m)*
security borg *(f)*
security for a loan ānwedd *(n)*
set right gebētan *w*
  • rihtan *w*
spare (ge)sparian *w*
sponsor forespeca *(m)*
steal stalian *w*
  (for)stelan *4*
stealing stalu *(f)*
stipulation gerād *(f)*
stocks hengen *(f)*
straight riht(līc)
straighten gerihtlǣcan *w*
tax nīedgyld *(n)*
tenant gafolgielda *(m)*
testament yrfegewrit *(n)*
testimony gewitennes *(f)*
theft ðīefð *(f)*
thief ðēof *(m)*
tradition ealdgesegen *(f)*
  ealdriht *(n)*
tribute gafol *(n)*
value weorð *(n)*
violation ǣswice *(m)*
voluntary agnes willan
will cwide *(m)*
  gesetednes *(f)*
  yrfegewrit *(n)*
witness gewita *(m)*
wrongful unriht
  wrang
wrongful custom unsidu *(f)*
wrongfully conceal forhelan *4*

LIVE

alive cucu
  cwic
breath ǣþm *(m)*
  blǣd *(m)*
breathing ǣðung *(f)*
camp gewīcian *w*
come alive cwician *w*
dwell būan *w*
  eardian *w*
  oneardian *w*
  onwunian *w*
  (ge)wīcian *w*
  (ge)wunian *w*
dwelling cotlīf *(n)*
  eardung *(f)*
  (on)wunung *(f)*
  setl *(n)*
  stoc *(n)*
dwelling-place stoclīf *(n)*
  stocwīc *(n)*
earn a living drohtnian *w*
encamp wīcian *w*
encampment wīcstōw *(f)*
experience onfundelnys *(f)*
frequent gelōmlic
  gewunian *w*
habitation eardung *(f)*
inhabit būan *w*
  onwunian *w*
inhabitant bīgenga *(m)*
life blǣd *(m)*
  ealdor *(n)*
  feorh *(m,n)*
  līf *(n)*
live libban *w*
  lifian *w*
live on ālibban *w*
livelihood bigleofa *(m)*
living bīleofa *(m)*
  ealdor *(n)*
lone-dweller ānhoga *(m)*
middle-age midfeorh *(m,n)*

neighbour nēahgebūr *(m)*
occupy weardian *w*
  wīcian *w*
outlive oferbīdan *1*
remain (ā)wunian *w*
separate dwelling sundorwīc *(n)*
spend one's life drohtnian *w*
survive gedīgan *w*
  oferlibban *w*
way of life drohtnung *(f)*

LORD

almighty ælmihtig
arrange stihtian *w*
array trymian *w*
authority hlāforddōm *(m)*
  onweald *(m)*
benefactor (in wealth) bēahgifa *(m)*
benevolent ruler winedrihten *(m)*
bestow honour upon inwyrcan *w*
birth gebyrd *(f)*
brandish ācweccan *w*
  bregdan *3*
care heord *(f)*
chief æðeling *(m)*
  ealdor *(m)*
  frēa *(m)*
  lēod *(m)*
  ðēoden *(m)*
chief thane ealdorðegn *(m)*
coerce geðyn *w*
command bebēodan *2*
  diht *(m)*
commandment gebodscipe *(m)*
compel bǣdan *w*
  fornȳdan *w*
  (tō)genȳdan *w*
  geðyn *w*
  nīedan *w*

comrade genēat *(m)*
consume notian *w*
control geweald *(n)*
  (ge)wealdan *7*
  wieldan *w*
crown corenbēg *(m)*
  corōna *(m)*
  cynehelm *(m)*
custody heord *(f)*
decree bebod *(n)*
direction diht *(m)*
dispose fadian *w*
  stihtian *w*
distributor brytta *(m)*
draw a sword ābregdan *3*
  ūtātēon *1,2*
draw up stihtan *w*
  trymian *w*
duty nytt *(f)*
earl ealdorman *(m)*
  eorl *(m)*
elder ealdor *(m)*
  ealdorman *(m)*
emperor cāsere *(m)*
empress cāsern *(f)*
enjoy nēotan *2*
force geðȳn *w*
  ðrēa *(m)*
  ðrēat *(m)*
forced tribute nīedbād *(f)*
govern stȳran *w*
  wieldan *w*
great grēat
greatness dōm *(m)*
  grēatnes *(f)*
hall-governor selerǣdend *(m)*
head officer ealdorðegn *(m)*
high counsellor hēahwita *(m)*
high-born æðele
  byrde
high-ranking hēahðungen
in shining armour scīrham
king cyng *(m)*
  cyning *(m)*

king over a nation ðēodcyning *(m)*
kingdom cynedōm *(m)*
  (cyne)rīce *(n)*
kingship cynehād *(m)*
lady hlǣfdige *(f)*
  ides *(f)*
law regol *(f)*
lawful regollīc
leader brego *(m)*
  ealdor *(m)*
leaderless hlāfordlēas
lord dryhten *(m)*
  ealdor *(m)*
  frēa *(m)*
  hearra *(m)*
  hlāford *(m)*
  mondryhten *(m)*
lordless ealdorlēas
  hlāfordlēas
lordship hlāforddōm *(m)*
low-born unǣðele
master frēa *(m)*
  hearra *(m)*
  hlāford *(m)*
mighty rīce
  þyhtig
  wielde
nation geðēode *(m)*
  lēod *(f)*
  lēode *(mpl)*
  ðēod *(f)*
  ðēodscipe *(m)*
nobility (of birth) æðelborennes *(f)*
noble indryhten
noble family æðelu *(f)*
obedience hīersumnes *(f)*
obey hīeran *w*
  hīersumian *w*
officer gerēfa *(m)*
order diht *(m)*
  fadian *w*
palace cynestōl *(m)*
people ðēodscipe *(m)*
possession ǣht *(f)*
power ǣht *(f)*

  geweald *(n)*
  onweald *(m)*
  rīccetere *(n)*
powerful mihtig
  rīce
powerless unmihtig
prince æðeling *(m)*
  brego *(m)*
  ealdor *(m)*
  eodor *(m)*
  lēod *(m)*
  ðēoden *(m)*
profit nytt *(f)*
protector eodor *(m)*
  helm *(m)*
  weard *(m)*
province ealdordēm *(m)*
provincial governor ealdormann *(m)*
queen cwēn *(f)*
rank gebyrd *(f)*
reeve gerēfa *(m)*
regular regollīc
regulate besīdian *w*
reign rīxian *w*
restrain gehaþerian *w*
ring-giver bēahgifa *(m)*
royal cynelīc
royal family cynecynn *(n)*
rule rǣdan *w*
  regol *(f)*
  rīce *(n)*
  rīxian *w*
  wealdan *7*
  wieldan *w*
ruler weard *(m)*
ruler of a district londfruma *(m)*
serviceable stǣlwyrðe
shake ācweccan *w*
  (ā)scacan *6*
shake off tōbregdan *3*
society gefērscipe *(m)*
standard-bearer cumbolwiga *(m)*
steer stȳran *w*
subject underðēodan *7*
submit to underhnīgan *1*

successor æftergenga *(m)*
summon (ge)bannan *7*
sway geweald *(n)*
throne cynesetl *(n)*
  giefstōl *(m)*
tribe geðēode *(n)*
tyranny ofermægen *(f)*
  rīccetere *(n)*
under the control of gewylde
unintentionally ungewealdes
unlordly unæðele
use nēotan *2*
  notian *w*
  nytt *(f)*
useless unnytt
war-leader bealdor *(m)*
  folcāgend *(m)*
  folctoga *(m)*
  gūðweard *(m)*
  heretoga *(m)*
  wīgfruma *(m)*
weak unmihtig
wield wealdan *7*
  wieldan *w*
without dishonour unforcūð

LOVE

adulation oferlufu *(f)*
  twædding *(f)*
adultery æwbryce *(m)*
affable wordwynsum
agreeable gecwēme
  gemēde
allure ōlæcung *(f)*
appearance ansīen *(f,n)*
  wlite *(m)*
ardour hātheortnes *(f)*
  wylm *(m)*

aspire to fundian *w*
at will on lyste
attract getēon *2*
  spanan *6*
be pleasing to gelīcian *w*
beautiful ælfscīenu
  beorht
  blāchlēor
  cȳmlīc
  deall
  fæger
  hīwbeorht
  hwīt
  leoht
  scīene
  scīr
  smicer
  wlitig
  wrǣst(līc)
beauty blēoh *(n)*
  glǣm *(m)*
  lēoma *(m)*
  mægwlite *(m)*
  scīma *(m)*
  torht *(n)*
  wlīte *(m)*
beloved fǣle
  lēof
  luflīc
  swǣs
beloved companion wilgesīð *(m)*
  wilgeðofta *(m)*
blush blyscan *w*
bridesmaid hādswǣpe *(f)*
bridesman hādswǣpa *(m)*
care cearu *(f)*
care for begongan *7*
  gīeman *w*
  rēcan *w*
  reccan *w*
celebrate mǣran *w*
charm ōlæcung *(f)*
cherish clyppan *w*
  friðian *w*
  tyddrian *w*

choice cyre *(m)*
choose (ge)cēosan *2*
co-habit hǣman *w*
coitus (wīf)gemāna *(m)*
  wīfþing *(n)*
comely cȳmlīc
comfort gefrēfrian *w*
company gefērscipe *(m)*
comrade gefēra *(m)*
  genēat *(m)*
  geselda *(m)*
console frēfran *w*
consort gemæcca *(m)*
crave crafian *w*
  giernan *w*
dalliance with a woman wīfcȳððu *(f)*
darling dēorling *(m)*
dear dēore
  lēof
  luflīc
  weorð
delight gecwēmednes *(f)*
  wynn *(f)*
  wynsumnes *(f)*
delightful wynsum
desirable giernendlīc
  wilsumlīc
desire fundian *w*
  giernan *w*
  lust *(m)*
  willa *(m)*
  willan *a*
  (ge)wilnian *w*
  wilnung *(f)*
  wyscan *w*
desperate love sorglufu *(f)*
devotion wilsumnes *(f)*
draw getēon *2*
eager fūs
ecstasy elhygd *(f)*
elegant smicer
embrace (ymb)clyppan *w*
  fæðm *(m)*
enfold befealden *7*
engagement winetrēow *(f)*

enjoy to the full ðurhbrūcan *2*
entice getihtan *w*
  (ā)spanan *6*
fair fæger
  gemēde
fair of face blāchlēor
  wlitescīene
favour fremsumnes *(f)*
fervour wylm *(m)*
flatter ōlǣcan *w*
folly gāl *(n)*
  gālnes *(f)*
fornicate firenian *w*
  forlecgan *w*
fornication forliger *(n)*
  wōhhǣmed *(n)*
fraternity gefērscipe *(m)*
friend frēond *(m)*
  wine *(m)*
friendless winelēas
  wineðearfend
friendly blīðe
  blīðmōd
  frēondlīc
  welwillende
friendship cȳððu *(f)*
  frēondrǣden *(f)*
  frēondscipe *(m)*
gentle līðe
glad (ge)fægen
  lustlīc
gladden blissian *w*
greet grētan *w*
  hālettan *w*
grin grennian *w*
guest giest *(m)*
hail hālettan *w*
happy blīðemod
  fægen
harlot hōre *(f)*
  firenhicge *(f)*
harmonious gesībsum
  geðwǣre
heartfelt love ferhðlufu *(f)*
  mōdlufu *(f)*

heed gīeman *w*
hospitable giestlīðe
hug ymbclyppan *w*
incite desire lystan *w*
intimate friend wilgehleða *(m)*
joy blīðnes *(f)*
  wynn *(f)*
joyful blīðe
  lustlīc
  wynlīc
joyous lustbǣre
keep peace with friðian *w*
kindness fremsumnes *(f)*
kiss (ge)cyssan *w*
laugh hlihhan *6*
laughter breahtm *(m)*
  hleahtor *(m)*
like līcian *w*
longing fūs
  longað *(m)*
  lustbǣre
  mynela *(m)*
look after begongan *7*
love frēogan *w*
  frīge *(fpl)*
  lufian *w*
  lufu *(f)*
love-making restgemāna *(m)*
loved one drūt *(f)*
lovely cȳmlīc
  lufiendlīc
lover frēond *(m)*
  hǣmedwīf *(n)*
  hǣmend *(m)*
  hǣmere *(m)*
  lufestre *(f)*
  lufiend *(m)*
  wine *(m)*
loving lufiendlīc
  luflīc
lust gāl *(n)*
  gālnes *(f)*
  lust *(m)*
lustful gālferhð
  gālmōd

maidenhead mǣgðhād *(f)*
maidenhood mǣgðhād
make love with cnēowian *w*
marriage ǣwnung *(f)*
  hǣmed *(m)*
  legertēam *(m)*
mate gemǣcca *(m)*
mild līðe
  rōw
  smolt
  smylte
mirth bearhtm *(m)*
mislead forsponan *6*
noise bearhtm *(m)*
object of desire willa *(m)*
one's own beloved swǣs
partner gemǣcca *(m)*
passion ðrōwung *(f)*
passionate hātheort
peaceful geðwǣre
perversion forliger *(n)*
placate ōlǣcan *w*
playful plegol
pleasant gecwēmlīc
  līðe
  wynsum
please gecwēman *w*
  (ge)līcian *w*
  lystan *w*
pleasure gecwēmednes *(f)*
  lust *(m)*
  willa *(m)*
  wynsumnes *(f)*
precious dēor
  weorð
prefer bet lystan *w*
  foreberan *4*
  swīðor unnan *a*
pretty blāchlēor
  wlitescīene
protect friðian *w*
rather hraðor
ready fūs
rejoice blissian *w*

seduce costnian *w*
  forsponan *6*
select cēosan *2*
send greetings hǣlo bodian *w*
set free frēogan *w*
sex hǣmed *(m)*
  liger *(n)*
sexual intercourse hǣmedlāc *(n)*
sexual pleasure wynlust *(m)*
sigh over sīcan *1*
stroke ðaccian *w*
suffer ðrōwian *w*
suffering ðrōwung *(f)*
sweet līðe
take care of rēcan *w*
  reccan *w*
take note of gīeman *w*
tempt costnian *w*
tend begongan *7*
  lǣstan *w*
tickling smeartung *(f)*
troth winetrēow *(f)*
trouble cearu *(f)*
unfaithfulness ungetrȳwð *(f)*
virginity mǣgðhād
voluntary wilsumlīc
want willan *a*
wedding weddung *(f)*
wedding gift (groom to bride)
  morgengifu *(f)*
weep grēotan *2*
  rēotan *2*
welcome grēting *(f)*
  lēof
welcome guest wilcuma *(m)*
willing (ge)fægen
  lustlīc
willing companion wilgesīð *(m)*
winsome wynsum
winsome female wynmǣg *(f)*
wish willan *a*
  wȳscan *w*
with love frēondlīc
yearn for giernan *w*
yearning longað *(m)*

MATERIAL

alum efne *(f)*
amber eolhsand *(n)*
  glær *(m)*
  smelting *(f)*
atom mot *(n)*
bitumen eorðtyrewe *(f)*
bloom blōma *(m)*
brass ār *(n)*
  mæstling *(n)*
brazen ǣren
chalk cealc *(m)*
chipping sceafoða *(m)*
cloth godwebb *(n)*
coal col *(n)*
condensation īsenswāt *(m)*
copper ār *(n)*
corrode ābītan *1*
  forrotian *w*
crystal cristalla *(m)*
  ðurhscȳnestān *(m)*
dubbing gedrēog *(n)*
dust dūst *(n)*
filings gesweorf *(n)*
fine cloth godwebb *(n)*
flint flint *(m)*
glass glæs *(n)*
gold gold *(n)*
golden gylden
gypsum spærstān *(m)*
hardness heardnes *(f)*
  stīðnes *(f)*
hide hȳd *(f)*
horn horn *(m)*
iron īren *(n)*
  īsern *(n)*

ivory elpendbān *(m)*
　elpendtōð *(m)*
　ylpesbān *(n)*
knot in wood ōst *(m)*
lead lēad *(n)*
lime līm *(m)*
lime (whitewash) hwītingmelu *(n)*
limestone cealcstān *(m)*
lump blōma *(m)*
　wecg *(m)*
　wolcen *(m,n)*
made of beechwood bēcen
made of bone bǣnen
made of boxwood byxen
made of brass ǣren
made of glass glǣsen
made of gold gylden
made of iron īsern
made of ivory elpendbǣnen
made of lindenwood linden
made of linen līnen
made of otterskin yteren
made of planks breden
made of silk seolcen
made of stone stǣnen
made of wheat hwǣten
made of wood trēowen
made of wool wullen
marble marmastān *(m)*
oakum ācumba *(m)*
ore ār *(m)*
paste slypa *(m)*
perfume stēran *w*
　stōr *(m)*
pewter tin *(n)*
pitch pic *(n)*
red lead tēafor *(n)*
refined smǣte
refuse ðreax *(m)*
resin eolhsand *(n)*
　glær *(m)*
rust ābītan *1*
　ōm *(m)*
rusty ōmig
sheet metal platung *(f)*

silk seolc *(m)*
silver seolfor *(n)*
solid gold eallgylden
solid iron eallīren
soot hrūm *(m)*
sort cynn *(n)*
steel stȳle *(n)*
stone stān *(m)*
straw healm *(m)*
stubble healm *(m)*
sulphur swefel *(m)*
tar eorðtyrewe *(f)*
　teoru *(n)*
tin tin *(n)*
verdigris ārsāpe *(f)*
wax weax *(n)*
weft ōweb *(n)*
whitewash hwītingmelu *(n)*
wooden trēowen
wool wull *(f)*

MEASURE

a great deal micel
　wornfela
a little lyt(hwōn)
　sumes
all eall
almost fulnēah
　welnēah
amount andefn *(f)*
　worn *(m)*
amphor-full amber *(m,n,f)*
arm's length fæðm *(m)*
　fæðmrīm *(n)*
big grēat
　micel

bushel mydd *(n)*
cartload fōðor *(n)*
completely fullfremedlīce
   tō wissum
count (ā)rīman *w*
   talian *w*
   tellan *w*
counting by thousands
   ðūsendgerīm *(n)*
countless number un(ge)rim *(n)*
distance fyrlu *(f)*
double twīfeald
earliest ǣrest
   forma
ecclesiastical measure ciricmitta *(m)*
ell eln *(f)*
empty ǣmtig
   tōm
enough genōg
entire anwealh
especially swīþost
few fēa
fine smæl
first forma
foot fōtmǣl *(n)*
furlong furhlang *(n)*
gill pægel *(m)*
gourd cucurbite *(f)*
great grēat
   micel
greatly miclum, micle
half healf *(f)*
handful handfull *(f)*
   grīpa *(m)*
hard to count earfoðrīme
heavy hefig
hide of land hīd *(f)*
huge ormǣte
in addition on ðǣrtō
in any way on ǣnigum
in half emtwā
in two emtwā
inch ince *(m)*
innumerable unārīmed
just as much efnlīce

large grēat
   micel
   ormǣte
least lǣst
length langnys *(f)*
less lǣssa
light līht
little lytel
little by little dǣlmǣlum
long lang
lot(s) fela
   monig
   worn
manifold monigfeald
many fela
   manig
   worn
measure gemet *(n)*
   mǣð *(f)*
   metan 5
   mitta *(m)*
   trȳm *(n)*
measure by weight wǣge *(f)*
measure of bulk sester *(m)*
measure of corn sesðlar *(n)*
measuring cup cuppe *(f)*
metre gemet *(n)*
mile mīl *(f)*
more mā
   māra
most mǣst
much grēat
   micel
   worn fela
multiply gemænigfealdian *w*
multitude menigu *(f)*
nearly æthwōn
   fulnēah
   welnēah
none nān
   nǣnig
number gerīm *(n)*
   getæl *(n)*
   worn *(m)*
odd number ofertæl *(n)*

ounce yndse *(f)*
oxgang (eighth of a hide)
  oxangang *(n)*
pace stæpe *(m)*
part dæl *(m)*
partly be sumum dæle
penny peni(n)g *(m)*
pennyweight peningwæg *(f)*
pound pund *(n)*
  pundwæg *(f)*
quarter feorðandæl *(m)*
quite lythwōn
  sumes
rear endemæst
reckon rīman *w*
rod gyrd *(f)*
scale-bowl scealu *(f)*
separate ānlīpig
series getæl *(n)*
several manigfeald
severely ðearle
shilling scilling *(m)*
short scort
shortness sceortnes *(f)*
simple ānfeald
single ānge
  ānlīpig
size grēatnes *(f)*
  micelnes *(f)*
slight gehwæde
slim þynn
  wāc
small lytel
somewhat hwega
  nāthwōn
  sumes
sort cynn *(n)*
sparing spær
spoon(ful) sticca *(m)*
staff gyrd *(f)*
threefold ðrifeald
thrice ðriwa
too (much) forhwega
  tō
triple ðrifeald

twice tū
  twuwa
two thirds twæde
twofold twifeald
very ful
  swīðe
  wel
weight gewiht *(n)*
  hefignes *(f)*
  wæge *(f)*
whole ful
widely wīde
widespread rȳfe

MIND

ability cræft *(m)*
  mæð *(f)*
accomplishment gecneordnes *(f)*
accustom geliðian *w*
  wenian *w*
accustomed bewuna
adulation oferlufu *(f)*
  twædding *(f)*
advice ræd *(m)*
advisable rædlīc
advise gelæran *w*
  rædan *w*
afraid forht
against one's will unðonces
amazed āmasod
  ofwundrod
anger ierre *(f)*
angry ierremōd
  wrāð
annoyance æfðonca *(m)*
anxiety ymbhoga *(m)*
apply onself befēolan *3*

arrogance gielp *(m,n)*
  ofermōdignes *(f)*
aspire to fundian *w*
at leisure ǣmettig
aware gemyndig
awareness gewitnes *(f)*
awe ege *(m)*
bad-tempered gedreht
  hrēohmōd
bashful forhtful
be addicted to underðēodan *w*
be amazed wāfian *w*
be ashamed (ge)scomian *w*
be envious æfestian *w*
be in the habit of gewunian *w*
be intent hīgian *w*
be merciful to gemiltsian *w*
be sad sorgian *w*
  sweorcan *3*
be sane tela witan *a*
be troubled (ge)sweorcan *3*
  swincan *3*
be wary of warian *w*
bear in mind gemunan *w*
  gemyndian *w*
behave gebǣran *w*
bemoan besorgian *w*
  murnan *3*
benefit ār *(f)*
betoken tācnian *w*
big-hearted rūmheort
bitter wrāð
boast hrēman *w*
bold beald
  cāf
  collenferhð
  dēor
  dyrstig
  fram
  mōdelīc
boldness gebyld *(f)*
boredom ǣðrytnes *(f)*
bravado ellen *(m)*
  wlencu *(f)*
brave dēor

rōf
stīðmōd
unhēanlīc
brutish stunt
calm smylte
calm down (ge)sweðrian *(m)*
care cearu *(f)*
  gīeman *(f)*
  gīeming *(f)*
  murnan *3*
  ymbhoga *(m)*
  ymbhygd *(f)*
careful behȳdig
  hohful
careless mōdlēas
  wanhȳdig
careworn earmcearig
cause intinga *(m)*
celebrate frēolsian *w*
  rǣran *w*
cheerful rōtlīc
cherish friðian *w*
clever snotor
comfort (ge)frēfran *w*
  frōfor *(f)*
commotion styrenes *(f)*
  unstilnes *(f)*
compassion efensārgung *(f)*
condition wīse *(f)*
conduct gebǣre *(n)*
  ðēaw *(m)*
confidence gebyld *(f)*
confident ðrīste
  unearg
conscience ingeðanc *(m,n)*
consider behycgan *w*
  ymbðencan *w*
consolation frōfor *(f)*
contempt forhogdnes *(f)*
  oll *(n)*
contrary ambyre
courage ellen *(n)*
  mōd *(m)*
courageous ellenrōf
cowardice yrhðu *(f)*

cowardly earg
craftiness sierwung *(f)*
cruel heard
  slīðen
cunning list *(m,f)*
  lytig
  onglǣwlīc
  orðonc
  prættig
  searugrim
  sierwung *(f)*
curiosity fyrwit *(n)*
  fyrwitnes *(f)*
curious frymdig
  searolīc
custom gewuna *(m)*
  ðēaw *(m)*
customary geðȳwe
  gewuna *(m)*
damn fordēman *w*
dare durran *a*
  genēðan *w*
  geðristian *w*
daring dyrstig
  ðrȳste
deceive besyrwan *w*
deception swicdōm *(m)*
  wrenc *(m)*
deep neowol
  nīwol
delusion dyderung *(f)*
depression unmōd *(n)*
despairing ormōd
determined ārǣd
difference gescād *(n)*
dignity geðyncðu *(f)*
diligence gīeman *(f)*
  gīeming *(f)*
disappointed getrucod
disgrace scomu *(f)*
dishearten yrgan *w*
disheartened werigferhð
disinclination unðonc *(m)*
dismayed ācol
distress angsumnes *(f)*

gedrēfednes *(f)*
dizziness swīma *(m)*
dread ondrǣdan 7
drug-taking lyblāc *(n,m)*
dull dwǣs
eager cēne
  fūs
  georn(ful)
eager for glory dōmgeorn
eagerness ellenwōdnes *(f)*
  georn(ful)nes *(f)*
earnestness earnost *(f)*
echo onscillan *w*
  dweorg *(m)*
ecstasy elhygd *(f)*
encourage ehtian *w*
  hyrdan *w*
encouragement forbylding *(f)*
envious æfestful
  æfestig
envy anda *(m)*
excite hwettan *w*
  onbryrdan *w*
exciting hrōr
exhort monian *w*
  rǣdan *w*
  trymian *w*
expectation wēn *(f)*
  wēna *(m)*
expedient nytlic
  rǣdlīc
experienced frōd
exult behliehhan 6
  hrēman *w*
  mōdigian *w*
exultant hrēmig
fain gefægen
falter wandian *w*
fastidious cīs
favour fremsumnes *(f)*
fear forhtian *w*
fearful ācol
  egelic
  forht
feel pity ofhrēowan 2

fervent mōdig
  onǣled
fierce āfor
  grimm
  hrēoh
  hrēðe
firm (stede)fæst
  stīð(līc)
firmness ānmōdnes *(f)*
  fæstnes *(f)*
folly dysignes *(f)*
  gāl *(n)*
  gālnes *(f)*
  hygelēast *(f)*
  unrǣd *(m)*
foolish dwǣs
  dwollīc
  dysig
  stunt
forgetfulness ofergitolnys *(f)*
forward fram
free from sorrow sorglēas
frivolous dysig
  gālsmǣre
  oferblīþe
game gamen *(n)*
generous ginfæst
  rūmheort
gentle bilewit
ghost gāst *(m)*
  gǣst *(m)*
glad gefægen
  glæd
gloomy galgmōd
  sweorcendferhð
glorious torhtmōd
glory ār *(f)*
go mad wēdan *w*
gracious ārfæst
  glæd
grief brēostwylm *(m)*
  cearu *(f)*
  hrēow *(f)*
  mōdcearu *(f)*
  sorg *(f)*

grieving hrēowigferhð
  hrēowigmōd
  sorgende
grudge æfðonca *(m)*
  inca *(m)*
habit ðēaw *(m)*
happiness gesǣlignes *(f)*
  gesǣlð *(f)*
hasten fundian *w*
hatred anda *(m)*
heart ferhð *(m,n)*
  geðonc *(m,n)*
  gewitloca *(m)*
  mōd *(m)*
  mōdgeðonc *(m,n)*
  (mōd)sefa *(m)*
heed gīeman *w*
heedless gīemelēas
hesitate wandian *w*
honest eornost *(f)*
honour ār *(f)*
  ārian *w*
hope gehyhtan *w*
  hopian *w*
  hyht *(m)*
  tōhopa *(m)*
howling wōma *(m)*
human joy mondrēam *(m)*
humble ēaðmōd
humility ēaðmēdu *(n)*
  ēaðmētto *(f)*
  ēaðmōdnes *(f)*
hypocrisy līcetung *(f)*
idleness āsolcennes *(f)*
  īdel *(n)*
  īdelnes *(f)*
imitate æfterhyrgan *w*
  gelǣcan *w*
impetuous forðgeorn
  ungefōglīc
incline geliðian *w*
indolent īdelgeorn
inexorable ārǣd
injustice unriht *(n)*
innocence bilewitnes *(f)*

innocent bilewit
inspiration inbryrdnes *(f)*
intellect gewit *(n)*
   mōd *(n)*
intend hogian *w*
   mynian *w*
intent behygdig
   gemyndig
invention finding *(f)*
irritable ēaðbylige
joy gefēa *(m)*
   gomen *(n)*
   mondrēam *(m)*
joyful gelustful
keen cēne
   fram
   georn(ful)
keep peace with friðian *w*
kind ārfæst
   bilewit
   glæd
   mildelīc
kindness fremsumnes *(f)*
knowledge gewitnes *(f)*
   leornung *(f)*
   ongietennes *(f)*
lacking counsel rǣdlēas
lament geōmrung *(f)*
lamenting wōpig
language gereord *(n)*
   geðēode *(n)*
lax earg
   slāw
lazy īdelgeorn
learned gelǣred
leisure ǣmetta, ēmta *(m)*
light-hearted lēohtmōd
longing fūs
luck gesǣlignes *(f)*
   gesǣlð *(f)*
lust gāl *(n)*
   gālnes *(f)*
lustful gālmōd
mad gemād
   wōd

madness wōdnes *(f)*
malice anda *(m)*
malicious heteðancol
manner wīse *(f)*
matter intinga *(m)*
mean tācnian *w*
memory gemynd *(f,n)*
mental aberration onweggewit *(n)*
merciful milde
merry blīðe
   hlagol
   myrge
mighty ðearlmōd
mild milde
   rōw
   smolt
   smylte
mind ferhð *(m,n)*
   geðonc *(m,n)*
   gewitloca *(m)*
   hordcofa *(m)*
   hyge *(f)*
   mōd *(m)*
   mōdgeðonc *(m,n)*
   (mōd)sefa *(m)*
mindful gemyndig
   hohful
mirth myrhð *(f)*
misery iermðu *(f)*
   wēa *(m)*
   wracu *(f)*
   wræc *(n)*
mislead dwelian *w*
mistake misfēran *w*
moderation syfernys *(f)*
modest scomfæst
mood hyge *(m)*
   mōd *(m)*
mourn gnornian *w*
   hrēowan *2*
   murnan *3*
mourning gnornung *(f)*
move āstyrian *w*
nature gecynd *(n)*
neglect wandian *w*

noble torhtmōd
normal gewuna
obey gīeman *w*
oblivion ofergeatu *(f)*
outstanding ǣrgōd
pain sārnes *(f)*
  sārwracu *(f)*
painless unsār
patience geðyld *(f)*
patient geðyldig
peaceful smolt
penetrating glēaw
persuade gelǣran *w*
perverse wiðerweardlīc
piety ārfæstnes *(f)*
plan gerǣdan *w*
  hogian *w*
  rǣd *(m)*
play gomen *(n)*
pleasant myrge
  wynsum
powerful emotion brēostwylm *(m)*
prejudice fordēman *w*
pride bælc *(m)*
  gāl *(n)*
  gālnes *(f)*
  hyge *(f)*
  (ofer)mōd *(m)*
  mōdignes *(f)*
  oferhygd *(f,n)*
  ofermettu *(f)*
  pryte *(f)*
  ūpāhefednes *(f)*
  wlencu *(f)*
profound neowol
  nīwol
prompt gearu
propriety mǣð *(f)*
proud mōdelīc
  wlonc
providence forescēawung *(f)*
quick-witted horsc
rancour inca *(m)*
rash hātheort
ready fūs

  gearu
reckless reccelēas
reflect behycgan *w*
  smēagan *w*
rejoice gefēon *5*
remember gemunan *w*
  gemyndian *w*
remembrance mynegung *(f)*
remind gemonian *w*
  mynian *w*
repent gescomian *w*
  hrēowan *2*
resolute ānrǣd
  rǣdfæst
  stīðmōd
resolution ānrǣdnes *(f)*
restless unstille
  ūtfūs
reverance mǣð *(f)*
rightly āriht
risk genēðan *w*
rouse āwacan *6*
  onhrēran *w*
rue hrēowan *2*
sad geōmor
  hrēoh
  hrēowigferhð
  hrēowigmōd
  mēðe
  unrōt
sad at heart frēorigferð
  mōdcearig
  sārigferð
sad-spirited galgmōd
  wintercearig
sane gewittig
sanity gewit *(n)*
sated sæd
satisfaction bliss *(f)*
sensible gewittig
serious hefig
severe hefig
  hrēðe
  stearc
  stīð(līc)

shame scomu *(f)*
sharp cēne
shifty ðusenthīwe
shy scēoh
sign tācn *(n)*
simplicity of mind bilewitnes *(f)*
sincere bilewit
   eornoste
skilful gelǣred
skill list *(m,f)*
slackness sleacnes *(f)*
   yrhðu *(f)*
sloth āsolcennes *(f)*
soften lissan *w*
solace frōfor *(f)*
sorrow murcnung *(f)*
   sārnes *(f)*
   (gnorn)sorg *(f)*
sorrow for gnornian *w*
   (be)sorgian *w*
sorrowful sārig
   sārlīc
   sorgcearig
   sorhful
sorry sārig
   sārlīc
spirit gāst *(m)*
   gǣst *(m)*
   sāwol *(f)*
spirited mōdig
splendid ǣnlīc
sport gomen *(n)*
staidness gestæððignes *(f)*
steadfast ānhȳdig
   stedefæst
stern hrēðe
   ðearlmōd
stimulate scyrpan *w*
stir āstyrian *w*
stir up drēfan *w*
   onhrēran *w*
stirring hror
stout stīð(līc)
stout-hearted stearcheort
   stercedferhð

stīðhycgend
swīðmōd
strength ellen *(n)*
strong fæst
strong in mind ellenrōf
stubborn fæst
study begengnes *(f)*
   gecneordnes *(f)*
subdue lissan *w*
surprise besyrwan *w*
swoon swīma *(m)*
take note of gīeman *w*
teach gelǣran *w*
tearful tēargēotend
thank geðoncian *w*
thanks ðonc *(m)*
thought gehygd *(f)*
   ingeðonc *(m)*
   mōdgeðonc *(m,n)*
   mōdsefa *(m)*
   (ge)ðonc *(m,n)*
tired of sæd
token tācn *(n)*
tranquil smylte
treacherous flāh
treachery searu *(n)*
   searucræft *(m)*
trick besyrwan *w*
   wrenc *(m)*
trouble cearu *(f)*
trust gehyhtan *w*
   gelȳfan *w*
unawares unforscēawodlīc
undaunted ðyhtig
   unearg
understanding andgiet *(n)*
   ingehygd *(f)*
   ongietennes *(f)*
   (ge)wit *(n)*
unhappy unhȳðig
   unrōt
unique ǣnlīc
unswayable ārǣd
usual bewuna
   wunelīc

valour dryhtscipe *(m)*
  ellen *(n)*
virtue ārfæstnes *(f)*
want willan *a*
warn warnian *w*
weary mēðe
  sæd
weary-minded wērigferhð
wile lot *(n)*
  searu *(n)*
  searucræft *(m)*
willing gefægen
  gelustful
wily searogrim
wise frōd
  glēaw
wise of mind ferhðglēaw
wit witt *(n)*
with one accord ānmōdlīc
woe wēa *(m)*
zeal ellenwōdnes *(f)*
zealous nēodful

female spirit āglǣcwīf *(n)*
fierce spirit heoruwearg *(m)*
ghost scinngedwola *(m)*
giant ent *(m)*
  fifel *(n)*
  ðyrs *(m)*
goblin nihtgenga *(m)*
  pūca *(m)*
  pūcel *(m)*
hellish spirit hellegāst *(m)*
  helsceaða *(m)*
monster āglǣca *(m)*
  egesa *(m)*
night creature nihtgenga *(m)*
  nihtscūa *(m)*
phantom scīnlāc *(n)*
werewolf werwulf *(m)*

MONSTER

alien spirit ellorgāst *(m)*
aquatic monster brimwylf *(f)*
  meredēor *(n)*
  nicor *(m)*
  wæteregesa *(m)*
devil dēofol *(m,n)*
doomed spirit gēosceaftgāst *(m)*
dragon draca *(m)*
  līgdraca *(m)*
  nīðdraca *(m)*
  wyrm *(m)*
dwarf dweorg *(m)*
evildoer lāðgetēona *(m)*

NEED

as necessary tō ðearfe
be necessary nēodian *w*
behove behōfian *w*
bereave belēosan *2*
bereft berēafod
  benumen
  sceard
calamity heardsǣlð *(f)*
  ðrēa *(m)*
care gedrēfednes *(f)*
compel bǣdan *w*
  fornȳdan *w*
  nīedan *w*
deprive bedrēosan *2*
  belīðan *1*
  benǣman *w*
  beniman *4*
  bescyrian *w*

deprived of beliden
 gǣsne
 lēas
 sceard
difficulty nearu *(f)*
 nīed *(f)*
 nīedðearf *(f)*
distress nearunes *(f)*
experience drēogan *2*
 gefaran *6*
famine hungor *(m)*
go without forðolian *w*
grievous swār
 swǣr
hardship gewinn *(n)*
heavy swār
 swǣr
hunger hungor *(m)*
in need ðearfendlīc
 wǣdligend
lack forðolian *w*
 gād *(n)*
 onsȳn *(f)*
 wana *(m)*
lack of food metelīest *(f)*
lacking gewana
 orfeorme
miserable earm
 unlǣde
misfortune ungesǣlð *(f)*
necessary nīedbehefe
 nīedbeðearf
 nīedðearflīc
necessity nīed *(f)*
 nīedðearf *(f)*
 ðearf *(f)*
necessity for a task ondweorc *(n)*
need behōfian *w*
 gād *(n)*
 nīed *(f)*
 nīedðearf *(f)*
 ðurfan *a*
needful nīedbehefe
 nīedbeðearf
 nīedðearflīc

 ðearf
owe āgan *w*
 sculan *a*
passion ðrōwung *(f)*
poor ðearfendlīc
 unspēdig
poor man ðearfa *(m)*
 wǣdla *(m)*
poverty ðearfednes *(f)*
 wǣdl *(f)*
require beðurfan *a*
require of bǣdan *w*
suffer gefaran *6*
 ðolian *w*
 ðrōwian *w*
terrible distress firenðearf *(f)*
trouble ungesǣlð *(f)*
want gād *(n)*
wanting wana
worry gedrēfednes *(f)*

PERFORM

accomplish geæfnian *w*
achieve æfnan *w*
 begān *a*
 gehēgan *w*
act dǣd *(f)*
 gewyrht *(n)*
act out plegian *w*
active hwæt
allow lǣtan *7*
apply onself to gefeallan *7*
attempt fandian *w*
 tilian *w*
be able magan *a*
be empowered to onhagian *w*
beaten sigelēas

behave gebǣran *w*
behaviour gebǣru *(npl)*
bring about (ge)fremman *w*
  geweorcan *w*
carry on ðurhtēon *2*
carry on (an activity) begongan *7*
carry out begān *a*
  (ge)dōn *7*
  (ge)forðian *w*
  gefremman *w*
  gehēgan *w*
  (ge)lǣstan *w*
  ðurhtēon *2*
complete fullfremman *w*
  fullgān *a*
  fyllan *w*
  geendian *w*
copy onhyrian *w*
deed dǣd *(f)*
  gewyrht *(n)*
deserve geearnian *w*
disobey forgīemelēasian *w*
  forgȳman *w*
  mishȳran *w*
do dōn *a*
earn geearnian *w*
easily īeð
  īeðelīce
easy īeðe(līc)
emulate gelǣcan *w*
  onhyrian *w*
exceed oferstīgan *1*
exultant sigehrēðig
fall to (an action) gefeallan *7*
feat dǣd *(f)*
fell fyllan *w*
  gehnǣgan *w*
forget forgietan *5*
  ofergietan *5*
fulfill fyllan *w*
further (an aim) (ge)forðian *w*
  fremian *w*
  (ge)fremman *w*
game gamen *(n)*
  lāc *(n)*

  plega *(m)*
gestures gebǣru *(npl)*
hesitate forwandian *w*
inactive blēaþ
intervene swīfan on *1*
keen hwæt
labour deorfan *3*
  winnan *3*
make ready fȳsan *w*
  gearwian *w*
manage gedōn *7*
  manian *w*
  stihtan *w*
merit geearnung *(f)*
neglect forgīemelēasian *w*
  forgietan *5*
  forgȳman *w*
overcome beswīcan *1*
  gehnǣgan *w*
  gereccan *w*
  ofercuman *4*
  oferdrīfan *1*
  oferflītan *1*
  oferwinnan *3*
overpower oferflītan *1*
  oferswīðan *1*
  oferwīgan *1*
overthrow tōbrecan *4*
  tōweorpan *3*
perform begān *a*
  gefremman *w*
  gelǣstan *w*
play gamen *(n)*
  lāc *(n)*
  plega *(m)*
  plegian *w*
practice begān *a*
prepare gearcian *w*
  (ge)gearwian *w*
  gierwan *w*
prevail rīcsian *w*
prevalent genge
prevent forwiernan *w*
refuse forwiernan *w*
reward geearnung *(f)*

see (something) through
  fullfremman *w*
  gelæstan *w*
severe swīð
steadfastly unwāclīc
strive sacan *6*
strong rōf
  swīð
subdue gereccan *w*
  ofercuman *4*
  oferdrīfan *1*
  oferflītan *1*
  oferwinnan *3*
subject gereccan *w*
succeed spēdan *w*
  spōwan *7*
success spēd *(f)*
successful spēdig
surpass oferstīgan *1*
  oferðēon *1*
sweep away forswāpan *7*
thrive ðēon *1*
toil deorfan *3*
undo undōn *a*
unprepared ungearu
victorious lord sigedrihten *(m)*
victorious nation sigeðēod *(f)*
victory sige *(m)*
  sigor *(m)*
vigorous rōf
wage (war) ðurhtēon *2*
  wīgian *w*
win by exchange gewrixlan *w*
win by fighting gefeohtan *3*
  geslēan *6*
  gewinnan *3*
win by going gefēran *w*
win by riding geærnan *w*

PLANT

aconite ðung *(m)*
agrimony gārclife *(f)*
albumen hwēte *(n)*
alder alor *(m)*
antirrhinum hundeshēafod *(n)*
apple-tree apulder *(m,f)*
archangelica blindenetele *(f)*
ash æsc *(m)*
asparagus eorðnafola *(m)*
aspen æspe *(f)*
bark rind *(f)*
barley bēow *(n)*
  bere *(m)*
barley crop berewæstm *(m)*
basil mistel *(m)*
bast bæst *(m)*
bean bēan *(f)*
bed of flowers wyrtbedd *(n)*
beech bōc *(f)*
beetroot bēte *(f)*
berry berge *(f)*
betony betonice *(f)*
  brūnwyrt *(f)*
bindweed wiðowinde *(f)*
birch berc *(f)*
blackberry bremel *(m)*
blackthorn slāhþorn *(m)*
bloom blōstma *(m)*
  blōwan *7*
blossom blōstma *(m)*
  blōwan *7*
bog myrtle gagel *(m)*
box tree box *(m)*
  boxtrēow *(n)*
bramble brember *(m)*
  brēmel *(m)*
branch blēd *(f)*
  bōg *(m)*
  telga *(m)*
brook lime hleomoce *(f)*
broom brōm *(m)*
bryony hymele *(f)*
buckbean glæppe *(f)*

buckthorn ðȳfeðorn *(m*
bugle ðunorclæfre *(f)*
bunch of berries lēactrēog *(m)*
burdock clāte *(f)*
  clifwyrt *(f)*
  ēawyrt *(f)*
burr clāte *(f)*
bush ðȳfel *(m)*
  wrid *(m)*
buttercup clufwyrt *(f)*
cabbage cawel *(m)*
cannabis hænep *(m)*
carline thistle eoforðrotu *(f)*
carrot more *(f)*
catmint nepte *(f)*
cedar ceder *(m?)*
centaury curmelle *(f)*
chaff egenu *(f)*
charlock cedelc *(f?)*
chestnut tree cystel *(f)*
chervil cerfille *(f)*
chickweed cicena mēte *(m)*
cleavers clāte *(f)*
clover clæfre *(f)*
cockspur grass āttorlāðe *(f)*
cole cāwel *(m)*
comfrey galluc *(m)*
coriander celendre *(f)*
corn spelt *(m)*
corncockle coccel *(m*
couch grass cwice *(m,f)*
cow parsley wuducerfille *(f)*
cowslip cūslyppe *(f)*
cress cærse *(f)*
crocus croh *(m)*
crosswort wrætte *(m)*
cucumber eorðæppel *(f)*
  hwerhwette *(f)*
cummin cymen *(n)*
cyclamen slite *(m,f)*
daisy dæges ēage
dandelion ægwyrt *(f)*
deadly nightshade ælfðone *(f)*
deciduous hrurul
dill dile *(m)*

dock (wudu)docce *(f)*
dog rose hēopbrēmel *(m)*
  wudurose *(f)*
drug lybb *(n)*
dwarf elder līðwyrt *(f)*
elder ellen *(n)*
elder ashtree ellenahse *(f)*
eyebright eāgwyrt *(f)*
fennel finol *(m)*
fern fearn *(n)*
feverfew feferfuge *(f)*
fir-tree furhwudu *(m)*
flax fleax *(n)*
flower blōstma *(m)*
  cropp *(m)*
flower-bed wyrtbedd *(n)*
flower festival blōstmfrēols *(m)*
fragrance stenc *(m)*
fragrant welstincend
fruit blēd *(f)*
  ofett *(n)*
  wæstm *(m)*
furze gors *(m)*
garden wyrtgeard *(m)*
gardener ediscweard *(m)*
  wyrtweard *(m)*
garlic gārlēac *(n)*
  hramsa *(m)*
  hramse *(f)*
gentian feldwyrt *(f)*
gorse gors *(m)*
grass gærs *(n)*
groundsel grundswylige *(f)*
hassock cassuc *(m)*
hawthorn ðȳfeðorn *(m)*
hazel hæsel *(m)*
healing herb lǣcewyrt *(f)*
heart's ease bānwyrt *(f)*
heather hǣþ *(m,n)*
hedge bewindla *(m)*
hemlock hymlic *(m)*
  hymlice *(f)*
hemp hænep *(m)*
henbane belene *(f)*

hip hēopbrēmel *(m)*
  hēope *(f)*
hoarhound hūne *(f)*
holly hole(g)n *(m)*
hop plant hymele *(f)*
houseleek ðunorwyrt *(f)*
hyacinth iācinctus *(m)*
iris glædene *(f)*
iris illyrica hwatend *(m)*
ivy īfig *(n)*
juice of a plant wōs *(n)*
juniper cwīcbēam *(m)*
laurel lawertrēow *(n)*
leaf lēaf *(n)*
leek lēac *(n)*
lettuce lactuce *(f)*
lichen ragu *(f)*
lily of the valley glofwyrt *(f)*
linseed līnsǣd *(n)*
log bēam *(m)*
  stocc *(m)*
lovage lubastice *(f)*
lupin elehtre *(f)*
luxuriant geþūf
madder mædere *(f)*
made of roses gerōsod
mallow hocc *(m)*
  hoclēaf *(n)*
maple tree hlin *(m)*
  mapuldor *(m)*
marigold sigelhweorfa *(m)*
marshmallow merscmealuwe *(f)*
meadowsweet medowyrt *(f)*
medlar æpening *(m)*
  openears *(m)*
millet hers *(f)*
mint minte *(f)*
mistletoe mistel *(m)*
  mistiltān *(m)*
moss ragu *(f)*
mugwort mucgwyrt *(f)*
mulberry byrigberge *(f)*
mustard senep *(m)*
myrtle wīr *(m)*
narcissus halswyrt *(f)*

narcotic substance lybb *(n)*
nasturtium lēaccærse *(f)*
nettle netle *(f)*
nut hnutu *(m)*
oak āc *(m)*
odour stenc *(m)*
onion (hwīt)lēac *(n)*
ooze sīpian *w*
  wāse *(f)*
oxeye gescādwyrt *(f)*
oxslip oxanslyppe *(f)*
palm palmtrēow *(m)*
parsley petersilie *(f)*
parsnip feldmoru *(f)*
  more *(f)*
pea pīse *(f)*
peach persic *(m)*
pennyroyal brōðerwyrt *(f)*
  dweorgedrostel *(m)*
  hǣlwyrt *(f)*
  pollegie *(f)*
peony peonie i(f)
pepper pipor *(m)*
pimpernel brysewyrt *(f)*
pine tree furhwudu *(m)*
plant þȳfel *(m)*
  wyrt *(f)*
plant juice wōs *(n)*
plough beswincan *3*
pomegranate cornæppel *(n)*
pungent gestence
quince coddæppel *(m)*
rapeseed nǣpsǣd *(n)*
raspberry hindberge *(f)*
rattlewort hrætelwyrt *(f)*
reed hrēod *(n)*
ribwort ribbe *(f)*
ripe rīpe
ripen gerīpian *w*
root more *(f)*
  moru *(f)*
  wyrtruma *(m)*
rose rōse *(f)*
rosehip hēope *(f)*

rosemary boðen *(m,n)*
  feldmædere *(f)*
rosy rōsen
rue rūde *(f)*
saffron croh *(m)*
sage salfie *(f)*
sap sæp *(n)*
savoury sæðerige *(f)*
saxifrage sundcorn *(n)*
seaweed sǣwār *(n)*
sedge dūðhamor *(m)*
seed cīð *(m)*
  corn *(n)*
  sǣd *(n)*
shoot blēd *(f)*
  cīð *(m)*
snapdragon hundeshēafod *(n)*
sorrel sure *(f)*
sow sāwan *7*
sowthistle ðufeðistel *(m)*
speedwell hleomoce *(f)*
spikenard nard *(m)*
sprout spryttan *w*
stichwort æðelferðingwyrt *(f)*
stink (fūl)stincan *3*
stock stocc *(m)*
straw strēaw *(n)*
strawberry strēaberge *(f)*
stubble gedrif *(n)*
sulfurwort cammoc *(m)*
tansy helde *(f)*
teazel tǣsel *(f)*
  wulfes camb *(m)*
thicket gewrid *(n)*
thistle ðistel *(m)*
thorn ðorn *(m)*
thorn thicket ðorngrǣfe *(f)*
thyme boðen *(m)*
  wuducūnelle *(f)*
till beswincan *3*
toadstool feldswamm *(m)*
tree bēam *(m)*
  trēow *(n)*
trefoil ðrilēfe *(mpl)*
turnip nǣp *(m)*

twig twig *(n)*
vervain æscðrotu *(f)*
violet bānwyrt *(f)*
  symeringwyrt *(f)*
viper's bugloss haransprecel *(m)*
water lily ēadocce *(f)*
  fleoðe *(f)*
waybread wegbrǣde *(f)*
weed wēod *(n)*
wheat hwǣte *(m)*
wild thyme wuducūnelle *(f)*
willow windeltrēow *(n)*
  wīðig *(m)*
withy wīþig *(m)*
woad wurma *(m)*
  wurme *(f)*
wood sorrel ðrilēfe *(mpl?)*
woodbine wudubend *(m)*
woodruff wudurofe *(f)*
woody nightshade ælfþone *(m)*
wormwood wermōd *(m)*
wychelm wice *(m,f)*
yarrow gearwe *(f)*
yew ēoh *(m)*
  īw *(m)*

POSITION

abide ābīdan *1*
above bufan
  ofer
  (on-, be-)ufan
absent æfweard
  ofhende
after æfter
against ongēan
alongside emnlang
  tōemnes
  onemn

amid onmiddan
tōmiddes
among ongemang
anywhere āhwǣr
apart (on)sundor
around onbūtan
attend andweardian *w*
ǣtwesan *a*
await ābīdan *1*
back-to-back bæcling
be at rest restan *w*
sittan *5*
standan *6*
wunian *w*
be present ǣtwesan *a*
behind behindan
below(-mentioned) hērbeæftan
beneath (be)neoðan
between betwēonum
betwuh (betwux)
beyond begeondan
bide (ge)bīdan *1*
cast weorpan *3*
close getenge
nēah
close together getenge
getenglīc
combine fēgan *w*
gesamodlǣcan *w*
continue ðurhwunian *w*
diagonally across ðwȳres
divide tōlicgan *5*
downward niðerweard
due east ēastrihte
east ēast
encompass ymbhwearfan *3*
ymblicgan *5*
everywhere ǣghwǣr
expect onbīdan *1*
extend licgan *5*
face-to-face nebb wið nebb
fasten gefæstenian *w*
following hērbeæftan
from behind æftan
from beneath neðan

from every direction ǣghwonan
hang hōn *7*
hongian *w*
in front foran(tō)
forne
onforan
in succession æfter
in the lower part neoðeweard
in the middle middeweard
onmiddan
tō middes
indoors inne
install onstellan *w*
instead on his lōh
internal innanweard
kneel cnēow(l)ian *w*
lay (ā)lecgan *w*
lean hlinian *w*
left hand side wynstra
lie licgan *5*
lie between tōlicgan *5*
lie round ymblicgan *5*
lie supine upweard licgan *w*
lock lūcan *2*
loose unfæst
low lāh
niðerlīc
lower niðera
lurk lūtian *w*
middle midde *(f)*
middel *(n)*
midway midd
near nēah
neglect forsittan *5*
nether neðera
nigh nēah
north norð
nowhere nāhwǣr
on this side behionan
opposed ondweard
out of doors onūtan
outside būtan
wiðūtan
over ofer
part ende *(m)*

persist ðurhwunian *w*
place stede *(m)*
  stōw *(f)*
position stede *(m)*
  stōw *(f)*
  till *(n)*
presence ondweardnes *(f)*
present ondweard
prevent forstandan *6*
remain (ā)wunian *w*
  (ge)bīdan *1*
  seomian *w*
remote fyrlen
remove ofdōn *a*
resist wiðstandan *6*
rest hlinian *w*
  seomian *w*
resting place strēowen *(f)*
right hand side swīðra
roundabout onbūtan
  ymbūtan
seat setl *(n)*
secure fæst
  gefæstenian *w*
separate (on)sundor
settle gesittan *5*
sit sittan *5*
sit down gesittan *5*
sit round ymbsittan *5*
skulk lūtian *w*
socket stæpe *(m)*
south sūð
southern side sūðhealf *(f)*
stand (ge)standan *6*
stand by bestandan *6*
stand firm stemnettan *w*
stand in the way forstandan *6*
stay away from forsittan *5*
stay behind lāst weardian *w*
stick (ge)cleofian *w*
sticky clibbor
stiff stīf
  stīð
straight ahead gerihte *(n)*
surround ymbsellan *w*

take a seat onsittan *5*
throne setl *(n)*
throughout geond
throw weorpan *3*
together ongeador
undermentioned hērbeæftan
until oð(ðæt)
up to oð(ðæt)
upon on
  onufan
  uppan
wait (on)bīdan *1*
wait for onbīdan *1*
west west
west, from the westan
within (on-, in-, be-)innan
withstand wiðstondan *6*

PROTECT

armour herewǣde *(n)*
barrier eodor *(m)*
cherish friðian *w*
cover helm *(m)*
  ðeccan *w*
  wrēon *1*
defence of one's home wīcfreoðu *(f)*
defenceless griðlēas
defend werian *w*
embrace fæðm *(m)*
fasten sǣlan *w*
favour hyldu *(f)*
fortified place burg *(f)*
guard warian *w*
  weard *(m)*
  werian *w*
guardian of a country londweard *(m)*
help fylstan *w*
  help *(f)*
  helpan *3*

hold (safe) warian *w*
  weardian *w*
keep gehabban *a*
  healdan *7*
  weardian *w*
keeper hyrde *(m)*
  weard *(m)*
keeping wǣr *(f)*
lordly protector eodor *(m)*
maintain gehealdan *7*
  gelǣstan *w*
make fast fǣstan *w*
  sǣlan *w*
make good gebētan *w*
power of protection mundcræft *(m)*
preserve beorgan *3*
protect āwerian *w*
  (ge)beorgan *3*
  (ge)ealgian *w*
  friðian *w*
  griðian *w*
  healdan *7*
protection fæðm *(m)*
  gebeorg *(n)*
  gescyldnes *(f)*
  hlēow *(m)*
  hlēowð *(f)*
  hyldu *(f)*
  mund(byrd) *(f)*
  trēownes *(f)*
  wǣr *(f)*
protector eodor *(m)*
  gehola *(m)*
  healdend *(m)*
  helm *(m)*
  mundbora *(m)*
  weard *(m)*
redeem ālīesan *w*
repair ednīwian *w*
  gebētan *w*
rescue āhreddan *w*
safe gebeorglīc
  gesund
  hæghāl
  unplēolīc

safe keeping gedrēog *(n)*
safe quarters friðstōl *(m)*
salvation gesyntu *(f)*
save āhreddan *w*
  ālīesan *w*
  beorgan *3*
  (ge)nerian *w*
saviour hǣlend *(m)*
secure fæst
  gefæstenian *w*
  sǣlan *w*
secure from orsorg
sheath scēað *(f)*
shelter hlēow *(m)*
  hlēowð *(f)*
sheltered hlēowfæst
shield (ge)scyldan *w*
support ācuman *4*
  fylstan *w*
surety borg *(f)*
truce trēownes *(f)*
undefended fierdlēas
  unwered
war fugitive hereflīema *(m)*
ward hyrde *(m)*

RECREATION

actor trūð *(m)*
alehouse ealuhūs *(n)*
arena pleghūs *(n)*
  wæferhūs *(n)*
bell clucge *(f)*
celebrate frēolsian *w*
charm galdor *(n)*
clear hlūtor
  swutol
comic song scēawendwīse *(f)*

cry hlēoðrian *w*
dance intrepettan *w*
dancer tumbere *(m)*
death song fūslēoð *(n)*
drum bydenbotm *(m)*
  tunnebotm *(m)*
drummer-girl glīwbydenestre *(f)*
entertainer trūð *(m)*
fiddle fiðele *(f)*
fiddler fiðelere *(m)*
  fiðelestre *(f)*
flautist hrēodpipere *(m)*
  hwistlere *(m)*
flute hwistle *(f)*
game gamen *(n)*
gymnasium bæðstede *(m)*
harp glīwbēam *(m)*
  hearpe *(f)*
harpstring hearpestreng *(m)*
hearing hlyst *(f)*
horn sweglhorn *(m)*
hunt huntian *w*
hunter hunta *(m)*
hunting huntoð *(m)*
  wāð *(f)*
incantation onsang *(m)*
lament sorglēoð *(n)*
listen hlosnian *w*
loud hlūd
lyre hearpe *(f)*
make verses wordum wrixlan *w*
melody hlēoðor *(n)*
  swinn *(m)*
  swinsung *(f)*
minstrel glīwmon *(m)*
minstrelsy glīwdrēam *(m)*
mirth blīðnes *(f)*
music sōncræft *(m)*
  swēg *(m)*
musical skill swēgcræft *(m)*
musical sound orgeldrēam *(m)*
musician trūð *(m)*
noise wōp *(m)*
organ organa *(m)*
organist organestre *(f))*

swegesweard *(m)*
piper pīpere *(m)*
play gomen *(n)*
play the harp hearpian *w*
plectrum hearpenægel *(m)*
poem lēoð *(n)*
  lēoðsong *(m)*
poet scop *(m)*
poetic language scopgereord *(n)*
poetic skill lēoðcræft *(m)*
public entertainer ealuscop *(m)*
quick (at dice) hrædtæfle
rattlestick clædersticca *(m)*
rope-walker rāpgenga *(m)*
shout hlēoðrian *w*
sing (ge)giddian *w*
  (ā)singan *3*
sing out (ā)galan *6*
singer scop *(m)*
song (cwide)giedd *(n)*
  (lēoð)song *(m)*
song of joy blissesang *(m)*
song of longing fūslēoð *(n)*
song of praise lofsang *(m)*
song of victory sigelēoð *(n)*
sound hlēoðor *(n)*
  swēg *(m)*
speak in verse hlēoðrian *w*
spell gealdor *(n)*
tambourine wīfhearpe *(f)*
trumpet bȳmere *(m)*
  trūðhorn *(m)*
  tube *(f)*
verse fers *(n)*
whistle hwingian *w*
  hwistle *(f)*
  hwistlian *w*
  pīpe *(f)*
whistling hwistlung *(f)*
wind instrument sweglhorn *(m)*

SAY

account gerecednes *(f)*
  racu *(f)*
acknowledge (and-)ondettan *w*
address tōspēcan *5*
admit andettan *w*
advise lǣran *w*
advocacy forspǣc *(f)*
advocate forspeca *(m)*
agree gecweðan *5*
ambiguous twifeald
announce (ā)bēodan *2*
  bodian *w*
answer andswaru *(f)*
  andwyrde *(n)*
  ondswerian *6*
  oncweðan *5*
  ondwyrdan *w*
argument mǣl *(f)*
avow gebēotian *w*
bad news lāðspell *(n)*
belie ālēogan *2*
bequeath (be-,ge-)cweðan *5*
bewail cwiðan *w*
blame ætwītan *1*
boast (ge)bēot *(n)*
  (ge)bēotian *w*
  gielp *(m,n)*
  gielpan *w*
  gielpword *(n)*
  hrēman *w*
broadcast tōbrǣdan *w*
  wīdmǣrsian *w*
calumny hōl *(n)*
clear swutol
command bebēodan *2*
  bebod *(n)*
  bēodan *2*
  hǣs *(f)*
  hātan *7*
complain besprecan *5*
complain of mǣnan *w*
concern ontimber *(n)*

confess (ge)andettan *w*
confirm fæstnian *w*
contend fettian *w*
  flītan *1*
conversation gewosa *(m)*
  sprǣc *(f)*
correct account rihtracu *(f)*
correct word wordriht *(n)*
credible gelēaflēc
curse werhð *(f)*
  wyrgðu *(f)*
debate mōtian *w*
deceive bedydrian *w*
  beswīcan *1*
  dwelian *w*
  gelēogan *2*
decide gereccan *w*
declare āreccean *w*
  āsecgan *w*
  benemnan *w*
  bodian *w*
  (ā)cȳðan *w*
  gecweðan *5*
  gereccan *w*
  onbēodan *2*
  swutelian *w*
decree ārǣdan *7*
  āstihtan *w*
  gereccan *w*
  scyrian *w*
  word *(n)*
deny ætsacan *6*
  forsacan *6*
  wiðsacan *6*
direction diht *(m)*
discourse mǣl *(f)*
discuss maðelian *w*
  wordum wrixlan *w*
discussion gesprec *(n)*
disgrace bismerian *w*
dispose fadian *w*
dispute fettian *w*
dissemble lytegian *w*
dissuade belēan *6*

distinct ānlīpig
  swutol
  ānlic
eloquence getingnes *(f)*
English language Englisc *(n)*
  Engliscgereord *(n)*
evil tidings lāðspell *(n)*
excuse belādung *(f)*
  lād *(f)*
  talu *(f)*
explain reccan *w*
express (ā)cweðan *5*
exult hrēman *w*
fairspoken swǣswyrde
faith trēow *(f)*
forbid forbēodan *2*
forementioned foresǣd
forename fulwihtnama *(m)*
foretell foresecgan *w*
  forewītegian *w*
forswear forswerian *6*
gasp orðian *w*
greet (ge)grētan *w*
  hālettan *w*
grumble grēotan *2*
  missprecan *5*
grumbling ceorung *(f)*
guidance lāttēowdōm *(m)*
  stēor *(f)*
  wissung *(f)*
hail hālettan *w*
harangue mǣlan *w*
hasty in speech hrædwyrde
hear gehlȳstan *w*
  (ge)hīeran *w*
hearing gehȳrnes *(f)*
  hlȳst *(f)*
herald ār *(m)*
  ǣrendraca *(m)*
  boda *(m)*
hesitate forwandian *w*
hiss hwinsian *w*
  hwistlian *w*
history spell *(n)*
  stǣr *(n)*

hoarse hās
ignore forsuwian *w*
  forswigian *w*
in truth sōðe
  tō sōðe
incite getyhtan *w*
  stihtian *w*
indescribable unāsecgendlīc
informer melda *(m)*
instruct behwyrfan *w*
  tēon *2*
  (ge)tȳn *w*
instruction lārcwide *(m)*
insult bismer *(m,n,f)*
  bismrung *(f)*
  hearm *(m)*
  hosp *(m)*
  misgrētan *w*
insulting bismerlīc
intellect ondgit *(n)*
  ongitennes *(f)*
intelligible ondgitfullīc
intercede for geðingian *w*
intercession ðingung *(f)*
interpret reccan *w*
  trahtian *w*
invite gelaðian *w*
issue geðinge *(n)*
jesting gegafsprǣc *(f)*
  hygelēast *(f)*
joke glēowian *w*
lament seofian *w*
language gereord *(n)*
  geðēode *(n)*
learn hīeran *w*
letter ǣrendgewrit *(n)*
liar lēogere *(m)*
lie (ā)lēogan *2*
  forlēogan *2*
listen gehlȳstan *w*
listen for hlosnian *w*
logic flitcræft *(m)*
  wordloc *(n)*
loquacious cwidol
loud hlūd

lying lēasung *(f)*
magic word galdorword *(n)*
make clear swutelian *w*
make known cȳðan *w*
manual sign hondseten *(f)*
matter geðinge *(n)*
  ontimber *(n)*
  ðing *(n)*
mean forstandan *6*
meaning ondgit *(n)*
meeting gemāna *(m)*
  ðing *(n)*
mention secgan *w*
message ǣrende *(n)*
  lāc *(n,f)*
  spell *(n)*
messenger ār *(m)*
  ǣrendwreca *(m)*
  boda *(m)*
mislead bedydran *w*
  dwelian *w*
moan cwiðan *w*
mourn cwiðan *w*
name benemnan *w*
narrative gerecennes *(f)*
noise hrēam *(m)*
oath āð *(m)*
obey gehīeran *w*
offer bēodan *2*
ordain scyrian *w*
order diht *(m)*
  hātan *7*
outwit lytegian *w*
pass in silence forsuwian *w*
  forswīgan *1*
perjure forlēogan *2*
perjury āðbryce *(m)*
persuasion swǣp *(n?)*
plead mōtian *w*
pledge wordbēotung *(f)*
poet wōðbora *(m)*
point out (ge)wīsian *w*
  wissian *w*
praise herenes *(f)*
  hering *(f)*

proclaim (ā)bēodan *2*
  wīdmǣrsian *w*
professed geanwyrde
promise behātan *7*
  gebēot *(n)*
  gehāt *(n)*
  gehātan *7*
  weddian *w*
prophesy forewītegian *w*
proposing forspǣc *(f)*
quiet swīge
rave wēdan *w*
  woffian *w*
refuse forsacan *6*
regulate fadian *w*
remind gemonian *w*
renounce wiðsacan *6*
report gesǣgen *(f)*
reproach hosp *(m)*
respond andswerian *w*
rumour hlīsa *(m)*
salute hālettan *w*
say āsecgan *w*
  cweðan *5*
  (ge)secgan *w*
saying cwide *(m)*
  sagu *(f)*
semi-vowel healfclypigend *(m)*
sentence fers *(m)*
settle gecweðan *5*
shame bismer *(m,n,f)*
  bismrung *(f)*
shout hlūdan *w*
  hlynnan *w*
show tǣcan *w*
  tǣcnan *w*
  wīsian *w*
  wissian *w*
sigh seofian *w*
sign gebēacn *(n)*
  getācnung *(f)*
signify forstandan *6*
  mǣnan *w*
silence swīgian *w*
soothsayer hwata *(m)*

speak cweðan *5*
  maðolian *w*
  (ge)mǣlan *w*
  secgan *w*
  (ge)sprecan *5*
speak about mǣnan *w*
speak out (ā)cweðan *5*
speaker reordberend *(m)*
speaking a foreign language elreord
speech cwide *(m)*
  gereord *(n)*
  gesprec *(n)*
  mǣl *(f)*
  sp(r)ǣc *(f)*
  word *(n)*
  wordcwide *(m)*
spoken message ǣrendsprǣc *(f)*
stammer stam *(f?)*
  stamettan *w*
  wlæffian w
statement (ge)sægen *(f)*
story racu *(f)*
  spell *(n)*
strange of speech elreord
swear (ge)swerian *6*
syllable stæfgefēg *(n)*
tale talu *(f)*
talk gemaðel *(n)*
  maðelian *w*
talkative specul
  swīðsprecel
teach lǣran *w*
  tǣcan *w*
tell gesecgan *w*
  reccan *w*
  tellan *w*
  wīsian *w*
  wissian *w*
thing ðing *(n)*
threat bēot *(n)*
threaten ðrēagan *w*
threatening words ðēowracu *(f)*
token getācnung *(f)*
translate āreccean *w*
  āwendan *w*

  oferlǣdan *w*
translator wealhstōd *(m)*
trick lytegian *w*
true sōð(līc)
true to one's word wordfæst
truth sōð *(n)*
  trēow *(f)*
unspeakable unāsecgend
uproar cierm *(m)*
  hrēam *(m)*
urge on getyhtan *w*
  stihtian *w*
utter gesprecan *5*
  wrecan *5*
verbal skill wōðcræft *(m)*
verbose wordig
voice reord *(n)*
  stefn *(f)*
vow bēotian *w*
  gebēot *(n)*
warn (ge)warnian *w*
wheedle geswǣslǣcan *w*
whine hwīnan *1*
whinge hwinsian *w*
whisper hwisprian *w*
whispering rēonung *(f)*
word word *(n)*

SEE

appear wrongly misðyncan *w*
behold gesēon *5*
  lōcian *w*
blind blind
come upon becuman *4*
cover behelian *w*
  bewrēon *1*

cover up behrēosan *2*
dark dimm
deceptive gedwimorlīc
despise forsēon *5*
dim dimm
dimness dimnes *(f)*
display oðȳwan *w*
espy scēawian *w*
exploration scēawung *(f)*
feign līcettan *w*
gaze hāwian *w*
  wlītan *1*
hide bedīglian *w*
  behelian *w*
  behȳdan *w*
  bewrēon *1*
  (ge)hȳdan *w*
  mīðan *1*
illusion dyderung *(f)*
illusory gedwimorlīc
invisible ungesewenlīc
look besēon *5*
  hāwian *w*
  lōcian *w*
  (ge)scēawian *w*
  wlātian *w*
look down on forsēon *5*
look (out) for wlātian *w*
make known (ge)cȳðan *w*
make manifest geswutelian *w*
meet gemētan *w*
meeting gemēting *(f)*
  gemitting *(f)*
  gemōt *(n)*
mirror scēawere *(m)*
mislead misðyncan *w*
mistake misðyncan *w*
observe ofersēon *5*
  (ge)scēawian *w*
obvious ēaðfynde
  ēaðgesyne
  sweotol
open onhlīdan *1*
  ontȳnan *w*
perceive gesēon *5*

pretend līcettan *w*
remote dīgel
reveal cȳðan *w*
  onhlīdan *1*
  ontȳnan *w*
  yppan *w*
scan geondscēawian *w*
scarce seldsīene
search (ge)sēcan *w*
secrecy dīgolnes *(f)*
secret dīgel
  dyrne
see lōcian *w*
  scēawian *w*
  (ge)sēon *5*
seem sēon *5*
  ðyncan *w*
show ætīewan *w*
  gecȳðan *w*
  oðȳwan *w*
sight gesihð *(f)*
  wlitesēon *(f)*
spectacle wæfersȳn *(f)*
spectator hāwere *(m)*
  scēawere *(m)*
spy scēawere *(m)*
squinting sceolh
stare starian *w*
survey geondscēawian *w*
turn to besēon *5*
uncover onwrēon *1*
view scēawian *w*
visible gesewenlīc
  gesīene
vision gesihð *(f)*
watch wacian *w*
watch over weardian *w*
wink wincian *w*
wrongfully conceal forhelan *4*

SKY

air lyft *(f)*
bad weather unweder *(n)*
blast blǣst *(m)*
  fnǣst *(m)*
blow blāwan *7*
  wāwan *7*
blow against ondhweorfan *3*
blow round bewāwan *7*
chill cyle *(m)*
cloud genip *(n)*
  wolcen *(n)*
cold ceald
  cyldu *(f)*
cold with frost hrīmceald
constellation tungol *(n)*
darkness dimnes *(f)*
  genip *(n)*
  heolstor *(n)*
eternal cold sincaldu *(f)*
fog mist *(m)*
freeze frēosan *2*
frost forst *(m)*
  hrīm *(m)*
frosty frēorig
  hrīmceald
frozen frēorig
gloomy mirce
grow dark (ge)nīpan *1*
  (ge)sweorcan *3*
grow wintry winterlǣcan *w*
hail hagol *(m)*
  hægl *(m)*
hailstorm hæglfaru *(f)*
heat hǣtan *w*
  hǣtu *(f)*
horizon lyftedor *(m)*
hot hāt
ice īs *(n)*
icy īsig
lightning līget *(n,m)*
  līgetu *(f)*
  onǣlet i(n)
lightning flash līgræsc *(m)*

magnificent micellic
  sweglwered
melt away gemeltan *3*
mist mist *(m)*
moon mōna *(m)*
Orion Eoforðring *(m)*
Plough Wǣnes Đisla *(fpl)*
radiant sweglwered
rain regn *(m)*
  rīnan *w*
rainbow heofonlic boga *(m)*
resound hlynnan *w*
  ðunian *w*
rime hrīm *(m)*
serene smolt
serenity smyltnes *(f)*
shining heavens sweglwundor *(n)*
sky heofon *(m,f)*
  lyft *(f)*
  rodor *(m)*
  swegl *(n)*
snow snāw *(m)*
  snīwan *w*
snowstorm hrīð *(f)*
  snāwgebland *(n)*
  wintergeweorð *(n)*
  winterscūr *(m)*
star steorra *(m)*
  tungol *(n)*
storm storm *(m)*
  styrman *w*
storm-beaten hrīðig
storm-cloud wederwolcen *(n)*
sun sunne *(f)*
sunbeam sunnbēam *(m)*
sunset setlgang *(m)*
thunder ðun(r)ian *w*
  ðunor *(m)*
thunderclap ðunorrād *(f)*
Ursa Major Wǣnes Đisla *(fpl)*
weather gewider *(n)*
  weder *(n)*
wind blǣst *(m)*
  fnǣst *(m)*
  wind *(n)*

wind-propelled lyftgeswenced
windy windig
winter shower winterscūr *(m)*
winter's hour winterstund *(f)*
wintry winterlīc

SLEEP

arouse āweccan *w*
awake onwæcnan *w*
be fast asleep swodrian *w*
be weary ātēorian *w*
become tired tēorian *w*
bed bedd *(n)*
  bedrest *(f)*
  ræst *(f)*
bedfellow gebedda *(m)*
  gemæecca *(m)*
  hǣmere *(m)*
bedroom slǣpern *(n)*
blanket hwītel *(m)*
bleary-eyed sīwenēge
bolster bolster *(m)*
  heafodbolster *(n)*
bower būr *(f)*
chamberlain būrðegn *(m)*
cot cradol *(m)*
cover of darkness nihthelm *(f)*
cradle cradol *(m)*
curtain wāgrift *(n)*
dark deorc
  dimm
  heolstor
  ðēostre
darkness dimnes *(f)*

  heolstor *(f)*
  ðēostru *(f)*
den denn *(n)*
dim dimm
dimness dimnes *(f)*
dormitory slǣpærn *(n)*
doze hnappung *(f)*
dream swefn *(n)*
drowsiness hnappung *(f)*
early awake ǣrwacol
evening's rest ǣfenræst *(f)*
fall asleep onslǣpan *w*
gloomy ðēostre
grow dark sweorcan *3*
half-asleep healfslǣpende
insomnia slǣplēast *(f)*
lying down leger *(n)*
nightmare ælfsiden *(f)*
pillow bolster *(m)*
  pyle *(m)*
pillow-down healsrefeðer *(f)*
prone neowol
  nīwol
put to sleep āswebban *w*
repose (ge)restan *w*
rest leger *(n)*
  ræst *(f)*
  (ge)restan *w*
sheet hopscȳte *(f)*
  scēat *(m)*
  scīte *(f)*
sleep ræst *(f)*
  (ge)restan *w*
  slǣp *(m)*
  slǣpan *7*
  slūma *(m)*
  swefan *5*
  sweofot *(n)*
sleeping chamber būr *(f)*
sleepy slāpol
  slǣpor
snore fnǣrettan *w*
soporific slǣpbǣre
stay awake wæccan *w*
tire tēorian *w*

vigil wæccen *(f)*
wake weccan *w*
waken āweccan *w*
watch wæccan *w*
weary getēorod
  wērig
yawn gīnan *w*

original position frumstaðol *(m)*
part ende *(m)*
ready to start ūtfūs
set about fōn on *7*
source ordfruma *(m)*
start ōr *(n)*
  ord *(m)*
undertake underfōn *7*
  underginnan *3*

START

begin āginnan *3*
  beginnan *3*
  onginnan *3*
  onstellan *w*
beginning fruma *(m)*
  ord *(m)*
close betȳnan *w*
close off beclȳsan *w*
  tȳnan *w*
close up belūcan *2*
complete fullfremman *w*
  fullgān *a*
  gefyllan *w*
creation frumsceaft *(f)*
end ende *(m)*
  endian *w*
ending geendung *(f)*
endure ādrēogan *2*
  ðolian *w*
enterprise onginn *(n)*
envelop forðylman *w*
finish (ge)endian *w*
initiate onstellan *w*
open openian *w*
open up geopenian *w*
origin fruma *(m)*
  frymð *(m,f)*
  ord *(m)*

STRANGE

abroad elðēodige
  ūtanbordes
  ūt(e)
Africans Affricani *(mpl)*
alien elelendisc
  ellende
  fremde
alien spirit ellorgāst *(m)*
Alps Alpīs
Angeln Angel *(f)*
Angles Angelcynn *(n)*
  Engle *(mpl)*
Baltic Sea Ōstsǣ *(f)*
Bavarians Bǣgwǣre *(mpl)*
Bedfordshire Bedanfordscīr *(f)*
Berkshire Bearrucscīr *(f)*
Bernician people Beornice *(mpl)*
Biarmians (White Sea people)
  Beormas *(mpl)*
Bohemians Bǣme *(mpl)*
  Bēhēmas *(mpl)*
Britain Bryten *(f)*
British Byttisc
  Wylisc

Britons (Bret)wēalas *(mpl)*
　Wēalcynn *(n)*
Buckinghamshire
　Buccingahāmscīr *(f)*
Bulgarians Pulgare *(fpl)*
Burgundians Burgendan *(mpl)*
Cambridgeshire Grantabrycgscīr *(f)*
Carinthia Carendre *(f)*
Cheshire Cestrescīr *(f)*
　Legeceasterscīr *(f)*
Chiltern (Hills) Ciltern *(m)*
Cornish (people) Cornwēalas *(mpl)*
Cornwall Cornwēalas *(mpl)*
　Triconscīr *(f)*
Cumberland Cumbraland *(n)*
Cumbrians Cumbras *(mpl)*
Dacia Datia *(f)*
Dalaments (Polish people)
　Dalamentsan *(mpl)*
Danelaw Denelagu *(f)*
Danes Dene *(mpl)*
Danish Denisc
Danube Dōnua *(f)*
Deiran (people) Dēre *(mpl)*
Denmark Denamearc *(f)*
Derbyshire Deorbyscīr *(f)*
Devonish (people) Defnas *(mpl)*
Devonshire Defnascīr *(f)*
distant feorr
　fyrlen
distant land feorweg *(m)*
Don (river) Danais *(f)*
Dorset Dornsǣtan *(mpl)*
dwarf dweorg *(m)*
East Angles Ēastengle *(mpl)*
East Franks Ēastfrancan *(mpl)*
East Kent (people)
　Ēastcentingas *(mpl)*
East Saxons Ēastseaxe *(mpl)*
Egyptian Egiptisc
Egyptians Ægypte *(mpl)*
Elbe (river) Ælf *(f)*
Elbing (river) Ilfing *(m)*
else elles
　elleshwæt

elsewhere ellor
England Englalond *(n)*
English Englisc
English Nation Angelcynn *(n)*
　Angelþēod *(f)*
　Engle *(mpl)*
Essex Ēast Seaxe *(mpl)*
Estonia Estland *(n)*
Estonians Este *(mpl)*
Ethiopian Sigelhearwa *(m)*
far-off feorr
　fyrlen
folk folc *(n)*
foreign elðēodig
　feorcund
　feorrancumen
　fremde
　ofersǣwisc
　ūtancumen
foreign land uncȳððu *(f)*
France Francland *(n)*
Franks Francan *(mpl)*
French Frencisc
　Gallisc
Frenchmen Galwalas *(mpl)*
Frisches Haff Estmere *(m)*
Frisia Frīsland *(n)*
Frisian Frysisc
Frisian (man) Frīesa *(m)*
from afar feorran
from overseas ofersǣwisc
Gloucestershire Gleawcestrescīr *(f)*
Goths Gotan *(mpl)*
Greek (people) Crēcas *(mpl)*
guest cuma *(m)*
　fletsittend *(m)*
Hampshire Hāmtūnscīr *(f)*
Hebrew Ebraisc
Hebrews Ēbrēas *(mpl)*
　Israhēla folc *(n)*
Herefordshire Herefordscīr *(f)*
Hertfordshire Heortfordscīr *(f)*
Huntingdonshire Huntadūnscīr *(f)*
Indian Syndonisc
Indians Indie *(mpl)*

Ireland Īraland *(n)*
Irish Īrisc
Irishmen Scottas *(mpl)*
Isle of Man Mænīg *(f)*
Isle of Wight Wihtland *(n)*
Italians Eotolware *(mpl)*
Jews Ēbreas *(mpl)*
Jordan (river) Iordānen *(f)*
Jutes Ēote *(mpl)*
Jutish Ēotisc
Kent Cent *(f)*
Kentish (people) Cantware *(fpl)*
    Centingas *(mpl)*
Lappish Finnisc
Lapps Finnas *(mpl)*
Latins (people) Lædenware *(fpl)*
Leicestershire Lægreceastrescīr *(f)*
Lincolnshire Lincolnscīr *(f)*
Lindisfarne Lindisfarnēa *(fpl)*
Lindisfarne (people)
    Lindisfaran *(mpl)*
Lindsey Lindesīg *(f)*
Lindsey (people) Lindisse *(mpl)*
Livonia Sermende *(mpl)*
Lombards (people)
    Langbeardan *(mpl)*
Lombardy Langbeardnarīce *(n)*
Mediterranean Sea Wendelsæ *(f)*
Mercia Mierce *(mpl)*
Mercian Miercisc
Mercians (people) Mierce *(mpl)*
Middlesex Middelseaxan *(mpl)*
monstrous unhȳre
Moravians (people) Marware *(fpl)*
native land cȳðõu *(f)*
    eard *(m)*
    ēðel *(m,n)*
negro ælmyrca *(m)*
Norfolk Norðfolc *(n)*
Normandy Ricardesrīce *(n)*
Northamptonshire
    (Norþ)Hāmtūnscīr *(f)*
Northumberland Norðhymbre *(mpl)*
Norway Norðweg *(m)*
Norwegian Norðmannisc

Norwegians (people) Norðmenn *(mpl)*
Nottinghamshire Snotingahāmscīr *(f)*
Obodrites (Baltic people)
    Afdrede *(mpl)*
of this country ūrelendisc
Oland (Baltic island) Ēowland *(n)*
otherwise elcor
    elles
outsider unmæg *(m)*
Oxfordshire Oxnafordscīr *(f)*
Peak District Peācland *(n)*
people folc *(n)*
Persian Persisc
Persians (people) Perse *(mpl)*
Picts (people) Peohtas *(mpl)*
pilgrimage abroad elðīodignes *(f)*
Polish Wendisc
Quains (Finnish people)
    Cwenas *(mpl)*
rare seldcūð
    seldsīene
Rhaetia Rētie *(f)*
Rhine (river) Rīn
Roman Rēmisc
    Rōmānisc
Romans (people) Lædenware *(fpl)*
    Rōmāne *(fpl)*
    Rōmwēalas *(mpl)*
Rome Rōmeburg *(f)*
Rutland Roteland *(n)*
Saxon Seaxisc
Saxons Seaxe *(mpl)*
Saxons (Continental) Ealdseaxe *(mpl)*
Scandinavia Scedenīg *(f)*
    Scōnēg *(f)*
Schleswig Sīlende
Scotland Scottaland *(n)*
Scots (people) Scottas *(mpl)*
Scottish Scyttisc
Scythia Sciððiu *(f)*
Scythians Sciððie *(mpl)*
Shropshire Scrobbesbyrigscīr *(f)*
some other thing elleshwæt
Somerset Sumersætan *(mpl)*
Sorbians (Baltic people) Surpe *(mpl)*

Spanish Spēonisc
Staffordshire Stæffordscīr *(f)*
strange elelendisc
stranger gīest *(m)*
Suffolk Sūðfolc *(n)*
Surrey Sūðrige *(n)*
Sussex Sūð Seaxe *(mpl)*
Swabians (German people)
  Swæfe *(mpl)*
Sweden Swēoland *(n)*
Swedes Swēon *(mpl)*
Thuringians (German people)
  Þyringas *(mpl)*
Trojans Trōiāna *(mpl)*
unknown uncūð
Vandals Wendle *(mpl)*
Wales Norðwalas *(mpl)*
Warwickshire Wæringwīcscīr *(f)*
Weald, The Andrēdesweald *(n)*
well-known cūð
Welsh Wylisc
Welsh (people) Norðwalas *(mpl)*
  Norðwēalcynn *(n)*
West Kent (people)
  Westcentingas *(mpl)*
West Saxons West Seaxe *(mpl)*
Westmorland Westmōringaland *(n)*
White Sea Cwēnsæ *(f)*
Wiltshire Wiltūnscīr *(f)*
Worcestershire Wireceastrescīr *(f)*
Yorkshire Eoforwīcscīr *(f)*

THINK

acceptable ðoncwyrðe
advise gerǣdan *w*
adviser geðeahtere *(m)*
  rǣdbora *(m)*

agree gecweðan *5*
apply oneself befēolan *3*
assess dēman *w*
  geeahtian *w*
be ashamed gescomian *w*
be intent hīgian *w*
be occupied ābisgian *w*
bear in mind beðencan *w*
belie gelēafa *(m)*
believe gelīefan *w*
beware of warnian *w*
careful hohful
cause intinga *(m)*
choose (ge)cēosan *2*
compare (ge)ānlīcian *w*
comparison wiðmetennes *(f)*
complain mǣnan *w*
condemn fordēman *w*
condition gerǣden *(f)*
consider behealdan *7*
  bescēawian *w*
  beðencan *w*
  eahtian *w*
  geðencan *w*
  smēagan *w*
  ymbðencan *w*
consideration smēa(g)ung *(f)*
contemplate geondðencan *w*
contempt forhogdnes *(f)*
counsel geðeaht *(n,f)*
  (ge)ðeahtung *(f)*
counsellor geðeahtere *(m)*
damn fordēman *w*
dare gedyrstlǣcan *w*
deceive bepǣcan *w*
  besyrwan *w*
decide gecēosan *2*
  gerǣdan *w*
deliberate smēagan *w*
deliberately willes
delude bepǣcan *w*
delusion dyderung *(f)*
deny forsacan *6*
despise forhogian *w*
  forsēon *5*

determine gerǣdan *w*
device orðanc *(m,n)*
devise āsmēagan *w*
diligent nēodlīc
discretion gescēadwīsnes *(f)*
disdain forhogdnes *(f)*
displease ofðyncan *w*
doubt twēo *(m)*
  twēogan *w*
  twēonian *w*
entrust befæstan *w*
  betǣcan *w*
error gedwild *(n)*
  gedwola *(m)*
  wōh *(n)*
esteem prōfian *w*
estimate (ge)eahtian *w*
examine smēagan *w*
explain gereccean *w*
exult behliehhan *6*
fame dōm *(m)*
feel drēogan *2*
  ongietan *5*
foolish dol(gilp)
forget forgietan *5*
  ofergietan *5*
  ofergitolian *w*
forgetfulness ofergitolnys *(f)*
gratitude ðoncung *(f)*
grieve ofðyncan *w*
have mercy on miltsian *w*
heart geðonc *(m,n)*
hesitate forwandian *w*
  twēogan *w*
  twēonian *w*
hope gehyhtan *w*
  hopian *w*
idea geðōht *(m,n)*
imagine wēnan *w*
impute gestǣlan *w*
incredible ungelīefedlīc
inspire onbærnan *w*
  onbryrdan *w*
intellect mōd *(n)*
intend hycgan *w*

  mynian *w*
  teohhian *w*
  ðencan *w*
  willan *w*
interpret gereccean *w*
  trahtian *w*
interpretation gereccennes *(f)*
it occurs to me beirnð mē on mōde
judge dēma *(m)*
  dēman *w*
  dēmend *(m)*
judgement dōm *(m)*
lament mǣnan *w*
laugh over behliehhan *6*
look forward to cēpnian *w*
loyalty trēow *(f)*
matter intinga *(m)*
  ondweorc *(n)*
memory gemynd *(f,n)*
mind geðonc *(m,n)*
mindful hohful
mistake misfōn *7*
mourn mǣnan *w*
neglect forgiefan *5*
  oferhebban *6*
notice onfindan *3*
  ongietan *5*
omit oferhebban *6*
option cyre *(m)*
pardon forgiefan *5*
pay attention to onmunan *w*
perceive ongietan *5*
  understandan *6*
plan gerǣdan *w*
  hogian *w*
  rǣd *(m)*
pleasing ðoncwyrðe
precept lār *(f)*
prejudice fordēman *w*
pride prȳte *(f)*
purpose gemynd *(f,n)*
  myndgian *w*
  teohhian *w*
puzzle cnotta *(m)*
  rǣdels *(m,f)*

reckon rīman *w*
reflect behycgan *w*
 smēagan *w*
refuse forsacan *6*
regard behealdan *7*
rely on getrūwian *w*
remember gemunan *w*
 gemyndian *w*
 geðencan *w*
remind gemonian *w*
repent gescomian *w*
resolve gecweðan *5*
 gescēadan *7*
resume gedyrstlæcan *w*
risk nēðan *w*
satisfied with gehealden on
settle gecweðan *5*
stupid dysig
 inðicce
 medwīs
subject ondweorc *(n)*
suppose myntan *w*
 wēnan *w*
surprise besyrwan *w*
sympathize midðolian *w*
tedium æleng *(f)*
thank (ge)ðoncian *w*
thankful ðoñcful
thanksgiving ðoncung *(f)*
think hogian *w*
 hycgan *w*
 myntan *w*
 (ge)ðencan *w*
think about behycgan *w*
think deeply geondðencan *w*
think of behycgan *w*
 gehycgan *w*
think out āðencan *w*
thought gehygd *(f)*
 geðeaht *(n,f)*
 geðeahtung *(f)*
 geðōht *(m)*
 ðonc *(m)*
treat with contempt forhogian *w*
 forsēon *5*

trick besyrwan *w*
trust gehyhtan *w*
 gelȳfan *w*
 getrūwian *w*
trust in trīewan *w*
 trūwian *w*
truth trēow *(f)*
understand understandan *6*
urge ðȳwan *w*
venture nēðan *w*
wary wær
 wærlīc
watchful behȳdig
 wærlīc
wish wȳscan *w*
worth remembering gemyndwyrðe
wrongthinking gedwild *(n)*
 gedwola *(m)*

TIME

after æfter
 siððan
again eft
 ongēan
age yldo *(f)*
ago gēo
all day long andlangne dæg
already īu
always ā(wā)
 ealne weg
 ealnig
 on symbel
 simble
anew edneowe
anniversary gemynddæg *(m)*
anticipate forecuman *4*
appointed day āndaga *(m)*
April Eastermōnað *(m)*
at last sīð ond late
 æt niehstan

at once ǣdre
    instæpe
    sōna
at one time ... at another
    hwīlum ... hwīlum
at the moment on ondweardnesse
at times tīdlīc
    hwīlum
August Rugern *(m)*
    Wēodmōnað *(m)*
autumn hærfest *(m)*
awake early ǣrwacol
become dark genīpan *1*
become day dagian *w*
before ǣr
by night nihterne
change edhwyrft *(m)*
    edwenden *(f)*
Christmas Eve Mōdraniht *(f)*
continually simble
    singallīc
daily dæghwāmlīc
    on dæg
darkness genip *(n)*
date datārum *(m)*
dawn ǣrnemergen *(f)*
    dagian *w*
    dægrǣd *(m)*
    ūhta *(m)*
day dæg *(m)*
    dōgor *(n)*
daybreak dægrǣd *(n)*
December ǣrra Gēola *(m)*
    Gēol *(n)*
    Gēolmōnað *(m)*
delay elcian *w*
    elcung *(f)*
    slacian *w*
duration hwīl *(f)*
    ðrāg *(f)*
earliest ǣrest
    forma
early awake ǣrwacol
early morning ǣrnemergen *(m)*
    ūhta *(m)*

Easter Sunday Ēasterdæg *(m)*
Eastertide Ēastertīd *(f)*
end edwenden *(f)*
endless endelēas
Epiphany Bæðdæg *(m)*
equinox efniht, emniht *(f)*
erelong nīehst
    sōna
    ungēara
eternal ēce
eternity ēcnes *(f)*
eve niht *(f)*
evening ǣfen *(m,n)*
    ǣfentīd *(f)*
evening twilight cwildseten *(f)*
ever ā
    ǣfre
everyday dæghwǣmlīc
February Solmōnað *(m)*
first ǣrest
    ǣrra
    forma
fix a day āndagian *w*
fleeting lǣne
follow (æfter)fylgian *w*
forever ā
    ā on ēcnesse
    ǣfre
    tō worulde
former days ǣrdagas *(mpl)*
formerly gēara
    gefyrn
    gēo
forthwith āninga
    ǣdre
    instæpe
    lungre
    semninga
    sōna
frequent gelōmlic
frequently gelōmlīce
Friday Frigedæg *(m)*
from now on heonanforð
full moon mōnaðfylen *(f)*

future forðgesceaft *(f)*
  tōweard
harvest time onrīptīd *(f)*
hasty recen
henceforth heonanforð
here and there ongemang ðissum
hour stund *(f)*
  tīd *(f)*
hour of winter winterstund *(f)*
immediately sōna
impending tōweard
in future forð
in the day on dæg
in the first place æt ærestan
in the meantime betwēnan
  betweoh ðon
  ongemang ðissum
  ðendan
in time sīðlīc
in turn ðurh endebyrdnesse
instantly bearhtme
  sōna
January æfterra Gēola *(m)*
July æfterra Līða *(m)*
June ærra Līða *(m)*
  Midsumermōnað *(m)*
  Sēremōnað *(m)*
kalend cālend *(m)*
last night tōniht
late læt
  sīð
later æfterra
lengthy longsum
Lent Lencten *(m)*
long ago gefyrn
March Hlȳda *(m)*
  Hrēðmōnað *(m)*
May Ðrīmeolce *(n)*
  Ðrīmilcemōnað *(m)*
meeting day mēting *(f)*
midday middæg *(m)*
midnight middeniht *(f)*
midsummer middansumer *(m)*
midwinter middanwinter *(m)*

moment bearhtmhwæt *(f)*
  prēowthwīl *(f)*
Monday Mōnandæg *(m)*
month mōnað *(m)*
morning dægredlīc
  mergen *(m)*
  mergenlīc
  morgentīd *(f)*
never nā
  næfre
new nīw
next æfterra
next year ōðergēara
night niht *(f)*
nightlong nihtlong
Nones (3pm) nōn *(f)*
November Blōtmōnað *(m)*
now nū
  nūða
occasion byre *(m)*
  cirr *(m)*
  sīð *(m)*
  tīma *(m)*
October Winterfyllēð *(m)*
often gelōmlīce
  oft(rædlīc)
  oftsōna
old eald
once gēara
  gēo
  on ænne sīð
  on ænre tīde
opportunity byre *(m)*
  sæl *(m,f)*
order endebyrdnes *(f)*
passing læne
past on ærdagum
  on geardagum
  wyrd *(f,n)*
period of time fæc *(n)*
  þrāg *(f)*
precede foregangan 7
present andweard
presently eftsōna
  sīðlīc

previous time ǣrdagas *(mpl)*
prompt cāf
  recen
proper time tīma *(m)*
quick cāf
quickly hraðe
  recene
ready gegearwod
  recen
recently nīwan
renewed edneowe
repeatedly eftsōna
  on oftsīðas
reversal edhwyrft *(m)*
  edwenden *(f)*
Saturday Sæternesdæg *(m)*
season sǣl *(m,f)*
second æfterra
  ōðer
seldom seldan
September Hāligmōnað *(m)*
  Hærfestmōnað *(m)*
set a day āndagian *w*
shortly scortwyrplīc
since siððan
singly ānlīpig
slow longsum
  slāw
sometimes hwīlum
soon eftsōna
  hraðe
space of time hwīl *(f)*
  stund *(f)*
spend the winter oferwintrian *(w)*
spring lencten *(m)*
still forð
  (nū-, ðā-)gīen
  (nū-, ðā-)gīet
sudden fǣrlīc
suddenly fǣringa
  semninga
summer sumor *(m)*
Sunday Hāligdæg *(m)*
  Sunnandæg *(m)*

sundial dægmǣl *(m,n)*
  sōlmerca *(m)*
temporary hwīlen
  lǣne
then ðā
  ðonne
Thursday Ðunresdæg *(m)*
  Ðursdæg *(m)*
tide tīd *(f)*
time byre *(m)*
  fierst *(m)*
  sǣl *(m,f)*
  tīma *(m)*
  tīd *(f)*
  ðrāg *(f)*
time of day mǣl *(n)*
time of one's birth gebyrdtīd *(f)*
timely tīdlīc
  tōtīman
today tōdæg
tomorrow morgenlīca dæg *(m)*
  tōmergen
too often foroft
too soon forhraðe
  forsōna
Tuesday Tīwesdæg *(m)*
turn endebyrdnes *(f)*
unending ungeendod
Wednesday Wōdnesdæg *(m)*
week wucu *(f)*
while hwīl *(f)*
  þenden
winter winter *(m,n)*
wintertime wintertīd *(f)*
without delay unaswundenlīc
year gēar *(n)*
yesterday gierstandæg *(m)*
  giestran
yet gīen
  gīet
young geong
youth geogoð *(f)*
Yule Gēol *(n)*

TOOL

adze adesa *(m)*
awl æl *(m)*
axe æcs *(f)*
axle eax *(f)*
ball clīewen *(n)*
 ðōðor *(m)*
bar scyttels *(m)*
barrel byrla *(m)*
basket spyrte *(f)*
 windel *(m)*
be of use dugan *a*
beaten geðrūen
bellows blæstbelg *(m)*
 bylig *(m)*
blade īren *(n)*
bolster cweornbill *(n)*
bolt scyttels *(m)*
bore into borian *w*
 ðurhdrīfan *1*
box cist *(f)*
 teag *(f)*
branding iron ceorfingīsen *(n)*
broom besma *(m)*
bucket byden *(f)*
bushel mydd *(n)*
cauldron citel *(m)*
 fæt *(n)*
 hwer *(m)*
chain racente *(f)*
 racentēag *(f)*
chisel brædīsen *(n)*
chisel for stone cweornbill *(n)*
chopping block onhēaw *(m)*
clasp gespong *(n)*
cloth shears hræglscēara *(fpl)*
comb camb *(m)*
cooking vessel ālfæt *(n)*
coulter culter *(m)*
creel spyrte *(f)*
curling tongs wealcspinl *(f)*
dibble spitel *(m)*
dice tæflstān *(m)*

drill bor *(m)*
 ðurhdrīfan *1*
engraving tool græfseax *(m)*
equip scyrpan *w*
fan fann *(f)*
fastening gespong *(n)*
 ðwang *(m,f)*
file fēol *(f)*
file-hardened fēolheard
fine sieve hērsyfe *(f)*
 tæmespīle *(f)*
 temse *(f)*
firedog brandīren *(n)*
fish-hook angil *(m)*
fish-trap hæcwer *(m)*
forceps hæferbīte *(m)*
forged geðrūen
fork forca *(m)*
frying pan hierstepanne *(f)*
glue lēag *(f)*
 līm *(m)*
goad gād *(m)*
 gādīsen *(n)*
griddle brandrād *(f)*
guyrope stæg *(n)*
hairpin hǣrnǣdl *(f)*
hammer homer *(m)*
 slecg *(f)*
handle hylfe *(n)*
harrow egðe *(f)*
hatchet wudubil *(m)*
helve hylfe *(n)*
hoe tyrfhaga *(m)*
hook ancgil *(m)*
 hōc *(m)*
hub nafeða *(m)*
 nafu *(f)*
insert borian *w*
key cǣg *(f)*
knife seax *(n)*
ladder hlǣder *(f)*
ladle hlædel *(m)*
leadline sundrāp *(m)*
lid hlid *(n)*

line līne *(f)*
lye lēag *(f)*
machine searu *(n)*
mallet slic *(n)*
mattock becca *(m)*
mortar (bowl) mortere *(m)*
mousetrap mūsfealle *(f)*
muzzle cāma *(m)*
nail scēað *(f)*
nailtrimmer næglseax *(n)*
needle nǣdl *(f)*
net max *(n)*
   nett *(n)*
noose ðelma *(m)*
oilpress wringe *(f)*
oven ofen *(m)*
pail byden *(f)*
   pægel *(m)*
   sā *(m)*
pan panne *(f)*
peg pinn *(n)*
pin pinn *(n)*
   prēon *(m)*
pitchfork forcel *(m)*
plane locor *(m)*
   scafa *(m)*
plough sulh *(f)*
ploughing equipment sulhgeteog *(n)*
ploughshare scear *(m,n)*
plumbline weallþrǣd *(m)*
pointed tool pīl *(n)*
pot crocca *(m)*
pot (with a handle) stelmēle *(m)*
rake egðe *(f)*
raw material ondweorc *(n)*
   ontimber *(n)*
razor scearseax *(n)*
reel gearnwinde *(f)*
   hrēol *(m)*
rod gyrd *(f)*
   stæf *(m)*
rope līne *(f)*
   rāp *(m)*
   sāl *(m)*
rope for prisoners wealsāda *(m)*

saucepan stelmēle *(m)*
saw sagu *(f)*
scalpel ceorfsæx *(n)*
scissors scēarra *(fpl)*
sharpen scyrpan *w*
shovel scofl *(f)*
skewer sticca *(m)*
sledgehammer slecg *(f)*
smithy smiðða *(f)*
spade delfīsen *(n)*
   spadu *(f)*
spike scēað *(f)*
   spīcing *(m)*
spindlewhorl hweorfa *(m)*
spoon cuculer *(m)*
spoon(ful) sticca *(m)*
staff gyrd *(f)*
   stæf *(m)*
stake staca *(m)*
   stocc *(m)*
stick stæf *(m)*
string streng *(m)*
thimble ðȳmel *(m)*
tongs (ge)tang *(fpl)*
tool īren *(n)*
   tōl *(f)*
torture implement wītesteng *(m)*
trappings gerǣde *(n)*
tray bǣrdisc *(m)*
trivet trefet *(m)*
trough trog *(m)*
twine twīn *(n)*
use brūcan *2*
   bryce *(m)*
   nytnes *(f)*
   nytt *(m)*
useful behēfe
   nytt
   nytwyrðe
   til
utensils andlōman *(mpl)*
utility nytnes *(f)*
vessel fæt *(n)*
waterwheel hlǣdtrendel *(m)*
whetstone hwetstān *(m)*

whip swipu *(f)*
winch wince *(f)*
wire wīr *(m)*

WARFARE

argument beadurūn *(f)*
arm syrwan *w*
army fierd *(f)*
   folc *(n)*
   getrum *(n)*
   getruma *(m)*
   prass *(m)*
army division fierdstemn *(m)*
   gefylce *(n)*
army of spearmen æschere *(m)*
assail gestandan *6*
assist fultumian *w*
   helpan *3*
attack gesēcan *w*
   gestandan *6*
   onrǣs *(m)*
   onscyte *(m)*
attacking onsǣge
balista stæfliðere *(f)*
band gedryht *(f)*
   gesīðmægen *(n)*
   hlōð *(f)*
   þrēat *(m)*
battle beadu *(f)*
   (ge)camp *(n)*
   camphād *(m)*
   getoht *(n)*
   gūð *(f)*
   hild *(f)*
   lāc *(n,f)*
   wīg *(n)*
   wīgrǣden *(f)*
battlefield campstede *(m)*

   wælfeld *(m)*
   wælstōw *(f)*
beat down bēatan *7*
   cnyssan *w*
beaten gefliemed
   sigelēas
behead behēafdian *w*
besiege besittan *5*
betray forrǣdan of līfe *w*
bloodshed blōdgyte *(m)*
blow slege *(m)*
   swinge*(f)*
bodyguards werod *(n)*
bold cāf
   dǣdcēne
booty lāc *(n,f)*
brave felamōdig
brave deed ellendǣd *(f)*
campaign campian *w*
   fierd *(f)*
   fierdian *w*
   fyrding *(f)*
carry off forniman *4*
cavalryman rīdwiga *(m)*
challenger oretta *(m)*
champion (sige)cempa *(m)*
cheekpiece hlēorberg *(f)*
clash (of opponents)
   cumbolgehnāst *(n)*
company flocc *(m)*
compete gesacan *6*
   winnan *3*
comrade-in-arms gedryhta *(m)*
conflict geflit *(n)*
   gemōt *(n)*
   sacu *(f)*
contend flītan *1*
   gehnǣstan *w*
   winnan *3*
contest geflit *(n)*
cut down (ā-, ge-)hēawan *7*
cut to pieces forhēawan *7*
defeat gewinnan *3*
   oferflītan *1*
   oferwinnan *3*

defy wiðerian *w*
destructive foray forhergung *(f)*
die cringan *3*
doughty dyhtig
dub dubbian *w*
encourage byldan *w*
enemy fleet unfriðflota *(m)*
enemy troops unfriðhere *(m)*
equip syrwan *w*
exhort byldan *w*
expedition fyrding *(f)*
fall in battle cringan *3*
fight (ge)feohtan *3*
  feohte *(f)*
  gefeoht *(n)*
fight on foot fēðewīg *(m)*
footsoldier fēða *(m)*
foreign army ūthere *(m)*
fort burg *(f)*
  ceaster *(f)*
  fæsten *(n)*
fully-armed fullwēpnod
gore heolfor *(m,n)*
  wældrēor *(m,n)*
grappling with ætgrǣpe
great ēacen
greave bānbeorge *(f)*
hand-to-hand handlinga
harry (for)hergian *w*
help out fultumian *w*
hero beorn *(m)*
  brego *(m)*
  guma *(m)*
  hæleð *(m)*
home forces fierd *(f)*
  innhere *(m)*
hostile encounter ætsteall *(m)*
  wǣpengewrixl *(n)*
hostility unfrið *(m)*
impending onsǣge
infantryman fēða *(m)*
invading force flocrād *(f)*
kick spurnan *3*
kill ācwellan *w*
  āfyllan *w*

forniman *4*
forwegan *5*
gecwylman *w*
(ā)swebban *w*
leader heretoga *(m)*
lifeless belifd
mass against ðrēatian *w*
mighty ēacen
  felameahtig
military punishment fierdwīte *(n)*
militia londfyrde *(f)*
mounted troop ēored *(n)*
  ēoredcyst *(m)*
  rǣdehere *(m)*
murder monslyht *(m)*
  morðdǣd *(f)*
  morðor *(n)*
nation folc *(n)*
overrun ofergān *a*
peace grið *(n)*
period of service stemn *(m)*
plunder hīðan *w*
press ðringan *3*
put to flight flīeman *w*
  flīgan *w*
quarrel beadurūn *(f)*
  geflit *(n)*
raiding force here *(m)*
rally against ðrēatian *w*
reinforcements ēaca *(m)*
  fultum *(m)*
resistance wiðre *(n)*
retreat mylma *(m)*
rout flīeman *w*
  flīgan *w*
shieldwall bordweall *(m)*
  wīghaga *(m)*
shoot down (of-, on-) scēotan *2*
slaughter dēaðcwealm *(m)*
  wæl *(n)*
  wælsleaht *(m)*
  wīghryre *(m)*
slay (for-, of-) slēan *6*
slayer bana *(m)*
sling stæfliðere *(f)*

smack plætt *(m)*
  plættan *w*
spearman æscmann *(m)*
stab to death ofstician *w*
  ofstingan *3*
standard fana *(m)*
standard bearer cumbolwiga *(m)*
strengthen getrymman *w*
strife geflit *(n)*
  gewinn *(n)*
  sacu *(f)*
  sæcc *(f)*
strike bēatan *7*
  beslēan *6*
  cnyssan *w*
strike down forslēan *6*
  gefyllan *w*
  offellan *w*
strive sacan *6*
stroke slege *(m)*
strong dyhtig
stronghold burg *(f)*
  ceaster *(f)*
  fæsten *(n)*
sudden attack fær *(m)*
summer expedition sumorlida *(m)*
surround begān *a*
tested warriors duguð *(f)*
throng ðringan *3*
tower wīghūs *(n)*
troop flocc *(m)*
  gedryht *(f)*
  gemong *(n)*
  hlōð *(f)*
  ðrēat *(m)*
truce grið *(n)*
turret wīghūs *(n)*
two-edged twiecge(de)
uncontested unbefohten
undefended fierdlēas
  unwered
unfought unfohten
vanguard warrior ordfruma *(m)*
vigorous felahrōr
wage (war) ðurhtēon *2*

wīgian *w*
war beadu *(f)*
  gewinn *(n)*
  gūð *(f)*
  hild *(f)*
  wīg *(n)*
warfare beadu *(f)*
warrior beorn *(m)*
  cempa *(m)*
  dreng *(m)*
  fruma *(m)*
  (dryht)guma *(m)*
  (gūð)rinc *(m)*
  secg *(m)*
  wīga *(m)*
  wīgend *(m)*
wound benn *(f)*
wound mortally forwundian *w*
wrest from beslēan *6*
  gewinnan *3*
wrestler wrāxlere *(m)*
  wrǣstliend *(m)*

WATER

absorb bedrincan *3*
anchor ancer *(m)*
anchor-chain oncerbend *(m,f)*
barque flota *(m)*
  naca *(m)*
barrel tunne *(f)*
bath bæð *(n)*
bathe baðian *w*
bathhouse bæðern *(n)*
bathing ðwēal *(n)*
bathing place bæðstede *(m)*

be moist fūhtian *w*
beach strand *(m)*
boat bāt *(m)*
  naca *(m)*
boatkeeper bātweard *(m)*
body of water lagu *(f)*
  wæterscipe *(m)*
boil āwyllan *w*
  gesēoðan *2*
  weallan *7*
bottle cylle *(m)*
  flaxe *(f)*
  pinne *(f)*
bottom botm *(m)*
bright scīr
brine-stained wārig
brook brōc *(m)*
canal wæterweg *(m)*
channel flōde *(f)*
  sund *(n)*
clean clǣne
cleanness clǣnnes *(f)*
cleanse clǣnsian *w*
  fǣlsian *w*
clear scīr
coast sǣrima *(m)*
coastal defence sǣweall *(m)*
coastguard londweard *(m)*
cool cōl
current (brim)strēam *(m)*
curve-prowed ship hringedstefna *(m)*
damp ðān
  wæt
deck cēolðel *(n)*
deep bront
  dēop
  hēah
deep water dēop *(n)*
depth dēopnes *(f)*
dew dēaw *(m,n)*
din dynian *w*
dip dyppan *w*
dirt gor *(n)*
  meox *(n)*
dive dūfan *2*

dive through ðurhdūfan *2*
dock hyð *(f)*
drain drē(a)hnian *w*
draw water hlādan *6*
drench begēotan *2*
drip drȳpan *w*
drop dropa *(m)*
dry drȳgan *w*
  drȳge
  sīere
dung gor *(n)*
  meox *(n)*
  scearn *(n)*
  scytel *(m)*
  tord *(n)*
  tyrdelu *(npl)*
  ðost *(m)*
earwax drōs *(f)*
ebb (ā)ebbian *w*
ebbtide ebba *(m)*
embark āstīgan *1*
  scipian *w*
filth horh *(m,n)*
filthy horig
  unclǣne
fishtrap sprincel *(m)*
flask cylle *(m)*
fleet flota *(m)*
  scipfierd *(f)*
  sciplið *(n)*
float flēotan *2*
flood bestēman *w*
  faroð *(m)*
  flōd *(m)*
  wæd *(n)*
floodwave flōdȳð *(f)*
flow dennian *w*
  flōwan *7*
  iernan *3*
  weallan *7*
flow away tōflōwan *7*
  tōrinnan *3*
flow under underflōwan *7*
flux flēwsa *(m)*
foam fām *(m)*

foamy-necked fāmigheals
foreshore ȳðlāf *(f)*
freeze frēosan *2*
freight hlæst *(m)*
fresh fersc
frozen over oferfroren
go on board gestīgan *1*
gourd cucurbite *(f)*
half-boiled healfsoden
handbasin mundlēow *(f)*
harbour hȳð *(f)*
haven hæfen *(f)*
  hȳð *(f)*
high seas hēahsǣ *(f)*
  sǣlīce dǣlas *(mpl)*
ice īs *(n)*
icicle cylegicel *(m)*
  wælrāp *(m)*
icy īsig
in flood flēde
island ēalond *(n)*
  īggað *(m)*
  īglond *(n)*
journey sund *(n)*
lake wæterscipe *(m)*
larboard bæcbord *(n)*
lather fām *(n)*
leave on an ebb-tide beebbian *w*
liquid wǣta *(m)*
load hlæst *(m)*
  hlæstan *w*
  scipian *w*
lukewarm wlæc
lye lēah *(f)*
marine sǣlīc
maritime sǣlīc
marshy land ēalond *(n)*
  fenn *(n,m)*
  mōr *(m)*
mast mæst *(m)*
melt meltan *3*
millstream hwēolrīðig *(n)*
moisten wǣtan *w*
naval expedition scipfyrding *(f)*
naval force scipfyrd *(f)*

sciphere *(m)*
oar ār *(f)*
oars gerēðru *(npl)*
ocean brim *(n)*
  ēar *(m)*
  gārsecg *(m)*
  geofon *(n)*
  hēahsǣ *(f)*
  holm *(m)*
ooze sīpian *w*
open sea ūtermere *(m)*
  wīdsǣ *(m,f)*
pearl meregreot *(n)*
pirate flotman *(m)*
pleasure craft plegscip *(n)*
plunder taken at sea sǣlāc *(n)*
polishing feormung *(f)*
polluted fūl
  unclǣnlīc
pool wǣl *(m)*
port-side bæcbord *(n)*
pour (ā)gēotan *2*
prow frumstemn *(m)*
purge afeormian *w*
pure clǣne
  swutol
  unwemmed
purify geclǣnsian *w*
  merian *w*
quay hȳð *(f)*
quench ācwencan *2*
resound hlynnan *w*
  ðunian *w*
riding the waves sundplega *(m)*
rigging mæstrāp *(m)*
river ēa *(f)*
riverbank stæð *(m,n)*
  strand *(n)*
rivermouth mūða *(m)*
rolling waves gewealc *(n)*
row rōwan *7*
row around berōwan *7*
row away oðrōwan *7*
rowing rēwet *(n)*
rowlock hā *(m)*

rubbish geswǣpa *(fpl)*
  ðreax *(m?)*
run aground āsittan *5*
sail faran *6*
  segl *(m,n)*
  seglian *w*
  siglan *w*
sail to geseglian *w*
  gesiglan *w*
sailor flotman *(m)*
sauna stofbæð *(n)*
sea brim *(n)*
  flot *(n)*
  gārsecg *(m)*
  geofon *(n)*
  holm *(m)*
  lagu *(f)*
  mere(flōd) *(m)*
  sǣ *(m,f)*
  seolhbæð *(n)*
  sund *(n)*
sea journey ȳðfaru *(f)*
sea-bed (sǣ)grund *(m)*
sea-bird brimfugol *(m)*
sea-going vessel sǣgenga *(m)*
seaboard sǣrima *(m)*
seafarer sǣlida *(m)*
  sǣmon *(m)*
  sǣrinc *(m)*
  scipflota *(m)*
seaman brimlīðend *(m)*
  brimman *(m)*
  lidmonn *(m)*
  merefara *(m)*
seawall sǣweall *(m)*
seaweed wāroð *(n)*
seep sīpian *w*
seethe (ge)sēoðan *2*
set sail lagu drēf'an *w*
shallow undīop
shampooing hēafodbæð *(n)*
sheer nīowol
  scīr
ship bāt *(f)*
  brimwudu *(m)*

  bundenstefna *(m)*
  cēol *(m)*
  fær *(n)*
  flota *(m)*
  lid *(n)*
  (sǣ)naca *(m)*
  scip *(n)*
  sundwudu *(m)*
  wǣghengest *(m)*
  wæterðīsa *(m)*
  ȳðhengest *(m)*
ship's hold wranga *(m)*
ship's rope sciprāp *(m)*
ship's stem stefn *(m)*
shipwreck forlidennes *(f)*
shore ōfer *(m)*
  stæð *(m,n)*
shove off āscūfan *2*
shower scūr *(m)*
sink besencean *w*
  besincan *3*
small ship cnearr *(m)*
soak socian *w*
soap sāpe *(f)*
source æwielme *(m)*
  wiella *(m)*
  wielle *(f)*
speck mot *(n)*
spout wæterðrūh *(f)*
spray sprengan *w*
spring æwielme *(m)*
  wæteræddre *(f)*
  wiella *(m)*
  wielle *(f)*
spring up āspringan *3*
springwater wiellewæter *(n)*
sprinkle begēotan *2*
starboard stēorbord *(n)*
steam stēam *(m)*
strand strand *(n)*
stream ēastrēam *(m)*
  faroð *(m)*
  rīð *(m)*
  (lagu)strēam *(m)*
submerge besincan *3*

suffer shipwreck forlīðan *1*
surge wylm *(m)*
sweep swāpan *7*
swift ship scegð *(m)*
swim swimman *3*
swimming sund *(n)*
tap tæppa *(m)*
tempest stormsǣ *(m,f)*
thaw ðāwian *w*
thirst ðyrstan *w*
tide faroð *(m)*
travel faran *6*
  sīðian *w*
troubled waters ēargebland *(n)*
urinate micgan *w*
  mīgan *1*
urine hland *(n)*
  migoða *(m)*
vapour ǣðm *(m)*
vessel naca *(m)*
  sǣgenga *(m)*
vessel of nailed construction
  nægledcnearr *(m)*
wash ðwēan *6*
  wascan, waxan *6*
wash away ādwǣscan *w*
washing ðwēal *(n)*
water lagu *(f)*
  leccan *w*
  wǣta *(m)*
  wæter *(n)*
  wǣterian *w*
waterfall ðēote *(f)*
wave waðum *(m)*
  wǣg *(m)*
  ȳð *(f)*
well wiella *(m)*
  wielle *(f)*
well up weallan *7*
wellspring wyllsprynge *(m)*
wet bestēman *w*
  leccan *w*
  wǣt
  wǣtan *w*
wharf hwearf *(m)*

with the tide æfter faroðe
wooden ship bēam *(m)*
wring wringan *3*
yardarm seglrōd *(f)*

WEALTH

accrue ārīsan *1*
  ēacian *w*
acquire gestrȳnan *w*
afford it, he can hē spēdeð tō ðǣm
  him tō ðǣm gehagige
alms ælmesse *(f)*
assess dēman *w*
  geeahtian *w*
bail borg *(m)*
bargain bycgan *w*
  nǣming *(f)*
barter cēap *(m)*
  cēapian *w*
beggar ælmesmann *(m)*
  wǣdla *(m)*
belong belimpan *3*
benefit feorm *(f)*
bequeath becweðan *5*
borrow (ā)borgian *w*
bountiful rōp
bounty blǣd *(m)*
  bōt *(f)*
bracelet bēag *(m)*
  būl *(m)*
  dalc *(m)*
brooch dalc *(m)*
buy (ge)bycgan *w*
  gecēapian *w*
cattle cēap *(m)*
  feoh *(n)*

charter londbōc *(f)*
cheap undēore
coin sceatt *(m)*
common property gemāna *(m)*
compensate gebētan *w*
dear dēore
  weorð
dowry brȳdgifu *(f)*
  wituma *(m)*
enrich geweligian *w*
exaction manung *(f)*
exchange gehwearf *(n)*
  gewrixl *(n)*
frankincense stōr *(m)*
gain gestrȳnan *w*
gemstone gimm *(m)*
  gimstān *(m)*
get (be)gietan *5*
gift of money feohgift *(f)*
give giefan *5*
  sellan *w*
gratis būtan cēape *(m)*
ground-rent londfeoh *(n)*
have āgan *w*
  habban *w*
high price dēop cēap *(m)*
hoard hord *(n,m)*
householder boldāgend *(m)*
impoverish foryrman *w*
income ār *(f)*
inheritance ierfe *(n)*
jewels frætwa *(fpl)*
kindness ār *(f)*
landed wealth londār *(f)*
lend (on)lænan *w*
loan gelænan *w*
lordly wealth eorlgestrēon *(n)*
marketplace cēapstōw *(f)*
merchant cȳpmonn *(m)*
money feoh *(n)*
  sceat *(m)*
obtain begietan *5*
  gefōn *7*
own āgan *w*
  agen

  swǣs
pay gieldan *3*
  mēd *(f)*
pay for angieldan *3*
  gebētan *w*
  (fore)gieldan *3*
payment gafol *(n)*
  gescot *(n)*
penny peni(n)g *(m)*
pennyworth sceat *(m)*
plunder berēafian *w*
  herehȳð *(f)*
poor earm(līc)
portion dǣl *(m)*
possession ǣht *(f)*
precious weorð
private property sundorfeoh *(n)*
  (syndrig) ǣht *(f)*
profit bryce *(m)*
  gedīgan *w*
  geðēon *1*
  nytt *(f)*
prosper geðēon *1*
prosperity ēad *(n)*
  gesyntu *(f)*
prosperous blǣdfæst
  spēdig
  welig
prove a claim geāgnian *w*
purchase cēapian *w*
rent feorm *(f)*
repayment ǣgift *(m,n)*
reward geearnung *(f)*
rich welig
riches blǣd *(m)*
  gestrēon *(n)*
rid ālīesan *w*
  geryddan *w*
right to alms ælmesriht *(n)*
ring bēah *(m)*
  hring *(m)*
rob berēafian *w*
scot (tax) gescot *(n)*
security for a loan anwedd *(n)*
sell cȳpan *w*

share out dǣlan *w*
spare (ge)sparian *w*
spear strap sceaftlō *(m?)*
spend (ā)spendan *w*
squander forspendan *w*
steal forstelan *4*
surety borg *(f)*
tax gescot *(n)*
trade cēapung *(f)*
treasure frætwa *(fpl)*
  hord *(n,m)*
  gestrēon *(n)*
  māðm *(m)*
treasure-cave hordærn *(n)*
treasurer hordere *(m)*
tribute gafol *(n)*
uncompensated ǣgylde
unpaid unāgiefen
  unlēanod
unsold unbeboht
value geeahtian *w*
wealth ǣht *(f)*
  cēap *(m)*
  feoh *(n)*
  spēd *(f)*
  wela *(m)*
wealthy spēdig
  welig
without inheritance ierfelēas
without money feohlēas
worthless fracod
  unnyt
worthy weorð
yield up gieldan *3*

WEAPON

arm syrwan *w*
  wǣpnian *w*
armour herewǣde *(n)*
arrow flān *(m,f)*
  strǣl *(m,f)*
axe æcs *(f)*
banner segen *(m,n)*
blade ecg *(f)*
blood-stained drēorig
boarspear eoforspere *(n)*
  eoforsprēot *(n)*
bow boga *(m)*
bright-edged brūnecg
club casebill *(n)*
cudgel cycgel *(m)*
  sāgol *(m)*
  steng *(m)*
dagger (hand)seax *(n)*
dart daroð *(m)*
  scytel *(m)*
draw a sword bregdan *3*
  ūtātēon *1,2*
edge ecg *(f)*
gird on begyrdan *w*
group of spears æscholt *(n)*
handle gripe *(m)*
hard-edged heardecg
helmet helm *(m)*
hilt gripe *(m)*
  hilt *(m,n)*
in shining armour scīrham
javelin daroð *(m)*
  franca *(m)*
  pǣl *(m)*
lance gār *(m)*
mailcoat beadohrægl *(n)*
  byrne *(f)*
  byrnhoma *(m)*
  hringloca *(m)*
  hringnett *(n)*
missile scotung *(f)*
point ord *(m)*

poisoned ættren
quiver bogefōdder *(m)*
sabre seax *(n)*
sharp scearp
sharpened mylenscearp
sheath scēað *(f)*
shield bord *(n)*
   lind *(f)*
   rond *(m)*
   scyld *(m)*
shield formation bordweall *(m)*
   scyldburh *(f)*
sign segen *(m,n)*
spear æsc *(m)*
   franca *(m)*
   gafeluc *(m)*
   gār *(m)*
   spere *(n)*
spearpoint ord *(m)*
spearstrap sceaftlō *(m?)*
staff cycgel *(m)*
   stæf *(m)*
stick cycgel *(m)*
studded (shield) cellod
sword bile *(m))*
   bill *(n)*
   heoru *(f)*
   mēce *(f)*
   sweord *(n*
visor būc *(m)*
war-gear heregeatu *(f)*
war-spear wælspere *(n)*
   wælsteng *(m)*
warrior (byrn)wīga *(m)*
weapon wǣpn *(n)*

WORK

act dǣd *(f)*
administer ðegnian *w*
adviser geðeahta *(m)*
   geðeahtend *(m)*
   rǣdbora *(m)*
bailiff wīcgerēfa *(m)*
baker bæcere *(m)*
   bæcestre *(f)*
barmaid tæppestre *(f)*
barman tæppere *(m)*
behave drohtnian *w*
binder bindere *(m)*
birdcatcher fuglere *(m)*
bondsman ðēowmon *(m)*
bondswoman ðēowen *(f)*
   wȳln *(f)*
boxer bēatere *(m)*
breadmaker dǣge *(f)*
build beweorcan *w*
business bisgu *(f)*
busy bisig
captive hæft *(m)*
care for gīeman *w*
carpenter trēowyrhta *(m)*
catch birds fuglian *w*
chancellor canceler *(m)*
chief thane ealdorðegn *(m)*
clang swēging *(f)*
comb cemban *w*
computer circolwyrde *(m)*
cook cōc *(m)*
coppersmith ārsmið *(m)*
counsellor rǣdbora *(m)*
   wita *(m)*
craft cræft *(m)*
cultivate būan *w*
   tilian *w*
dairy woman smeremangestre *(f)*
dancer tumbere *(m)*
day's work dægeweorc *(n)*
deed dǣd *(f)*
deputy ðegn *(m)*

dock-keeper hȳðweard *(m)*
doctor lǣce *(m)*
doorman duruðegn *(m)*
duty ðegnung *(f)*
earn āwyrcan *w*
  earnian *w*
earn a living drohtnian *w*
  tilian *w*
embroidery borda *(m)*
  tæpped *(n)*
employ bisgian *w*
engrave āgrāfan *6*
enslave ðēowian *w*
eunuch cwēnhirde *(m)*
  hwasta *(m)*
exert oneself strūtian *w*
feat dǣd *(f)*
female pupil lǣringmǣden *(n)*
fish fiscian *w*
fisherman fiscere *(m)*
flautist hrēodpipere *(m)*
  hwistlere *(m)*
follow gelǣstan *w*
following folgað *(m)*
footman fōtsetla *(m)*
forge slēan *6*
fowler fuglere *(m)*
freeman ceorl *(m)*
  frēomann *(m)*
gain earnian *w*
  gewinnan *3*
gardener ediscweard *(m)*
  wyrtweard *(m)*
goldsmith goldsmið *(m)*
guard weard *(m)*
  werian *w*
guide lātteow *(m)*
  stīeran *w*
  weard *(m)*
  (ge)wīsian *w*
  (ge)wissian *w*
guild gesomnung *(f)*
guildsman gegilda *(m)*
harvest rīp *(n)*
head officer ealdorðegn *(m)*

heed gīeman *w*
help gelǣstan *w*
herdsman hyrde *(m)*
  swān *(m)*
high reeve hēahgerēfa *(m)*
hollow out holian *w*
horse-handler horsðegn *(m)*
  horswealh *(m)*
hunt huntian *w*
hunter hunta *(m)*
  huntere *(m)*
hunting huntoð *(m)*
  wāð *(f)*
idleness īdel *(n)*
innkeeper wīnbrytta *(m)*
inspector inscēawere *(m)*
jeweller gimwyrhta *(m)*
judge dēma *(m)*
  dēmend *(m)*
kinsman-retainer maguðegn *(m)*
labour earfoð *(n)*
  deorfan *3*
  gedeorf *(n)*
  winnan *3*
lawful slave rihtðēowa *(m)*
leatherworker scōwyrhta *(m)*
look after gīeman *w*
make āsmiðian *w*
  dōn *a*
  gewyrcan *w*
  macian *w*
maker smið *(m)*
  wyrhta *(m)*
manager fadiend *(m)*
mason stāncræftiga *(m)*
mechanics weorccræft *(m)*
member of a guild gegilda *(m)*
merchant cȳpmann *(m)*
merit earnung *(f)*
midwife byrþþīnen *(f)*
moneyer mynetere *(m)*
mow māwan *7*
obedience gehīersumnes *(f)*
obedient gehīersum
  ðēowlīc

obey gehīersumian *w*
obliging gehīersum
occupation bisgu *(f)*
occupied bisig
occupy bisgian *w*
office hād *(m)*
    notu *(f)*
    ðegnung *(f)*
officer ambyhtscealc *(m)*
official gerēfa *(m)*
oxherd oxanhyrde *(m)*
peasant ceorl *(m)*
pierce stician *w*
play (be)lācan *7*
plough (ge)erian *w*
ploughman ierðling *(m)*
    sȳla *(m)*
plumber lēadgota *(m)*
potter pottere *(m)*
prostitute forlegnis *(f)*
provide with horses horsian *w*
pursue a craft begongan *w*
rank hād *(m)*
reap (ge)rīpan *1*
reaping rīp *(n)*
reeve gerēfa *(m)*
retainer ðēningman *(m)*
reward earnung *(f)*
    mēd *(f)*
roar swēging *(f)*
saltmaker sealtere *(m)*
scholar bōcere *(m)*
    leornere *(m)*
servant ambyhtscealc *(m)*
    esne *(m)*
    geongra *(m)*
    hæft *(m)*
    scealc *(m)*
    selesecg *(m)*
    ðēow(a) *(m)*
serve gehīersumian *w*
    gelǣstan *w*
    ðegnian *w*
    ðēowan *w*
serve well tō gōdre āre cuman *4*

service folgað *(m)*
    ðegnscipe *(m)*
    ðegnung *(f)*
    ðēow(ot)dōm *(m)*
servile ðēow
serving-man ðēningman *(m)*
serving-woman ðīnen *(f)*
shepherd (scēap)hyrde *(m)*
shoemaker scēowyrhta *(m)*
silversmith seolforsmið *(m)*
skill cræft *(m)*
skilled craftsman smēawyrhta *(m)*
slave ðēow(a) *(m)*
    ðēowman *(m)*
slavery ðēowdōm *(m)*
    ðēowot *(m)*
smith smið *(m)*
sow (ā)sāwan *7*
stamp stempan *w*
strength cræft *(m)*
strike slēan *6*
strive winnan *3*
sweep away forswāpan *7*
sword-polisher sweordhwīta *(m)*
tailor sēamere *(m)*
tanner tannere *(m)*
targe targa *(m)*
temper temprian *w*
tenant genēat *(m)*
thane ðegn *(m)*
thrall ðrǣl *(m)*
thrall's duty ðrǣlriht *(n)*
toil deorfan *3*
    gedeorf *(n)*
    geswinc *(n)*
    swincan *3*
    wyrcan *w*
town-reeve tūngerēfa *(m)*
tracker spyremon *(m)*
trader cīepemann *(m)*
    mangere *(m)*
undertaking anginn *(n)*
use notian *w*
    notu *(f)*
vassal genēat *(m)*

warder ræplingweard *(m)*
way of life drohtnung *(f)*
weaver webba *(m)*
wet nurse cildfēstre *(f)*
whore hōrcwene *(f)*
   hōre *(f)*
woodsman wudere *(m)*
work āwyrcan *w*
   beweorcan *w*
   geweorcan *w*
   gewinn *(n)*
   (ge)weorc *(n)*
   winnan *3*
   wyrcean *w*
workman bīgengere *(m)*
   wyrhta *(m)*
workmanship geweorc *(n)*
workshop oden *(f)*
wright wyrhta *(m)*
writer bōcere *(m)*
yoke iucian *w*

WRITE

adjective nama *(m)*
adverb bīword *(n)*
   wordes gefēra *(m)*
alphabet stæfrǣw *(f)*
already mentioned foresprecen
ambiguous twifeald
bible biblioðece *(f)*
   cȳðnes *(f)*
book bōc *(f)*
book of instruction lārbōc *(f)*

bookcase bōcfōdder *(m)*
carry a message geærendian *w*
carve āgrafan *6*
   ceorfan *3*
cause intinga *(m)*
charter bōc *(f)*
charterland bōcland *(n)*
compose (ge)settan *w*
conjunction fēging *(f)*
   gefēgnys *(f)*
   geþēodnys *(f)*
copy down āwrītan *1*
copy out bewrītan *1*
corrupt gewemmodlīc
declension declīnung *(f)*
   gebigednys *(f)*
describe āmearcian *w*
document gewrit *(n)*
dot prica *(m)*
   pīc *(m)*
English language Englisc *(n)*
   Engliscgereord *(n)*
engrave āgrafan *6*
epilogue endespǣc *(f)*
example bīsen *(f)*
explain trahtian *w*
grammar stæfcræft *(m)*
grant by charter (ge)bōcian *w*
herald ār *(m)*
   ǣrendraca *(m)*
   boda *(m)*
historian wyrdwrītere *(m)*
historical wyrdelīc
historical narrative spellcwide *(m)*
ignore forsuwian *w*
   forswigian *w*
ink blæc *(n)*
inkwell blæchorn *(m)*
Latin Lǣdengereord *(n)*
   Lǣdengeðēode *(n)*
letter of the alphabet stæf *(m)*
library biblioðece *(f)*
   bōchord *(n)*
   bōchūs *(n)*
literary composition gesetednes *(f)*

literary Latin bōclæden *(n)*
literature bōccræft *(m)*
 stafas *(mpl)*
martyrology martirlogium *(n)*
matter intinga *(m)*
mean forstandan 6
message ǣrendgewrit *(n)*
messenger ār *(m)*
nib græf *(n)*
nota bene! lōc nū!
noun nama *(m)*
page cine *(f)*
 lēaf *(n)*
paper carte *(f)*
parchment cine *(f)*
participle dǣlnimend *(m)*
pass in silence forsuwian *w*
 forswīgan *1*
pen hrēod *(n)*
 wrītingfeðer *(f)*
 wrītingīsen *(n)*
 writseax *(n)*
pronoun bīnama *(m)*
quill fiðer *(f)*
read rǣdan *w*
read out ārǣdan *7*
read through oferrǣdan *w*
reader rǣdere *(m)*
reading bēcrǣde *(f)*
 (bēc)rǣding *(f)*
rulebook regol *(m)*
ruler reogel *(m)*
rune rūn *(f)*
 rūnstæf *(m)*
scroll ymele *(f)*
seal geinseglian *w*
sentence fers *(n)*
set down settan *w*
signify forstandan 6
 mǣnan *w*
stand for forstandan 6
stylus græf *(n)*
syllable stæfgefēg *(n)*
syllogism smēagelegen *(f)*
symbol tācen *(n)*

translator wealhstōd *(m)*
undermentioned hēræfter
 hērbeæftan
ungrammatical gewemmodlīc
verb word *(n)*
write gesettan *w*
 wrītan *1*
write out āwrītan *1*
writer bōcere *(m)*
 writere *(m)*
writing bōccræft *(m)*
 gewrit *(n)*
 stafas *(mpl)*
writing instrument græf *(n)*
writing tablet weaxbred *(n)*

Some of our other titles

An Introduction to the Old English Language and its Literature
Stephen Pollington

The purpose of this general introduction to Old English is not to deal with the teaching of Old English but to dispel some misconceptions about the language and to give an outline of its structure and its literature. Some basic knowledge about the origins of the English language and its early literature is essential to an understanding of the early period of English history and the present form of the language. This revised and expanded edition provides a useful guide for those contemplating embarking on a linguistic journey.

£4.95   A5   ISBN 1–898281–06–8   64 pages

First Steps in Old English
An easy to follow language course for the beginner
Stephen Pollington

A complete, well presented and easy to use Old English language course that contains all the exercises and texts needed to learn Old English. This course has been designed to be of help to a wide range of students, from those who are teaching themselves at home, to undergraduates who are learning Old English as part of their English degree course. The author is aware that some individuals have little aptitude for learning languages and that many have difficulty with grammar. To help overcome these problems he has adopted a step-by-step approach that enables students of differing abilities to advance at their own pace. The course includes many exercises designed to aid the learning process. A correspondence course is also available.

£16.95   ISBN 1-898281-19-X   9½" x 6¾"/245 x 170mm   224 pages

Ærgeweorc: Old English Verse and Prose read by Stephen Pollington
This audiotape cassette can be used in conjunction with *First Steps in Old English* or just listened to for the sheer pleasure of hearing Old English spoken well.
Tracks: 1. Deor. 2. Beowulf – The Funeral of Scyld Scefing. 3. Engla Tocyme (The Arrival of the English). 4. Ines Domas. Two Extracts from the Laws of King Ine. 5. Deniga Hergung (The Danes' Harrying) Anglo-Saxon Chronicle Entry AD997. 6. Durham 7. The Ordeal (Be ðon ðe ordales weddigaþ) 8. Wið Dweorh (Against a Dwarf) 9. Wið Wennum (Against Wens) 10. Wið Wæterælfadle (Against Waterelf Sickness) 11. The Nine Herbs Charm 12. Læcedomas (Leechdoms) 13. Beowulf's Greeting 14. The Battle of Brunanburh 15. Blacmon – by Adrian Pilgrim.

£7.50   ISBN 1–898281–20–3   C40 audiotape

Leechcraft: Early English Charms, Plantlore and Healing
Stephen Pollington

An unequalled examination of every aspect of early English healing, including the use of plants, amulets, charms, and prayer. Other topics covered include Anglo-Saxon witchcraft; tree-lore; gods, elves and dwarves.
The author has brought together a wide range of evidence for the English healing tradition, and presented it in a clear and readable manner. The extensive 2,000-entry index makes it possible for the reader to quickly find specific information.
The three key Old English texts are reproduced in full, accompanied by new translations.
Bald's Third Leechbook; *Lacnunga*; *Old English Herbarium*.

£35 ISBN 1–898281–23–8 10" x 6¾" (254 x 170mm) hardback 28 illust. 544 pages

Looking for the Lost Gods of England
Kathleen Herbert

Kathleen Herbert sifts through the royal genealogies, charms, verse and other sources to find clues to the names and attributes of the Gods and Goddesses of the early English. The earliest account of English heathen practices reveals that they worshipped the Earth Mother and called her Nerthus. The tales, beliefs and traditions of that time are still with us and able to stir our minds and imaginations.

£4.95   ISBN 1–898281–04–1   A5   64 pages

A Handbook of Anglo-Saxon Food: Processing and Consumption
Ann Hagen

For the first time information from various sources has been brought together in order to build up a picture of how food was grown, conserved, prepared and eaten during the period from the beginning of the 5th century to the 11th century. No specialist knowledge of the Anglo-Saxon period or language is needed, and many people will find it fascinating for the views it gives of an important aspect of Anglo-Saxon life and culture. In addition to Anglo-Saxon England the Celtic west of Britain is also covered. Subject headings include: drying, milling and bread making; dairying; butchery; preservation and storage; methods of cooking; meals and mealtimes; fasting; feasting; food shortages and deficiency diseases.

£9.95   ISBN 0–9516209–8–3   A5   192 pages

The Battle of Maldon
Text and Translation
Translated and edited by Bill Griffiths

The Battle of Maldon was fought between the men of Essex and the Vikings in AD 991. The action was captured in an Anglo-Saxon poem whose vividness and heroic spirit has fascinated readers and scholars for generations. *The Battle of Maldon* includes the source text; edited text; parallel literal translation; verse translation; notes on pronunciation; review of 103 books and articles. This new edition (the fourth) includes notes on Old English verse.

£4.95   ISBN 0–9516209–0–8   A5   96 pages

Note: *The Battle of Maldon* and *Beowulf* have been produced with edited Old English texts and parallel literal modern English translations which will be of help to those learning Old English.

Beowulf: Text and Translation
Translated by John Porter

The verse in which the story unfolds is, by common consent, the finest writing surviving in Old English, a text which all students of the language and many general readers will want to tackle in the original form. To aid understanding of the Old English, a literal word-by-word translation is printed opposite the edited text and provides a practical key to this Anglo-Saxon masterpiece. The literal translation is very helpful for those learning or practicing Old English, however, it is not a good way to read the story. For that, we recommend *Beowulf* by Kevin Crossley-Holland – published by Penguin.

£8.95   ISBN 0–9516209–2–4   A5   192 pages

Aspects of Anglo-Saxon Magic
Bill Griffiths

Magic is something special, something unauthorised; an alternative perhaps; even a deliberate cultivation of dark, evil powers. But for the Anglo-Saxon age, the neat division between mainstream and occult, rational and superstitious, Christian and pagan is not always easy to discern. To maintain its authority (or its monopoly?) the Church drew a formal line and outlawed a range of dubious practices (like divination, spells, folk healing) while at the same time conducting very similar rituals itself, and may even have adapted legends of elves to serve in a Christian explanation of disease as a battle between good and evil, between Church and demons; in other cases powerful ancestors came to serve as saints.

In pursuit of a better understanding of Anglo-Saxon magic, a wide range of topics and texts are examined in this book, challenging (constructively, it is hoped) our stereotyped images of the past and its beliefs.

Texts are printed in their original language (e.g. Old English, Icelandic, Latin) with New English translations. Contents include:– twenty charms; the English, Icelandic and Norwegian rune poems; texts on dreams, weather signs, unlucky days, the solar system; and much more.

£14.95   ISBN 1–898281–15–7   250 x 175mm / 10 x 7inches   hardback 256 pages

The Mead-Hall
The feasting tradition in Anglo-Saxon England
Stephen Pollington

This new study takes a broad look at the subject of halls and feasting in Anglo-Saxon England. The idea of the communal meal was very important among nobles and yeomen, warriors, farmers churchmen and laity. One of the aims of the book is to show that there was not just one 'feast' but two main types: the informal social occasion *gebeorscipe* and the formal, ritual gathering *symbel*.

Using the evidence of Old English texts - mainly the epic *Beowulf* and the *Anglo-Saxon Chronicles*, Stephen Pollington shows that the idea of feasting remained central to early English social traditions long after the physical reality had declined in importance.

The words of the poets and saga-writers are supported by a wealth of archaeological data dealing with halls, settlement layouts and magnificent feasting gear found in many early Anglo-Saxon graves.

Three appendices cover:
- Hall-themes in Old English verse;
- Old English and translated texts;
- The structure and origins of the warband.

£14.95   ISBN 1-898281-30-0   9 ¾ x 6 ¾ inches 248 x 170mm   hardback 288 pages

Tastes of Anglo-Saxon England
Mary Savelli

These easy to follow recipes will enable you to enjoy a mix of ingredients and flavours that were widely known in Anglo-Saxon England but are rarely experienced today. In addition to the 46 recipes, there is background information about households and cooking techniques.

£4.95   ISBN 1-898281-28-9   A5 80 pages

Rune Cards
Brian Partridge & Tony Linsell

"This boxed set of 30 cards contains some of the most beautiful and descriptive black and white line drawings that I have ever seen on this subject."
Pagan News

30 pen and ink drawings by Brian Partridge
80 page booklet by Tony Linsell gives information about the origin of runes, their meaning, and how to read them.

£9.95   ISBN 1-898281-34-3   30 cards & 80 page booklet - boxed

The English Warrior from earliest times to 1066
Stephen Pollington

"An under-the-skin study of the role, rights, duties, psyche and rituals of the Anglo-Saxon warrior. The author combines original translations from Norse and Old English primary sources with archaeological and linguistic evidence for an in-depth look at the warrior, his weapons, tactics and logistics.
A very refreshing, innovative and well-written piece of scholarship that illuminates a neglected period of English history"
Time Team Booklists - Channel 4 Television

This is not intended to be a bald listing of the battles and campaigns from the Anglo-Saxon Chronicle and other sources, but rather it is an attempt to get below the surface of Anglo-Saxon warriorhood and to investigate the rites, social attitudes, mentality and mythology of the warfare of those times.

Revised Edition
An already highly acclaimed book has been made even better by the inclusion of additional information and illustrations.

£14.95 ISBN 1–898281–27–0   9½" x 6¾"/245 x 170mm   +50 illustrations   288 pages

Ordering Please check latest prices before ordering.
Payment may be made by Maestro, Visa, and Mastercard. Telephone orders accepted.
Payment may also be made by a cheque drawn on a UK bank in sterling.
If you are paying by cheque please make it payable to Anglo-Saxon Books and enclose it with your order. When ordering by post please write clearly.
UK deliveries add 10% up to a maximum of £2-50
Europe – including **Republic of Ireland** - add 10% plus £1 – all orders sent airmail
North America add 10% surface delivery, 30% airmail
Elsewhere add 10% surface delivery, 40% airmail
Overseas surface delivery 5–8 weeks; airmail 5–10 days
For details of other titles and our North American distributor see our website or contact us at:

Anglo-Saxon Books
Frithgarth, Thetford Forest Park, Hockwold-cum-Wilton, Norfolk IP26 4NQ
web site: www.asbooks.co.uk   e-mail: enq@asbooks.co.uk
Tel: 01842 828430   Fax: 01842 828332

Organisations

Þa Engliscan Gesiðas

Þa Engliscan Gesiðas (The English Companions) is a historical and cultural society exclusively devoted to Anglo-Saxon history. Its aims are to bridge the gap between scholars and non-experts, and to bring together all those with an interest in the Anglo-Saxon period, its language, culture and traditions. The Fellowship publishes a journal, *Wiðowind*. For further details see www.kami.demon.co.uk/gesithas/ or write to: The Membership Secretary, Þa Engliscan Gesiðas, BM Box 4336, London, WC1N 3XX, England.

Regia Anglorum

Regia Anglorum was founded to accurately re-create the life of the British people as it was around the time of the Norman Conquest. Our work has a strong educational slant. We consider authenticity to be of prime importance. Approximately twenty-five per cent of our members, of over 500 people, are archaeologists or historians. The Society has a large working Living History Exhibit and a forty-foot wooden ship replica
For further information see www.regia.org or contact: K. J. Siddorn, 9 Durleigh Close, Headley Park, Bristol BS13 7NQ, England, e-mail: kim_siddorn@compuserve.com

The Sutton Hoo Society

Our aims and objectives focus on promoting research and education relating to the Anglo-Saxon Royal cemetery at Sutton Hoo, Suffolk in the UK. The Society publishes a newsletter SAXON twice a year. For details write to: Membership Secretary, Sutton Hoo Society, 258 The Pastures, High Wycombe, Buckinghamshire HP13 5RS, England
website: www.suttonhoo.org

Wuffing Education

Wuffing Education provides those interested in the history, archaeology, literature and culture of the Anglo-Saxons with the chance to meet experts and fellow enthusiasts for a whole day of in-depth seminars and discussions. Day Schools at Tranmer House, Sutton Hoo, Suffolk. Wuffing Education, 4 Hilly Fields, Woodbridge, Suffolk IP12 4DX, England education@wuffings.co.uk   web www.wuffings.co.uk Tel. 01394 383908 or 01728 688749

Places to visit

Bede's World at Jarrow

Bede's world tells the remarkable story of the life and times of the Venerable Bede. Bede's World, Church Bank, Jarrow, Tyne and Wear, NE32 3DY
Tel. 0191 489 2106; Fax: 0191 428 2361; website: www.bedesworld.co.uk

Sutton Hoo near Woodbridge, Suffolk

Sutton Hoo is a group of low burial mounds. Excavations in 1939 brought to light the richest burial ever discovered in Britain. Some original objects as well as replicas of the treasure are on display. National Trust - 2 miles east of Woodbridge on B1083   Tel. 01394 389700

West Stow Anglo-Saxon Village

An early Anglo-Saxon Settlement reconstructed on the site where it was excavated consisting of timber and thatch hall, houses and workshop. There is also a museum containing objects found during the excavation of the site. For details see www.stedmunds.co.uk/west_stow.html or contact: The Visitor Centre, West Stow Country Park, Icklingham Road, West Stow, Bury St Edmunds, Suffolk IP28 6HG Tel. 01284 728718

Index of Word Lists and Codes

Index of Word Lists and Codes

(continued)